Trauma and Romance in Contemporary British Literature

Drawing on a variety of theoretical approaches including trauma theory, psychoanalysis, genre theory, narrative theory, theories of temporality, cultural theory, and ethics, this book breaks new ground in bringing together trauma and romance, two categories whose collaboration has never been addressed in such a systematic and in-depth way. The volume shows how romance strategies have become an essential component of trauma fiction in general and traumatic realism in particular. It brings to the fore the deconstructive powers of the darker type of romance and its adequacy to perform traumatic acting out and fragmentation. It also zooms in on the variations on the ghost story as medium for the evocation of trans-generational trauma, as well as on the therapeutic drive of romance that favors a narrative presentation of the working-through phase of trauma. Chapters explore various acceptations and extensions of psychic trauma, from the individual to the cultural, analyzing narrative texts that belong in various genres from the ghost story to the misery memoir to the graphic novel. The selection of primary sources allows for a review of leading contemporary British authors such as Peter Ackroyd, Martin Amis, Ian McEwan, Salman Rushdie, Graham Swift, Sarah Waters and Jeanette Winterson, and less canonical ones such as Jackie Kay, Alan Moore and Dave Gibbons, Justine Picardie, Peter Roche and Adam Thorpe.

Susana Onega is Professor of English Literature at the University of Zaragoza, Spain.

Jean-Michel Ganteau is Professor of Contemporary British Literature at the Université Paul Valéry-Montpellier 3, France

Routledge Studies in Contemporary Literature

Trauma and Romance in Contemporary British Literature

Edited by Jean-Michel Ganteau
and Susana Onega

Routledge
Taylor & Francis Group
NEW YORK   LONDON

First published 2013
by Routledge
711 Third Avenue, New York, NY 10017

Simultaneously published in the UK
by Routledge
2 Park Square, Milton Park, Abingdon, Oxon OX14 4RN

*Routledge is an imprint of the Taylor & Francis Group,
an informa business*

Library of Congress Cataloging-in-Publication Data

Trauma and romance in contemporary British literature / edited by
Jean-Michel Ganteau and Susana Onega.
    p. cm. — (Routledge studies in contemporary literature ; 8)
    Includes bibliographical references and index.
    1. English fiction—21st century—History and criticism.   2. Wounds
and injuries in literature.   3. Psychic trauma in literature.   I. Ganteau,
Jean-Michel.   II. Onega Jaén, Susana.
    PR756.W69T73 2012
    823.009'3561—dc23
    2012032846

ISBN13: 978-0-415-66107-2 (hbk)
ISBN13: 978-0-203-07376-6 (ebk)

Typeset in Sabon
by IBT Global.

Contents

Acknowledgements

The idea for this book originated in two academic events: the "Trauma and Ethics in Contemporary British Literature" seminar that was convened by the editors of the present volume during the ESSE 2008 conference in Aarhus (Denmark); and the "Between the Need to Know and the Urge to Deny" conference that was held at the University of Zaragoza in March 2009. Those are the two main events that triggered off the idea of devoting a seminar and a volume of collected essays to the collaboration of trauma and romance in contemporary British fiction. Both events were concerned with ethics, a dimension that seeps into most of the articles in the present collection, the alliance between trauma and ethics being fairly well documented in contemporary criticism and theory.

The co-authorship of the Introduction and the co-editing of the book by Jean-Michel Ganteau are part of a project funded by the French Ministry of Education through the laboratory to which he belongs (EMMA-EA 741). The co-authorship of the Introduction and the co-editing of the book by Susana Onega belong in a research project funded by the Spanish Ministry of Science and Innovation (MICINN) and the European Regional Development Fund (ERDF) (code HUM2007-60135). She also wishes to acknowledge the support of the Government of Aragón and the European Social Fund (ESF) (code H05) for the development of this project.

We would like to thank the editors of the online *Journal of Popular Romance Studies* for their kind permission to reproduce part of Lynne Pearce's article on repetition in Sarah Waters's *The Night Watch*.

Introduction

Traumatic Realism and Romance in Contemporary British Narrative

Susana Onega and Jean-Michel Ganteau

Over the last two decades, a great deal of attention has been devoted to the literary representation of trauma and, more particularly, to the ethics of trauma (see Ganteau and Onega). On both sides of the Atlantic, following on the pioneering work of critics like Cathy Caruth, Geoffrey H. Hartman and Shoshana Felman and Dori Laub, a spate of critical studies have contributed to drawing attention to the perplexed relations between trauma and literature. As indicated in the bibliography on which this introduction is based, Dominick LaCapra and Michael Rothberg in the USA, Anne Whitehead and Roger Luckhurst in Britain, Stef Craps and Marc Amfreville in continental Europe among many others have not only helped discover, contextualise and define trauma studies from a literary perspective, but have also managed to hone out theoretical and critical tools that any new discussion of the poetics and ethic of trauma cannot but take into account. Such emphasis on the literary paradigm of trauma is not fortuitous, needless to say. It is symptomatic of a generalised attempt to narrativise, and so work through, collective traumas often correlated with moments of historical crisis (in our age, the two world wars, the Holocaust, the horrors of colonisation and its aftermath, the spectre of terrorism, among others), as well as the less overt, though equally damaging individual and structural traumas associated with patriarchal ideology, unmitigated capitalism and globalisation (from the punctual traumas produced, for example, by abuse or harassment to the endemic violence directed against sexual, racial and socio-cultural minorities as a whole). Such narratives may choose realism as a means of conveying the experience of trauma in the seemingly transparent terms of fictional testimony. Thus, for example, Pat Barker's war novels privilege a realism of the gritty type to evoke life in the trenches or in the military hospitals where WWI "shell-shocked" soldiers used to undergo treatment at the hands of the first generation of psychiatrists. In this case, why bring in romance at all, a medium cut out to express paroxystic affect and evoke extreme situations, and being so generally opposed to realism, most often in terms of one-to-one confrontation? One reason is that trauma fiction and traumatic realism seem to evince a formal affinity with the poetics of romance, as shown in the selfsame novels by Pat Barker, where romance seems to be solicited whenever realism fails to evoke limit-case situations. From a methodological point of view, another reason is that, as literary scholars, the authors in this collection set great store by working with concepts or categories imported from the field of philosophy (ethics), and psychoanalysis (trauma), while resolutely striving to till the field of literary criticism. Still, the main reason is the need to establish a crucial collaboration between traumatic realism and romance in contemporary trauma fictions which has been generally neglected so far, the pages that Lynne Pearce devotes to the trauma of love and romance writing being a glaring exception (Pearce 2007, 17–19). Furthermore, the scanty, though by no means negligible critical literature devoted to romance has tended to develop approaches that do not take into consideration its ethical and deconstructive powers. It is our contention that this has contributed to the critical neglect of the similarities of the effects and functions of romance and trauma fiction.

But again, why bring in romance at all? In the spate of works devoted to contemporary British literature and ethics since the "ethical turn" in philosophy and criticism that took place in the 1980s, the words that crop up most often are "novel" or "fiction," the latter term purporting to accommodate shorter or longer versions of what is generally known as fictional prose narrative in English. Focusing on romance has implications from a generic or, more specifically, modal point of view. From the work of early commentators, like Northrop Frye, to that of more recent contributors walking in his wake (see Vitoux), either favouring a deconstructive approach to romance (Parker 5), adopting a Marxist perspective (Jameson 137), or working within an altogether more general framework (Fuchs 5), the status of romance as mode, as opposed to the narrower category of genre, seems to have been fairly well established over the last few decades. Admittedly, the label "genre" is still retained in some seminal texts—if only to stress its limitations, as does Corinne Saunders in her Introduction to *A Companion to Romance, from Classical to Contemporary* (5). Yet, romance as a mode is envisaged, among other things, as a *strategy* by Barbara Fuchs:

> Under this definition, the term describes a concatenation of both narratological elements and literary *topoi*, including idealization, the marvellous, narrative delay, wandering, and obscured identity that, as Parker suggests, both pose a quest and complicate it. I find this the most useful notion of romance because it accounts for the greatest number of instances, allowing us to address the occurrence of romance within texts that are clearly classified as some other genre and incorporating the hybridization and malleability that [. . .] are such key elements of romance. (Fuchs 9)

Resorting to the idea of modal strategy (as opposed to genre) is a way of suggesting the iterability and ubiquity of romance, its urge to transcend groupings based on criteria such as period, form and theme and permeate texts of all types and generic labels. Such malleability is referred to by Fuchs (9), who also speaks in terms of flexibility (2), as well as by other critics who prefer the notion of resilience (Norris 180), or the resolutely metaphorical figure of impurity (Elam 158). One may surmise from this briefest of panoramas that, whether the object of study be classical, modern or contemporary romance; whether it draw on the conventions of courtly love or chivalry; or whether it concern the Gothic and other fantastic developments of romance, or totally different instantiations, what is foregrounded is the malleability of the mode or, more generally, the sense of a collaborating, all-encompassing essence of romance, all such features implying a fair measure of ubiquity. This may account for Pierre Vitoux's conception of romance as an essentially reactive mode, i.e., existing in reaction and in relation to the other *mythoi* identified by Frye (Vitoux 392). Furthermore, the fact that, from the earliest modern period, romance has been defined in opposition to the novel[1] may account for its function as a dialogical component of fiction. This is the case with the excessively mawkish, euphoric, conservative versions of the mode that have prevailed as the backbone of sentimental literature. It is equally true of the darker versions, tapping and peddling the Gothic, fantastic, spectral tradition that, both in the American and British contexts, stand in diametrical opposition to the reassuring transparency of realism by promoting subversion and disarticulation, shunning rationality and totality the better to leave room for openness and the paroxystic expression of the irrational.

Such ubiquity seems to characterise the literary representations of trauma in contemporary literature, as underlined in one of our previous publications (see Onega and Ganteau, especially Ganteau and Onega 16–17) and in numerous works devoted to this aspect of contemporary literature (see Whitehead 87). From the 1980s onwards, the fictional presentation of trauma has come to colonise contemporary literary production through its evocation of the haunting consequences (both for individuals and collectivities) of such armed conflicts as the two world wars, the wars of decolonisation and, more recently, the menace of international terrorism, the trauma of segregation and other forms of institutionalised ethnic hate, not to mention sexual trauma, or else the trauma of love that qualifies as a key *topos* of all narratives rehearsing the discourse of romantic love (Pearce 2004, 527–30; Pearce 2007, 17–19). In all such instances of trauma fiction, literature has come to be envisaged as one of the privileged *loci* of testimony, being endowed with the power of saying/complementing what other types of narratives, including history cannot say (Whitehead 4). As argued by Françoise Davoine and Jean-Max Gaudillière, fiction has even turned into a necessary instrument of historisation (116). As mentioned above, the analysis of the representation of trauma in contemporary fiction goes back to the pioneering work of a group of critics and historians associated with the Yale School of Deconstruction, like Cathy Caruth,

Shoshana Felman, Geoffrey H. Hartman and Dominick LaCapra (see Ganteau and Onega 8–9), who set to re-reading and adapting for the analysis of Holocaust narratives the founding texts of trauma studies by Pierre Janet, Sandor Ferenczi, Josef Breuer and Sigmund Freud among others. According to these critics, trauma has provided a new historiographic paradigm that gainsays the assumed transparency and objectivity of the Hegelian definition of world history as endless progress endorsed by modernity. For example, Caruth defines trauma as the symptom of the unconscious of history (Caruth 1995, 5), as encapsulated in the following paradox: "a history can be grasped only in the very inaccessibility of its occurrence" (Caruth 1995, 8). The haunting presence of trauma, its ubiquity and concomitant elusiveness or ungraspability have come to dwell in contemporary literary production, in the selfsame way as a spectre haunts an individual or a community, through its intermittent though endlessly reproducible visibility. In its many thematic actualisations, trauma would, thus, appear to be latent in the contemporary fictional corpus, ready to materialise. And when absent, its absence would be both the very symptom of its latency, its necessary inaccessibility, and the promise of a violent manifestation. In keeping with this, the idea for this volume starts from the observation of a double omnipresence in contemporary British fiction: that of romance strategies and that of trauma-related themes and forms (hence strategies, in Fuchs's definition). There is no confusion, then, between our intended use of the term "mode" attributed to romance, and "genre" or "sub-genre" employed to designate those contemporary trauma fictions that share with the *genre* of romance its *modal* strategies to create a new hybrid form capable of putting trauma into words. Our contention is that it is this urgent and irrepressible need to represent trauma that has forced fiction to problematise the traditional conventions of transparent realism by moving toward the pole of non-fictional testimony, while simultaneously incorporating the most salient modal strategies of romance, and so paradoxically moving towards the contrary pole of unabated fictionality and fantasy.

When assessing the degree of collaboration and deeper affinity between romance and the fictional presentation of trauma, one should look for the nodal points where both categories meet in order to address the "but why romance at all?" question properly. One might claim that there is an obvious poetic or aesthetic affinity between romance and fictional trauma narratives. If one takes the paradigmatic example of Pat Barker's fiction, it becomes obvious that it more often than not taps the resources of the mode of romance by borrowing from the ghost-story tradition and evincing a strong taste for the presentation of spectrality—as is clearly the case in *Double Vision* (2003) and in the *Regeneration Trilogy* as a whole. The darker tradition, that which summons spectrality in its more violent guises, literally informs other extreme instances of contemporary narratives, most notably those devoted to the evocation of the Holocaust, like Eva Figes's *Konek Landing* (1969), D. M. Thomas's *The White Hotel* (1981), or Martin

Amis's *Time's Arrow* (1991), complete with doublings and haunting, as documented by María Jesús Martínez-Alfaro. Admittedly, this is a far cry from what might be expected as instances of romance, if we are to rely on the evidence provided by the airport bookstore genre, which seems to have contaminated the general perception of the mode. One has to remember that not all romances are re-workings of the courtly love conventions, and that the darker side of the mode has also infiltrated contemporary literary production. Still, love is a prominent element in Jeanette Winterson's consistent re-working of the romance as mode that has led her to tap from the genre of the fairy tale, complete with magical occurrences. This appears clearly in *The Passion* (1987) or in *The.PowerBook* (2000), two novels which also mix the historical with the wonderful, the mimetic with the non-mimetic and, in William Congreve's words, set up an illusion of verisimilitude, the better to denounce it as a lie.[2] Albeit diverging from the romantic love type of narrative, another obvious example would be Peter Ackroyd, whose *œuvre* may be seen as a dialogue with the tradition of romance, and whose "English music" is in fact the melody of romance in many ways, as it repeats and rehearses the mysteries of the past more than it seems to remember them, not only in *English Music* (1992) but most of his narratives. In so doing, Ackroyd pays homage to T. S. Eliot's famous call for the presence of the past even while performing the Freudian paradox according to which trauma is not remembered but *repeated* in the present (Freud 18). Ackroyd revisits a (more or less) submerged visionary canon, from Chaucer to Dickens through Shakespeare and Mary Shelley, in which he identifies quintessential Englishness in terms that are very much akin to romance, as demonstrated elsewhere (Ganteau 2008). It would thus seem that, in Ackroyd's *œuvre*, the cultural trauma of some violently repressed Catholic, Non-conformist, visionary culture he ascribes to "London Luminaries and Cockney Visionaries" is perpetually haunting the cultural present under the guise of a darker shade of romance flirting with the fantastic, the uncanny and even the sublime.

The purpose of this sketchiest of panoramas is to show that some of the canonical representatives of contemporary British fiction fairly often resort to romance in order to produce trauma narratives. By romance, then, what is meant here is a form that is distinct from the novel but collaborates with it or dynamises it; a form whose favourite themes are love, war, the past and its mysteries, and which, from a formal point of view, privileges excess, unbalance, and the spectacular (Pearce 2007, 2). Seen in this light, romance would be conversant with a form of expressionism and a disruption of mimetic codes. These writers may obviously work within the tradition of romance—as is the case with Jeanette Winterson and her systematic quest structures (Onega 2006), Sarah Waters and her ghost stories, or Justine Picardie and Pat Barker, with their insistence on trans-generational haunting, as addressed in Part I, "Ghost Stories, Repetition and the Transmission of Trauma." Or they may import romance elements within a framework that is not especially or explicitly defined as that of romance, as is the case of Graham Swift, but also of Alan Moore and David Gibbons, Adam Thorpe and Martin Amis, whose works are addressed in Part III, "Collective Trauma, History and Ethics." As the analyses show, many of those contemporary British writers are very much indebted to romance strategies. However, romance is obviously not the prerogative of postmodern narrative, and nor is it the only medium through which trauma may be represented, as underlined above. So, it would seem somewhat rash to endorse Diane Elam's most general statements and equate romance with postmodernism. Yet it might be justified and appropriate to argue that romance strategies are prevalent in contemporary fictional trauma narratives. This raises in turn the question of whether such a thing as a fictional trauma narrative couched in a strictly realistic idiom may exist or, more precisely, if a trauma narrative couched in an idiom relying solely on the conventions of traditional realism may exist. As such a thing as undiluted realism (or, for that matter, undiluted romance) is hardly available, the answer is certainly negative. But one should underscore the invasive, labile powers of romance in its relation to the novel, as indicated by Radford (12) among others (see above).

Raising such issues requires that we distinguish between "trauma fiction," the umbrella category (which may be content with representing or thematising trauma), and "traumatic realism," the category coined by Hal Foster in *The Return of the Real* to describe the work of avant-garde artists like Andy Warhol, and employed by Michael Rothberg in his analysis of Holocaust fiction. While Foster, drawing on Freud's notion of repetition-compulsion, argues that the apparently flat repetitiveness of Warhol's commodity fetishes and media stars "may point less to a blank subject than to a shocked one" (130–31), Rothberg contends that the perplexities of understanding and representing the Holocaust, with its peculiar combination of ordinary and extreme elements, has brought to the fore "the problem of realism" in trauma narratives and triggered off the need to rethink the categories of realism, modernism and postmodernism simultaneously, rather than sequentially. His main argument is that the combination of these three modes, together with the blurring of boundaries between fictional and non-fictional genres, is meant to create a "complex system of understanding" aimed at making readers think history in relational, rather than sequential terms, thus substituting montage for the linearity of teleological world history. Rothberg compares this relational structure with Walter Benjamin's constellation, "a sort of montage in which diverse elements are brought together through the act of writing [. . .] meant to emphasize the importance of *representation* in the interpretation of history" (10, original emphasis). As argued elsewhere (Onega 2012, 90), the fact that Benjamin's constellation works on the principle of accumulation and repetition-*cum*-variation of apparently disparate elements, may be said to echo the mechanism of acting out of trauma, whereas his association of sequential narrative forms with the excess of the ideology of progress that abutted in Nazism adds an ethical dimension to his endeavour to arrest narrative progression. The same ethical dimensions may be said to lie at the heart of traumatic realism, a form built on anti-linear montage and generic hybridity that "exceeds mimesis and cannot free itself from mimesis" (Rothberg 140). In this excessive bringing together of two idioms that have been traditionally kept separate in literary studies, traumatic realism might be said to extend the age-long dialogue between the novel and romance, and to problematise mimesis as a way to set into question the reliability and objectivity of Hegelian world history. The working hypotheses on which the present volume develops are, firstly, that the secular mixing (that always falls short of turning into a blending) of those reputedly antagonistic modes in their various thematic actualisations and periods of literary history might well provide the aesthetic soil on which the current trends of traumatic realism thrive, since these ever-growing contemporary trends never completely jettison the mimetic even while they tap the incommensurable powers of the inassimilable, and, secondly, that the "mixed fiction" strategy that characterises traumatic realism is a hallmark of romance discourse in its secular collaboration with the novelistic idiom (Vitoux 407).

One of the reasons why romance strategies are germane to the literary evocation of trauma may reside in the hyperbolical nature of the language of romance, a language notoriously geared on to the paroxystic expression of violent affect (Radford 8). One should remember that excess in general is the first trait that Elam signals in her study of postmodern romance (1). This excessiveness is also consistent with the nature of trauma, as trauma is characteristically registered as a surplus of affects that cannot be accounted for or channelled properly. As indicated by several critics (Amfreville 44; Caruth 1996, 3-6; Kasper 59), the central characteristic of trauma is the unknowability and inassimilability by the conscious mind of the event that has triggered the traumatic condition, so that trauma always has an element that remains *in excess of* representation and understanding. This is particularly in agreement with the literary representation of trauma, as Whitehead reminds us when she singles out intensification (84–86) as one of the most effective devices of trauma fiction, based on repetition, but also on correspondences and coincidences, rhythmical characteristics that belong to the stock in trade of romance strategies and go against the grain of conventional mimesis. In the violently repetitive and poetically resonant worlds of Ackroyd, Barker, Waters or Winterson, some suspension of disbelief often goes hand in hand with the assumption of textual opaqueness, when the text refers to its own textuality and to the uncanny, destabilising web of echoes and repetitions that it keeps weaving and unweaving. In such instances, the readers' affects are violently solicited and performed by the text, romance thereby enhancing the status of trauma fiction as ethical event (see Attridge 126–31; Ganteau 2011). As suggested above, the ethical concern looms large over the articles collected in Part III, but it also seeps into most of the chapters. For instance in Part II, "Narratives of Distress and Individual Trauma," ethics is envisaged in relation with the works of Peter Roche, Jackie Kay, Sarah Waters and Ian McEwan, allowing for an ethical reading of character, narrator and reader trauma.

Still, the most obvious zone of collaboration between romance and trauma fiction may be said to lie in its obsession with time, and more specifically with the warping of time. As indicated by most definitions of the mode, romance is the province of the there and then, of the far and the bygone, as stipulated by Sir Walter Scott in his "Essay on Romance" (129), and also notably by Nathaniel Hawthorne in his preface to *The House of the Seven Gables* (xi) or Henry James in his preface to *The American* (9). This is one of the points that most of the following articles address, keeping in mind that such return is always tentative and provisional in both romance and traumatic realism. However, if anachronism is the stuff of romance, as we are forcibly reminded by Mariadele Boccardi (13), the past is not recognised as such, as demonstrated by Diane Elam:

> [. . .] within postmodernism, grand or master narratives lose their explanatory power, and we are forced to reconsider, re-member the historical event—no longer in the form of realism but through the genre of generic uncertainty, through romance. The relationship between postmodernism and romance becomes a way in which to rethink narrative and its legitimation of historical knowledge. Thus while periodicity attempts to make the past represented as "past," romance and postmodernism attempt to be flagrantly *anachronistic*, upsetting our ability to recognize the past as past, challenging the way in which we "know" history. (Elam 12, emphasis added)

One of the effects of such a situation is, of course, to challenge the certainties of historiography, as Elam (68) and Rothberg (see above) contend, since remembrance and the narrativisation of past events are constantly troubled by repetition and haunting, in a way that brings to mind Freud's concepts of traumatic belatedness and *Nachträglichkeit*.[3] Still, even if a good deal of ironisation goes along with the fictional revisiting of the past, irony is not the only way in which romance reworks historical discourse. In its historical and literary dimensions, the revisiting of the past is not purely subversive but seems to coexist with a more mimetic or *iconic* purpose. As already pointed out, trauma narratives evince some deep affinity with romance in that they share a taste for contradiction. This is powerfully expressed by Elam when she argues that romance "makes the past unforgettable *and* points out that it is impossible fully to remember" (15, emphasis added). In the treatment of a past which is not a past, of a time that does not pass, of a past that is *repeated* in the present for want of being remembered, romance and trauma fiction share a conception of time which is all middle, which does not have a beginning or an end, a time characterised by what Patricia Parker calls the category of "dilation" resorted to by Spenser and, to a lesser degree, by Milton as well (Parker 76, 138). This characteristic of romance time has led Fuchs to envisage the dynamics of romance as one of "narrative entropy" (72).

In the light of these temporal considerations, it may be stated that what romance does is to accommodate naturally the temporality of trauma and provide the anti-lineal and relational temporal structure of traumatic realism and trauma fiction in general, be it under the guise of haunting/spectrality, as happens in Waters's neo-Victorian fictions; or under the guise of dilation, as in McEwan's *The Child in Time* or *Saturday*. Elam has written that postmodern romance does "not [stage] a 'now' but a haunting, excessive return of past events" (23). The same would apply to traumatic realism, since both prise open the totalising realistic idiom and the narrative of history so as to present us with a past that is both present and endlessly deferred, thrown out of joint through the violence of *Nachträglichkeit*. In this sense it might be stated that romance and trauma, as narrative strategies, seem to owe most of their power to their temporal strategies.

What emerges from the evocation of the paradoxical temporality of trauma fiction and romance is a poetics of contradiction as the foundation of both forms. In fact, for all the problematic workings of anachronism, romance has regularly been defined as the site of a tension between anticipation and return (Fuchs 19), the mimetic and the non-mimetic (Beer 10), the conventional and the disruptive, the serious and the parodic, the escapist and the edifying, etc. This has led Parker to posit contradiction as one of the defining traits of the mode (105), while Michael O'Neill, in his analysis of the romance inflection in the poetry of the Romantic period, has drawn a parallelism between the workings of the mode and the way in which the Romantic poets fused their own with earlier types of poetry: "Romance, like a metaphysical conceit, yokes together the dissimilar, fusing or holding together in tension the ancient and the novel, the marvellous and the ordinary" (306). Romance, then, becomes the site of illogicality, of the failure or stammering of causality, of the impossibility of certainty and of the subversion of any teleological imperative, while at the same time it welcomes the euphoric tendencies of the emphatic happy ending that helps formulate the possibility of a resolution of trauma. In fact, in some of the narratives addressed in this volume, romance does favour the evocation of the healing phase of trauma known as the phase of "working through" (LaCapra 2001, 21–22), in which the hyperbolical fragmentation, repetition and temporal dilation of the phase of "acting out" (21) are eventually resolved, allowing for the emergence of a happy ending/the healing of trauma, as in some of McEwan's, Ackroyd's or Rushdie's works, as will appear in Part IV, "Therapeutic Romance." From this perspective, the ethical suspicion around the use of happy ending in fictional trauma narratives is attenuated or even dispelled, as such structures are means to address the ultimate, healing phase of trauma and help evoke the move *beyond* trauma.

However, more often than not, the main effect of romance is one of liminality and irresolution, a characteristic analysed by Parker, who evokes a "half knowledge" (5) and a "conditional mode" (43) that is germane with traumatic realism's emphatic tentativeness, its staging and performance of its epistemological limits, its loudly signposting of its impossibility to say/represent: what Caruth has famously described in terms of "unknowing" (1996, 3) and as the "collapse of [. . .] understanding" (1995, 6). In fact, when, referring to the strategies of romance, Fuchs contends that: "[w]hat is most striking is the central narrative of a quest that the characters only barely understand, and which in some cases is completely opaque to them" (29), and one has the impression that she is commenting on the power of trauma fiction to make absence achingly visible. Interestingly, Fuchs's words ring with the echoes of Parker's evocation of early modern romance as privileging a state of "half knowledge" (5), as if the hallmark of the mode were its epistemological failings, its rejection of any totalising claims. Now, we should recall that, in the most extreme cases of psychic trauma, the patient has access to the symptoms of his/her affection only, all possibility of effraction being so blocked out that he/she becomes haunted by an "internal foreign body" (Press 69; Michaud 64) that remains inassimilable and inadmissible. Romance would thus seem to be intrinsically suited to the evocation of that which escapes cognition, being a hyperbolical idiom bent on conveying that there is something in excess of representation, in a way that is strongly reminiscent of the negative presentation of the Kantian and Lyotardian sublime and very much in the vein of the philosophy of the limit analysed and vindicated by Drucilla Cornell. As the mode of the tentative and the liminal (Parker 171), meant to explore boundaries (O'Neill 309), or ceaselessly and failingly probe at the limits of representation and understanding, romance becomes the privileged vehicle for trauma fiction in that it ostentatiously presents that there is something unpresentable, inaccessible, inassimilable. Romance is a monstrous mode that performs the groping and privation inherent in the literary presentation of trauma in the efficiently performative drive of traumatic realism and which allows for some asymptotic evocation of trauma always moving towards it and rarely managing to spell it, remaining on the verge of, or around the other of trauma—"au bord de l'autre," according to Ponet (52). Said differently, romance is a mode particularly suited to evoke the radical alterity of trauma that, in Dominick LaCapra's terms, can only be recorded prospectively, through the testimonial powers of fiction:

> what is particularly striking in this singular experience [of trauma] is that its insistent re-enactments of the past do not simply serve as testimony to an event, but may also, paradoxically enough, bear witness to a past that *was never fully experienced as it occurred*. Trauma, that is, does not simply serve as record of the past but precisely registers the force of an experience *that is not yet fully owned*. (110, original emphasis)

If romance appears as the privileged vehicle of trauma fiction it is certainly thanks to its intrinsic ethical power: its openness, its ceaseless probing at the provinces of the unknown, in a movement reminiscent of Emmanuel Levinas's *excendance*. By helping flaunt trauma as the site of alterity, romance becomes the privileged medium of testimony, in its double acceptation of testimony as "crisis of truth" and "crisis of evidence" (Felman 17), and testimony as "speaking beyond understanding" (Whitehead 7). Ultimately, it would seem that romance, a mode that is proud of its opaqueness and which constitutes some sort of a concentration of the literary and of the poetic (or at least of the fictional), provides a means for fiction to attempt to say what historiography, history and perhaps critical theory fail to grasp and convey. This would make fiction, and more particularly this concentration of fiction that romance is, the most suited vehicle for an anti-totalising textual strategy (Gibson 8) that meets the requirements of the literary representation of trauma. Such specificity may largely justify its presence in contemporary fictional narratives of trauma, the fact that it legitimates fictional testimony and is used as an operator of disruption (Pearce and Wisker 15) or disarticulation (Attridge 69), whose purpose is overwhelmingly ethical.

NOTES

1. For a synthesis of the traditional definitions of romance in the literary tradition, from Congreve to James, through Scott, see Ganteau 2011, 80–81.
2. Referring to the effect of the formidable romances of chivalry produced by Mlle. de Scudéry and other French authors, and their offspring, the Heroic Play, Congreve said that Romances "elevate and surprise the Reader into a giddy Delight, which leaves him flat upon the Ground whenever he [. . .] is forced to be very well convinced that 'tis all a lye'." (Congreve 5).
3. The English translation of *Nachträglichkeit* as "belatedness" or "deferred action" designates the acting out of an unsolved traumatic experience through which the past recurs in the present as present, while in his original use of *Nachträglichkeit*, Freud included the subsequent process of working through of the traumatic experience through reinterpretation and adscription to the past where it belongs. On the lexical analysis of the term making explicit the double temporal orientation of the category, both meaning "subsequently" and "backwards," see Laplanche 23–24.

WORKS CITED

Ackroyd, Peter. "London Luminaries and Cockney Visionaries." The L.W.T. London Lecture (Victoria and Albert Museum, 7 December 1993). Edited extract from lecture printed as "Cockney Visionaries." *Independent* 18 December 1993: 27. Print.

Amfreville, Marc. *Écrits en souffrance. Figures du trauma dans la littérature nord-américaine.* Paris: Houdiard, 2009. Print.

Amis, Martin. *Time's Arrow, or, The Nature of the Offence.* 1991. Harmondsworth: Penguin, 1992. Print.

Attridge, Derek. *The Singularity of Literature*. London and New York: Routledge, 2004. Print.

Barker, Pat. *Double Vision*. 2003. London: Penguin, 2004. Print.

Beer, Gillian. *The Romance*. London: Methuen, 1970. Print.

Boccardi, Mariadele. "A Romance of the Past: Postmodernism, Representation and Historical Fiction." *Études britanniques contemporaines* 29 (December 2005): 123–32. Print.

Caruth, Cathy. *Unclaimed Experience: Trauma, Narrative and History*. Baltimore: The Johns Hopkins UP, 1996. Print.

Caruth, Cathy, ed. *Trauma: Explorations in Memory*. Baltimore: The Johns Hopkins UP, 1995. Print.

Congreve, William. *Incognita, or Love and Duty Reconciled*. 1692. London: Hesperus, 2003. Print.

Cornell, Drucilla. *The Philosophy of the Limit*. London and New York: Routledge, 1992. Print.

Craps, Stef. *Trauma and Ethics in the Novels of Graham Swift*. Brighton: Sussex Academic P, 2005. Print.

Davoine, Françoise and Jean-Max Gaudillière. *History beyond Trauma*. New York: Other Press, 2004. Print.

Elam, Diane. *Romancing the Postmodern*. London and New York: Routledge, 1992. Print.

Felman, Shoshana. "Education and Crisis, or the Vicissitudes of Teaching." *Trauma: Explorations in Memory*. Ed. Cathy Caruth, 1995. 13–60. Print.

Felman, Shoshana and Dori Laub. *Testimony: Crises of Witnessing in Literature, Psychoanalysis and History*. New York and London: Routledge, 1992. Print.

Ferenczi, Sandor. *Le traumatisme*. 1982. Paris: Payot, 2006. Print.

Figes, Eva. *Konek Landing*. 1969. London: Panther, 1972. Print.

Freud, Sigmund. "Beyond the Pleasure Principle." 1929. *The Standard Edition of the Complete Psychological Works of Sigmund Freud* Vol. XVIII. Ed. James Strachey London: Vintage, 2001. 7–64. Print.

Foster, Hall. *The Return of the Real: The Avant Garde and the End of the Century*, Cambridge, Mass.: MIT Press, 1996. Print.

Frye, Northrop. *Anatomy of Criticism: Four Essays*. Princeton, NJ: Princeton UP, 1957. Print.

Fuchs, Barbara. *Romance*. London and New York: Routledge, 2004. Print.

Ganteau, Jean-Michel. *Peter Ackroyd et la musique du passé*. Paris: Houdiard, 2008. Print.

———. "The Logic of Affect: Romance as Ethics." *Anglia. Zeitschrift fur Englishe Philologie*. Special Issue on Literature and Ethics 129.1–2 (August 2011): 79–92. Print.

Ganteau, Jean-Michel and Susana Onega. "Introduction." *Trauma and Ethics in Contemporary British Literature*. Eds. Susana Onega and Jean-Michel Ganteau, 2011. 7–19. Print.

Gibson, Andrew. *Postmodernity, Ethics and the Novel: From Leavis to Levinas*. London and New York: Routledge, 1999. Print.

Hartman, Geoffrey H. *The Longest Shadow: In the Aftermath of the Holocaust*. Bloomington and Indianapolis, IN: Indiana UP, 1996. Print

Hawthorne, Nathaniel. *The House of the Seven Gables*. 1851. London: Everyman, 1982. Print.

James, Henry. *The American*. 1907. New York: Norton, 1978. Print.

Jameson, Fredric. "Magical Narratives: Romance as Genre." *New Literary History* 7.1 (1969–1970): 135–63. Print.

Kasper, Judith. "L'espace traumatisé." *Trauma et texte*. Ed. Peter Kuon. Frankfurt: Peter Lang, 2003. 59–67. Print.

LaCapra, Dominick. *History and Memory after Auschwitz*. Ithaca, NY: Cornell UP, 1998. Print.

———. *Writing History, Writing Trauma*. Baltimore, MD: Johns Hopkins UP, 2001. Print.

Laplanche, Jean. *Problématiques VI. L'après-coup*. Paris: Presses Universitaires de France, 2006. Print.

Levinas, Emmanuel. *De l'évasion*. Montpellier: Fata Morgana, 1935. Print.

Luckhurst, Roger. *The Trauma Question*. London and New York: Routledge, 2008. Print.

Luckhurst, Roger and Peter Marks. *Literature and the Contemporary: Fictions and Theories of the Present*. Harlow: Longman, 1999. Print.

Martínez-Alfaro, María Jesús. "Where Madness Lies: Holocaust Representation and the Ethics of Form in Martin Amis' *Time's Arrow*." *Trauma and Ethics in Contemporary British Literature*. Eds. Susana Onega and Jean-Michel Ganteau, 2011. 127–54. Print.

McEwan, Ian. *The Child in Time*. 1987. London: Vintage, 1997. Print.

———. *Saturday*. 2005. London : Vintage, 2006. Print.

Michaud, Ginette. "Crypte et trauma." *Actualité du trauma*. Ed. Patrick Chemla. Ramonville: érès, 2002. 55–69. Print.

Norris, Jay Lacy. "The Evolution and Legacy of French Prose Romance." *The Cambridge Companion to Romance*. Roberta L. Krueger, ed. Cambridge: Cambridge UP, 2000. 167–82. Print.

Onega, Susana. *Jeanette Winterson*. Manchester: Manchester UP, 2006. Print.

———. "Affective Knowledge, Self-awareness and the Function of Myth in the Representation and Transmission of Trauma. The Case of Eva Figes' *Konek Landing*." *Journal of Literary Theory* 6.1 (2012): 83–102. Print.

Onega, Susana and Jean-Michel Ganteau, eds. *Trauma and Ethics in Contemporary British Literature*. Amsterdam and New York: Rodopi, 2011. Print.

O'Neill, Michael. "Poetry of the Romantic Period: Coleridge and Keats." *A Companion to Romance, from Classical to Contemporary*. Ed. Corinne Saunders, 2004. 305–20. Print.

Parker, Patricia. *Inescapable Romance: Studies in the Poetics of a Mode*. Princeton, NJ: Princeton UP, 1979. Print.

Pearce, Lynne. "Popular Romance and its Readers." *A Companion to Romance, from Classical to Contemporary*. Ed. Corinne Saunders, 2004. 521–38. Print.

———. *Romance Writing*. Cambridge: Polity, 2007. Print.

Pearce, Lynne and Gina Wisker, eds. *Fatal Attractions: Reinscripting Romance in Contemporary Literature and Film*. London: Pluto, 1998. Print.

Ponet, Blandine. "Au Bord de l'autre." *Actualité du trauma*. Ed. Patrick Chemla. Ramonville: érès, 2002. 39–52. Print.

Press, Jacques. *La Perle et le grain de sable. Traumatisme et fonctionnement mental*. Lausanne: Delachaux et Niestlé, 1999. Print.

Radford, Jean, ed. *The Progress of Romance: The Politics of Popular Fiction*. London and New York: Routledge, 1989. Print.

Rothberg, Michael. *Traumatic Realism: The Demands of Holocaust Representation*. Minneapolis: U of Minnesota P, 2000. Print.

Saunders, Corinne. *A Companion to Romance, from Classical to Contemporary*. Oxford: Blackwell, 2004. Print.

Scott, Walter. "Essay on Romance." *The Miscellaneous Prose Works of Sir Walter Scott* Vol. 6. 1824. Edinburgh: Robert Cadell, London: Whitaker, 1834. 127–217. Print.

Thomas, D. M. *The White Hotel*. 1981. London: Phoenix, 1999. Print.

Vitoux, Pierre. "The Mode of Romance Revisited." *Texas Studies in Literature and Language* 49.4 (Winter 2007): 387–410. Print.

Whitehead, Anne. *Trauma Fiction*. Edinburgh: Edinburgh UP, 2004. Print.
Winterson, Jeanette. *The Passion*. 1987. London: Vintage, 1996. Print.
———. *The.PowerBook*. 2000. London: Vintage, 2001. Print.

Part I

Ghost Stories, Repetition and the Transmission of Trauma

1 "The past won't fit into memory without something left over"

Pat Barker's *Another World*, in between Narrative Entropy and Vulnerability

Jean-Michel Ganteau

Pat Barker's *Another World* has received abundant critical attention since it was published in 1998, most of the reviews and commentaries focussing on the theme of trauma and finding their inspiration in trauma criticism and theory—Whitehead's famous "The Past as Revenant: Trauma and Haunting in Pat Barker's *Another World*" is a case in point. So why return to a narrative that has been so widely reviewed and commented on? The most obvious reason lies in the fact that even though the theme and literary inscription of trauma have been well researched, scant attention has been paid to the trauma-romance collaboration that informs the novel and provides the focus of this volume. In *Trauma Fiction*, Whitehead herself comments on the "disruption of referentiality" that lies at the heart of trauma and insists that trauma fiction in general, and Barker's novel in particular, points to a "new form of referentiality" (28). The issue of representation is equally central to the article that Catherine Bernard devotes to Barker's novels: she explains that in Barker's production realism is "on trial," and that even if self-reflexiveness is "harnessed to the mimetic agenda," her work "shares with 'historiographic metafiction,' a same concern with the repressed voices of history" (174). Admittedly, the way in which Barker's novels raise the issue of an ethics of representation—even if they are not overtly experimental and even though they remain reasonably metafictional—looms large on the critics' agendas and appears as one of the novelist's main preoccupations. This is made clear in an interview discussing *Double Vision* (2003), in which Barker confesses that she is more preoccupied with "the ethics of representation" than with the "ethics of action" (Brannigan 2), a concern that seems to dominate *Another World*.

My contention in this article is that one of the privileged modal means through which the ethics of representation as applied to the evocation of trauma is conveyed in *Another Word*—alongside historiographic metafiction and without radically turning its back on realism—is romance. This does not mean that I consider Barker's narrative as an instance of pure romance. Rather, in line with the introduction to this volume, I shall argue that it imports what Barbara Fuchs calls "romance strategies" (Fuchs 2) whose disarticulating function warps and problematises the dominating realistic idiom from within. This is tantamount to signposting the limits of traditional mimesis and suggesting a way in which romance strategies amplify and buttress what critics like Hal Foster and Michael Rothberg have defined as "traumatic realism" (Foster 1996, Rothberg 2000). I am more specifically interested in the ways in which traumatic realism takes its power from contradiction, demanding both documentation and self-reflexivity, and shattering realism while refusing to "free itself from the claim to mimesis" (Rothberg 140), in a way that is reminiscent of the workings of romance, a mode that prises open the realistic idiom in its relentless ethical yearnings.[1]

Another World has sometimes been read as undiluted realism,[2] but most critics take into account—more or less explicitly—its concern with the ethics of representation, as linked with the issue of the literary rendering of trauma, without invalidating a vision of the book as realistic, overall. Such a position is easily understandable, as *Another World* naturalises trauma in many ways, essentially by thematising instances of psychological duress. This is done most obviously through the character of Geordie, the WWI veteran whose last days and seconds are scrutinised throughout and whose health, past and present, is envisaged in terms of PTSD: he is prey to such early symptoms as bed wetting and stammering (59) or to more belated manifestations like nightmares, hallucinations, delusions and various forms of re-enactment of the traumatic scene of fratricide possibly perpetrated on the battlefield (62, 69, 74, 86, 146, and *passim*). The thematisation of his trauma is achieved by means of embeddings reproducing the script of Geordie's interviews (148–58, 260–65), or also through the resort to authoritative voices—close to the narrator's, in fact—conveying a great deal of technical information about PTSD and the collective reception of war testimonies. Thus Nick, Geordie's grandson, who is a professor of psychology, and Helen, the colleague of his who conducted Geordie's interviews, help naturalise the trauma issue in the novel, treating it in fairly documentary fashion.

Yet, in the following pages, I shall try to demonstrate that the novel displays features of a darker type of romance that work to bolster up the deconstructive inflexions of traumatic realism by privileging narrative verticality, temporal disjointing and hermeneutic failure.

NARRATIVE VERTICALITY

In his seminal study on the structure of romance, *The Secular Scripture*, Northrop Frye sets up the romance paradigm in opposition to that of the novel in terms of structural development: while the novel favours horizontal action and causality—a narrative dynamics taking the reader to the end of the story—the romance aspires to a verticality—whose correlatives are sensationalism, discontinuity, and a narrative impulse taking the reader to the top of the story (47–52). Such a time-honoured distinction provides an economical way to account for the flaunted implausibility of romance narratives that are more concerned with the there and then than with the here and now, and that set great store by coincidences, correspondences, and other instances of improbability oblivious of phenomenal realism.[3] And indeed, what should be pointed out is that repetition—the arch characteristic of trauma and traumatic realism—appears as the main modality of verticality, hence qualifying as one of the central poetic and structural devices that allows for the close collaboration of romance and trauma.

As exemplified in *Another World*, one of the tonal components of romance is the Gothic, whose ubiquity has been underlined by Sarah Gamble. She comments on the role of space, and focuses on the family home, Lob's Hill—now inhabited by Nick's family, and formerly the home of a local Victorian paterfamilias—as a stock Gothic mansion (Gamble 74), complete with dark recesses, haunted garden, and also shadows and reflections of various types. She is also quick to spot the various intertextual references to Gothic precedents, like *Wuthering Heights* or *Jane Eyre*, and she devotes some textual space to the structural and thematic similarities with Henry James's *The Turn of the Screw* (75–76), in so doing highlighting the borrowings from the fantastic in general and the ghost story in particular. This leads Gamble to uncover an "unsettling pattern of repetition" (79) that she envisages in the light of Gothic's essential reliance on the staging of secrets that are concealed and revealed (71). Needless to say, the revelation paradigm crops up throughout the novel in the guise of the recurrent image of that which is hidden or held back and irresistibly returns to the surface as a metaphor for the manifestations of trauma. One may remember that *Another World* is organised around a series of traumas—individual and collective—that are presented as being both separated and connected. At the individual level, Geordie's is the trauma most obviously thematised, but it must be considered alongside Gareth's (Nick's son in law), Miranda's (Nick's daughter), and Nick's own traumatised states, the last one being presented in a more indirect way. One step further, this series of familial traumas echoes those of the Fanshawes—their Victorian predecessors—and, more widely, the social and cultural trauma of the First World War which finds direct echoes in the gratuitous violence of the contemporary urban and suburban worlds.[4] Indeed, those traumas seem to be individualised and separated the better to be connected, which accounts for the proliferation of motifs and correspondences evoking the rising of colours and shapes behind screens or membranes of sundry types: from a girl's breasts under her white cotton dress in the opening paragraph (1), to the central scene of the excavation of an obscene fresco representing the Fanshawe family from under the living-room wallpaper:

> [Nick's] last impression, before he drifts off into sleep, is that the portrait had risen to the surface of its own volition, that it would have been impossible to keep it hidden any longer, rather as a mass of

rotten vegetation, long submerged, will rise suddenly to the surface of a pond. (43)

The archetypal water imagery, suggesting the return of memories long inadmissible, clinches the analogy between the two examples and contributes to the rather loud eloquence of the text that signposts its own paradigmatic organisation. Such a flaunting is made even more inescapable through the striking use of the present tense as associated with the pluperfect ("had risen"), when the simple past would be more natural, indicating the untimely though irrepressible emergence of the image, and singling it out as a powerfully visual event. The fact that allusions to the central scene of the emergence of the painting should crop up later as, for example, in the closing paragraphs (277), testifies to its haunting power and weaves its disrupting effects into the structure and rhythm of the text, thereby performing the symptoms of trauma on top of representing them.

In such passages, the multiplication of correspondences displays the vertical organisation of romance and contributes to the opaqueness of the text, in breach of realistic transparency, so as to evoke what Whitehead terms the "inexorable surfacing of consciousness" (23), soliciting the reader's suspension of disbelief while at the very same time making traumatic repetition and obsession affect him/her. Throughout, the narrative compels the reader to experience emotion recollected in extremity, in conformity with romance's logic of sensation, a trait shared with the mode's inherent concern with paroxystic affect and the transports of passion. And passion might be adopted as a relevant term to evoke the compelling nature of trauma, in which the subject's agentivity is eclipsed in favour of passivity and submission to the crushing power of traumatic recurrence, a suppression of agency not incompatible with the fundamental tenets of an ethics of alterity relying on the surrender of identity. Such profoundly destabilising effects are further performed on the reader in the abounding passages in which Gothic inflexions rely on the powers of the uncanny. This is obviously the case whenever the figure of the double is introduced through reflections in mirrors and darkened windowpanes, the characters failing to recognise themselves completely and being presented with a picture of the non-familiar within the familiar, as is the case with Nick peering into his grandfather's mirror and seeing a face that is not really his own (164), or listening to his own voice on the answering machine (129). In all such episodes, the title of the novel reverberates with accrued meanings and points at the very proximity of some otherness situated in familiar contexts and faces, destabilising the same from within, performing the manifestations of traumatic re-enactment and thereby straining the mimetic logic to breaking point. This is achieved by means of powerful visual images that Barker, as mentioned in interview, has come to favour in her fictional presentation of trauma: "because [those icons are] beyond language, they're beyond our control as well. It's the image of trauma for which there is no talking cure." (Brannigan 383). The logic of violent affect that traditionally inhabits romance comes to be felt in its raw power in such iconotextual moments, when the text seems to hesitate on the verge of spatialisation so as to tap the violence of the cumulatively iconic as a modality of the haunting visual nature of traumatic hallucinations.

This leads me to one of the most obvious *loci* that trauma and romance inhabit, i.e., the image of the ghost, and the ghost-story dimension of the narrative. For in fact, even if, in Gamble's terms, *Another World* falls short of becoming a real ghost story (76), the ghost motif that has come to be associated with Gothic cannot pass unnoticed. Beside the recurring hallucinations that haunt Geordie's nights, whose pathological nature is ascertained by the realistic, authoritative discourse of the narrative, a spectre haunts the pages of the narrative and hardly seems to be laid at the end of the novel. Nick, Miranda and Gareth do come to partially apprehend the elusive but forceful apparition of a girl whom Nick thinks he has run over when driving back home one night (87, 176–77, 190, 211). This girl may be a flesh-and-blood girl (the one whom Gareth has to come to terms with in a violent encounter on his way from school, or also Miranda, as she looks very much like her, especially during one of the uncanny sleepwalking scenes). But she may also be at least another weakly ontologised creature, i.e., the Fanshawe daughter, who presumably perpetrated a fratricide in 1904 and who is reputedly haunting the grounds of Lob's Hill, as Gareth would have Miranda believe at the beginning of the novel (27, 36). Such an uncanny, fantastic character, in conformity with the *topoi* of the Gothic genre and of romance, provides a striking correlative for one of the salient features of trauma, and more especially of trauma of the trans-generational type, even while it strains the reader's suspension of disbelief to breaking point.

As analysed by Nicolas Abraham and Maria Torok, the mimetically subversive image of the ghost or phantom would help illustrate the notion of "cryptophoria," relevant to the extreme cases of impossible mourning turning into melancholia and leading to the setting up of a secret tomb or crypt for the objectal correlative of the loss within the suffering subject. In Abraham and Torok's terms, the incorporated phantom dwelling in the crypt would come to haunt and obsess the suffering, traumatised subject transformed into a phantom bearer or cryptophore (266–67). And one must admit that it looks as though *Another World* were obsessed with the theme and related images of cryptophoria, and as if its protagonists were inhabited by "internal foreign bodies" (Press 69, translation mine; Steveker 31) without their knowing. It would appear that the common internal foreign body that has come to haunt the various characters is the same one: the lost Fanshawe daughter, for whom Nick and the family members of the next generation have become cryptophores. This is evidenced in all passages in which the latter are made to act compulsively, performing actions that escape their volition, as in the episode of the stoning of the baby already referred to (192, 232). Interestingly, this provides the reader with an instance of trans-generational haunting which is not to be accounted for in scientific terms and which strains the realistic logic even while it seems to respect it, as the only concrete link between Nick's family and the Fanshawes is that they lived in Lob's Hill at some point. Here, romance conventions take the upper hand over realism in investing the ghost image with the magical and supernatural powers of the traditional ghost story, as the only trans-generational connection is spatial and, on no account, emotional or psychological (neither Nick nor the children may have been in a position to mourn, or rather to fail to mourn). The narrative tricks the reader into admitting the possibility of a trans-generational case of haunting while at the same time asserting its impossibility. It seems as though the rule of contradiction according to which traumatic realism favours anti-mimetic devices without relinquishing mimesis (Rothberg 137) were brought in through the disarticulating power of Gothic romance. Such apparent derealisation of trauma would paradoxically lend realistic impetus to the evocation of extreme psychic states. By multiplying such instances, romance manages to assert the ordinariness of vulnerability that is also conveyed through a vision of disjointed time.

TEMPORAL DISJOINTING

As suggested in the Introduction to this volume, one of the main areas of natural collaboration between romance and trauma lies in their intrinsic concern with the warping of time. The idea is present in embryonic form in most traditional definitions of the mode of romance and has received more recently a great deal of emphasis. This is substantially evidenced in Diane Elam's work, fundamentally devoted to "romance's troubled relationship to both history and realism" (3). Indeed, Elam tells us, postmodern romance "challenges the certainties of Modernist history" (68), and this it does through its essentially anachronistic nature, so much so that one of the most striking effects of postmodern romance is that it

> re-members the past, re-situates its temporality, in order to make the past impossible to forget. To render the past in this sense unforgettable is to point out that it is impossible fully to remember, fully to come to terms with the past. It is this sense of the past as *an excess over consciousness* that is shared by postmodernism and romance. (15, emphasis added)

The contradiction or paradox that Elam articulates here is both at the heart of postmodernism and of romance, and it is also germane to trauma's relation with a past that is central to the literary evocation of trauma and fictional testimony. Said differently, in its dealings with the past, romance also seems to be primarily concerned with its partially inassimilable nature, a structural and functional characteristic analysed by Northrop Frye in *The Secular Scripture*. When addressing the type of darker romance characterised by its fascination with descent, Frye mentions a recurrent phase of romance narratives that, he insists, corresponds to a state of "amnesia" or (quoting Wordsworth) "sleep and forgetting" (102). In other words, during his/her quest for the ideal object, the romance hero or heroine has to go through a "break of consciousness" (102). Frye even goes so far as to claim that throughout this nightmarish, amnesiac phase, the subject of romance experiences "a change so drastic as to give the sense of becoming someone else altogether" (103).[5] In its very structure romance would thus seem to lend itself naturally to the evocation of traumatic temporality, whose characteristics are a-chronology and non-linearity (Whitehead 91) as expressions of the fundamental Freudian principle that the traumatic past is not remembered as past but *repeated* in the present (Freud 18).

Belatedness as linked with the manifestation of individual trauma is the most obvious temporal distortion dominating *Another World* but, interestingly, it is essentially mediated in a realistic way, as it centres around Geordie's acting out of the fratricidal act of mercy killing performed on the front. The obsessive effects of the repetition of this moment of fixation, in which the past is not seen as past but experienced as present, are perceived from outside, from Nick's or Aunt Frieda's (Geordie's daughter's) perspectives and rather objectively analysed without the text structurally performing any of this distortion. Only perhaps through the web of verbal echoes reverberating through the narrative and applying to various generations does the more magical and implausible temporality of romance manifest itself. In fact, in a passage that sends metafictional reverberations through the text, Nick's mind wanders to Geordie's striking statement delivered at the end of a violent hallucinatory bout: "I am in Hell" (246, 250). And the academic in Nick surfaces to give an enlightened commentary on the temporal implications of the statement:

> Present tense, the tense in which his memories of the war went on happening. A recognized symptom of post-traumatic stress disorder, a term Geordie probably never knew. Though he knew the symptoms well enough, he knew what it did to the perception of time. The present—remote, unreal; the past, in memory, nightmare, hallucination, re-enactment, becoming the present. I *am* in hell. (270, original emphasis)

In such passages, where realism is the main vehicle of traumatic experience, *Another World* remains a piece of trauma fiction by resorting to statement and description. Yet, other pages resort to the more indirect though more violent presentation of trauma that privileges the ways of performance and qualifies as traumatic realism, including its reliance on romance strategies.

Significantly, the present tense is also used in a phrase reminiscent of Geordie's statement to metaphorically apply the war imagery to the activities of baby Jasper, when something unpleasant befalls him. At the beginning of Chapter 3, as the family are getting ready to tear off the paper from the walls of the living room (an action that will reveal the Fanshawe painting), Nick comments on his son's teething pains in the following words: "You're in the wars, aren't you, son?" (31), a sentence that will crop up again when Nick discovers the bruise on Jasper's skull, on the night when Gareth dropped his baby half-brother on purpose: "You have been in the wars" (144). The metaphorical conversion points to a similarity between the baby and the dying veteran, at both extremities of life, both periods characterised by vulnerability and dependency. By multiplying such occurrences, what the narrative suggests is a temporal model in which sequence and linearity are not necessarily privileged. In a narrative that follows the rules of linearity, overall, even if it is concerned with the evocation of trauma's warping of time and of temporal dislocation, the figure of the baby "being in the wars" becomes a powerful image of belatedness that reveals a circularity indicating that time cannot elapse. Significantly, the verbal motifs echoing Geordie's "I am in hell" play with the reader's memory and introduce an uncanny sense of identification between great-grandfather and infant, giving a fragmented image of trauma itself, as if it were spread among various individuals. This might be said to reactivate the idea of the curse, so often associated with the figure of the revenant, and forcefully reminds the reader of dissociated traumatic states.

It is also telling that the belatedness of trauma should be interpreted through the filter of "Rip Van Winkle" (1819)—one of the founding texts of American romance—in the evocation of Geordie's advanced case of PTSD. This is indicated in an extract from Helen's book of testimonies about the First World War, and more specifically in one of Geordie's interviews: "Like Rip Van Bloody Winkle, I suppose. [. . .] I remember [. . .] thinking all the time about this man going to sleep on the hillside, and waking up years later, and nobody knowing who he was. It haunted me." (81). Thanks to the intertextual allusion, the temporal compression famously expressed through a defamiliarising ellipsis in Washington Irving's short story becomes a powerful device to economically signal the presence of the past, or more particularly the fact that the past leaks into the present and *vice versa*. Paradoxically then, acceleration may be considered here an image of stagnation, an image that is all the more powerful as it is compounded of amnesia and presents the reader with an obvious instance of the "crisis of truth" (Caruth 8) that is characteristic of traumatic states and concomitant with a collapse of temporality. This may explain why in extreme instances of trauma like Geordie's, belatedness applies to the deferred and recurrent manifestation of the moment of fixation and also to the understanding of the causes of trauma, as if delay were to be suffered systematically, as if time were indefinitely warped and seemed to become elastic, as if, in other terms, time thickened and stopped, as analysed by Davoine and Gaudilière (28, 158).

The dilated temporality of romance has been insisted on by some critics, among them Patricia Parker, who, in her analysis of Spenserian romance, comments on such categories as expansion, irresoluteness, openness, and, especially, dilation, before concluding that the narrative of romance "is all middle" (54–113). From this point of view, it may not be irrelevant to suggest that *Another World* evokes a critical temporality not only in terms of disorder, but also in terms of rhythm. This is the case with the two companion passages in which the characters experience a strong sense of acceleration. The first one, in the first part of the novel, evokes the fast-forward motion of a film or VCR, as Nick seems to experience an epiphany centring on his daughter Miranda:

> He seems to be living in one of those speeded-up sequences beloved of wildlife photographers. Fran's stomach swelling, the children growing, the house roses blooming and decaying, Geordie dwindling into death before his eyes. Time must move at a constant pace, he supposes, but that's not how we experience it. (124)

This seems to contradict the "all-middle" hypothesis posited above, but not so when put in relation with the later passage of acceleration, showing a fast-rewind type of motion this time, as the family is spending the afternoon in a leisure park. Here, the focus is not on individual but collective history, and there is a hesitation as to the identity of the focaliser, Nick being one of many candidates and the impersonal narrator qualifying as the most plausible hypothesis:

> The time wagon travels backwards, pulling them away from the present. On either side figures slip past and vanish: an air-raid warden from the Blitz, an unemployed man in a cloth cap, a First World War officer, his arm raised, cheering, a lady in a crinoline, and so on until the wagon backs into the roar and crackle of flames, shouts, cries, a woman with a wounded baby in her arms, screaming. (231)

In the two passages—the first one naturalised as epiphanic experience, and the second through the realistic evocation of a historical show—what is foregrounded is the ordinariness of trauma and violence, as articulated in individual and collective terms. Moreover, the effect in both cases is one of hyperbolical intensification, one of the criteria of trauma fiction according to Whitehead (84), as associated with temporal disruption, both being suggestive of traumatic states. I would argue that those passages are emblematic of the temporal disorder and refusal of linearity to be encountered in trauma fiction and that they come close to *performing* the temporal warping that they evoke by being so obviously paired and so uncannily playing on the reader's memory and capacity for association. As with "Rip Van Winkle," and because it is submitted to a double contradictory vector, acceleration may be said to paradoxically neutralise time so as to figure the collapse of linearity and the prevalence of an arrested middle with which both trauma and romance feel naturally conversant.

The same sense of dilation is seen to emerge when the scene of the stoning of the infant, which Rawlinson reads as intertextual reference to William Golding's *Lord of the Flies* (6), is seen from various perspectives— i.e., Gareth's and Miranda's (190–91, 214)—, performing a repetition that slows down the narrative rhythm and becomes iconic of the repetitive occurrences of the family trauma running through the generations. In this instance, as in many others, time slows down and "the moment does not pass," as in the case of one of Gareth's own hallucinatory experiences in which he is visited by the ghost girl who has become the correlative of his fear (211). However, the warped temporality of trauma is most effectively manifested through an obvious yet fairly invisible device: the use of the present tense that dominates the narrative and that is reminiscent of Whitehead's "eternal traumatic present" (18). I would argue that the effect of such a radical use of the present tense on the scale of a whole novel partakes of two choices.[6] On the one hand, it does give the impression of attending the events as they were unfolding, and it should be noted that, far from giving an impression of neutrality and objectivity, such presentification is a powerful dramatic device that helps solicit the reader's attention and (violent) affects in the sensational scenes of haunting and hallucination that abound in the novel. In so doing, *Another World* meets the sensationalist criteria of romance by discreetly undermining the more balanced narrative choices of the realistic idiom. On the other hand, the use of the present of narration as opposed to the aorist presents the reader with an open temporality: that of time and history in the making. This implies that the events are not closed and set definitely in place, but that we are placed "in the middle" of them, perhaps in between two occurrences of traumatic manifestations, and in the arrested middle of a crisis that is not history, that escapes sequence, hence that is not stopped or laid—meaning that the ghosts haunting the characters and the diegesis are not laid to rest.

In summary, the time of *Another World* may be seen as quite other: another time, different from that of realism, the critical time of romance which becomes iconic of the open, disrupted temporality of trauma, the time of the narrative and of testimony in the making. This is an echo of the "tick of the different clock" that looms over Geordie's trauma (148), and it is another way of evoking the eternal present of trauma that Nick ponders over during Geordie's funeral: "Suppose time can slow down. Suppose it's not an ever-rolling stream, but something altogether more viscous and unpredictable, like blood. Suppose it coagulates around terrible events, clots over them, stops the flow" (271). I would argue that the difference between such a sentence and the rhythmical disruptions of the narrative evoked above is that the former makes explicit the workings of trauma while the latter imitate its symptoms, allowing for the emergence of traumatic realism thanks to the natural plasticity of the romance idiom and its hyperbolic, disruptive diction.

HERMENEUTIC FAILURE

Barker has remarked in interview on what she sees as a recurring concern in her fiction, namely, the way in which people are silenced and the way in which trauma makes them particularly silent (Brannigan 385). Of course, her interest in silenced, vulnerable populations has been copiously commented on, particularly, the violence perpetrated on women in her earlier novels and the effect it had on masculinity in wartime Britain from the trilogy onwards.[7] And it must be added that it has become a commonplace of criticism that Barker's novels evince a sustained interest in the trauma of individuals and groups caught in the vice of history, in such historical and "social convulsions that tend to eliminate the subject," as Davoine and Gaudillière put it (25). Besides, as repeatedly demonstrated, the history of trauma is a history of gaps and silences, a vulnerable type of narrative that cannot be made to cohere and that remains incomplete and ridden with holes. And the fact that trauma is characterised by a lack of understanding has similarly been established from the earlier clinical descriptions onwards. As suggested above, such a hypothesis has been given pride of place in trauma studies by Caruth—not exclusively but prominently—in her deconstructive approach to trauma narratives and testimony. At the same time, psychoanalysts and clinicians, like Press, keep defining trauma in conformity with the etymology of the term, as the hole or "empty zone" or else "blank" at the heart of the subject (69, 75). Press himself insists on trauma's doubly disruptive power when he mentions the suffering subject's incapacity to think, and consequently impossibility to figure or represent trauma (62, translation mine), which cannot be apprehended but only felt paroxystically, through pain.

One realises that traumatic realism, if it tries to provide the most iconic evocation of trauma, cannot be content with traditional mimesis and the latter's intended exhaustiveness in accounting for the phenomenal world. The challenge of traumatic realism is to make the reader share in the experience of trauma, which is indirect experience as impossibility to comprehend concomitant with a sense of irresistible passivity. My point, then, is that such an agenda can only be met by the idiom of romance, not only because it is germane to the intensification devices and the expression of temporal warping, as explained above, but also because the natural vocation of romance is to trade in the unknowable and the mysterious. Once again, such traits are specified in the earliest literary definitions of the mode, and they also loom large in the more recent productions, as evidenced in the work of Parker, who considers that romance is dominated by a state of "half knowledge" defeating all certainties (5).[8] She also comments on the logic of contradiction at work in romance, a point that Elam harps on throughout her study of postmodern romance. She insists that such narratives are intent on telling a story while refraining from doing so fully, which is particularly true of the type of romance that she associates with the historical sublime and the "unrepresentable"—her main focus of interest, admittedly (Elam 76). Once again, romance and traumatic realism seem to share common interests and abilities, and I will argue that *Another World* is more indebted to romance strategies than merely meets the eye.

This is notably shown in Whitehead's analysis of the ghost motif, when she rightly comments on the unresolved nature of the ghost girl and, comparing the novel with Henry James's *The Turn of the Screw*, resorts to the category of the fantastic, dominated by an irresolution as to the type of explanation to be provided in order to account for a given mysterious occurrence (22–23). For, in fact, the ghost girl whose haunting presence recurs throughout, affecting Nick, Gareth and Miranda—especially Gareth, if Waterman is to be believed (50)—might qualify as Miranda's double, a flesh-and-blood girl, and also the Fanshawe daughter's double, as indicated above. Interestingly, significantly, such versions of the same occurrence remain contradictory more than complementary, as each one of the hypotheses is invalidated at least in one of the occurrences of the motif, so much so that the reader is deprived of a panoramic view of the situation and has to be content with instability of interpretation, or half knowledge. This implies that the reader is compelled to share in the traumatic experience of the contemporary characters, who are aware of the anxiety-provoking presence of the revenant without really identifying her as spectral and without dismissing the possibility either, without being sure whether she is there or not, and above all without having access to the origin of their own individual, and familial, trauma. Such a state of half knowledge or chiaroscuro effect is characteristic of romance and allows for the powerful emergence of traumatic realism.

One could add that the narrative is full of moments of denial and evasion, as emblematised by the characters who prefer lying or denial to confession. This is the case with Gareth who, after attempting to stone Jasper to death, re-writes the episode radically: "And it was an accident. It's fixed in Gareth's mind now, what happened that afternoon, and it won't change. The pebbles he threw will never grow back into stones. None of them will ever connect with Jasper's head" (232). In the first two sentences, the shift from free indirect discourse to the narrator's authoritative voice illustrates the process of denial being obliterated as denial, as if the violence of the stoning had become a moment of fixation after a period of denial, as if the trauma were brought about less by the stoning than by the adult pressure put on Gareth in the aftermath of the event, as if, in a word, the narrator were suggesting that what the reader is witnessing is the encysting process of trauma in the making. But perhaps the most striking instance of denial may be found in Nick (Waterman 50), who literally whitewashes the Fanshawe painting—"Apple white, it says on the tin. Alzheimer white" (118)—and refuses to reveal to the rest of the family what he learns about the Fanshawe tragedy, metaphorically sweeping the dust under the narrative carpet, as suggested in the following words: "He opens the car boot, throws in the book, and after a moment's thought, pulls a plastic bin bag over it. Right, that's settled then" (115). In so doing, Nick recognises and validates the irrational articulation between his family's and the Fanshawes' traumas, and above all lets it be supposed that he may be himself suffering from a trauma whose origins are never revealed. Here again, *Another World* chooses the ways of romantic half-knowledge to become iconic of the workings of trauma, to suggest that there is trauma, without indicating the origins of trauma, and without making it clear that there *is* trauma, ultimately. What the perplexed reader is left with is the hypothesis that Nick's is yet another case of cryptophoria, either because he has suffered a severe loss whose conditions and the identity of whose object are not specified, or because he is the victim of some silence or lacuna active in a prior generation, some parent's or ancestor's secret coming back to haunt him recurrently. Seen from this angle, the idiom of romance might be said to complement and relay that of realism to evoke this specific occurrence of what Abraham has called "the phantom" (Abraham and Torok 426). This might help account for the various episodes when Nick cannot achieve full access to memories or impressions, as is the case with the incipient yet incomplete reminiscence triggered off by "a smell that recalls some childhood excitement, though Nick can't place the memory" (105). We are here presented with one of the specificities of romance, which, as Mariadele Boccardi reminds us, is compounded of longing and irretrievability (12), a structure evocative of the workings of trauma in which resolution is never achieved but endlessly delayed, though sought after.

Ultimately, the main crux lying at the heart of the narrative seems to be connected with the evocation of trans-generational trauma, an issue which has come to be associated with the novel. Gamble focuses on this notion and favours a reading in the light of Abraham and Torok's theories on the phantom. This leads her to conclude that the novel is a study of the masculine psyche "as a series of vacant spaces echoing down generations," in her analysis of the inter-generational trauma affecting Nick's family (Gamble 80). Now, even if such a conclusion is perfectly relevant as regards that strand of the plot (though one has to accept that the novel only gives access to the symptoms of the trauma, without asserting the existence of such a complex of traumas), it does not take into consideration the link between the Fanshawe family trauma and the trauma running in Nick's family. The implication is that the cryptophoria/phantom model analysed by Abraham and Torok can be applied only metaphorically to the whole of the plot. It is as if *Another World* called for the linking of the two plots in terms of trans-generational trauma (the ghost of the Fanshawe girl visiting the members of Nick's family) even while the fact that those are different families whose members never came into contact but through the successive occupation of the same place, prevents a literal, realistic reading of the two plots. Waterman analyses the points of connection between the two families and shows how the only real plausible connection is between Robert, the Fanshawe elder son, and Geordie, as both spent the war in the trenches, a fact which he sees as providing "a flesh and blood link between the two stories" (56). Still, nowhere are we given textual evidence as to the reality of the meeting between the two young soldiers, and the connection remains a matter of conjecture, some magical hypothesis invalidating any claim at a realistic evocation of trans-generational trauma, and privileging the reading of the text as a variation on the ghost story through the filter of romance.

Unless of course there *was* some contact between the two young soldiers, and Robert Fanswhawe was murdered in circumstances that Geordie had to know of, or was implied in, in which case his impossible memory of killing his brother Harry would only be a screen memory, some second trauma reactivating an earlier one that is never mentioned by the text. Indeed, the gaps and silences of the narrative leave room for such an interpretation. More concretely, it is because of the contradictory, impossible nature of the narrative, because it presents the reader with a model of trans-generational trauma even while rendering it inacceptable in realistic terms that another interpretation is solicited, one that remains a mere possibility and produces but half knowledge, plunging the reader into what might be considered a state of agitated or perplexed negative capability—unless one chooses to read the novel through the prism of what Marianne Hirsch has called "postmemory" (106), that is, which would multiply possibilities and further blur the whole picture. The "central silence" of the narrative that Nick comments on very explicitly would thus become the candidate for various interpretations: "All Geordie's words, Nick realizes suddenly—and there are thousands of them in [Helen's] interview alone—orbit round a central silence, a dark star" (158). This comment could be read realistically, as an external description of Geordie's trauma triggered off by his act of fratricide, or according to the radically suspensive logic of traumatic realism, in which a central silence is never voiced. Seen in this light, *Another World* becomes an efficient instance of traumatic realism, whose power derives from the contradictory propositions that it puts forward and that leave the reader with the sublime impossibility of gathering things together, of making things cohere, even while s/he is both dimly and acutely aware that something is cruelly amiss. The dynamics of *Another World* does espouse those of romance by ceaselessly encouraging a coherent reading even while banning access to such a possibility, in conformity with the collapse of causality or "disruption of referentiality" (Whitehead 28) characteristic of both trauma fiction and romance.

From this perspective, one may have the impression that the narrative is metafictionally modelled on the pre-written postcards that soldiers used to send from the front, without being allowed to write any extra piece of information. The content of such a card is reproduced on pages 229 and 230, accompanied by the following instruction: "NOTHING is to be written on this side except the date and signature of the sender. Sentences not required may be erased." (229). I would then say that this is precisely what the victim of trauma and the reader of *Another World* must be content with doing: short of reconstructing the narrative of events, causes and emotions, they can merely erase the least inappropriate formulas, in an endless groping for the inadmissible truth that will not come to light. Despite the narrative scruple of the last chapter, which seems to shift *in extremis* to the lighter tone of the romance of ascent (to take up another of Frye's categories), and despite the appearance of the possibility of healing brought about by external causes in the last paragraphs of the text, the open-endedness of the narrative cannot be toned down.

CONCLUSION

Ultimately, I would argue that such a tentative, determined yet defeated gesture that consists in clinging to the least inappropriate choices is an apt image not only of the characters' trauma(s) but also of the way in which *Another World*, that arch-representative of trauma fiction, works. The novel comes as close as possible to an imitation of the symptoms of trauma (which may constitute the only genuinely realistic way to present trauma) by, in Rothberg's terms, "representing the felt lack that is the real in trauma" (104). By hyperbolically signposting motifs and correspondences, the narrative points at a central disruption of temporality and of understanding, true to the workings of romance, that flaunts its paroxystic diction the better to signal a hole, signalling that there is some invisibility without giving access to its object. The apparently loud idiom of romance may be considered as a vulnerable form, in fact, and its vulnerability lies in its constitutive gaps and holes that are displaced and kidnapped as a medium naturally prone to the presentation of trauma. What Barker comes up with in *Another World* and in her preceding novels, whether they be about the First World War or not, is a sense of the essential vulnerability of the subject. As opposed to the triumphant model of a subject in full possession of his/her capacities, she ethically asks the reader to consider the contemporary subject as defined by his/her capacity to fail, and to do so employs the medium of a vulnerable literary form and mode dominated by its own capacity to err and fail.

Ultimately then, I would argue that what makes trauma fiction and romance collaborate so as to produce a special brand of traumatic realism, as evidenced in *Another World*, is an ethical faithfulness to the historical, cultural, social and psychic contents of vulnerability and to its narrative ethics and aesthetics. On account of these choices, Barker manages to get the reader to experience some form of narrative entropy, while at the very same time ceaselessly hankering after some form of working through whose advent is relentlessly postponed. It is such a situation that her practice of traumatic realism captures and performs in a new mode of referentiality especially honed out to account for the contemporary, (post-) traumatic condition.

NOTES

1. For more details on the ethical claims of romance, see Ganteau 2011.
2. Witness an American review of the novel by E. J. Graff that finds fault with the "deeply flawed plotting" and is ignorant of the trauma content and of the ways in which trauma may be represented (6). Needless to say, such an apprehension of the novel may derive from what may be termed the "gritty realism" at work in many passages dealing with historical and sociological evocations, and especially bodily functions and anatomical details in scenes where the body is shown in various states of vulnerability: a pregnant woman (Fran) having sex with her husband (Nick), Geordie's intestinal haemorrhage, etc.
3. For a brief archaeology of the canonical, literary definitions of romance, see Ganteau 2003.
4. For a brief analysis of the novel's evocation of violence as ethos see Rawlinson 103–04.
5. Of course, the affinity seems to go further, as the sense of loss of identity and becoming someone else signposts the natural possibility of welcoming images of the double and of the internal foreign body associated with the cases of severe trauma, as indicated above.
6. The same grammatical choice is at work in Ian McEwan's *Saturday*, as has been noticed by critics, the time frame of the novel corresponding to one day in the life of the protagonist. Things are altogether different, however, in a narrative whose main story spans a few weeks, and critics have been rather discreet about this grammatical choice.
7. The theme is to be found in Whitehead 22; Steveker 22–26; or Kirk 623, among a host of commentators.
8. Fuchs prefers the terms "peculiar vagueness" (56).

WORKS CITED

Abraham, Nicolas and Maria Torok. *L'Ecorce et le noyau*. 1987. Paris: Flammarion, 2001. Print.
Barker, Pat. *Another World*. 1998. Harmondsworth: Penguin, 1999. Print.
———. *Double Vision*. London: Picador, 2003. Print.
Bernard, Catherine. "Pat Barker's Critical Work of Mourning: Realism with a Difference." *Etudes anglaises* 60.2 (Spring 2007): 173–84. Print.
Boccardi, Mariadele. "A Romance of the Past: Postmodernism, Representation and Historical Fiction." *Études britanniques contemporaines* 26 (June 2004): 1–14. Print.

Brannigan, John. "Interview with Pat Barker." *Contemporary Literature* 46.3 (Autumn 2005): 367–92. Print.

Caruth, Cathy, ed. *Trauma: Explorations in Memory*. Baltimore and London: Johns Hopkins UP, 1995. Print.

Davoine, Françoise and Jean-Max Gaudillière. *History Beyond Trauma*. Trans. Susan Fairfield. New York: Other Press, 2004. Print.

Elam, Diane. *Romancing the Postmodern*. London and New York: Routledge, 1992. Print.

Foster, Hal. *The Return of the Real: The Avant Garde and the End of the Century*, Cambridge, Mass.: MIT Press, 1996. Print.

Freud, Sigmund. "Beyond the Pleasure Principle." 1920. *The Standard Edition of the Complete Psychological Works of Sigmund Freud* Vol. XVIII. Ed. James Strachey, London: Vintage, 2001. 7–64. Print.

Frye, Northrop. *The Secular Scripture: A Study of the Structure of Romance*. Cambridge, MA: Harvard UP, 1976. Print.

Fuchs, Barbara. *Romance*. London and New York: Routledge, 2004. Print.

Gamble, Sarah. "North-East Gothic: Surveying Gender in Pat Barker's Fiction." *Gothic Studies* 9.2 (November 2007): 71–82. Print.

Ganteau, Jean-Michel. "Fantastic but Truthful: The Ethics of Romance." *Cambridge Quarterly* 32.3 (2003): 225–38. Print.

———. "The Logic of Affect: Romance as Ethics." *Anglia* 129.1–2 (August 2011): 79–92. Print.

Graff, E.J. "Time's Bombs." *The Women's Review of Books* 16.12 (September 1999): 5–6. Print.

Hirsch, Marianne. "Generations of Postmemory." *Poetics Today* 29.1 (Spring 2008): 103–28. Print.

Kirk, John. "Recovered Perspectives: Gender, Class and Memory in Pat Barker's Writing." *Contemporary Literature* 40.4 (Winter 1999): 603–26. Print.

McEwan, Ian. *Saturday*. 2005. London: Vintage, 2006. Print.

Parker, Patricia. *Inescapable Romance: Studies in the Poetics of a Mode*. Princeton, NJ: Princeton UP, 1979. Print.

Press, Jacques. *La Perle et le grain de sable. Traumatisme et fonctionnement mental*. Lausanne: Delachaux et Niestlé, 1999. Print.

Rawlinson, Mark. *Pat Barker*. Houndmills: Palgrave Macmillan, 2010. Print.

Rothberg, Michael. *Traumatic Realism: The Demands of Holocaust Representation*. Minneapolis and London: U of Minnesota P, 2000. Print.

Steveker, Lena. "Reading Trauma in Pat Barker's *Regeneration Trilogy*." *Trauma and Ethics in Contemporary British Literature*. Eds Susana Onega and Jean-Michel Ganteau. Amsterdam and New York: Rodopi, 2011. 21–36. Print.

Waterman, David. "The Family, Constructed Reality and Collective Traumatic Memory: Pat Barker's *Another World*." *Etudes britanniques contemporaines* 36 (June 2009): 43–46. Print.

Whitehead, Anne. "The Past as Revenant: Trauma and Haunting in Pat Barker's *Another World*." *Trauma Fiction*. Edinburgh: Edinburgh UP, 2004. 12–29. Print.

2 Hauntology as Compromise between Traumatic Realism and Spooky Romance in Sarah Waters's *The Little Stranger*

Georges Letissier

History features prominently in contemporary British fiction as a way of creatively re-appropriating the past. Romance, taken here as a mode and not as genre, finds itself in close association with a renewed form of historiography. Romance may be briefly defined in contrast to the novel as "eschew[ing] verisimilitude, prefer[ing] [. . .] the far to the near, because it replaces the horizontal linear description of the phenomenal world by either more vertical probings into mystery (in the case of the Gothic) or elevations towards the transcendent (in religious romances)" (Ganteau 226).

In the case of Sarah Waters the far is relative; it has never gone beyond the nineteenth century, and more recently has confined itself to the mid-twentieth century. However, the breaks from the codes of fictional realism, though subtle, are nonetheless clearly noticeable. Waters's novels may be seen as offering a sequel to, or rather a mutation from, the historical romance, which had become "predominantly a woman's genre" (Hughes 3)[1] by the 1950s. In her neo-Victorian lesbian trio,[2] the novelist availed herself of the fictional liberty afforded by a genre in which the "distant setting is [. . .] realised in great detail, and emotional reactions and relationships are presented with a fullness which gives an impression of verisimilitude, despite the unlikelihood of much of the action" (Hughes 2). Waters's major interference with the popular genre consisted in altering its ideological message, by promoting a form of progressive sexual politics within a traditionally conservative form. With *The Little Stranger*, the imaginary flights of the historical romance are set at one remove. The novelist's engagement is indeed with a more recent past, one whose traumatic persistence is still palpable. The historical romance is the submerged textual layer of a palimpsest—it is spectral. In many respects, Waters inaugurated a new way of coming to terms with the past, by maintaining a balance between the historical imagination and a constant faithfulness to a degree of factuality. This double allegiance is what Marie-Luise Kohlke, a neo-Victorian scholar, calls new(meta)realism (156). This means that instead of opting for a flippant and playful, albeit devastating, deconstruction of traditional representations of the past, like Jeanette Winterson in *The Passion* (1987) and *Sexing the Cherry* (1989), Waters apparently endorses the format of realist, historical fiction. Thus, in her novels, she refrains from exhibiting the codes of narrativity: all that makes up the emplotment technique according to Hayden White.

In *The Little Stranger*, as in *The Night Watch*, the novel she had published before, Waters set herself new challenges. The main shift was not so much in selecting a new era—i.e. the move from the Victorian age to WW2 and its aftermath—as in confronting recent history. Not only was there the need to sift through a vast amount of unrecorded primary sources, but also the ethical responsibility of being answerable to surviving witnesses. This recent past, unlike the Victorian age, could no longer be regarded as merely recreational. In an article for *The Guardian*, published in 2006, Waters writes:

> The nineteenth century always felt to me to a certain extent like a stage-set, already mythicized by its own extravagant fictions and by a century's worth of period novels and nostalgia; the era and its motifs seemed up for grabs, available for playful reinvention. For all our overuse of wartime stereotypes—the Blitz spirit, the nylons, the gum-chewing GIs—I would have felt a bit of an upstart taking liberties like that with the 1940s. (Waters 2006b, 4)

Whereas Waters departed from the codes of romance in *The Night Watch*, by choosing the relative objectivity of third-person narration, by making extensive use of memoirs and diaries from the period and by resorting to the historical anthropological method, in *The Little Stranger* she deals approximately with the same context, by adopting a radically different literary approach. To address the still traumatic repercussions of the transitory post-war years, Waters borrows the ghost story's plotline and symbolically foregrounds its favourite locus: the haunted house. The novelist is, of course, familiar with ghost stories as *Affinity*, her 1999 neo-Victorian fiction of same-sex romance, tropes the historical invisibility of lesbian identity in the nineteenth century through paranormal, supernatural phenomena—thus equating phantoms with phantasms. However, in *The Little Stranger*, Waters's purpose is significantly different.

The aim of this essay is to argue that in this recent novel the use of the ghost story partakes of an attempt to artistically recreate a comparatively recent traumatic past, by means of a fluid, unfixed temporality, precluding the possibility of a totalising vision from the vantage point of a firmly fixed present. Granted that reading ghost tales is an experience likely to elicit unrest, loss and angst, it will be shown that this existential malaise interferes with the relation to the past which is built up through the act of reading. Indeed, the logic of the ghost story informs the historical discourse underpinning Waters's fiction, by positing the "disadjustment of the contemporary" (Derrida 123), which is in itself the condition to express trauma, i.e. the belated iteration of some unassimilated event, the fact that: "[t]rauma is a disorder of memory and time" (Baer 9).

REVENANCE AND THE "CONDITION OF ENGLAND NOVEL"

When Jacques Derrida published *Specters of Marx* in 1993 most Marxist regimes had already collapsed. The ideal of communism had therefore been nipped in the bud even before it could be tested. Neo-liberal intellectuals like Francis Fukuyama saw in the disappearance of Marxism the end of a historical process resting on class conflicts and championed the advent of liberal democracy as the ideal finality, i.e. the ultimate stage of a long eschatological progress. The prime mover of historical materialism lay in the antagonism between the conflicting interests dividing social classes. Marxist philosophy had contended that the triumph of the working classes, followed by the temporary dictatorship of the proletariat, was ultimately to lead to the emergence of a pacified, fully egalitarian society. Nevertheless, due to historical circumstances, to put it euphemistically, the final communist stage was bound to remain forever a virtual, never-to-be fulfilled prospect. Because it was never actualised, Derrida speaks of the spectrality of communism. What had first been dreaded as a terrifying menace to come, in the middle of the nineteenth century, by the powers of all old Europe: "the 'specter of communism' (*das Gespenst des Kommunismus*)" (Derrida 46) had, by the end of the twentieth century, become a past spectre, an illusion, or a phantasm. However, the eradication of Marxist regimes in the course of the late twentieth century could in no way abolish the *specter* of communism, because it is in the nature of a ghost never to die: "it remains always to come and to come back" (Derrida 123).

The distinction between the spectre of the past and the spectre of the future, therefore, proves to be immaterial in the sense that spectrality undoes any clear-cut opposition between the past, present, and future and, by extension, between the actual, effective presence and the virtual, unactualised prospect still in the offing. Because the spectre eludes temporal boundaries and because its comings and goings may not be neatly ordered along a linear axis clearly divided between a before and an after, or between real time and deferred time, it entails a specific relation to the historical past which is structurally traumatic. Dominick LaCapra has pointed out the desirability of relating deconstructive and psychoanalytic concepts by suggesting that the collapse of the distinction between present and past, and between the actual and the virtual "are related to transference and prevail in trauma and in post-traumatic acting out in which one is haunted or possessed by the past and performatively caught up in the compulsive repetition of traumatic scenes" (21).

Precisely, the compulsive repetition of the past, correlated with a form of temporal stasis precluding the possibility of any projection into an untainted future, implies a form of a-chronicity which is rendered palpable through *The Little Stranger's* diegesis. Before being a spooky romance, Waters's fiction sets up a form of spectral temporality first of all by reviving, and amplifying, the topic of social class difference. This theme harks back to the Condition of England Novel which has now largely gone out of fashion. Waters revives the Angry Young Men's social discontent of the late 1950s and early 60s by recreating England in 1947 at the war's end, from the perspective of the beginning of the new millennium. She also smuggles the agenda of the social novel into the realm of the historical romance, characterised by its dream vision of the rich and wealthy, which was known to appeal chiefly to a popular readership. This overlap of different time schemes, actual and real, fantasised and imaginary, but also implicit or virtual, conjures up a halo of spectrality in a seemingly realistic fiction.

Everything starts with the choice of a middle-aged male bachelor as narrator-focaliser. Dr. Faraday, the intradiegetic-homodiegetic narrator, enters a story which should not have been his own by right, even if his past is inscribed within it: "You're the doctor, are you? We were expecting Dr. Graham" (6). The Ayres, who have called for the doctor, are the local upper-class members. Their family circle is now reduced to a widowed mother and her two unmarried children, Caroline, the tall spinsterish daughter, and her brother Roderick, a former pilot, suffering from Post-traumatic Stress Disorder (PTSD). Hundreds Hall, their property, has seen better days, and the novel records its final architectural and moral collapse as two of its occupants die while the third is sent off to a lunatic asylum. Waters, who is especially interested in showing how WW2 shook up the British class system, gives a new lease on life to the post-war ghost and detective fictions, acknowledging Josephine Tey and Angela Thirkell, among others, as literary influences.[3]

Angst plays at a first level through the introduction of the class question, which goes beyond the purely realistic to include the traumatic and the spectral. By deliberately choosing as persona a character who is poles apart from her more familiar figures, Waters gives a skewed angle to the story to be told. Faraday, who is a lackluster, no-nonsense heterosexual bachelor, has none of the flamboyance of the likes of Kitty and Nancy, or Sue and Lily, in respectively *Tipping the Velvet* and *Fingersmith*. Actually, the doctor is the typical embodiment of the man of science stumbling upon a mysterious case, which he is at pains to rationalise. He is also a catalyst who unwittingly arrives at a critical juncture in the history of the Ayres/ heirs dynasty. That Faraday, through a traumatic, social stigma may not be a fully reliable narrator, is evidenced by the text itself. So his biased account of facts calls for competing versions, doomed to remain as spectral narrative alternatives (27).

In retrospect, Faraday's own train of thoughts during his first visit appears to trigger the events to follow. Yet, the process is twofold, not solely turned towards the future, but also directed backwards towards the past. Indeed, the doctor intrudes into a story whose script was not destined for him but which, nevertheless, bears the imprint of his own family romance, or "back-door romance" (28) rather. His mother met his father, a grocer's boy then, when she worked as a maid at Hundreds Hall, and it is sadly ironical that on the picture that Mrs. Ayres presses him to accept as a memorandum, Faraday should fail to identify her for certain, as if this trace of the past was to remain like an optical unconscious (Baer 87), pointing at a dimension of reality which must have been there even if its tangibility will never be ascertained: "the nursemaid had tilted back her head in fear of flailing elbows. Her gaze, as a consequence, was drawn from the camera, and her features were blurred" (29).

The world of Hundreds Hall is indeed characterised by temporal disjointure, by a permanent state of anachrony which entails the non-contemporaneity of the present with itself. The denizens of the Hall cannot be merely their own selves because they are seen simultaneously as the spectral doubles of their putative ancestry. Roderick Ayres is emptied of his own contemporary self, both as failed war pilot and social parasite, to be described through the association that his status as heir of Hundreds Hall conjures up: "Lord of the Manor" (193). History repeats itself as farce through the vagaries of the same Roderick fantasising that he and his sister are hanged from the beam just like the Royalists in the days of Cromwell. The retrospective narrative further adds to this effect of temporal displacement. Not only are the fateful events stretching over a one-year period recounted with the benefit of hindsight, but an odd time gap precedes the epilogue. Three years elapse between the story's ending and the last chapter, which introduces an odd sort of *faux* dénouement. The coda somewhat peremptorily shows the final episodes as fulfilling some kind of historical *telos*: "Hundreds was, in effect, defeated by history, destroyed by its own failure to keep pace with a rapidly changing world" (498). In the meantime, the egalitarian ideal of a classless society consecutive on the collective war effort seems to have been achieved: "The council houses on the edge of Hundreds Park have been a great success" (495). Such a utopian picture, with its pastoral Morrissian echoes, artificially forces an ideal finality upon the ongoing historical process.[4] This somewhat idealistic picture may also be interpreted as a typical illustration of this halting of a future which "is blocked or fatalistically caught up in a melancholic feedback loop" (LaCapra 21).

In 2009, when *The Little Stranger* was published, readers could only have been perplexed by the eerie collusion between the end of the diegesis and the unexpected inclusion of an eschatological perspective. In fact, the irenic representation of the restoration of peace in social relationships may be no more no less than a final *trompe-l'œil*. Through an ultimate sleight-of-hand trick, Waters misleads the reader into believing that a ghost still haunts the now derelict Hundreds Hall, when actually, the only remaining ghost is none other than the spectre of history: "The most popular tale, I gather, is that the Hall is haunted by the spirit of a servant-girl who was badly treated by a cruel master" (495).

The maid's ghost is anecdotal, a mere concession to folklore. On the opposite, the spectre of history, however implicit it may be, has to be reckoned with. It is a combination of absence and presence, of virtuality and actuality, because, first of all, the state of social reconciliation hinted at in the last pages of *The Little Stranger* calls for historical contextualisation. Many social disturbances and an overall process of national decline have indeed intervened between 1950, which marks the ending of the narrated events, and 2009, the time of telling. This silenced temporal gap casts a pall over the forced conciliatory tone of the narrative closure, whilst reminding the reader that "[a]t bottom, the specter is the future, it is always to come, it presents itself only as that which could come or come back" (Derrida 48).

THE SPIRAL OF EVIL

Ghost tales have something to tell us about the nature of evil; they are the reverse of the enlightened stories of education, a form which Waters experimented with, to a certain extent, in *Tipping the Velvet*. Evil is closely linked to the spectral through its propensity to recur endlessly. This is an aspect which Slavoj Žižek underlined in one of his most recent studies: "Evil is something which threatens to return for ever [. . .] a spectral dimension which magically survives its physical annihilation and continues to haunt us" (56). In the meantime, in the age of the politically correct, there seems to be some reluctance to tackle the issue of evil in any depth: "The word 'evil' is generally a way of bringing arguments to an end, like a fist in the solar plexus. [. . .] it is an end-stopping kind of term, one which forbids the raising of other questions" (Eagleton 8). Alain Badiou points to a related form of denial by showing that evil is considered rather abstractly as a self-evident category defining itself through its total and radical antinomy to law and civilisation (27–29). Such perfunctory approaches aiming principally at reinforcing the foundations of moral principles taken for universal and absolute in the Kantian tradition of categorical imperatives, dismiss the transcendence of evil too rapidly: "Evil, then, is a form of transcendence, even if from the point of view of good, it is a transcendence gone awry. Perhaps it is the only form of transcendence left in a post-religious world." (Eagleton 65)

Waters in *The Little Stranger* draws explicitly on the correspondence between supernatural apparitions and polymorphous evil. However, by allowing doctors—Faraday the first-degree narrator but also Dr. Seeley—to deliver their rational discourses, she opens the possibility of piercing through the mystery of spectral phenomena, without fully endorsing these explanations as the ultimate key to lift the veil on what she intends to remain as essentially and fundamentally riddling and elusive. Symptomatically, Waters situates her story immediately after WW2, when Britain through an unprecedented all-out war effort had just defeated barbarity or, said differently, when the light of a long-established humanist tradition had just triumphed over the dark powers of evil. However, she underlines the persistence of evil, not as an alien, all-devastating storm blowing from outside the borders of mother England, but as a pernicious, malevolent infection corrupting what is nearest and dearest: i.e., society's own foundations, chiefly the patriarchal family, through the squire and his lady, both traditionally set up as models to ensure the community's stability. To put it shortly, just when the threat of barbarity from without has been victoriously eradicated, Waters shows the return of evil from within through "a sort of orgy of surrender" (203). The ghost story permits her to investigate the iterative nature of evil, and correlatively, to address the notion of guilt, which in its turn may spawn further evils.

The rotary structure, with a gradual intensification of malevolent powers, gestures towards Henry James's *The Turn of the Screw*. The narrative pace speeds up thanks to a meticulously concatenated chain of unfortunate events: "One upset summons up a crowd of others" (Waters 2009a, 220). Waters's novel takes up all the usual ingredients of the typical ghost story, and the rise of the tension she builds up is flawless. The crescendo succession of the nuisances and mysterious tricks plaguing the peace of the household can be summarised as follows: first Gyp, the house's dog, under a wicked influence viciously bites a little girl from the neighbourhood; then, Roderick, the young Master of Hundreds Hall, falls under the delusion that inanimate objects, including a mirror, attack him. Waters successively introduces as embedded narratives or reported speeches the testimonies of Hundreds Hall's occupants: Roderick's, Mrs Ayres's and Caroline's. Tangible signs of major disturbances are evoked, such as scorch marks and scribbles on the walls, unexplainable smudges on the ceilings, much knocking and tapping, and repeated ringings of the telephone bell at night with no one at the other end of the line, not to forget the mischievous tricks played by a Victorian speaking-tube, from the basement kitchen to the nurseries at the very top of the stairwell.

Waters borrows the motif of the animated looking-glass from the phantom tale. Not only does it make for one of the novel's creepiest episodes, it also sets off the contaminating effect necessary to all ghost stories, through the reverberation of specular reflections, ultimately sparing no one—including the reader. Significantly, in the coda, the narrator, who had hitherto managed to keep at some distance from the events he had reported, finds himself caught up in the web of the haunted house. This retrospectively elicits doubt in the reader, who may suspect Faraday of having been a quasi-ghost haunting not only the house, but the text itself. Ultimately, narrating spooky events would have induced the narrator's self-alienation:

> If Hundreds Hall is haunted, however, its ghost doesn't show itself to me. For I'll turn, and am disappointed—realising that what I am looking at is only a cracked window-pane, and that the face gazing distortedly from it, baffled and longing, is my own. (499)

To quote Shoshana Felman, this final epiphanic confession might seal: "the absolute transience and the absolute indelibility of a moment of missed encounter with reality, an encounter whose elusiveness cannot be owned and yet whose impact can no longer be erased" (167).

In Waters's fiction, the spooky romance is the first step towards a deep engagement with the traumas of recent history, through what may be seen as an etiology of evil and guilt. Evil is first broached through the instinctive misgivings of an impressionable maid faking illness in an attempt to inform an exterior witness of the preoccupying situation in the house (12). Then, Waters's approach consists in calling up various plausible explanations from different witnesses to account for this spell of nervousness; absence of parental care according to the Ayres, isolation from other youths for Dr. Faraday, and later a more positivistic type of justification from Dr. Seeley, who demonstrates how unreleased sexual impulse amongst pubescent girls may turn out to have the most extreme consequences (381).

In a way that is familiar to readers of postmodernist, self-reflexive narratives, the novel provides keys for the interpretation from within the fictitious fabric. However, in this case, Dr. Seeley's explanations are both formulaic and dictated by the type of pseudo-scientific cant that prevailed in the late fifties amongst the "more informed" circles of the British society. As a result, today's readers cannot fail to see through the arbitrariness of such prefabricated schemata. And thus there remains an irreducible part of mystery to the maid's fits of panic.

Similarly, the correspondences between war trauma and ghostly apparitions are clearly asserted. Roderick Ayres, in the confinement of his room, is the victim of what looks like hallucinations. These torturing visions are obvious reminders of the tragic circumstances in which the plane that he piloted during the war crashed, killing his navigator. The evidence points to Roderick as suffering from what has been recently diagnosed as survivor's guilt. Delayed war-shock takes for him the shape of powerful hallucinations or fantastic delusions. The fact that these nightmarish scenes involving phantoms are phantasmal revivals of an initial traumatic war episode is plainly perceptible through Roderick's words evoking a mirror inching forward in his direction: "'I knew it wished me harm. It wasn't even like being on an op and picking up an enemy fighter [. . .] This was mean and spiteful and wrong [. . .] I felt as though the very blankets I was sitting on might rise up and throttle me!'" (164)

Admittedly, Waters writes at a time when war trauma studies have benefited from the input of many different areas such as psycho-neurology, cognition, psychodynamics, behaviourism and social theory. What is recounted as spooky romance might equally be read as a medical record of blatant symptoms of PTSD. Roderick's recurrent obsession with death, for instance, could fall under the comorbidity label: "Most research into PTSD has shown that there is nearly always a comorbid disorder—often depression, sometimes generalised anxiety, substance abuse, or aggression or violence-related problems." (Hunt 56–57). More closely related to this reflection on the overlap between the spooky (fictitious romance meant to elicit sensations of fear and awe in the reader) and the spectral (intangible persistence of the historical past) is the fact that the traumatised subject is more perceptually aware of environmental stimuli that might remind him/her of a traumatic event. Added to this, the traumatised person is unable to separate the traumatic situation from the normal environment. So, in a sense, entering the psyche of a traumatised subject would present many similarities with the artistically created universe of spooky romance. This raises the question of where psycho-pathology ends and art begins, or vice versa. Likewise, ghostly tales dramatise the question of the origin, since they are chiefly concerned with the belated effect or after-images resulting from a cause(s) bound to remain elusive. It is worth noting that, correlatively, the same type of logic applies in the case of PTSD. A distinction must indeed be drawn between the event and the psychological response to the event, as there is not necessarily a direct causal link between a specific traumatic stressor and a subsequent psychopathological condition. In a way, there is always something mysterious and unfathomable about the different responses of single individuals to a same event, or about the time it takes for them to build up some kind of response. The very nature of the event itself can never be fully recovered because it may only be assessed from a range of different, potentially contradictory reactions (Waters 2009a, 56). Roderick Ayres's survivor's guilt translates into a feeling of inadequacy; the obsessive conviction that he fails to live up to the image of Master of the House (180). Here again, psychological trauma coils back on the central social class question.

FAMILY TRAUMA AND SPECTRALITY

In *The Little Stranger* the ghost romance tropes the topic of the extinction of the Ayres's dynasty, and by extension the disappearance of a social class tightly bound up with the British establishment, more specifically the Army and the fading glory of the Empire. The intrinsic link between familial trauma and historical change underpins the whole novel. From his childhood memories, Dr. Faraday has known of the existence of Susan, the first Ayres daughter, who died of diphtheria when she was still a child. What he discovers in the course of the novel, though, is the extent of the trauma caused by this early demise. Retrospectively, Susan Ayres's death triggers family anomie and irreversible decline. Spectral phenomena accelerate the downfall and disappearance of the last Ayres survivors. Scribbles on the saloon walls draw the name Sukee, for Susan, as a vampiric reminder of the family's tragedy. "A faint, moist sussuration" (345) is also attributed to the visitant intent on drawing in her wake the still living members of her family. Mrs. Ayres, the mother, dies of self-inflicted injuries aimed to acknowledge the presence of her daughter in her own flesh and blood. Under the delusion that mutilating nips, cuts and bruises are responses to the exacting demands of her dear dead child, the old Mistress of Hundreds Hall willingly submits herself to her own destruction and to the dismantlement of her property and estate: *"My little girl, she isn't always kind"* (414, original emphasis). That the whims of a deceased daughter, through her mother's agency, should decide upon the plight of the last occupants of the Georgian mansion is the surest and shortest way to assert the irreversible process of their extinction.

Allusions to the first daughter's burial ceremony are interspersed throughout the narrative (35, 424) so that the following funerals, Mrs. Ayres's and Caroline's, take on a spectral quality, they are like "photograph[s] of [the original scene], oddly developed and slightly unreal" or like "a film on loop" (472). Mrs. Ayres never got over the loss of her first-born child. Her exclusive passion may be construed as no less than a psychopathological hypostatisation of the exclusive passion of a mother for her first-born baby. It followed from this deviancy that her other children were never fully recognised and remained unborn, as it were: "We've been disappointing her all our lives, my sister and I, I think we disappointed her simply by being born" (194). So, the script of their (non-)destiny was sealed from the outset, it was to complete the parts ascribed to them by "going out of [their] way to make themselves extinct" (190). The estate that Dr. Faraday (far a day) enters is not so much that of the undead—"Dracula's daughter" (435)—as that of the unborn, or perhaps half-born. Precisely, Mrs. Ayres explains that what she felt for her second and third child could not measure up to her total, passionate commitment to her first-born one: "She was my one true love" (219). What came after was a pale copy of the original: "a very dull and half-alive thing that love has seemed to me, sometimes! Because *I* have been half alive, you see . . . Caroline, I think, it hasn't harmed. Roderick was always the sensitive one." (220, original emphasis). Consequently, Mrs. Ayres's failure to bring her later born offspring into full existence, by unconditional filial love, results in what may be described as the spectral condition of the entire household:

> If there is something like spectrality, there are reasons to doubt this reassuring order of presents and, especially, the border between the present, the actual or present reality of the present, and everything that can be opposed to it: absence, non-presence, non-effectivity, inactuality, virtuality, or even the simulacrum in general, and so forth. (Derrida 48)

Waters goes one step further in her treatment of the non-presence or inactuality of the present, by transforming the prospect of a progeny at Hundreds Hall into the metaphoric birth of a monstrous phantom/phantasm which entraps the last surviving Ayres in a spectral curse. The ghost tale is thus taken full circle by this transformation of the natural succession of generations by procreation into a degeneration fed by the distorted vagaries of a fixated mind. "No heirs for the Ayres" could sum up the last part of the novel, focusing upon the preparations for the unlikely wedding between Dr. Faraday and Caroline Ayres. The natural conclusion to romance, in this case the love-match between the peasant and the princess, is fated to remain in limbo, or rather, parodically, at a non-effective, inactual level.

Right from the start, romance is claimed and denied in the same breath: "None of this, of course, was particularly inspiring to romance; and our affair, for the moment rather languished" (372). Caroline merely goes through the motions of the wedding preparations and what the narrator puts down to "pre-wedding jitters" (461) is actually the ultimate sign of "the Ayres family taint" (398), when the bride-to-be is discovered to have committed suicide. Through the paradigmatic plot of the ghost tale, Waters treats of the extinction of a dynasty. Evil is the overwhelming, all-devouring impulse for self-annihilation. The vital spirits of procreation have been sealed up as "some sort of ravenous frustrated energy," and as a result "some queer seed" (382) has been sown. Sarah Waters investigates, if only tentatively, the liminal spaces between biological (pro)creation, phantasms and spectrality. She blends different approaches to document her novel, notably writings from Victorian scholars like Edmund Gurney and Frederic William Henry Myers, who link ghosts and poltergeists to the mysteries of the human psyche: "Unconscious parts, so strong or so troubled they can take on a life of their own" (364).

Through this secularisation of the ghostly romance, no longer exclusively approached from a transcendental, metaphysical angle, the novelist tackles the historical question from an unwonted perspective. The Ayres lineage is brought to its termination by what amounts to an act of miscreation. In the words of the positivistic Dr. Seeley, the eponymous "Little Stranger" thus comes in for another explanation: it may be interpreted as the germ fed by malice, envy and frustration in the subliminal mind, as it grows, metaphorically like a child in the womb, in the unconscious of the socially ostracised: "'Suppose, unconsciously, she [Caroline] had given birth to some violent shadowy creature, that was effectively haunting the house?'" (400). The little stranger would be the shadow self, the spectral *Doppelgänger*, morphing into different phantasmal projections over the ages, from Caliban to Mr. Hyde.

Waters does not so much insist upon entropic decline, as she shows the spiral of evil operating through some self-generative process, whereby the dread of the ghostly cannot be discriminated from the bewildered churning of ideas of ghosts and phantoms. The giddy, circulatory logic of the tale suggests, intertwined with the actual, tangible life, a spectral life "twisting round its head to snap at its own tail" (424). The Hall itself must be the central locus of the supernatural influence.

A HAUNTED TEXT FOR A SPECTRAL DEMESNE

Waters's interest in architecture, in the configuration of edifices, was already perceptible in her depiction of Millbank prison in *Affinity* (Armitt and Gamble). In *The Little Stranger*, Hundreds Hall deserves attention in its own right. It may be wondered if it is not even the central protagonist since it is often presented as having a life of its own, regardless of human decisions. In this respect, the link between the fall of the Ayres's House and the House of Usher is indeed seminal. The novel's progression is predicated upon the different perceptions of the house. The latter is never stabilised as a fixed, anchoring reference. On the contrary, both the building's plasticity and mutability are foregrounded, as it is mediated through a whole range of filters, from accurate architectural accounts to subjective reconstructions, blurring the dividing line between the actual and the phantasmal. Further, the house is the site of spectral narratives, whose vestigial traces add a further degree of inactuality through intertextual layering. The house is first the fulcrum of diverging perspectives. It belongs to the historical maze of Warwickshire as a typical representative of the Georgian style alongside the Elizabethan manor or the Victorian neo-Gothic eyesore. It may no longer be seen as the absolute mansion, because it is caught in historical evolution at a time when age-old constructions can be shipped over to America and faithfully re-built from scratch on the new continent. At a historical turning point, Hundreds Hall is in a transitory stage of its own, curiously insubstantial on account of its being torn between its glorious past and the ruin it is on the way to becoming. The temporal perspective is reinforced through narrative focalisation as the red-brick pile is filtered successively through the double lenses of Faraday as a child and as an adult. The aggrandising vision of the former, marvelling at the Gothic vaulted corridors and mysterious crypts and dungeons, is revised by the more practical perception of the adult struck by the house's state of disrepair. In all, the house is a composite mix of the tangible and concrete, vividly rendered by means of over-precise details: "cockled window glass [. . .] weathered sandstone edgings" (1), and of the ethereal, aerial reminiscent of Blakean etchings: "staircase ascending into shadows [. . .] glassdome suspended in the darkness, a great translucent disc" (81).

Waters takes up the Gothic *topos* of the body/home dyad,[5] turning the safety of hearth and home: *Heim* into an alienating environment: *unheimlich*. The house is anthropomorphised by being on several occasions identified as the active subject holding the characters as puppets or mannequins in its grip. Hundreds Hall arouses fantastic conjectures of manipulative strategies exerted at the expense of its helpless occupants, who fear they may be tricked or kept under close surveillance. The house is alleged to be privy to the characters' shortcomings, and has the power to entice them to serve its dark, cryptic purpose. Isomorphic correspondences between the house and its inhabitants replace the metonymic chain of association of the realist novel. Verisimilitude is sacrificed for the benefit of odd and uncanny effects, as when the house is said to develop scars of its own in response to Roderick's own scorch marks. The war, which left the young man with facial stigma and a bashed-up knee, also spoilt the property. Rusting barbed wire and sheets of iron are strewn on the estate and scratches and cigarette burns deface the upper floors where soldiers were billeted. Besides, the motif of vampirism tilts the narrative towards the hyperbolic grotesque. The mansion is an insatiable ghoul sucking the vital forces of the Ayres, before being chewed up by realtors "spit[ting] it all out again in nasty lumps" (246) with their housing schemes. In addition, the thematics of feasting on rustic fares is slipped in, as a baroque counterpoint aiming to play up the notion of quaint Englishness, when a character reads out a few lines by Robert Herrick (139). In sharp contrast with this bucolic variation, the gut metaphor and the ingestion and cannibalistic imagery are historically coded; they call to mind caricatures of replete landlords gorging themselves on victuals whilst their hard-pressed labourers died of starvation. By extension, it calls up a whole network of associations including the Irish famine and absentee landlords, which have been shown to constitute the historical subtext of Stoker's *Dracula*, mentioned in passing by Waters (435). Through the evocation of Hundreds Hall as a living organ, the trauma of past genocides is touched upon, if only obliquely, because it is in the nature of the paradigmatic English mansion to be historically connoted.

However, the hallmark of Waters's fiction-writing is probably to be found in her masterly, albeit discreet, use of intertextuality. All her fictions to date may be said to be multi-layered and fraught with fragments from well-known, canonical texts. *The Little Stranger* is no exception; it offers itself as a haunted text for a spectral demesne. Furthermore, the ghostly effect is heightened through deferral, as the most easily identifiable hypotexts are themselves texts depicting more or less haunted houses that have cast their spell over generations of readers. Interestingly, these texts, chiefly *La Belle au Bois Dormant* (referred to in French in the novel), *Great Expectations* and *Jane Eyre*,[6] through their dialogic correspondences within the novel, set off unprecedented echoes among each other, which is conducive to a deepening, enthralling effect. The first allusion to *bois dormant* is casual and jocular and must be understood in the context of the victory of Attlee's Labour government, which led some old disgruntled families to dream that their estates might providentially fall asleep to be awakened by the next Conservative government.

A peculiar ambience, amounting to death-in-life, life-in-death, characterises the mansion, whose shrouded furniture is like so many ghosts awaiting some hypothetical return to life. The suspension of time can be seen as an enchantment, or as a curse, wedged as it is in a period of historical limbo when the future is hard to foretell. Dr. Faraday, for instance, is proven wrong in his predictions when at the beginning of the novel he anticipates a drastic fall in his practice as a consequence of the introduction of the new

Health Service. In the epilogue, it turns out to have been just the opposite. The spell of lethargy at Hundreds estate, with its fairy-tale echoes, overlaps with another equally famous retreat from the course of time in the field of literature: Satis House in *Great Expectations*. The Ayres's property is over-run with nettle and bindweed just as Miss Havisham's garden is overgrown with tangled vegetation. In addition, Mrs. Ayres's voice is like cobwebs (240), and the fateful hour of twenty to nine, when all the clocks were stopped at Satis House to freeze for eternity the moment when the bridegroom should have showed up to claim his beloved, is also to be read on the timepieces at the Hundreds. Waters weaves together the fairy-tale castle plunged into a hundred-year-long slumber and the novelist's invention of a house purport-ing to stay beyond the reach of time, to comment on the collective trauma caused by the incapacity to keep pace with the changing course of history. Such textual interweaving may come with tongue-in-cheek, though: "There the air of general enchantment was even more pronounced, the stable clock still fixed at twenty to nine in that grim Dickensian joke [. . .] all thick with cobwebs too" (388).

Finally, by evoking the improbable prospect of a wedding between Far-aday, the uncouth booby, and Caroline Ayres, the aunt-maiden squire's daughter, Waters stumbles on both a famous aborted wedding and the no-less celebrated place with which it is associated: Jane Eyre and Roches-ter at Thornfield, another haunted hall. Clues are scattered to read *Jane Eyre* through *The Little Stranger*, and Thornfield Hall through Hundreds Hall. Fires first, and the riddle of how they started out, which subsequently invites an unexpected parallel between the imprisoned creole Mistress of Thornfield Hall and the confined-to-his-room Master of Hundreds Hall, both being in their own way alienated. The verticality of both places, so crucial to the Gothic, is pointed at by Dr. Faraday in a remark oddly redo-lent of what is probably the most famous attic room in literature the world over: "It looks like a lunatic's cell up there" (350). What clinches the textual interplay between these haunted and reader-haunting literary places and Waters's own version of a haunted manor is the moment of the realisa-tion of the failure of the wedding, when it transpires that everything is *not* going according to plans. At this fateful moment, there is both a bit of Jane Eyre and a bit of Miss Havisham about Dr. Faraday's own matrimonial discomfiture, barring the ostentatiously detached tone, of course: "At one o'clock—the hour fixed for our wedding—I was sitting at the bedside of an elderly patient [. . .] wondering vaguely which other couple had taken our slot at the registry office, that was all" (468).

CONCLUSION

Waters's *The Little Stranger* illustrates the potential ties between romance and contemporary history which, over the past two decades, has developed new fields of research into the issues of memory, trauma and war.[7] The ghost story falls under the romance category in so far as it testifies to the remanence of a vestigial past through after-images or hallucinatory transfigurations of actual experiences.

By drawing extensively on the capacity of the phantom tale to blur the boundary line between the objective and the subjective, the actual and the phantasmal, and to confront the limits of the representable, Waters propounds a thought-provoking return to an uneventful, transitory period in English history: the lull of the immediate post-war years. By so doing, she implicitly questions the possibility of telling the event, what positivist history has always been concerned with. In Graham Swift's *Waterland*, Tom Crick, the main character-narrator, who happens to be a history teacher, speaks of history as "The Grand Narrative, the filler of vacuums, the dispeller of fears of the dark" (53). And the phenomenological sensation of history is neatly summarised as "Plenty of Here and Now" (66). Waters's stance is the exact opposite of Crick's definition of history in *Waterland*. She deliberately sets her fiction in the uneventful, historical vacuum of 1947–48, singularly devoid of "Here and Now" to address the spectrality of an unhinged time period, totally emptied of the plenitude and substance of the Now. This epistemic posture retrospectively puts the troubled war years into some uncanny perspective, as it seems to suggest that the cognitive knowledge of the event, because of the non-contemporaneity of language to what it relates, and due to the generality of the linguistic medium, characterised by its iterability, is always bound to miss in some way the specificity of the event evoked. This halo of unsaid, or rather of unsayable, would be the tribute history has to pay (Derrida, Soussana and Nous 81–112). The ghost tale may be an attempt at a compromise to remedy, poetically at least, this epistemological lack.

NOTES

1. The allusion to Georgette Heyer, a major representative of this (sub)genre, in Sarah Waters's novel is, of course, not purely coincidental. See *The Little Stranger*, where a character in the portrait gallery at Hundreds Hall is introduced as "just like a Georgette Heyer rake" (65).
2. *Tipping the Velvet* (1998), *Affinity* (1999) and *Fingersmith* (2002).
3. Both writers are cited by Waters herself as decisive influences in writing this novel. Speaking about Josephine Tey's novel *The Franchise Affair* (1948), Waters, in an article for *The Guardian*, points out that though it is not a ghost fiction, but a detective story, it helped her imagine elements for both the setting and the plot of *The Little Stranger*: "*The Franchise Affair* is an ingenious book, a crime novel without a corpse, a detective story in which the victim is justice itself and the main weapons are ignorance, prejudice and careless journalism. The essential mystery is wonderfully established; the claustrophobic building up of the apparently seamless case [. . .] is impeccably done" (Waters 2009b, 2). The acknowledgement of Angela Thirkell's influence, whose novels are, according to Waters "at times [. . .] unbearably

snobbish," may seem more unexpected. It is probably through their treatment
of both the class question and society's changes in post-war England that
their link with *The Little Stranger* is the most obvious, as Waters explained
in an interview when she was shortlisted for the Man Booker Prize (Waters
2009c).
4. A passing allusion to the pastoral utopia dreamed up by William Morris in
his *News from Nowhere* (1890).
5. On this point see Annie Le Brun.
6. All three hypotexts are closely linked to the question of trauma. *Sleeping
Beauty* has been taken as a paradigm to investigate the trauma of awakening
after long comas (Minjard). In the context of *The Little Stranger* this may be
understood metaphorically as affording a tragically ironic perspective, since
Hundreds Hall is awakening to a world in which it no longer has any part
to play. Miss Havisham in *Great Expectations* has been shown to betray all
the symptoms diagnosed by Freud in "Mourning and Melancholia." More
recently, Anny Sadrin has drawn from Nicolas Abraham and Maria Torok's
notion of crypt to analyse the recluse's melancholia in *Great Expectations*
(223). As for *Jane Eyre*, the complementary relationship between the eponymous Jane and Bertha Mason has been recently analysed as symptomatic of
a failure to comply with "normal feminine" development in Victorian England. The culturally induced trauma of growing into the Angel of the House
would be fictionally recorded through the process of repetition underpinning
the Gothic novel (Ellis).
7. For an updated bibliography on the question see Hunt 206–21.

WORKS CITED

Armitt, Lucie and Sarah Gamble. "The Haunted Geometries of Sarah Waters's
Affinity." *Textual Practice* 20.1 (2006): 141–59. Print.
Badiou, Alain. *L'Éthique, essai sur la conscience du mal.* Caen: Éditions Nous,
2009. Print.
Baer, Ulrich. *Spectral Evidence, The Photography of Trauma.* Cambridge, MA. &
London: MIT Press, 2002. Print.
Brontë, Charlotte. *Jane Eyre.* 1847. Ed. Dunn R.J. New York & London: Norton,
1987. Print.
Derrida, Jacques. *Specters of Marx.* 1993. Trans. Peggy Kamuf. New York & Lon-
don: Routledge, 2006. Print.
Derrida, Jacques, Gad Soussana and Alexis Nous. *Dire l'événement, est-ce possi-
ble ? Séminaire de Montréal, pour Jacques Derrida.* Paris: L'Harmattan, 2001.
81–112. Print.
Dickens, Charles. *Great Expectations.* 1860–61. Ed. Rosenberg E. New York &
London: Norton, 1999. Print.
Eagleton, Terry. *On Evil.* New Haven and London: Yale UP, 2010. Print.
Ellis, Kate Ferguson. "Can you Forgive Her? The Gothic Heroine and her Critics."
A New Companion to The Gothic. Ed. David Punter. Oxford: Blackwell Pub-
lishing, 2012. 457–68. Print.
Felman, Shoshana. "The Betrayal of the Witness: Camus' *The Fall.*" *Testimonies. Cri-
ses of Witnessing in Literature, Psychoanalysis, and History.* Eds. Shoshana Fel-
man and Dori Laub. New York and London: Routledge, 1992. 165–203. Print.
Freud, Sigmund. "Mourning and Melancholia." *The Standard Edition of the Complete Psychological Works of Sigmund Freud* Vol. XIV. Trans. Joan Riviere.
London: The Hogarth P, 1975. 237–58. Print.

Fukuyama, Francis. *The End of History and the Last Man*. New York: Avon, 1992. Print.

Ganteau, Jean-Michel. "Fantastic, but Truthful: The Ethics of Romance." *The Cambridge Quarterly* 32.3 (2003): 225–38. Print.

Hughes, Helen. *The Historical Romance*. London & New York: Routledge, 1993. Print.

Hunt, Nigel C. *Memory, War and Trauma*. Cambridge: Cambridge UP, 2010. Print.

James, Henry. "The Turn of the Screw." 1898. *The Turn and the Screws and Other Stories*. Harmondsworth: Penguin, 1977. 7–121. Print.

Kohlke, Marie-Luise. "Into History through the Back Door: The 'Past Historic' in *Nights at the Circus* and *Affinity*." *Women: A Cultural Review* 15.2 (July 2004): 153–66. Print.

LaCapra, Dominick. *Writing History, Writing Trauma*. Baltimore and London: The Johns Hopkins UP, 2001. Print.

Le Brun, Annie. *Les Châteaux de la subversion*. Paris: Folio Gallimard, 1982. Print.

Minjard, Raphaël. "Pourquoi la belle au bois dormant est sortie de son château?" *Perspectives Psy* 46.4 (October-December 2007): 368–75. Print.

Morris, William. *News from Nowhere*. 1890. Harmondsworth: Penguin Classics, 1998. Print.

Poe, Edgar Allan. "The Fall of the House of Usher." 1839. *The Selected Writings of Edgar Allan Poe*. Ed. G.R. Thompson. New York and London: Norton, 2004. 199–216. Print.

Sadrin, Anny. *Great Expectations*. 1988. Paris: Éditions du Temps, 1999. Print.

Swift, Graham. *Waterland*. London: Picador, 1983. Print.

Waters, Sarah. *Tipping the Velvet*. London: Virago, 1998. Print.

———. *Affinity*. London: Virago, 1999. Print.

———. *Fingersmith*. London: Virago, 2002. Print.

———. *The Night Watch*. London: Virago, 2006a. Print.

———. "Romance among the Ruins." *The Guardian* 28 January 2006b: 4. Print.

———. *The Little Stranger*. London: Virago, 2009a. Print.

———. "The Lost Girl." *The Guardian* 30 May 2009b: 2. Print.

———. "I am a sucker for a good ghost story." Interview by Sophie Rochester. http://www.themanbookerprize.com/perspective/articles/1261. 2009c. Retrieved on 26/02/2012. Web.

White, Hayden. *Metahistory, The Historical Imagination in Nineteenth-Century Europe*. Baltimore & London: The Johns Hopkins UP, 1973. Print.

———. *The Content of the Form, Narrative Discourse and Historical Representation*. Baltimore & London: The Johns Hopkins UP, 1987. Print.

Žižek, Slavoj. *Violence: Six Sideways Reflections*. London: Profile Books, 2008. Print.

3 Personal Trauma, Romance and Ghostly Traces in Justine Picardie's *Daphne*[1]

Rosario Arias

[T]he desire, the pure quintessential need of my readers for escape,
[is] a thing I myself understood only too well. Life had been hard on
them and they had not fought back, they'd collapsed like soufflés in a
high wind. Escape wasn't a luxury for them, it was a necessity [. . .].
(Atwood 34)

A recent exhibition at the Brontë Parsonage Museum, "Sex, Drugs and Literature: The Infernal World of Branwell Brontë" (1 June 2009–June 2011), focused on the disreputable figure of Branwell Brontë and his influence on his sisters' works and lives. In visiting this exhibition, one could feel the literary genius of the Brontë brother gone to waste.[2] It is not coincidental that the subtitle of the exhibition received the title of the critical piece Daphne du Maurier (1907–1989) wrote about Branwell Brontë in 1960, captivated as she was by the Brontë family and the literary mystery of Branwell's life. *The Infernal World of Branwell Brontë* was dedicated to J. Alex Symington, former curator of the Brontë Parsonage Museum Library and keeper of the Brotherton Collection at the University of Leeds, who corresponded with the novelist for several years until his death.

This chapter analyses Justine Picardie's *Daphne* (2008) against the backdrop of personal trauma, romance and a myriad of ghostly traces. Picardie's novel mirrors du Maurier's obsession with the protagonist of her famous novel *Rebecca* (1938), a Gothic romance full of unspeakable secrets and incestuous feelings. In turn, *Daphne*, an example of what is now termed "biofiction," which can be defined as a "hybrid genre [. . .] highlighting the tension between biography and fiction, as well as marking the overlap between them" (Kaplan 65), shows du Maurier's increasing fascination with Branwell Brontë in an attempt to leave *Rebecca* behind, and as the result of her ambivalent relationship with her husband (which in turn can be read alongside du Maurier's unresolved conflicts with her father). Therefore, not only *Rebecca* (and its protagonists), but also the figure of Branwell Brontë, hauntingly return in Picardie's *Daphne*. This novel has a complicated threefold structure: firstly, the first-person narrative, set in contemporary London, centres on an unnamed young PhD student, recently married to a well-established senior academic, who strives to find a topic for her thesis and eventually turns to her life-long obsession with

Daphne du Maurier; secondly, du Maurier's strand of the plot, written in the third person, together with the story of Alex Symington, whose mutual passion for Branwell Brontë's life fuels the narrative, set in the 1950s; and finally, their interspersed letters over the years. These three characters are haunted by secrets, silences and shadows of the past. In what follows I will consider Picardie's novel, in between biography and fiction, from the point of view of the haunting presence of personal trauma (a sense of dislocation is commonly shared by the second wife of *Rebecca*, the fictional du Maurier, and the unnamed narrator in Picardie's novel), coupled with the soothing influence of the world of romance and escapism. As I hope to show, romance strategies in this novel facilitate "the evocation of the healing phase of trauma" (Introduction 10).

Daphne's generic hybridity points to its own status as a piece of "biofiction," or, if we prefer, of "fictography" (Carpenter 89) as it shows the overlapping of life and fiction, particularly in the depiction of the novelist Daphne du Maurier and of Alex Symington, whose attraction to the figure of Branwell Brontë underpins the pervasive presence of the past. *Daphne* proves to be an echo-chamber, full of resonances of du Maurier's biography and works, namely *Rebecca*, whose main intertext is acknowledged to be Charlotte Brontë's *Jane Eyre* (1847). Therefore, Picardie's novel explores an overwhelming past whose presence is powerfully felt in the present in various ways, and in so doing, it attempts to uncover the dark side of Daphne du Maurier as well as shed light onto the neglected brother of the Brontë family.

Daphne opens with du Maurier's struggles to put together the broken pieces of her family, torn apart after her husband and ex-soldier, Lieutenant General Sir Frederick Browning, has just had a nervous breakdown, while simultaneously she gets the news of his affair with a woman du Maurier calls the Snow Queen. After one visit to her husband during his convalescence in London, she returns to Menabilly, the real-life counterpart of Manderley, the mansion in *Rebecca*. She cannot help but feel permanently haunted by the image of Rebecca and her own similarities with her literary creation(s): the first and the second wife of Mr. de Winter. Du Maurier's Gothic romance has been studied as manifestation of the uncanny, that is, as a modality of the return of the repressed as defined by Sigmund Freud (1919): "[the] uncanny element is actually nothing new or strange, but something that was long familiar to the psyche and was estranged from it only through being repressed" (2003, 148). More recently, *Rebecca* has been approached from the critical standpoint of haunting and spectrality as theorised by the psychoanalysts Nicolas Abraham and Maria Torok (Arias and Pulham xi–xxvi). Re-interpreting Freud's case of "the Wolf Man," Abraham and Torok sustained "the claim that the patient may be the bearer of *someone else's* trauma" and developed "two related but distinct terms, the crypt and the phantom," which signal "the survival of the dead in the unconscious of the living" (Davis 77, original emphasis). Allan Lloyd Smith has examined *Rebecca* from the perspective of the "phantom," which in turn derives from Abraham and Torok's previous work on secrets and the crypt, published in *The Shell and the Kernel* (1987). The phantom refers to "the unspeakable," as "[t]he presence of the phantom indicates the effects, on the descendants, of something that had inflicted narcissistic injury or even catastrophe on the parents" (Abraham and Torok 174). The dead can survive in two different ways in Abraham and Torok's sense, and the phantom, Rebecca's enduring presence, haunts the subject of the husband, Maxim de Winter, whose life is tormented by his first wife's secrets. He lived a double life with Rebecca, as five days after their marriage she disclosed her real nature to her husband, who made a bargain with her about keeping up appearances. And after marrying his second wife, the unnamed narrator of the novel, he took her to the same place where secrets had been disclosed, in order "to remember":

> 'I found her out at once,' he was saying, 'five days after we were married. You remember that time I drove you in the car, to the hills above Monte Carlo? I wanted to stand there again, to remember. She sat there, laughing, her black hair blowing in the wind; she told me about herself, told me things I shall never repeat to a living soul. I knew then what I had done, what I had married. Beauty, brains, and breeding. Oh, my God!' (305)

Lloyd Smith applies this notion of the phantom and cryptonymy (Abraham and Torok's interpretive method) to the relation between Rebecca, the first wife, and Maxim de Winter and he shows that "Rebecca somehow persists, as a phantom, in *his* life, using *phantom* in Abraham and Torok's sense, that is, as a haunting by the secret of another" (302, original emphasis). The phantom is the haunting of the other within the self and s/he returns to prevent secrets and mysteries from being discovered. However, I would argue that there is another phantom or secret buried in du Maurier's life and fiction, as well as in Picardie's novel: the story of "[du Maurier's] remarkable and paradoxical family, the ghosts which haunted her life and fiction" (Kelly). In this sense, du Maurier's life and fiction can be considered "phantom texts," defined by Nicholas Royle as "textual phantoms which do not necessarily have the solidity or objectivity of a quotation, an intertext or explicit acknowledged presence" (280). And perhaps the phantom text might be seen here as an architext, as suggested by Teresa Petersen who convincingly argued that du Maurier uses the Gothic genre, specifically doubles and mirror images, to indicate "a narrative of incest and lesbian desire" (53).

FAMILY AND LITERARY TRACES

Granddaughter of George du Maurier, the author of *Trilby* (1894–95) and *Peter Ibbetson* (1891), and daughter of Sir Gerald du Maurier, the late Victorian and early twentieth-century actor and manager, Daphne du Maurier devoted several works to her family tree: *Gerald: A Portrait* (1934) is a biography of her father; *The du Mauriers* (1937) mainly focuses on her grandfather; *The Glass-blowers* (1963) is concerned with her ancestors. Lastly, *Myself When Young* (1977), an autobiography that centres on her youth, written at the age of seventy, engages with du Maurier's search for sexual identity and ambiguous attraction for her father, Sir Gerald, who is also clearly depicted in novels such as *I'll Never Be Young Again* (1932), *The Progress of Julius* (1933), *My Cousin Rachel* (1951) and, most tellingly, *Rebecca*, in which

> [the unnamed narrator's] search for identity would [. . .] be seen as played out through the father/daughter relationship that borders on the incestuous between the narrator and her father/husband, Maxim de Winter, *and* the dual performance of the narrator and the Rebecca/Danvers relationship with its lesbian undertones. (Petersen 54, original emphasis)

The shadow of incestuous attraction and lesbian desire looms large over du Maurier's fiction, and also over Picardie's *Daphne*. The second storyline re-interprets *Rebecca* in the present time: the unnamed narrator (only in the final pages the reader is to know that her name is Jane, hauntingly reminding us of Charlotte Brontë's Jane Eyre) is an orphan with a "quite Victorian" story (39), as much as Rebecca's second wife and Jane Eyre herself. While she "was shy [. . .] and looked childish beside [her husband, who was] an academic in London" (Picardie 2008a, 35), her husband is confident and treats her like a little child, thus echoing the father-daughter relationship in *Rebecca*. Several reviewers of the novel have noted that this contrived secondary plot is not as successful as the main one dealing with du Maurier's writing of her book on Branwell Brontë (Parker). Nevertheless, it seems that this contemporary re-appraisal of *Rebecca* underlines the hidden sexual uncertainties in du Maurier's life (already suggested by Margaret Forster in her biography of the author), since Jane and Rachel (the first wife whose presence is ominous in the novel until she finally materialises as an extremely successful academic, flamboyant and sophisticated) can again be taken as composite of du Maurier herself. Fiction and reality are difficult to distinguish in the genre of biofiction, in which Picardie, the author of this novel, attempts to answer the following question: "what was the reality that du Maurier feared facing?" (2008c). In my opinion, the answer is twofaced but related to the oedipal triangle and du Maurier's inability to move away from the fascination her father exerted upon her. In turn, her mother, who "might have been the Snow Queen in disguise" (Taylor xv), inspired rejection and disapproval in du Maurier. Interestingly enough, in Picardie's novel du Maurier's husband has an illicit affair with the so-called Snow Queen, the main figure of Hans Christian Andersen's fairy tale about the evil queen capable of turning children's hearts into ice and their memories into oblivion.

Arguably, Gerald du Maurier's desire for a son made du Maurier his favourite and she embarked on developing her masculine side, the "boy-in-the box," which accounted for the ambiguous feelings the nameless narrator of *Rebecca* displays. Teresa Petersen, Sue Zlosnik and Avril Horner have examined du Maurier's ambivalence towards her father, which borders on the incestuous, and have delved into the way in which her writing "might have functioned both to resolve such feelings and to give voice, simultaneously, to deep concerns about the various ways in which fathers threaten daughters" (Petersen 55; Zlosnik and Horner 10). Although there are clearly incestuous relationships in her novels, du Maurier's relation with her father cannot be considered incestuous *stricto sensu*.[3] However, as I hope to demonstrate, in Picardie's novel, as in *Rebecca*, the blurring of boundaries between fantasy and reality, imagination and real life, together with the complex web of intertextual links, enacts the repression of du Maurier's traumatic incestuous feelings, since she has carefully expurgated these from the biography of her father and her autobiography. On a summer holiday at the age of fourteen, she had an extremely close relationship with her middle-aged cousin, Geoffrey, who constantly reminded her of her father, as stated in du Maurier's *Myself When Young*: "D [Daddy] and he were the greatest of friends and companions, for there were only twelve years between them [. . .] I knew, instinctively, that we shared a secret" (61). She goes on to suggest that "[they began] a relationship that was curiously akin to what I felt for D, but which stirred me more, and was also exciting because I felt it to be wrong" (62–63). Du Maurier insists on the absence of kisses or any sort of physical contact between them at that stage in her autobiography, but when she is twenty they meet again and on that occasion Geoffrey and Daphne kiss in the drawing room (130). In *Daphne*, Picardie re-writes this key episode in du Maurier's youth and reduces the lapse of time by recounting these two episodes together. In so doing, Picardie takes pains to show more explicitly her sexual awakening in relation to both her cousin and D:

> Geoffrey was kissing her, his tongue pushing between her lips [. . .]. [S]he saw her father standing there, staring down at them [. . .]. It had seemed so natural to kiss Geoffrey [. . .] and he was so sweet and lovable, but it was also just like kissing Daddy. 'Perhaps this family is the same as the Borgias,' she wrote [in her diary], 'a sort of incest [. . .]'. And had she not thought of her father as she kissed Geoffrey [. . .]? (2008a, 222–23, 227)

Her writing allowed du Maurier to exorcise her ghosts and to explore the darker side of her own personality once and again. Her family secrets and ghostly traces from the past (especially, her dubious relationship with her father) are replayed in du Maurier's fiction and this may be taken as "acting out," in Dominick LaCapra's terms (713). This obsessive return to her (family) past should be understood as compulsive repetition, which defines melancholia, "in some way related to an object-loss which is withdrawn from consciousness, in contradistinction to mourning, in which there is nothing about the loss that is unconscious" (Freud 1984, 254). Tommy, du Maurier's husband, also suffered from melancholia as he was deeply affected by the wounding traces of WWI and II, as well as by a personal trauma closely related, in Picardie's interpretation of their relationship, to du Maurier's affair with Gertrude Lawrence, one of her father's actress lovers. According to Nina Auerbach, this affair "reaffirmed [Daphne and her father's] fraternity" (35), but it seems that the pang of guilt was buried in du Maurier's unconscious, and it also erupted in Tommy's mental breakdown: "could it be this that was the real root of Tommy's despair?" (Picardie 2008a, 274).

Once again *Rebecca* has to be mentioned as this novel showcases a subtext of lesbian desire in Mrs. Danvers's fixation on Rebecca's presence at Manderley. Mrs. Danvers provides the Gothic atmosphere, as she makes it clear that the house is haunted by the apparition of Rebecca, who watches the comings and goings of both the second wife and Mr. de Winter. On the face-to-face encounter between Mrs. Danvers and the unnamed narrator, the former asserts that Rebecca is "still mistress here, even if she is dead. She's the real Mrs. de Winter, not you. It's you that's the shadow and the ghost" (275). Paulina Palmer has aptly noted that the Gothic has served the lesbian discourse well since three defining features of this genre—excess, thematic concerns like female subjectivity, and the concept of the "uncanny" to illustrate repressed fears, libidinal desires, and silences—favour the re-inscription of lesbian subjectivity. Palmer and Petersen mention Terry Castle's theory of the spectralisation of the lesbian to refer to the ways in which lesbian desire has been decorporealised in literature and culture since the eighteenth century by associating lesbians with spectral images such as the ghost, the spectre and the apparition (Palmer 124; Petersen 59–60). According to Terry Castle, "[this] metaphor has functioned as the necessary psychological and rhetorical means for objectifying—and ultimately embracing—that which otherwise could not be acknowledged" (60). In *Rebecca* du Maurier utilises the Gothic romance in order to revise and transform it from within. The silences that the main characters maintain about Maxim de Winter's past married life can signify the repression of ambiguous desires, the "unspeakable" secrets which are eventually disclosed (although not leading to the promised happy resolution of the romance genre).[4]

In *Daphne*, du Maurier's Gothic romance takes a different turn as there is no seemingly lesbian desire between du Maurier and Tod, her governess when she was a child and her own children's governess, and now part of the household; although Tommy called her "Mrs. Danvers, after Rebecca's macabre housekeeper," du Maurier contradicts this as "there was nothing unnerving about Tod [. . .] and though she was devoted to Daphne, it was not at all the same as Mrs. Danvers's obsessive love for Rebecca" (16). However, in the contemporary storyline Picardie re-enacts the lesbian subtext found in *Rebecca* in the covert relationship that the nameless narrator keeps with Rachel, the first wife. If, conventionally speaking, romance as genre fulfils the need to be re-united with the pre-oedipal mother by transferring this desire onto the effectual hero, in this strand of the plot it is Rachel who dashes in to rescue Jane from her claustrophobic existence and from her disastrous married life. Jane cannot help but show contradictory feelings towards Rachel, even at the end of the novel when she is beginning a new life (Picardie 2008a, 358). Consequently, as in *Rebecca*, Picardie's novel textualises and releases fantasies of lesbian desire, and those of incestuous attraction.

TRAUMA AND ROMANCE

Now I would like to establish links between du Maurier's father, cousin and husband, with Branwell Brontë and Alex Symington, the two other men involved in Picardie's narrative. It remains clear that all the important men in her life (her father, her cousin Geoffrey, her husband "Boy," the literary figure of Branwell Brontë and, ultimately, Alex Symington) can be analysed as extensions of Daphne's father. It has already been suggested that her middle-aged cousin and her father were alike and that this affinity caused sexual disturbance in Daphne du Maurier. On the other hand, Gerald and Tommy, father and husband, were not dissimilar after several years of marriage: both drank heavily, suffered bouts of depression and melancholia, "[b]ut more disturbing to du Maurier were her mounting fears that her husband might mirror Maxim de Winter (a character who also bears some resemblance to her father [. . .])" (Picardie 2008c). These fears are expressed at the beginning of *Daphne* (12). Although Picardie's novel never states this openly, it seems that the author sustains the notion that Daphne's obsession with the life of Branwell Brontë owes much to her relationship with her father. In Picardie's novel Daphne du Maurier keeps in touch with one of the Llewelyn boys, his cousin Peter,[5] who chronicles the family story or "[t]he family morgue," as he calls it, at the time she is writing her book on Branwell:

> [S]he found her mind drifting towards her cousin, [. . .] wondering how he was getting on. But Daphne tried to concentrate only on Branwell, who had suffered himself, after all, dogged by misery and brought down further by drink, *like Gerald*; no, stop now, stop thinking about Gerald, this was not about him [. . .]. (Picardie 2008a, 250, emphasis added)

As mentioned before, Sue Zlosnik and Avril Horner consider that the paternal influence "continued to inspire and inform her writing in ways that suggest a continuing *unconscious* negotiation with her father's personality [. . .]" (13, original emphasis). It is my contention that du Maurier's decision to devote herself to writing her biography on Branwell Brontë had much to do with her husband's breakdown, as well as with her father's presence in her life, "the two ghosts of her past" (Kelly), and *Daphne* seems to prove this argument. In the opening section of the novel the fictional du Maurier shows her attraction for this literary figure, "tormented by the knowledge of unfulfilled promise" (Picardie 2008a, 19). Partly to distract her mind from her husband's affair, partly to prove to the wider world that she was worthy of critical attention, du Maurier embarked on one of the two main biographies of Branwell Brontë to date: du Maurier's *The Infernal World of Branwell Brontë* (1960) and Winifred Gérin's *Branwell Brontë* (1961). According to one critic, these two biographies were timely as they came out when there was "recent research on the Brontë's miniature writings" (Norman 1961, 461). These biographies differed, in her view, in that Gérin solidified her conjectures by accumulating and adding data and fact, whereas du Maurier "relied more on psychological probing, in an effort to explain Branwell from within" (461).

Branwell Brontë was the only son in the Brontë household and his father held high expectations about him and his genius, which were frustrated by his untimely death at the age of thirty one. At the exhibition mentioned at the beginning of this essay Branwell's creative output is clearly perceived in sketches, paintings and portraits, put on display in the Bonnell room. He had several opportunities to become a successful writer or a painter, but he let them waste. Sylva Norman, early reviewer of *The Infernal World of Branwell Brontë*, asks the following question that haunted du Maurier and other Brontë critics: "What went wrong, and why, with Branwell Brontë?" (1960, 734). Du Maurier stressed the relevance of his epileptic fits, together with his propensity to heavy drinking and drug consumption. At eighteen he was appointed to be interviewed for admission as an art student at the London Royal Academy of Arts, but this was thwarted and there is "[n]o word [. . .] about what had happened at the Royal Academy" (1972, 51). One of the most important blows Branwell (and his family) received was his dismissal from the Robinson household. It is widely known that he felt a passionate attachment to Mrs Robinson, but du Maurier goes further in speculating the following:

> If Branwell had been writing love letters to Mrs Robinson, the husband would not have threatened him with 'exposure', for to expose Branwell would also expose the lady who received the letters [. . .]. It is possible that, left at Thorp Green with Edmund [the Robinson boy under Branwell's care and tuition], and free from the constraining presence

of his employer, he had attempted in some way to lead Edmund astray (1972, 163)

Picardie's novel takes this hypothesis as the most plausible reason behind Branwell's sudden dismissal, and she includes one concocted letter from *The Yorkshire Post* in which du Maurier is praised for her biography as an achievement, supporting the same view: "that the tutor was thought to be a dangerous influence on the child's mind and morals" (Picardie 2008a, 391). This indicates that du Maurier had sought "to understand [Branwell]" (Norman 1960, 734). It seems clear that, in trying to understand Branwell, du Maurier was also hoping to know her father and husband better.

Du Maurier dedicated this volume to Alex Symington, Brontë scholar, bibliophile and ex-curator of the Haworth Parsonage Museum and the Brotherton collection at the University of Leeds, with whom she maintained correspondence for three years until Symington's death. Picardie's novel imbricates history and fiction by including "the reproduction of the du Maurier-Symington correspondence, now archived at The University of Exeter Library's Special Collections" (Carpenter 89). When du Maurier began writing letters to him, it was a long time since he had published the Shakespeare Head edition of the collected works of the Brontës and his reputation was clouded with suspicion, as he was involved in the disappearance of a number of manuscripts while he was curator, to the extent that the Brontë Society even took legal action against him (although it came to nothing). Du Maurier is not aware of this fact and she takes Symington as a prestigious Brontë scholar who might be instrumental in providing her with unpublished material for her biography. Picardie's novel precisely begins at this point of their professional liaison, when Symington feels flattered at being needed by a well-known novelist who seeks his assistance to rescue Branwell from oblivion. If I established linkages between du Maurier's father and husband, critics of Picardie's novel have detected striking similarities between Branwell Brontë and Symington (Carpenter). Symington, on the brink of his physical and mental deterioration at the beginning of the novel, made Branwell the only reason for his existence, while his family suffered from his cold indifference, obsessed as he was with proving that Branwell was of literary merit and that his work had inspired the novels and poems of his famous sisters. Neither Symington nor Branwell managed to find their places in the world, and they turned to be heavy drinkers, overwhelmed by guilt. Ginette Carpenter not only relates Symington and Branwell—"Like Branwell, Symington lacks the ability to create his own story—either artistically or personally—and therefore falls foul of an addiction to drink and self-pity in equal measure" (92)—, she also finds uncanny resemblance between Symington and Tommy, "a rather pathetic man, unable to exorcise his own demons and resorting to alcohol as cure" (92).

In *Daphne* Symington also functions as a reminder of the powerful influence du Maurier's domineering father exerted upon her life and fiction, and he comes into scene again through the use of disguise or masquerade, which, according to Sue Zlosnik and Avril Horner, is the trope du Maurier utilises in her writing to refer to "the complexities of familial relationships" (9) and a too close familial bond. Gerald was a professional performer whose debauchery, akin to that of Tommy, gave a false impression of security and a stable sense of self. Interestingly enough, Picardie fictionalises one visit the novelist actually paid to Symington at his place in real life (2008b). In the novel Symington takes on a disguise, pretending to be his assistant, not being able to face his failed life and misery at the sight of the successful novelist. Picardie's novel includes the trope of disguise to indicate deviancy and the disjunction between appearances and reality, but it also denotes the similarities between the men in du Maurier's life, particularly in this case, her father, the actor-manager, and Symington:

> But the more that he thought of the moment when Daphne arrived at his front door, the more it seemed to him that his assumption of another identity was not a decision; the words had simply floated out of his mouth, before he could stop them [. . .]. (350)[6]

In the meeting du Maurier holds with Symington (under cover) in *Daphne*, he shows her a notebook of Emily Brontë's handwritten poems, a rarity which Brontë scholars wish to find. According to Picardie's research, Symington was the last person to see this rare volume, known as the Honresfeld manuscript. This was the result of Picardie's following of the clues of the correspondence between Symington and du Maurier. Quite fittingly, she describes *Daphne* as a "quest" and "a detective story" (2008b). The quest is one of the defining features of any type of romance as Northrop Frye categorised in *Anatomy of Criticism* (1957): "The completed form of the romance is clearly the successful quest" (187). To varying degrees, the protagonists of *Daphne* undertake a quest.

Symington and du Maurier are similarly involved in the quest to know the truth of Branwell Brontë's mystery for different reasons: Symington aspires to gain academic recognition in helping du Maurier carry on with her research and to give Branwell the literary credit he thinks the Brontë brother deserves. In turn, du Maurier is determined to be recognised as a serious writer in academic circles. Picardie comments on the role of the real-life du Maurier in pursuing her line of research, and she admits that "[du Maurier], too, turned literary detective, by seeking out Symington, who owned a large number of Branwell's manuscripts" (2008b). Parallel to this, and whilst the literary du Maurier engages in knowing Branwell from within (and, by extension, Tommy and her father, similar as they are), she also searches for self-knowledge. Following Northrop Frye, a quest usually involves two main characters, a protagonist and an anti-hero (187);

du Maurier, the protagonist, finds her enemy or anti-heroine in the "Snow Queen," the woman Tommy is having an affair with, whose existence propitiates du Maurier's near-breakdown. She only finds solace and tranquillity at Menabilly.

Du Maurier succeeds in overcoming the conflict with the enemy, the anti-heroine, and after this descent into psychological hell, she is able to surface and achieve her aim of writing the biography of Branwell Brontë (even publishing it a few months before her opponent, Winifred Gérin, who is also about to finish her volume on Branwell). She will have another conflict with another opponent in disguise: Symington. He represents desolation; therefore, du Maurier escapes from this waste land of his house to avoid contamination and failure: "But it wasn't just a fear of physical infection taking hold of her, in that dim, cold study; she was beginning to think that his failure would be contagious" (Picardie 2008a, 345). Following Pierre Vitoux, du Maurier's encounters with the figures of her opponents could be taken as replays of "the binary opposition broadly defined as Light versus Darkness" (392) commonly found in Gothic romances. Finally, in trying to understand Branwell, she shows her unconscious wishes to understand the men in her life—but the novel leaves this search inconclusive. In a similar fashion, the author of the novel, Picardie, acknowledges that:

> Like du Maurier, I became obsessed by these clues [about Branwell's youthful manuscripts], and embarked on a paper chase to discover the rest of her correspondence with Symington, and a quantity of his extensive papers and manuscripts, squirreled away in various archives, scattered from West Yorkshire to New Jersey. (Picardie 2008b)[7]

As remains clear, the quest, one of the defining traits of romance narratives, features prominently in Picardie's novel. Nevertheless, it is in the contemporary storyline that the novel's connections with the romance are more patent.

The nameless narrator/Jane and Rachel (Paul's first wife) also undertake a literary quest in search of the lost Honresfeld manuscript, "Emily Brontë's much sought-after notebook of poems" (Carpenter 89), but it cannot be forgotten that this strand of the plot offers a contemporary revision of *Rebecca*, du Maurier's Gothic romance. One intertextual link between *Rebecca* and its reworking is the notion of the romantic quest, which involves a process of self-development and personal evolution, from childhood to womanhood:

> As an orphan, lacking parental or other familial precedent, [the second wife] struggles to assert herself against a dead, powerful figure who keeps alive an alternative femininity against which she must prove herself [. . .]. The search for an analogue of the self via the figure of the absent mother is paralleled by the love story's frequent conjunction of

paternal and erotic scripts. In *Rebecca* this finds expression through the girl's combined sexual and social desire for a father figure, a desire which she projects on to her lover/husband. (Simons 124–25)

Jane is an orphaned girl too and constantly searches for a substitute for her long dead mother. Like the unnamed narrator of *Rebecca*, she relocates her need of maternal love and model of female subjectivity on to a father figure who does not fulfil her expectations: he ends up as an ineffectual husband. In other words, what Jane is really searching for is to re-unite with "the lost mother" (Roberts 227). Her mother died while Jane was doing English at Cambridge University, and it is understood that her weak sense of self and lack of ego boundaries are due to her relation with her mother, whose memory haunts her. Jane's guilty conscience, for not having told her mother that she loved her on the last night her mother was alive, shows how she is still clung to her infantile stage:

> And it was the thought of my mother—or her ghost—in that familiar old raincoat that made me feel somehow ashamed, but also more myself again [. . .] when she was dead, I was so sorry that I hadn't told her that I loved her before putting the phone down, that those should have been my last words to her. (Picardie 2008a, 184)

Freud already suggested in "Family Romances" that daydreaming "[serves] as the fulfilment of wishes and as a correction of actual life" (1977, 222). Jane spends her married life daydreaming, and finds escapism from her entrapment through fantasising and reading, to the extent that she cannot distinguish what is real and what is fantasy[8]:

> And yes, I confess, when I looked at [Paul], I thought of Heathcliff and Mr. Rochester and Maxim de Winter [. . .] and how could I not, when I had been waiting for them to step out of the pages of the books I loved; when I knew them so well, read them inside out and into myself? (Picardie 2008a, 38)

Her enthusiasm for literature and romance writing "imprisons her within a cycle of repeated textual re-enactments whereby her own experiences are both mapped onto, and mapped out by, familiar fictional narratives" (Carpenter 90) like those mentioned in the above-quoted passage. Surprisingly, Jane finds her escape through the dashing figure of the first wife, Rachel, who (representing a different female script from those she has so far had access to) comes to replace the husband/lover and, thus, provides an interesting re-writing of *Rebecca*. In fact, the ending of this plotline also points to a revised version of the final outcome of du Maurier's Gothic romance. Granted that she is still passive, Jane is at least able to find some outlet for her desires and wishes, and she frees herself from the entrapment her life with

Paul stood for. Nevertheless, in Carpenter's view, the fact of finding a job in a bookshop, engaged in selling and recommending books to prospective customers, "maintains her identification with the world of the text" (90). All in all, she ultimately finds a Woolfian "room of [her] own" (Picardie 2008a, 374) towards the end of the novel, and this resonant phrase indicates that she has found some independence of mind and self-determination.

It is here that the tenuous division between biography and fiction in this novel becomes blurred. Reading (and writing) literature cannot be extricated from Jane's life, as shown above. Likewise, du Maurier could not stop writing literature as she considered this activity as part of her true self. Margaret Forster affirms that: "[t]hrough writing she lived more truly than she did in her daily life—it gave her satisfaction, release and a curious sense of elation" (416). Teresa Petersen closely relates Forster's comment with the subtext of incestuous feelings and the spectre of lesbianism in du Maurier's life and fiction, and with the question of how, through writing, she was able to come to terms with her identity.

I have elsewhere (Arias) discussed Doris Lessing's *The Sweetest Dream* (2008) and its textualisation of the spectral traces of traumatic childhoods by means of "scriptotherapy," defined by Suzette Henke as the process of narrative recovery of past traumatic experiences (xii). Along similar lines, Jeanie Warnock has analysed Doris Lessing's novel, *Memoirs of a Survivor* (1974) and the first part of her autobiography, *Under My Skin: Volume One of My Autobiography, to 1949* (1994) in the light of childhood trauma in relation to Lessing's ambivalent feelings towards her father. Warnock aptly notes that Lessing employs a nameless first-person narrator in *Memoirs of a Survivor*, who represents "Lessing's own attempts to use narrative to access and then hold together previously dissociated aspects of childhood experience" (13). It is interesting to draw similarities between this nameless first-person narrator and the unnamed second wife in *Rebecca*, as well as with the unnamed second wife in Picardie's novel: in Lessing's *Memoirs of a Survivor* the protagonist-narrator is clearly an *alter ego* of Lessing's, and there is critical agreement on the fact that the unnamed child-wife in *Rebecca* embodies du Maurier's troubled relationship with her father. To varying degrees, Lessing and du Maurier want to escape from "the nightmare repetition [sic]" (Lessing 104) by means of their writing activity. As Mark Llewellyn argues in relation to Sarah Waters's incest narrative, *Affinity* (1999), "writing provides an accessible medium, through which to demonstrate, articulate, and confront the trauma, which evades conscious experience when first undergone" (155). In du Maurier's case, it is the writing of romance and the use of romance strategies that facilitate the return of the repressed and the process of coming to terms with her ambivalence as far as her sexual identity and her father are concerned. Furthermore, I would like to contend that Picardie's novel, *Daphne*, proves how (Gothic) romance can provide coping strategies to the endless repetitions and replays of the ambivalent attractions in her narrative. We have shown how, although closely related to the Victorian Jane Eyre, this character is able to escape from stagnation and the compulsive repetitions that have long characterised her life with her husband Paul, by moving away and beginning a new life. Therefore, it seems that writing/reading (Gothic) romances alongside trauma allows for the incorporation of agency and a sense of power, as happens to Jane in Picardie's novel.

Daphne, following the thread of other contemporary biofictional novels such as Peter Ackroyd's *The Last Testament of Oscar Wilde* (1983); Julian Barnes's *Arthur and George* (2005), on Arthur Conan Doyle; or Colm Tóibín's *The Master* (2004) and David Lodge's *Author, Author* (2004) which are both on Henry James, dissolves the boundaries of the biographical and the literary. This raises a series of ethical questions about this intrusion into authors' lives, as the literary du Maurier poses in Picardie's novel (Carpenter 95). However, *Daphne* also works to recuperate "the romance of reading—and, by association, the reading of romance—[and] it also clearly wishes to reclaim du Maurier as a serious novelist" (Carpenter 94). This novel should be read, then, alongside the renewed critical interest that du Maurier has been recently attracting, testified by the celebration of an international conference in May 2007 at the University of Exeter (Munford and Taylor 1). As much as there is agreement on the figure of Daphne du Maurier and that she is a writer deserving further attention, there are attempts, every now and then, to re-consider Branwell Brontë's creative genius and his (possible) influence on the Brontë sisters. One such attempt was du Maurier's biography, published in 1960, and in this line, the Brontë Parsonage Museum organised an exhibition precisely to delve into unexplored areas of Branwell's creative outputs.

Picardie's *Daphne* is an extremely intertextual novel, with different storylines, that I have chosen to analyse in relation to trauma, incest and ghostly traces. In so doing, I have indicated how du Maurier's problematic relationship with her domineering father seeps into her romance narratives, where she is able to cope with her ambivalent feelings in disguised form, as happens in *Rebecca*. Her attempts at understanding and knowing her father are put on display in her decision to write the biography of another disreputable figure: Branwell Brontë. Picardie's *Daphne* stages du Maurier's complex familial web of feelings and attractions alongside a contemporary storyline which patently rewrites *Rebecca* with a difference. The novel is structured around the pattern of the quest, one of the defining features of the romance narrative and of the search for one's identity. As I hope to have demonstrated, romance writing (and reading) provides a satisfactory way of coming to terms with stagnation and the haunting presence of a traumatic past.

NOTES

1. The research carried out in this essay has been funded by the Spanish Ministry of Science and Innovation (MICINN) (code FFI2009–09242).

2. I wish to express my heartfelt gratitude to Professor Ann Heilmann (University of Cardiff) and Professor Mark Llewellyn (University of Strathclyde, Glasgow) for providing me with the opportunity to visit Haworth Parsonage Museum and the Branwell Brontë exhibition in October 2010.
3. Mark Llewellyn notes that "[t]he legal definition of incest in both the Punishment of Incest Act 1908 and the Sexual Offences Act 1956, into which the law was consolidated, requires penetration of the female body by a male blood relative" (141).
4. The romantic impulse that lies behind the unnamed narrator's actions is thwarted at the end of the novel when she and Maxim de Winter return to the South of France to live a companionate marriage, which "does not resurrect the passion in a re-oriented relationship" (Simons 125–26).
5. The du Maurier family held further connections with J. M. Barrie, the author of *Peter Pan* (1904) who adopted the five Llewelyn Davies brothers (also providing the inspiration for *Peter Pan*) in 1910 when Sylvia (née du Maurier) and Arthur Llewelyn Davies died. Gerald du Maurier played Captain Hook and Mr. Darling in the play, but he was really Peter Pan in real life: "essentially he was Peter Pan, a perpetual spoiled son for whom aging was death" (Auerbach 34).
6. The last sentence of the above passage reminds us precisely of the marriage between the young unnamed narrator (later, Jane) and Paul, the senior academic who spends his time lecturing his second wife on Henry James, whilst deploring the literary quality of du Maurier's romances.
7. At this point, one could find the pattern of the quest in this novel to be alike to that of A.S. Byatt's *Possession: An Academic Romance* (1990).
8. At this point Anita Brookner's *A Family Romance* (1993), a novel seeped into the romance world, comes to mind.

WORKS CITED

Abraham, Nicolas and Maria Torok. *The Shell and the Kernel: Renewals of Psychoanalysis* Vol. 1. Ed., trans., and intro. N. T. Rand. 1987. Chicago and London: U of Chicago P, 1994. Print.

Arias, Rosario. "'Aren't You Haunted by All This Recurrence?': Spectral Traces of Traumatised Childhoods in Doris Lessing's *The Sweetest Dream*." *Critique* (2012): 53.4 (2012): 355-65. Print.

Arias, Rosario and Patricia Pulham. "Introduction." *Haunting and Spectrality in Neo-Victorian Fiction: Possessing the Past*. Eds. Rosario Arias and Patricia Pulham. Basingstoke: Palgrave Macmillan, 2010. xi–xxvi. Print.

Atwood, Margaret. *Lady Oracle*. 1976. London: Virago, 1994. Print.

Auerbach, Nina. *Daphne du Maurier: Haunted Heiress*. 2000. Philadelphia: U of Pennsylvania P, 2002. Print.

Carpenter, Ginette. "Review of Justine Picardie's *Daphne*." *Women: A Cultural Review* 20.1 (2009): 89–96. Print.

Castle, Terry. *The Apparitional Lesbian: Female Homosexuality and Modern Culture*. New York: Columbia UP, 1993. Print.

Davis, Colin. *Haunted Subjects: Deconstruction, Psychoanalysis and the Return of the Dead*. Basingstoke: Palgrave Macmillan, 2007. Print.

du Maurier, Daphne. *Rebecca*. Afterword by Sally Beauman. 1938. London: Virago, 2003. Print.

———. *The Infernal World of Branwell Brontë*. 1960. Harmondsworth: Penguin, 1972. Print.

————. *Myself When Young: The Shaping of a Writer*. Intro. Helen Taylor. 1977. London: Virago, 2004. Print.

Forster, Margaret. *Daphne du Maurier*. 1993. London: Arrow, 2007. Print.

Freud, Sigmund. "Family Romances." *On Sexuality: Three Essays on the Theory of Sexuality and Other Works*. Trans. James Strachey. Ed. and comp. Angela Richards. 1908–09. Harmondsworth: Penguin, 1977. 221–25. Print.

————. "Mourning and Melancholia." *On Metapsychology: The Theory of Psychoanalysis*. Trans. James Strachey. Ed. and comp. Angela Richards. 1915–17. Harmondsworth: Penguin, 1984. 251–67. Print.

————. "The Uncanny." *The Uncanny*. Trans. David Mclintock. Intro. Hugh Haughton. 1919. London: Penguin, 2003. Print.

Frye, Northrop. *Anatomy of Criticism: Four Essays*. Princeton: Princeton UP, 1957. Print.

Henke, Suzette A. *Shattered Subjects: Trauma and Testimony in Women's Life-Writing*. New York: St. Martin's, 2000. Print.

Kaplan, Cora. *Victoriana: Histories, Fictions, Criticism*. Edinburgh: Edinburgh UP, 2007. Print.

Kelly, Richard. "Daphne du Maurier: An Obituary." *Daphne du Maurier Web Page* (21 April 1989). http://www.dumaurier.org/ obituary.html. Retrieved on 17 April 2011. Web.

LaCapra, Dominick. "Trauma, Absence, Loss." *Critical Inquiry* 25.4 (Summer 1999): 696–727. Print.

Lessing, Doris. *A Proper Marriage*. 1954. London: Flamingo-HarperCollins, 1993. Vol. 2 of *Children of Violence*. 5 vols. 1952–69. Print.

Llewellyn, Mark. "'Perfectly Innocent, Natural, *Playful*': Incest in Neo-Victorian Women's Writing." *Neo-Victorian Tropes of Trauma: The Politics of Bearing After-Witness to Nineteenth-Century Suffering*. Eds. Marie-Louise Kohlke and Christian Gutleben. Amsterdam and New York: Rodopi, 2010. 133–60. Print.

Lloyd Smith, Alan. "The Phantoms of Drood and Rebecca: The Uncanny Reencountered through Abraham and Torok's 'Cryptonymy'." *Poetics Today* 13.2 (Summer 1992): 285–308. Print.

Munford, Rebecca and Helen Taylor. "Introduction." Special issue on Daphne du Maurier. *Women: A Cultural Review* 20.1 (2009): 1–8. Print.

Norman, Sylva. "Brother and Sisters." Review of Daphne du Maurier's *The Infernal World of Branwell Brontë*. *Times Literary Supplement* 18 November 1960: 734. Print.

————. "The Black Sheep of Haworth." Review of Winifred Gérin's *Branwell Brontë*. *Times Literary Supplement* 28 July 1961: 462. Print.

Palmer, Paulina. "Lesbian Gothic: Genre, Transformation, Transgression." *Gothic Studies* 6.1 (March 2004): 118–30. Print.

Parker, Peter. Review of *Daphne*, by Justine Picardie. *Times Online* (2 March 2008). http://entertainment.timesonline.co.uk/tol/arts_and_entertainment/books/fiction/article3449279.ece. Retrieved on 29 January 2011. Web.

Petersen, Teresa. "Daphne du Maurier's *Rebecca*: The Shadow and the Substance." *AUMLA* 112 (2009): 53–66. Print.

Picardie, Justine. *Daphne*. London: Bloomsbury, 2008a. Print.

————. "The Great Brontë Mystery." *Times Online* (29 February 2008b). http:// entertainment.timesonline.co.uk/tol/arts_and_entertainment/books/article3459577.ece. Retrieved on 19 March 2011. Web.

————. "The Real Ghost of Manderley." *The Telegraph* (24 February 2008c). http://www.telegraph.co.uk/culture/donotmigrate/3671423/The-real-ghost-of-Manderley.html. Accessed on 29/01/2011. Retrieved on 21 March 2011. Web.

Roberts, Michèle. "Write, she said." *The Progress of Romance: The Politics of Popular Fiction.* Ed. Jean Radford. London: Routledge & Kegan Paul, 1986. 221–35. Print.

Royle, Nicholas. *The Uncanny.* Manchester: Manchester UP, 2003. Print.

Simons, Judy. "Rewriting the Love Story: The Reader as Writer in Daphne du Maurier's *Rebecca.*" *Fatal Attractions: Rescripting Romance in Contemporary Literature and Film.* Eds. Lynne Pearce and Gina Wisker. London: Pluto, 1998. 112–27. Print.

Taylor, Helen. "Introduction." *Myself When Young: The Shaping of a Writer.* By Daphne du Maurier. 2003. London: Virago, 2004. v–xviii. Print.

Vitoux, Pierre. "The Mode of Romance Revisited." *Texas Studies in Literature and Language* 49.4 (Winter 2007): 387–410. Print.

Warnock, Jeannie. "Unlocking the Prison of the Past: Childhood Trauma and Narrative in *The Memoirs of a Survivor.*" *Doris Lessing Studies* 23.2 (Winter 2004): 12–16. Print.

Zlosnik, Sue and Avril Horner. "Myself When Others: Daphne du Maurier and the Double Dialogue with 'D'." *Women: A Cultural Review* 20.1 (2009): 9–24. Print.

Part II

Narratives of Distress and Individual Trauma

4 Romance, Trauma and Repetition
Testing the Limits of Love

Lynne Pearce

The need for, yet denial of, repetition constitutes a paradox that has long confounded the theorisation of romantic love. Inasmuch as many of our most enduring definitions of love regard its non-repeatability as key ("love is forever," "you and no other," etc.), and others (particularly those stemming from psychoanalysis) regard the human subject's compulsion to repetition as equally non-negotiable, philosophical tension and dispute are guaranteed; and inasmuch as the romance genre depends upon an inexorable process of repeating and refiguring narrative and other conventions, so must the tension also live on in the love story itself. Repetition, in other words, is the seemingly inexhaustible, yet infinitely exhausting, life-blood of romance, regardless of whether the story in question is bound for tragedy (where death is invoked to vouchsafe love's non-repeatability) or a "happy ending" (where past relationships, as well as new ones glimmering darkly on the horizon, are temporarily dazzled and silenced by an all consuming present).

In this chapter I reflect further upon the theoretical and philosophical challenges that repetition poses for romantic love (the discourse and the genre), paying particular attention to its traumatic dimension. Following on from my discussion of the ways in which the moment of *ravissement* (Barthes 188–94) may be conceived as a traumatic incident in *Romance Writing* and an earlier essay (Pearce 2007, 17–19; 2004, 521–38) I explore the ways in which this first trauma is, itself, repeated in the course of a love affair before proposing, controversially, that the repetition of this unique distress, consequent upon the shattering of the self through the surrendering of one's ego to an/other (Nancy 96) is, perhaps, preferable to the dull misery of seeing that special love wither and the beloved (previously figured as "the One-and-Only") become banal and commonplace. Although, as literary fiction attests, it is this second scenario that allows broken-hearted lovers to live and love again ("as one door closes, another opens"), it is at the expense of a millennial-long belief in Love as non-negotiable absolute (de Rougemont). The moment we admit to love's repeatability, so, too, do we admit that the rapture of our first love was delusional and (following Lacan: see below) the Beloved no more than a fantastical attempt to remedy our "lack." In other words, love's repeatability acknowledges that *there is no Other* and no means of transcending the ravenous, imploded ego; such a humiliating return-to-the-self is, arguably, a far more brutal psychological reckoning than the traumas of first love and/or its loss.

After outlining, in more detail, the two formulations of romantic love (psychoanalytic and philosophical) that subtend this proposition, I draw upon the fiction of Jackie Kay—the short story collection, *Wish I Was Here* (2006)—and Sarah Waters—the best-selling novel, *The Night Watch* (2006)—, to explore further the ways in which the condition of repeatability threatens the integrity of romantic love. At the same time, both texts exemplify how the repetition of key incidents and experiences (most notably those associated with the trauma of *ravissement*) are the life-blood of the love-affair *per se* and may, on occasion, prove crucial in keeping the illusion/delusion of "love's exclusivity" alive (Pearce 2007, 9–11). The focus of this investigation is, thus, romantic love *per se* (the phenomenon rather than the genre), though the textual analysis will, I trust, confirm the signal role of literature in helping us unravel its complexities. By way of conclusion I also speculate as to whether "non-repeatable" love survives as a meaningful category in the Western world today. With theorists such as Anthony Giddens keen to argue that there are other, and better, ways of conducting intimate relations, it is possible that the nine-hundred year long "cultural moment" described by de Rougemont, has indeed, come to an end. Both popular romance and contemporary literary fiction may be seen to concur with this hypothesis in terms of a general trend; however, it seems unlikely that more intellectual explorations of "love" and "being" (whether in the context of philosophy or contemporary fiction) will ever cease to be fascinated by the limit-point represented by the popular understanding of Hercaclitus's *panta rhei*: that is, for better or worse, we can never step into the same stream twice.[1]

LOVE AS REPETITION-COMPULSION: THE VIEW FROM PSYCHOANALYSIS

Without wishing to rehearse in detail those psychoanalytic theories of subject and sexual development that offer, often incidentally, some insight into the set of emotions commonly referred to as love, it is useful to begin this discussion of romance and/as repetition with reference to the work of Freud and Lacan, whose writings on the subject are, of course, themselves complicit in the circulation of amorous discourse (Barthes).

For Freud, the patterns of adult love-relationships can be linked explicitly to early psychosexual developments in terms of both gender identity (and identification) and power. The Oedipal attachments of children to their parents are repeated in love relationships in later life, including both the initial idealisation of/obsession with the love-object and the accompanying jealousy and hostility felt towards any rivals for that object's affections (Freud 1984a). Although problematic in feminist terms—not least because of its assumption that all desire is, by default, phallocentric and heterosexual—the tensions Freud exposes in early childhood arguably do find their echoes in adult relationships, both in the subject's desire to possess *what is not strictly hers* (inasmuch as our parents belong, first and foremost, to each other) *and what is not easily had* (seduction, deviousness and general "bad-behaviour" may well be involved, as Gallop suggests). Furthermore, according to Freud's repetition-compulsion hypothesis (1984c), it is the difficulty and/or failure of these childhood attempts to win affection that causes us to want to repeat them later in life, sometimes to the extent of seeking out an overtly hostile or inaccessible love-object (Benjamin 1988). In his essay on "The Uncanny," Freud gives additional spin to his hypothesis by implying that "the compulsion to repeat" is stronger than "the pleasure principle," that is, the compulsion to sex itself. He writes:

> In the unconscious mind we can recognize the dominance of *a compulsion to repeat*, which proceeds from instinctual impulses. This compulsion probably depends on the essential nature of the drives themselves. It is strong enough to override the pleasure principle and lend a demonic character to certain aspects of mental life [. . .] (2003, 145)

The implications of this startling realisation for Freud were, of course, profound, but here I wish simply to note the gauntlet it throws down to all theories of love that are predicated upon the power exerted by an ideal "object." For Freud, in this instance, the object has completely disappeared: we repeat, not in order to find "the Other," nor even a missing part of "ourselves," but simply for the pleasure and empowerment of repetition itself. This, in turn, may cause us to speculate more generally on the extent to which love is a means rather than an end: the pretext, or "front," for any number of, as yet, imperfectly understood aspects of the human condition.[2] Similarly, many of the existential issues confronted in this chapter—not least, the issue of whether any portion of our lives is repeatable—are of metaphysical as well as romantic concern.

For Lacan, meanwhile, it is the fact that *all* desire is, by definition, unmet and "unmeetable"—the intolerable lack that grounds the human condition—that explains our compulsive tendency towards repetition in adult life (1992, 151). Because of the fundamentally narcissistic character of the human subject, whose first love affair is an idealised encounter with the self, all subsequent attempts at relationships are characterised by a desire to return to this original state of imagined "wholeness" ("immortality"); and all, of course, are doomed to fail: "For what is love other than banging one's head against a wall, since there is no sexual relation?" (Lacan 1982, 170). As Fred Botting observes, it is prognoses such as these that situate Lacan firmly to one side of all the theorists and artists that explain love as *"the self's completion of fulfilment*" (27, original emphasis). While this end point may, admittedly, be the *desire* that fuels the process, Lacan's narcissistic reflex is, in practice, far bleaker: for Lacan, the lover is banging his or her head against a wall not because the "thing" that s/he is seeking is no other than him/herself, but because that "self" is, itself, illusory and lost: a mere "sexed living being [. . .] no longer immortal" (Lacan 1982 qt. in Botting 27). While, at first sight, this claim may seem rather perversely counter-intuitive (surely the "sexed living being" *is* a subject of sorts, capable of participating in relationships that may deliver *mortal* comfort and satisfaction?), it is important to remember that Lacan's theory is not concerned with the everyday practice of desire but rather its psychic origins; in particular, the way in which our egotistical fantasies (where we aspire to be extra-ordinary beings) are repeatedly undermined by the disillusioning events of everyday life, including the romantic encounter. As Barthes's *A Lover's Discourse* dramatises so vividly, the condition of being-in-love is circumscribed by the threat that the other/lover will turn out to be rather less than "ideal"[3]: merely another "sexed living being," in fact, who can no longer deliver the subject from his/her own pitiful insignificance. In the Lacanian economy, then, the notion of a "pure love" that is exclusive and non-repeatable is quite simply unthinkable: love, inasmuch as it can be said to exist at all, is *only* repeatable. Because we are never going to find what we desire (since the "ideal" lover/other will always, ultimately, fail us) we are compelled to keep searching and thus stave off the nightmare encounter with our own profound ordinariness and mortality.

Both Freud and Lacan, then, can be seen to have produced theories that move repetition to the centre of adult sexual desire and, by implication, test the limits of more idealised, object-centred definitions of love. Jessica Benjamin, too, sees the habitual tendency to repetition within the (typically asymmetric) family unit as key to the perpetuation of unequal power-relationships in adult life, often with recourse to sadistic/masochistic subject positioning (Benjamin 1988), even though—in contrast to Freud and Lacan—she does not regard either the originating dynamics or their reproduction as necessary or inevitable. Although destructive patterns of relationship may have become habitual in the contemporary Western world, it is a repetition that can, with effort, be broken (Benjamin 1998). In general, however, it may be said that, for psychoanalysis, love is a palliative discourse that seeks to conceal the unrealisable and, hence, potentially traumatic desire(s) that subtend(s) it.

LOVE AS ESSENCE: THE PHILOSOPHICAL TRADITION

What any investigation of the history of romantic love quickly teaches us, however, is that psychoanalysis is a relatively recent and, in many respects, tangential, addition to the vast pantheon of philosophical and theological writings on the subject. Recent publications—for example, Ole M. Høystad's

A History of the Heart (2007)—reveal that there are still a large number of scholars investigating "Love" from within a tradition that looks back to Greek and other ancient cultures and has little interest in psychoanalytic explanations. For contemporary philosophers like Alan Soble, for instance, the quest remains rigorously metaphysical: the concern is not with how love functions (either as an ideology or as psychic mechanism), but with what it is, as an essence, as an aspect of Being. While there are many ways of attempting to answer this question within a metaphysical tradition, it is clear that temporality has always been a key determinant in both defining and ascribing value to love. Similarly, wherever one looks in the history of Western literature and popular culture—be it to folk songs, Arthurian legend, or, indeed, popular romantic fiction—there are few instances of love that are not tested, to a greater or a lesser extent, by time: be that through non-repeatability, simple longevity or love's capacity to survive the use, loss or death of the beloved object.[4] It is in the annals of philosophy, meanwhile, that we find the clearest proposition that love is an event defined by exclusivity and non-repeatability: inasmuch as "genuine love" is expected to survive the loss or death of the other, the issue of its repetition *via* a subsequent relationship becomes irrelevant. There is no need to repeat the experience since the first love lives on: "Love never dies." Such a view is consistent with the defining characteristics of what, in the classical tradition, is known as "Agapic Love" (Pearce 2007, 4–6). In contrast to "Erosic Love," which arises from a cognitive appreciation of another's qualities, Agapic love is predicated upon an idealised, some may even say fundamentalist, set of "first principles" that have exclusivity and non-repeatability at their core:

EROS	AGAPE
Love of individual	Love of God / Neighbour(s)
Based on personal properties	Involuntary / unconditional
Object-centred	Subject-centred
Repeatable	Non-repeatable
Indefinite	Infinite
Rational	Irrational
Bodily	Spiritual
Heaven-bound	Heaven-present

(5)

As may be seen from this table of comparative features, Agapic Love is distinguished from Erosic Love through a series of binaries that places it firmly within a transcendental philosophical tradition. As I observe in *Romance Writing* (2007, 4–5), there are significant problems with this set of oppositions (derived from a number of philosophical texts which invoke Eros and Agape in their quest for a credible definition of love). These include both their rather crudely oppositional relationship to one another (e.g., "object-centred" *versus* "subject-centred") and, in terms of internal consistency, the way in which Agape's association with the "love of God" and the "love of one's neighbours" (both familiar to us as Christian injunctions) implies a degree of conscious piety at variance with the attendant notion of "unconditionality" and, it must be said, any love that includes erotic elements. If we take spirituality as the key term binding all the Agapic elements, however, the collocation makes better sense because of its association with both subject-centred fulfilment and sublimation. What binds together all the terms in the right-hand column is arguably the notion that love comes to us in a sudden, involuntary access of emotion (often expressed as an "out-pouring") that, once-begun, is unstoppable and hence non-repeatable: the Agapic lover, thus construed, needs only to be struck once to be struck forever. A floodgate has been opened, and the waters of love will flow endlessly and effortlessly (towards God, towards neighbours and towards one's elective partner). The somewhat paradoxical conversion of this out-pouring towards an/other into intensely solipsistic spiritual satisfaction is familiar to us through the conventions of courtly love poetry which, according to de Rougemont, is ultimately an exercise in spiritual salvation: "Passion has thus played the part of a purifying ideal" (45–6). In signal contrast to the psychoanalytic models of desire discussed previously, Agapic love delivers so consummately that it is inexhaustible and without need of repetition.

As with all binaristic thought, moreover, it is not difficult to see how Agapic Love, which is so manifestly "on the side of the angels," has become the dominant term within metaphysics, and why more recent philosophers like Alan Soble have had to work so hard to prove that Erosic Love is not merely a mundane and compromised version of "the real thing." Further, as Soble himself argues, it is important to recognise that what we think of today as specifically romantic love very clearly combines features of both Eros and Agape; in particular, romantic love can sometimes seem to arise from the "personal properties" of the beloved (for example, their goodness and/or beauty), but on other occasions to manifest itself as an involuntary and unpredictable shot from the blue—as in the proverbial "love at first sight." I nevertheless believe that it is the persistence of the binary itself in our everyday thinking about love (in particular, our tendency to contrast something called "true love" with its ephemeral "imitation") that helps explain why, despite the persuasiveness of the psychoanalytic models, Western culture still clings to the notion that "true love" is both durable and non-repeatable: it is, by definition, an emotion that stands the test of time.

A similar absolutism is to be found in the work of contemporary French philosopher, Jean Luc Nancy, who, like myself, has preferred to understand and define love vis-à-vis the radical transformation experienced by the amorous subject at the moment of *ravissement* (Barthes 189). My own proposition, expressed through the equation $x + y \rightarrow x' + y'$ (2007, 1f.) is, quite simply, that it is the change wrought upon the lover at the moment of rapture that most surely prevents him or her from being capable of repeating the event a second time inasmuch as s/he is now no longer the person s/he once was. On the surface this is an unremarkable observation, but it is striking how rarely the changes to the lover (x) are considered when theorists and philosophers debate the reproducibility, or not, of love. All the attention has traditionally been focused, instead, on the (lost) love-object: whether *that* is, or is not, replaceable. However, Nancy, too, has observed that the trouble is rather with the lover who, having undergone a transformation akin to a chemical reaction is unable to return to his or her previous state. Working with the evocative motif of the "shattered heart," Nancy writes:

> I do not return to myself *from* love [. . .] I do not return from it, and consequently, something of *I* is definitively lost or dissociated in its act of loving. That is undoubtedly why *I* return [. . .] but *I* return broken: I come back to myself, or I come out of it, broken. The 'return' does not annul the break; it neither repairs it nor sublates it, for the return in fact takes place across the break itself, keeping it open. Love represents *I* to itself broken [. . .] (96, original emphasis)

A little later, Nancy reiterates the radical consequences of this break not only for the subject-in-love but for the subject *per se*:

> For the break is a break in his self-possession as a subject; it is, essentially, an interruption in the process of relating oneself to oneself outside of oneself. From then on, *I* is *constituted broken*. As soon as there is love, the slightest act of love, the slightest spark, there is the ontological fissure that cuts across and disconnects the elements of the subject-proper—the fibers of its heart. (96, original emphasis)

Although the cadences of Nancy's prose (in translation, at least) make this "shattering" of the heart and self in the act of love appear tragic, it is clearly also possible to embrace this uni-directional model of love as evidence of love's miracle: $x + y \rightarrow x' + y'$. Further, as I have suggested above, it is also possible to regard this trauma as more palatable and life-affirming than its notional opposite (i.e., the 'I' that remains intact, imploded: going nowhere).

To summarise, then: the question of whether love is, or is not, repeatable is at the very centre of attempts to both define and understand it. I have shown how, and why, certain theories and intellectual traditions (notably, the philosophical and theological) posit love as either metaphysically or practicably non-repeatable, while others (notably, the psychoanalytic tradition) have argued that love (albeit reconfigured as desire) is nothing but repetition.[5] It is, of course, possible to escape this impasse, as Soble has done with "Personal Love" (5), by signing up to an essentially Erosic definition of love which is fully rational and voluntary and predicated upon admirable qualities in the beloved (Pearce 2007, 4–6). Inasmuch as this love arises as the result of an individual being smitten by the unique properties of particular individuals it is acceptable for a subject to be enamoured of more than one individual in a lifetime: hence the logic of the widower who claims: "I can love my second wife as much as my first because they are so completely different." For the purposes of this article, however, I have chosen to leave the Erosic variant to one side in order that we may focus more closely on the more dramatic—and certainly more traumatic—tension that exists between the discourses of Agapic love and the "will-to-repetition" as figured by psychoanalysis.

In anticipation of the discussion of the literary texts that follow, my particular interest is in the crisis that arises when the non-repeatability implicit in the most ancient descriptors of "Love" as an involuntary affect which, once ignited, is both shattering and inexhaustible, is challenged by the desire or need to repeat the first, earth-moving event a second time (typically as the result of the death of or rejection by a former beloved). In other words, I shall be focusing on the tension—and agony—that proceeds from the fact that, rather than enter into a new experience with a different person (as is possible within the Erosic model), all the amorous subject wants is "the same again" even though s/he soon discovers that this will necessarily undermine the totality of the first love. This, of course, is the moment that Lacan comes knocking on the door, and the lover, thus held to account, may suddenly, if perversely, hope that his or her attempt to repeat the love affair will fail in order to prove that the first love was "true" and the beloved rather more than an (reproducible) *objet-idéal*.

In terms of its cultural representation, I would also suggest that, from the early-mid-twentieth century onwards, the paradox of love's compulsive (non)-repeatability has been actively embraced by the writers in search of a more honest account of how we wrestle with contending drives and belief systems when in pursuit of love. Rather than an ideological and aesthetic problem to be avoided, repetition, and its attendant traumas, has been moved to the centre of contemporary literary fiction (high-profile examples in the United Kingdom would include Doris Lessing, Muriel Spark, Anita Brookner, Ian McEwan, Hanif Kureishi and A. L. Kennedy). In the discussion that follows, I reflect upon the ways in which contemporary British authors Jackie Kay and Sarah Waters variously engage with repetition and/ as trauma, both as the constitutive life-blood of romance and, in the context of relationship-breakdown, its severest challenge (i.e., if love proves to be repeatable, can it be true?).

REPETITION, "RETURN" AND REPEATABILITY: THE "SHATTERED SELF" IN JACKIE KAY'S *WISH I WAS HERE* (2006) AND SARAH WATERS'S *THE NIGHT WATCH* (2006)

At the end of Annie Proulx's "Brokeback Mountain" (1999), Ennis del Mar—who has succumbed to a state of profound melancholia following the death (murder) of his cowboy-lover, Jack Twist—presents himself as a subject in urgent need of trauma-therapy. Psychically bound to Twist through (repeated) acts of memorialisation and introjection (symbolised in both fiction and film[6] by their entwined, blood-stained shirts), Ennis arguably needs to tell his story and "move on." Instead, both character and text remain stubbornly resistant to the healing process and stand by del Mar's earlier pronouncement: "If you can't fix it, you've got to stand it" (318). "Unhealthy" as this may seem to modern-day commonsense, it is arguable that del Mar's agony—with Twist's "image-repertoire" (Barthes 18–21, 25–28) still intact—is ultimately less nihilistic than that of many other heroes and heroines of contemporary fiction whose fruitless "serial monogamy" serves only to echo Lacan's view that "there is no sexual relation" (see above) and that love, at least as Ennis del Mar understands it, simply does not exist. And it is precisely this abyss that is glimpsed in the work of the two British authors to whom I now turn. In contrast to the "redemptive tragedy" represented by "Brokeback Mountain" (1999) and texts like it, the stories that comprise Jackie Kay's short-story collection, *Wish I Was Here*, articulate what is arguably, if somewhat surprisingly, a rather less optimistic account of love's capacity to preserve its first "dazzlement" (Barthes 24) and/or evade repetition. Widely celebrated for the warmth, wit and humour of her writing, Jackie Kay is not an author whom one would readily associate with despair and yet, as I shall argue here, several of the stories that comprise *Wish I Was Here* gesture towards something bleakly irredeemable and deeply traumatic in the nature of romantic love. Although making use of different characters, voices and dramatic scenarios (the family home, foreign holidays, the Trans-Siberian railway), many of the stories tell what is very obviously "the same story" of a relationship break-up in which one partner has taken a new lover and is prevailing upon the other to see sense and end the relationship. In each instance, the traumatic incident that encapsulates this crisis is spoken by the abandoned lover whose grief makes her an unreliable narrator and whose "madness" and delusion is frequently reflected back to the reader in the observations of her "sane" but cruel partner: "I would never have believed this of you, Esther, she said. That you could act so crazy [. . .]" (Kay 174).

As with all dramatic monologues, moreover, the final verdict on the story—and its narrator—is left to the reader, who is obliged to read between the speaker's lines. What this reader carried away was a vision of love that is arguably far bleaker than Proulx's inasmuch as the *objet-idéal* has failed to survive the test of time and the acts of repetition upon which the relationship has been built have succumbed to exhaustion: repetition, that is, without return to anything resembling the wonder and spectacle of the original encounter (Pearce 2004, 525–31; Pearce 2007, 18). Instead of reinforcing the singularity of the initial *coup de foudre* (i.e., every time I set eyes upon him/her, an electric shock passes through me) repetition, here, serves only to leach the other, and the "scene" (Barthes 192), of significance. In Kay's hands, many of the incidents that sound such death-knells are, of course, supremely comic—at the same time as being consummately tragic:

> When we got inside our cream kitchen, I thought she might have a cup of tea and a scone for old times' sake. 'Scones are a thing of the past,' Hilary said and I had the impression that she wasn't quoting from Martin Amis. (Kay 2006, 15)

Here, as in all the domestically-centred stories in the collection, the routines and habits of everyday life come to signify the lovers' failing relationship, as we see in "You go when you can no longer stay." Mundane rituals concerning food and television, which once endorsed the relationships, now expose its failings, and the departing lover repeatedly refers to these habituated activities to make visible differences between them:

> I didn't quite know what to do with myself because we usually watched *Frost* on the TV together or *Miss Marple* or *Midsomer Murders*. But lately Hilary had said, 'That isn't me, watching *Frost*. That's you.' She's started saying this a lot recently. 'I'm not the sort of person who does such and such or watches such and such.' (Kay 9)

Through this focus on the repeated rejection of the familiar and comforting, Kay demonstrates how the domestic routines that are the material bedrock of any long-term relationship can become positively *unheimlich* and, for the lover-left-behind, the scene of unacknowledged trauma and distress:

> I'm just wondering why you put three [jaffa cakes] on a plate for me if you're not having any yourself,' I said suspiciously. I was becoming very suspicious of her because she had started to change all her habits and it was very worrying to me. 'Do you know something?' she said, very nastily. 'I think you are going mad.' (Kay 2006, 5)

Across these stories, then (and the examples are multiple), repetition is, indeed, figured as the true enemy of romance. Once habits become habitual the end is nigh.

   Yet it is with regard to the weightier philosophical question of whether the love-affair, itself, is repeatable that I suggest we glimpse a deeper despair in Kay's collection: one that confirms the Freudian hypothesis that the compulsion to repeat is endemic to the human condition, and love nothing but the recycling of the trapped ego. The story in the collection which, perhaps, captures this most vividly is "Sonata," in which a young woman tells another (the narrator) the story of her failed relationship as the two take a long train journey across the snowy wastes of Russia. Exotic setting aside, the story being told is very similar in terms of domestic and dramatic detail to "You go when you can no longer stay" cited above, the more significant twist being that the narrator, as interlocutor, falls in love with the speaker in the course of the journey thus demonstrating the endless recyclability of love, a situation that recalls Barthes's "errantry": "he then realizes he is doomed to wander until he dies, from love to love" (101). The way in which love's ending becomes its beginning is made tangible on the page by Kay refusing the reader any textual clues as to when one speaker ends and the other begins; and while it is usually possible, after a couple of lines, to work out that we are back with Esther's story again, there are moments when we could credibly be in the mind of either woman, such is the uncanny similarity between the beginning and end of love (Pearce 2007, 92). The following passage, couched in the vocabulary of trauma, is probably the most striking in this regard:

> During this period I actually feel as if some part of myself has been banished to another part of the world. I feel as if I cannot live my life to the full and feel everything I am capable of feeling unless I have this love. The pleasure goes from me; the delight goes. Nothing means anything. I am dulled at the edges. I have a weight across my chest that is heavy and as surprisingly soft as a snake. I am sure that the weight is the weight of my broken heart. Two pieces of heart weigh more than one. I feel for the first time in my life that life and love are the same thing; without love you have no life. (Kay 160)

Beautiful and arresting as this sentiment is (with echoes, it will be noticed, of Nancy's "shattered self"), the "truth" of this love is sadly undermined by its dual (intradiegetic and diegetic) contexts: not only is the reader about to discover the full extent of Esther's jealous delusion (her lover was not being unfaithful; she was dying from cancer) but also that what was purportedly unique ("true love") is about to be recycled all over again as the two women (each other's mirrors) prepare to "begin all over again" (Barthes 103). For all its glamour and romance, then, this is a story in which the logic of Freud and Lacan most surely triumphs.

In Sarah Waters's *The Night Watch*,[7] meanwhile, love's repeatability—or not—is *the* existential question that propels the text's story-line and presses upon its characters as a trauma every bit as nerve-splitting as the Blitz. For readers not familiar with the novel, the action is set in London during and immediately after the Second World War, with the story of the novel's chief protagonists (Kay, Helen and Julia; Viv and Reggie; Duncan and Fraser) narrated backwards in three sections: 1947, 1944 and 1941. The effect of this temporal inversion is twofold: first, it renders starkly visible how events in our past make us the people we are today (*viz.* $x + y \rightarrow x' + y'$); secondly, it highlights the extent to which our lives are, indeed, inscribed by repetition: willed and unwilled, individual and institutional, local and national.

In *The Night Watch* repetition is a thematic pre-occupation as well as a narrative device. While its potential for dramatic irony, not to mention (poetic) justice and revenge, makes repetition a tempting plot embellishment for any fiction writer, Waters disguises her authorial orchestration well, not least because these are life-stories in which the characters' will to repetition is routinely thwarted or culminates in an unpleasant surprise. As Lacan puts it: "For what is love other than banging one's head against a wall since there is no sexual relation?" (170). Consequently, *The Night Watch* is characterised by a series of half-repeated, half-completed, events which expose the doomed will-to-repetition for what it is as well as the extent to which the war, itself, changed everything: made repetition a historical impossibility. The generic interplay between history and romance is, indeed, one of the things that distinguishes Waters's novel: a retrospective account of three sets of relationships that span the war and post-war period. In the manner of historical fiction, Waters also strives hard to connect the experiences of these central characters with those of the population at large by making two of them, Helen and Viv, work for a post-war dating agency. The task of finding new loves for men and women whose lives have been turned upside down by the war is seen to be very difficult indeed. As Helen observes:

> People came to look for new loves, but often—or so it seemed to her—only really wanted to talk about the loves they had lost [. . .] Recently, of course, business had been booming. Servicemen, returning from overseas, found wives and girlfriends transformed out of all recognition. They came into the bureau still looking stunned. Women complained about their ex-husbands. "He wanted me to stay in all the time." "He told me he didn't care for my friends." "We went back to the hotel we spent our honeymoon in, but it wasn't the same." (Waters 15)

The collective will-to-repeat, as the concluding sentence here suggests, is strong, but the common experience is one of disappointment: both pre-war existence, and the heightened sensibilities of wartime, are impossible to recapture: the breach in history suffered by the nation is similarly visited upon personal relationships. In a later conversation, Helen and Viv comment on the fact that the war, but two years' hence, already seems "a long time ago" (113). And yet it is manifestly clear that, in many respects, everyone is still living it, as Kay, the character who is arguably having the most trouble moving on confesses: "I don't want to think about it. But I don't want to forget it either" (109). Yet while the war's breach in history undoubtedly contributes to the demise of the relationships explored in the novel, it cannot be held fully responsible for it. This is especially true of the relationship(s) between Kay, Helen and Julia where a distinctly Freudian will-to-repetition is seen to be at work (at least, in the case of Helen and Julia). The dramatic twist is that Helen enters into a relationship with Julia in the knowledge that her present partner, Kay, was involved with Julia before the war. As the affair between Helen and Julia takes hold, both reveal—belatedly and, at first, unconsciously—that their attraction to each other has been fuelled by a desire to repeat the earlier relationship with Kay. Julia is curious to find out about "the wife" (Helen) that Kay preferred to her, while Helen—mistakenly believing that Kay was rejected by Julia—is fuelled by a vengeful desire to assume Kay's former role and succeed where the latter failed. After their second, sexually-charged encounter exploring the bomb-blasted houses, churches and streets of London Helen exclaims: "This is what Kay wanted, isn't it? I know why she did, Julia! God! I feel like—I feel like I'm her! I want to touch you, Julia. I want to touch you, like she would—" (375). The uncontrolled—indeed, hysterical—nature of this outburst works well to underline the unconscious and irrational nature of Helen's will-to-repetition. Her behaviour reminds us of Freud's reading of E. T. A. Hoffmann's *The Sandman* and his conclusion that human beings are driven to repeat in their desire to achieve control, not of the other, but of their own subjectivity (Freud 2003). By, albeit mistakenly, fantasising that she was repeating Kay's actions in making love to Julia, Helen is temporarily empowered. However, as subsequent events reveal, Helen's action has arguably very little to do with either Kay or Julia: not only is she mistaken about the nature of Kay's relationship with Julia—as Julia later tells her: "It wasn't like that you know [. . .] she was never in love with me" (424)—but so, too, are doubts cast about what she *sees*, quite literally, in Julia. Not only does Helen habitually regard Julia with Kay's eyes, but there is also the suggestion that her declaration of love is following an unconscious, yet calculating, script: "She hadn't known, until that moment, that she'd been going to utter those words; but as soon as she said them, they become true" (369). Further, as the relationship begins to unravel, both Helen and Julia are seen to call each other's bluff on why they got involved with one another in the first place. Although, on one level, we may be inclined to think that the demise of the relationship is the sole consequence of Helen's spiralling jealousy and paranoia, a crucial segment of conversation hints at the fact that both characters are addicted to affairs (and, perhaps especially, affairs with women) on account of the thrill of transgression and, of course, the pleasure of repetition, which is given an extra spike in a triangulated relationship such as this:

> "It always amazes me [said Julia], that's all, that it should be you who has this fucking—this fucking fixation. Is there something about affairs? Is it like—I don't know—Catholicism? One only spots the other Romans when one's practised it oneself?"
>
> She met Helen's gaze, and looked away again. They stood in silence for a moment. Then, "Work it up your arse," said Helen. She turned and went back downstairs to the sitting room. (150–51)

Suddenly, both women are quits. Julia, who has assumed the moral and emotional high-ground in the fight thus far is herself minded of her past, and present, behaviour. In retrospect, it becomes clear that neither woman entered into the relationship on account of the "special properties" she perceived in the other (*viz.* Erosic Love as defined above) but because of the thrill of repetition itself. What Helen and Julia's story exposes, however, is the horror that awaits those successful in the chase: instead of finding the happiness and completion that eluded you formerly through some synthesis of self and other (in this instance, the fantasy of merging oneself with one's former lover by assuming her role), all that is waiting is your shadow self, Lacan's "sexed living being" (qt. in Botting 27). This realisation, too clearly-grasped and sedimented to be confused with trauma, offers us a glimpse of the very bleakest horror that can attend the end of love: an endgame far worse, I would suggest, than the one experienced by Proulx's Ennis del Mar in his lonely trailer. Ennis, as noted previously, keeps his memory of Jack intact and will always have his dreams.

Entering into a relationship with one's partner's former lover is, it must be said, a fairly extreme means of re-igniting the spark of love and, elsewhere *The Night Watch* explores some rather less convoluted types of repetition. For instance, Viv may be seen to be repeating, in increasingly banal and glamour-less ways, her wartime romance with Reggie, a married man. The irreversible bodily and psychological scars that this relationship has left on Viv are palpable: not only has she suffered a horrendous abortion, but—despite being still only 25—she is described as having "something disappointed about her [. . .] a sort of greyness, a layer of grief, as fine as ash, just beneath the surface" (18). Thus, although this relationship was positively transformative of Viv at its outset, its demise has stripped her of agency and, two years after the war has ended, she is neither capable of ending it or falling in love afresh. And while Waters concludes her story with an action that is potentially redemptive (Viv finds Kay who "rescued" her on the night of her abortion), we are offered no assurance that she will go on to live and love again.

A similar uncertainty hangs over the fate of Viv's brother, Duncan, who has recently rediscovered Fraser: his friend and cell-mate from the war. Although the story-line suggests that Duncan's brave act of going to find Fraser at his house late one night might be the existential act that commits the men to a sexual relationship, there is no assurance of this either. Indeed, we have already been told how differently the men have recovered from the War (or not, in Duncan's case) and Fraser's homophobia is still evident in his attempts to chat up girls, including Duncan's sister.

Kay, too, begins and ends the 1947 section of the novel going, quite literally, nowhere. Her everyday, post-war existence consists of wandering the bomb-blasted streets of London, all the while appearing as though she has somewhere to go—when, in fact, she hasn't:

> She stepped like a person who knew exactly where they were going, and why they were going there—though the fact was, she had nothing

to do, and no one to visit, no one to see. Her day was a blank, like all of her days. (6)

Kay, it seems, may retrace her footsteps, but there is no sense that she will easily repeat her romantic attachment to Helen. As readers of the novel will recall, Kay's love for Helen—whom she rescues "fresh and [...] unmarked" (503) from a bomb-site—is the most simply romantic of all the relationships featured. Helen is Kay's *objet-idéal* and, to invoke Freud on melancholia (1984b, 252–53), has assumed a libidinal position in Kay's life that will not easily be replaced. Further, in terms of how her story is told, I would suggest that this has less to do with the impossibility of replacing Helen (or, indeed, recovering from the traumatic nature of the latter's betrayal) but rather (*viz.* Nancy's "shattered self") the extreme and irreversible nature of her own transformation: a transformation that owes both to the war, and to Helen. As she confides to her friend, Mickey: "I've got lost in my rubble, Mickey. I can't seem to find my way across it. I don't think I want to cross it, that's the thing. The rubble has all my life in it still." (Waters 2006, 108)

The Night Watch is, then, a text that can be used to think through, with some complexity, the ways in which repetition tests the limits of love. Several of the theoretical paradigms that I discussed in the first part of the article are given vivid, fictional expression in this text, each of them commenting upon the challenge posed by repetition in a different way. For example, while the behaviour of Helen and Julia may be seen to typify the Freudian will-to-repetition and its Lacanian demise, Kay may be seen to stand, heroically (but perhaps no less self-deceivingly?) for the non-repeatability of a "genuine love" that is focused on the other and entails a radical transformation of the self; meanwhile, Viv and Reggie's attempt to recycle their love would appear to be doomed to failure on account of the fact that it can never be brought to a satisfactory "romantic" conclusion: that is, marriage *or* death. Indeed, arguably the only relationship in the novel that holds out any possibility of hope for the future is that between Duncan and Fraser inasmuch as their reunion may be as a resumption of their original relationship and its "unfinished business" rather than a repetition *per se.*

CONCLUSION

In this chapter I have, with help of some germane contemporary literary texts, sought to untangle the ambiguous and seemingly paradoxical function of repetition in "the lover's discourse." In the course of these reflections it has, however, become clear that what may, initially, present itself as confusing and/or contradictory ("repetition is the life blood of romance," "repetition is the enemy of *true* romance") is consequent upon a failure to distinguish between the different applications of repetition within love-relationships, characterised in my discussion of the literary texts as the difference between "empty repetition" and inexhaustible "return"; further, that the question of whether the experience of "falling in love" can happen more than once (without, as Freud and Lacan would have it, exposing "Love" as a purely narcissistic reflex), is better understood as an exploration into the *conditions of repeatability* rather than as another expression of the (intradiegetic) repetition-paradox.

Allowing, as ever, for the fact that literary representations of romantic love operate according to conventions and resolutions not necessarily available to us in life, I have found the texts considered here extremely helpful in teasing out these hermeneutic complexities as well as keeping starkly visible the affective dimension of the theoretical and philosophical issues. Indeed, inasmuch as all the texts considered here deal with the death and aftermath of long-term and/or passionate love-affairs, the repetition of acts, scenes and sentiments necessarily exceed any intellectual enquiry we may throw at them and, as we have seen, frequently bind trauma and repetition together in the same breath. In the course of the analysis we have also seen many examples of the way in which the empty repetition of habits, routines and rituals in long-term relationships can slip from the banal and boring to the quietly horrific (as instanced in Kay's and Waters's use of kitchens and mealtimes as scenes for some of their most disturbing conflicts), at the same time that the trauma associated with *ravissement* (e.g., Kay finding Helen in the bombsite) may serve to animate the relationships concerned in perpetuity.

The further question this discussion raises is whether or not it is possible to identify a general movement away from what I have styled "redemptive-tragic romance" in contemporary fiction? My impression, based on an admittedly small sample of British fiction (the authors cited at the start of this article), is that it *is*: and for reasons that may be sourced to our social and literary zeitgeist. First, following the work of sociologists like Giddens and Bauman, there is now substantive evidence to suggest that, since the "sexual revolution" of the 1960s, Western cultures have adopted an increasingly pragmatic approach to inter-personal relations, based on the capacity "to deliver enough satisfaction to each individual to stay within it" (Giddens 58; Pearce 2007, 169). This cultural sea-change has also been absorbed—even relished—by contemporary popular romance ("Mills and Boon," "Harlequin," etc.), where it is now possible to fashion more complex back-stories for both hero and heroine and endorse plot-lines where the protagonists notionally "fall in love" more than once.[8] Secondly, it is possible to interpret the somewhat more despairing "recycling" of contemporary love in twenty-first century literary fiction as a continuum of the post-1945 cynicism, nihilism and angst that literary historians such as Malcolm Bradbury propose has cast a long shadow over the West's view of humanity *per se*. In other words, and following on from my earlier comments on love being a "means" rather than an "end in itself," there is a strong steer in a good deal of contemporary British fiction to read successive, futile attempts to repeat, or resurrect, love as symptomatic of a faltering belief in what Emmanuel Levinas characterised as "responsibility for the other" (Levinas 2004).

Whether or not we characterise such despair in human/sexual relations as traumatic will largely depend upon how we source, and fashion, our analysis. In Bradbury's case, the term is used advisedly inasmuch as it originates with the Holocaust (Bradbury 257). In terms of the more structural definition of love that I have been pursuing here, it may be argued that for love to be traumatic in and of itself it has, first, to be seared upon the metaphorical retina of the desiring subject in a manner akin to Barthes's *ravissement*; which is not to say that an "empty repetition" of the same is not without its own long-term—and potentially—psychological consequences (as exemplified by Helen's and Julia's narcissistic exploitation of one another). Further, if "tragic-redemptive" love of the kind identified by de Rougemont *has* now run its 900 year-long course as a literary and cultural phenomenon throughout the Western world, we must hope that it nevertheless survives as an intellectual, emotional and moral limit-point. As David Eng has argued in the Introduction to a book on "postcolonial melancholia" (Eng and Kazanjian 1–28), sometimes the events which impact upon our individual and collective lives are of *such* magnitude that "not forgetting"—and, likewise, "not-repeating"—is the appropriate response.

NOTES

1. My thanks to the Routledge reviewer for pointing out that my "tragic-redemptive" paradigm of love bears some similarity to the popular interpretation of Heraclitus's *panta rhei*; thanks, also, to Eleanor Fitton for explaining to me the limitations of the "everything changes" translation/interpretation and for providing a fascinating, alternative gloss to which I hope to return in the future.

2. See in this volume George Letissier's reading of Waters's *The Little Stranger*, which positions the historical romance as a "subtext" to the novel's deeper moral and aesthetic purpose.

3. See entry on "spoiling," in "The Tip of the Nose" (Barthes 125–28).

4. As I discuss in *Romance Writing* (2007, 19–23), it is important to keep in mind the fact that "love" and "desire" originate in very different discourses even though they are often used interchangeably in everyday speech. In my own writing, I am always mindful that desire is a psychoanalytic concept which understands affect as an expression of the psycho-sexual drives, while love (as noted in this article) is a concept that means differently across a wide range of historical and cultural discourses but which is typically bound up with metaphysical and spiritual belief-systems.

5. Within the folk tradition there are countless songs in which the (male) lover is separated from his beloved for long periods of time (typically, seven years) on account of war or other commitments, and the (female) beloved is required to wait patiently and faithfully for his return. In the tragic variants (e.g., "Lord Baker"; "Her Green Mantle," by Sinead O'Connor) the lover often returns just too late (the woman is dying or has finally given up and married another) though in many instances—"The Moorlough Shore" (O'Connor)—the songs include defiant professions of love (on both sides) that will follow the lovers

to the grave. However, popular music also includes many classics that cel-
ebrate the heart's capacity to heal and love again—"Falling in Love Again"
by Lerner and Hollander; "Second Time Around" by Cahn and van Heusen;
or "I'll Never Love Again" by Bacharach and David, which ends with the line
"so at least until tomorrow / I'll never fall in love again."

6. Many readers will be familiar with Ang Lee's film of the story, *Brokeback Mountain* (2005) starring Heath Ledger as Ennis del Mar.
7. I first broached the analysis on repetition in Sarah Waters's *The Night Watch* in an article published in the online *Journal of Popular Romance Studies* (Pearce 2011). I would like to thank the editors of the journal for their kind permission to reproduce the material.
8. My thanks to participants of the International Association of Popular Romance Studies conference in Brussels (August 2010), who informed me of these trends in popular romance fiction (see Pearce 2011).

WORKS CITED

Bacharach, Burt and Hal David. "I'll Never Fall in Love Again." Perf. Chuck Bax-
ter & Jill O'Hara. New York: Shubert Theatre, 1968. Performance.
Barthes, Roland. *A Lover's Discourse: Fragments.* 1977. Trans. Richard Howard.
Harmondsworth: Penguin, 1990. Print.
Benjamin, Jessica. *The Bonds of Love: Psychoanalysis, Feminism and the Prob-
lems of Domination.* 1988. London: Virago, 1990. Print.
———. *Like Subjects, Love Objects: Essays on Recognition and Sexual Differ-
ence.* New Haven, CT: Yale UP, 1998. Print.
Botting, Fred. *Gothic Romanced: Consumption, Gender and Technology in Con-
temporary* Fictions. London and New York: Routledge. 2008. Print.
Bradbury, Malcolm. *The Modern British Novel.* Revised edn. Harmondsworth:
Penguin, 2001. Print.
Cahn, Sammie and Jimmie van Heusen. "The Second Time Around." *High Time.*
Perf. Bing Crosby, 20th Century Fox, 1960. Film.
de Rougemont, Denis. *Love in the Western World.* 1940. Trans. M. Belgion. Princ-
eton, NJ: Princeton UP, 1983. Print.
Eng, David. "Introduction: Mourning Remains." *Loss: The Politics of Mourning.* Eds.
David L. Eng and David Kazanjian. Irvine: U of California P, 2002. 1–28. Print.
Freud, Sigmund. "On Narcissism." *On Metapsychology. Penguin Freud Library*
Vol. XI. 1914. Harmondsworth: Penguin, 1984a. 61–97. Print.
———. "Mourning and Melancholia." *Penguin Freud Library* Vol. XI. 1915. Har-
mondsworth: Penguin, 1984b. 247–68. Print.
———. "Beyond the Pleasure Principle." *Penguin Freud Library* Vol. XI. 1920.
Harmondsworth: Penguin, 1984c. 271–338. Print.
———. *The Uncanny.* 1919. London: Penguin Classics, 2003. Print.
Gallop, Jane. *The Daughter's Seduction: Feminism and Psychoanalysis.* New York,
Ithaca: Cornell UP, 1986. Print.
Giddens, Anthony. *The Transformation of Intimacy: Sexuality, Love and Eroti-
cism.* Cambridge: Polity, 1992. Print.
Høystad, Ole M. *A History of the Heart.* London: Reaktion Books, 2007. Print.
Kay, Jackie. *Wish I Was Here.* Basingstoke and Oxford: Picador, 2006. Print.
Lacan, Jacques. "Seminar of 21 January 1975." *Feminine Sexuality.* Eds. Juliet
Mitchell and Jacqueline Rose. London: Macmillan, 1982. 162–71. Print.
———. *The Ethics of Psychoanalysis.* Trans. Dennis Porter. London: Routledge,
1992. Print.

Levinas, Emmanuel. *Totality and Infinity: An Essay on Exteriority.* 1969. Pittsburgh: Duquesne UP, 2004. Print.

Lee, Ang. (dir). *Brokeback Mountain.* Universal Studios, 2005. Film.

Lerner, Sammy and Friedrich Hollaender. "Falling in Love Again (I Can't Help It)." *The Blue Angel.* Perf. Marlene Dietrich. UFA/Paramount, 1930. Film.

Nancy, Jean-Luc. "Shattered Love." *The Inoperative Community.* Minneapolis and London: U of Minnesota P, 1991. 82–109. Print.

O'Connor, Sinead. *Sean Nós Nua.* Netherlands: Roadrunner Records, 2002. CD.

Pearce, Lynne. "Popular Romance and its Readers." *A Companion to Romance: From Classical to Contemporary.* Ed. Corinne Saunders. Oxford: Blackwell, 2004. 521–38. Print.

———. *Romance Writing.* Cambridge and Malden, MA: Polity, 2007. Print.

———. "Romance and Repetition: Testing the Limits of Love." *Journal of Popular Romance Studies* 2.1. http://www.jprstudies.org. 2011. Retrieved on 12/03/2012. Web.

Proulx, Annie. "Brokeback Mountain." *Close Range: Brokeback Mountain and Other Stories.* 1999. London: Harper Perennial, 2006. 281–318. Print.

Soble, Alan. *The Structure of Love.* New Haven, CT and London: Yale UP, 1990. Print.

Waters, Sarah. *The Night Watch.* London: Virago, 2006. Print.

5   Some Versions of Romance Trauma as Generated by Realist Detail in Ian McEwan's *Atonement*

J. Hillis Miller

As the "Introduction" to this volume indicates, an enormous literature on trauma, on romance, on realism, and on their interconnection exists. I want in this essay first to establish my own brief outline of these topics and then turn to a reading of Ian McEwan's *Atonement* (2001).

The father of modern trauma theory, Sigmund Freud, in *Studies on Hysteria*, written with Josef Breuer, notoriously saw trauma as generated by some original event that may not have been experienced as traumatic at the time and that may now be completely forgotten, hidden away in the unconscious memory bank as a neural trace. Some later similar event, however, suddenly recovers the memory of the original event and makes it traumatic. The new event triggers lasting psychic suffering, all those symptoms Freud, following the medical nomenclature of his time, called "hysteria."

This happens by means of what Freud called "*Nachträglichkeit*." This term is translated by Alix and James Strachey in the Standard edition of Freud's works as "afterwardsness," or in Jacques Lacan's French: "*après-coup*."

Such traumas, as Cynthia Chase, among others, has observed, lie neither in the first event, which was not experienced as traumatic, nor in the second, which was often not objectively traumatic at all. It exists in between, in the blank space in the middle, and in the relation of similarity between the two events.[1] This relation can be called tropological, or, more specifically, metaphorical. The two events are similar, like the two halves of a metaphor.

Many modern trauma studies focus on the Holocaust as the locus of mass trauma, but the second form of trauma Freud studied was what was called, during and after WWI, "shell shock."[2] These early studies on shell shock forerun the formulation of Post-traumatic Stress Disorder (PTSD) carried out by the American Psychiatric Association in the *Diagnostic and Statistic Manual* of 1980. Soldiers return from war undergoing symptoms similar to those of Freud's hysterical women.

But what does trauma in these frightening senses have to do with postmodern fiction, specifically with Ian McEwan's *Atonement*, my example in this essay? It would seem that we read fiction for pleasure, to some degree to escape from the "real world." We enjoy entering a fictional realm where, as the phrase goes, "names can never hurt me." And yet no one can doubt that an incredible amount of traumatic violence is represented these days in novels, in films, and on television, even in such apparently innocuous television shows as PBS's "Nature" series.

INESCAPABLE ROMANCE

This chapter, however, relates trauma and romance. I want to account for the presence in those narratives we call "romances" of traumatic events. Romance is a loose and capacious genre or mode, as suggested in the Introduction to this volume. It comes in many flavours, from fairy tales, folk tales, and the medieval *Romance of the Rose*, through *Don Quixote* and the romances of chivalry that drove him mad, then up to Gothic novels of the Romantic period, and eventually to modern popular paperback "romances" and to high-brow postmodern novels like *Atonement*. Romances generally, though by no means always, are stories of an innocent girl growing up and marrying her Prince Charming. This happens after some terrifying mistakes brought about by misinterpretations.[3] Examples are Briony's childhood play, *The Trials of Arabella*, in *Atonement*, or all those romances that lead Emma Bovary astray and cause her to live through a dyslogistic version of the romance plot, or present-day paperback romances ("Harlequin" novels) that are fantasies of sexual and social fulfilment. These are read by millions of people worldwide, 90% of whom are women. Most novels from the beginning in the early seventeenth century to the present in one way or another fall into the capacious paradigm of the romance. It is not an accident that the French word for "novel" is "*roman*," the German word "*Roman*." The somewhat odd English word obscures the intimate connection of novels with romances.

The term "romance" is also important in Freud's works, in the technical psychoanalytical term "family romance" (*Familienroman*) (Freud 2001b, 235–41).[4] The "family romance" is the boy's or girl's fantasy that his or her parents are not the real progenitors. The child fancies that the true parents are more high-born than the actual real ones. The true parents must be at least an Emperor and Empress. Diverse versions of this fantasy find their way into many paperback romances or into parodies of these, like Briony's play in *Atonement*, *The Trials of Arabella*. When Arabella is sick unto death, a doctor who turns out to be a prince in disguise saves her. She marries her doctor-prince and lives happily ever after.

Four forms of trauma may be distinguished in novels: 1) some event performed, witnessed, or suffered by the characters that is traumatic for them; 2) some plot feature in which the fiction directly or indirectly expresses a trauma in its author, as Dickens transferred his childhood trauma in the blacking factory more or less verbatim into *David Copperfield*; 3) trauma suffered by the fictional narrator, whether a first- or third-person storyteller; 4) trauma suffered by the reader, perhaps caused by the vividness of the traumatic events described. Reader's trauma may, however, even include the trauma of being disappointed somehow in one's narratological expectations. This is certainly the case with *Atonement,* as I shall show. Such a traumatic disillusioning discovery by the reader leads to remembering the novel differently and to a re-reading, according to the Freudian law of trauma. Re-reading may activate a latent trauma repressed in the first reading in a way that confirms Freud's paradigm for the genesis of hysteria.

ERRING AND MISINTERPRETATIONS

I turn now to a closer look at *Atonement,* with special attention to trauma, romance, and realism as features in it. In order to do this I must commit two well-known fallacies of criticism. I must speak of the characters as if they were real people, and I must recapitulate crucial events, as succinctly and accurately as I can. I *know* the characters are fictive, but they seem like real people to me. My discourse bears witness to that. I write about the characters and their experiences in the present tense, though the novel uses the past tense, according to a curious convention of critical analysis. I write as though the events were going on happening in some strange perpetual re-enactment, as indeed they are inside the covers of the book. Though plot summary is in general otiose, in this case the central events and their repetitions, as they are told and retold from the perspectives of the different characters or are echoed by other events, are the generators of meaning in the novel. They, therefore, must be put before my readers' eyes.

Atonement, even on a first reading, generated in me fear and foreboding. Somehow I knew things were going to turn out badly, just as I do when I start a novel by Henry James, and just as the reverse is true when I begin a novel by Anthony Trollope. I know when I open a Trollope novel that it will most likely all come out happily in the end, as it does for Arabella in Briony's mock romance. Though the main narrative of *Atonement,* which might be called an adult romance, follows the pattern of *The Trials of Arabella,* including the happy ending, it turns out, as Briony in her old age notes, that matters are not quite so simple, as I shall show. The thirteen-year-old Briony matches neither Freud's model of the innocent girl-child who does not understand her father's sexual abuse of her, nor Freud's model of the adult woman who knows about sex and can, therefore, actuate the childhood potential trauma by way of deferred action or *Nachträglichkeit.* On the verge of puberty (she speaks at one point of fearing the onset of menstruation), Briony is betwixt and between. This, oddly enough, leads her to experience Freud's trauma pattern in reverse. She sees her older sister Cecilia behave strangely at a garden fountain with Robbie Turner. Both Cecilia and Robbie have just recently graduated from Cambridge, he with a strong first, she with a third. As the reader knows by seeing the episode first through Cecilia's eyes and Robbie's, Cecilia is angry with Robbie for his clumsiness in breaking the lip of a valuable Meissen vase she has brought to the fountain to get water for flowers. She takes off her skirt and blouse, and dives into the fountain in her underwear to retrieve the two broken pieces of the vase. She thinks she acts to demonstrate her independence from Robbie and her anger with her old friend, though actually (as the reader guesses) it is because she is unconsciously in love with him.

Catherine Morland, the heroine of Jane Austen's wonderfully funny, ironic, and profound parody of a Gothic romance, *Northanger Abbey* (1817–18), mistakenly interprets events around her according to the paradigm of the Gothic novels she has read, with disastrous results. McEwan's epigraph is from Austen's novel.[5] In a way that echoes Catherine Morland's mistakes, Briony misreads the scene she witnesses from the window as Robbie's sexual assault of Cecilia. The novel follows the Freudian sequence: first the innocent version, then the traumatic repetition. Briony makes the same kind of errors Catherine does, and for the same reason. Robbie Turner has, Briony thinks, forced Cecilia to undress. She describes the scene, as she has misinterpreted it, to her visiting slightly older cousin Lola. They agree that Robbie is a "maniac." That misinterpretation is confirmed later that day when Briony, who, the reader learns much later, still has a suppressed adolescent crush on Robbie, comes upon Robbie and Cecilia making love standing up in a dark corner of the library. Briony, perhaps motivated in part by jealousy, misreads this as Robbie's second sexual assault on an unwilling Cecilia. Robbie has sent a love letter to Cecilia that mistakenly includes a private erotic note, which uses a four letter word and which he did not intend to send. Robbie puts the wrong letter in the envelope. McEwan has Robbie tell himself that it is a true accident, not a Freudian slip. Briony wickedly intercepts and reads the letter before she passes it on to Cecilia. The letter and note paradoxically lead Cecilia to realise suddenly that she is as passionately in love with Robbie as he is with her. The narrator describes their lovemaking with circumstantial detail worthy of the most obscene of erotic romances. The explicitly mentioned model is Lawrence's *Lady Chatterley's Lover* (124).

The child's witnessing of adult copulation is a classic Freudian example of a trauma-causing event. It is seen as disgusting violence done by the male to the female, for example, by the father to the mother. The narrator's description in *Atonement* stresses the violence of copulation, with lots of biting and slapping, though Cecilia performs that violence even more than Robbie does. Briony, in any case, quite mistakenly views the event she interrupts as a violent attack on Cecilia by Robbie. It confirms her view that Robbie is an oversexed monster, a maniac. In this case, the first event was innocuous enough, while witnessing the second, in its repetition of the first innocent scene by the fountain, is traumatic for Briony. It is a turning point in her transition to adult knowledge. The scene in the library confirms her misreading of the fountain scene.

Briony's Catherine Morland-like misreadings are, she mistakenly thinks, confirmed later that night when she comes upon Lola outside the fake Greek temple on the estate being sexually assaulted in the darkness. The scene confirms the link of human sex to animal life. The first evidence to Briony that something is happening in the darkness ahead is a cry she wrongly assumes is being made by a duck: "a duck startled her with a high, unpleasant call, almost human in its breathy downward note" (154). Actually Lola makes the sound during the rape. Briony mistakenly assumes that the figure she sees slinking away is Robbie the sexual maniac, the monster. The reader learns much later in the novel that the rapist is Paul Marshall, a visiting friend of Briony's older brother Leon. Lola apologises to Briony for not having been able to resist the sexual assault: "I'm sorry, I didn't, I'm sorry [...]" (155). The novel stages the scene in chiaroscuro:

> [...] what she knew was not literally, or not only, based on the vis-
> ible. It was not simply her eyes that told her the truth. It was too dark
> for that. Even Lola's face at eighteen inches was an empty oval, and
> this figure was many feet away, and turned from her as it moved back
> around the clearing. But nor was this figure invisible, and its size and
> manner of moving were familiar to her. (158)

Briony thinks it looks like Robbie, even at a distance and in the darkness.

Paul Marshall is a vulgar and obnoxious war profiteer who is getting fabulously rich by manufacturing chocolate bars with no chocolate in them ("Amo bars"). He sells these to the Army that is mobilising for the imminent war. Somewhat grotesquely or improbably, Marshall later marries Lola. She thereby gets what she has always wanted, wealth and a high social position. The monsters are Paul Marshall and Lola. The reader will note that Briony's transition from innocent ignorance to adult knowledge is the reverse of Catherine Morland's. Catherine comes to see that she has been almost unforgivably in error. Briony moves from trusting Robbie Turner to mistakenly thinking he is a rapist. She fatuously congratulates herself for moving from childish innocence to the adult knowledge that will make her a mature novelist. The oscillating double irony here is the question of where the narrative voice stands in its implicit judgment of these echoing scenes. One could argue that the narrator (and perhaps McEwan as author) implies that "real life" does unfold according to the patterns of romance. The novel at its ending, however, as I shall show, argues against that presumption, while at the same time ironically supporting it. As with any novel using an apparently omniscient narrator who exploits all the powers of free indirect discourse, irony exists pervasively at the local level of style in *Atonement*. It exists, that is, in the discrepancy between the narrator's discreet, ambiguous wisdom and the characters' foolishness or ignorance. Irony is undecidable. It says: "both x and y."

Briony reports what she thinks she has seen to the family and to the police in what the narrator calls her "crime." She shows them Robbie's obscene letter. The result is that Robbie is arrested and taken away in handcuffs. He is convicted, labelled oversexed, and sent to prison. As he is led to the police car, Cecilia comes forward to tell him she believes he is innocent and that she will wait for him: *"I'll wait for you. Come back"* (190, original emphasis). Those sentences echo through the novel. They are repeated in all Cecilia's letters to Robbie and in his memory during the Dunkirk retreat scenes in *Part Two* of the novel. Once more Briony misreads what she sees at a distance. She interprets what she beholds according to her preconceived romance programme. She thinks she is seeing Cecilia's final accusation of Robbie as he is led off to jail (173). Briony is wrong again, disastrously wrong, at every point of her reading of what she witnesses in this scene. She sees the duck as a rabbit, to borrow from the famous Gestalt duck-rabbit diagram, just as, in another of her mistakes, she hears the cry of Lola being raped as the cry of a duck. Yet, no actual ducks exist in the novel, only a cry that Briony mistakenly interprets. Of course the figure in the Gestalt diagram is neither a duck nor a rabbit, but both, depending on how you undeliberately look at it one way or the other, just as a duck's nocturnal cry and a rape victim's cry are similar.

Cecilia angrily repudiates her family for believing Robbie is guilty. She leaves home. She will not speak to any of her family or answer their letters. Robbie joins the army after his release from prison and at the onset of WWII. He and Cecilia continue to exchange letters swearing their continued love. They meet and kiss publicly once before he is sent to France with his army unit. Cecilia becomes a nurse during the war, as does Briony. Briony has turned down her place at Cambridge as part of her attempt to expiate what she now understands to have been her disastrous crime of perjury. She has borne false witness. She swore she saw Robbie moving away in the darkness after the rape of Lola. She actually *saw*, however, only a looming figure in the darkness, a figure she mistakenly *knew* was Robbie, to borrow the narrator's play on these two words. The narrator defines this mistake as a narratological one. It is generated by Briony's dangerous gift for coherent storytelling. She now erroneously thinks this penchant is no longer childish. Her mistaken interpretations are necessary in order for her to make a consistent story of what she has seen. Robbie is a "maniac," therefore the unidentifiable figure must be Robbie (159). In her final such mistake, Briony assumes Cecilia must be accusing Robbie as he is about to be put in the police car: "[S]he had become a participant in the drama of life beyond the nursery. All she had to do now was discover the stories, not just the subjects, but a way of unfolding them, that would do justice to her new knowledge. Or did she mean her wiser grasp of her own ignorance? (150). That last phrase is a little ominous. It prepares obscurely for the surprise dénouement of the novel.

If Briony, like Catherine Morland, misreads events because she expects them to fall into a preconceived narrative pattern, which of us readers can deny doing the same, for example when we make certain assumptions about *Atonement* during a first reading? These assumptions turn out to be grotesquely mistaken, as the reader discovers at the end. The reader, I as reader at least, is led to become like Catherine Morland or like Briony Tallis. Our error also triggers trauma by deferred action when we are disillusioned. This might be called "Reader's Trauma."

POINTILLIST REALISM AND THE TRAUMA OF WAR

The long *Part Two* of *Atonement* is a detailed account of Robbie's experiences during the British retreat to Dunkirk. He laboriously walks many miles to the beach with two other men. This trek is recorded in disturbing detail. It is much more shocking for the reader than the dryer, more objective, statistical, and historical account in books about Dunkirk, or than my memory of news accounts at the time. As time passes, Robbie's septicemia from a shrapnel wound in his side gets gradually worse and worse. His thoughts get gradually more incoherent as his delirium increases. Robbie's inner life during the retreat is reported in standard free indirect discourse. It includes memories of his past life, of his lovemaking with Cecilia, of her promise to wait for him, of her letters (which he carries in his greatcoat), of his arrest and imprisonment, and of the possibility, reported in his last letter from Cecilia, that Briony may officially recant her false testimony and get him legally declared innocent. He could then make actual his dream of going to medical school. He could marry Cecilia and live happily ever after. He keeps thinking that he must survive and return to fulfil her promise: "*I'll wait for you. Come back*" (190, original emphasis).

Robbie's experiences are certainly traumatic for him and for the reader. Re-reading this section, especially in the light of revelations at the end of the text, is a good example of deferred action, good old *Nachträglichkeit*. I am old enough to remember Dunkirk being reported on the radio. It was not traumatic for me then, as a teenager. Reading *Atonement* now makes that recollection traumatic. The retreat to Dunkirk was truly horrible. The horror is in the details, as Freud knew, in the descriptions of innumerable rotting corpses, both military and civilian, in the roads and ditches, of the German dive-bombing and strafing, of the cries of the wounded, of the burned out vehicles, of grotesque scenes of British army men destroying their own equipment so the Germans won't get it.

The reader, like Robbie, is likely to be especially haunted by certain scenes and details in the novel. One example is the episode of the mother and child Robbie fails to save from obliteration by a German dive-bombing. Their killing leaves only a cone-shaped crater in a field with no signs of their bodies. Another example is the human leg Robbie sees in a tree.

This is one more awful mutilation brought about casually by German bombardment of the countryside and of the retreating British army. In Robbie's final hallucinated reverie he goes back obsessively in memory over those scenes. He wants to retrace his steps, to return and relive those events, and somehow to undo the guilt he unreasonably feels for the atrocities he has seen. In the same way, present-day soldiers suffering from PTSD endlessly relive in dreams or in imagination the trauma-causing scenes they have witnessed.

This leg in the tree achieves a quite unexpected traumatic effect for the reader when he or she re-reads the novel with an attentive eye. The re-reader may happen to notice, or even remember from the first reading, an earlier apparently insignificant detail. When Briony goes back by the house on her way to her fateful witnessing of Lola's rape, she sees through the drawing room window "one end of a sofa across which there lay at a peculiar angle a cylindrical object that seemed to hover. It was only after she had covered another fifty yards that she understood that she was looking at a disembodied human leg" (151). Briony soon recognises that it is her mother's leg and that it is only figuratively disembodied. Her mother is resting on the sofa with her leg stretched out waiting for the twins (Lola's brothers who have run away) to be found and for her errant husband to make his late evening telephone call. An innocent enough detail becomes traumatic for the reader when it reappears much later in Robbie's witnessing of that literally disembodied leg in the tree. Neither Briony nor Robbie experiences this traumatic doubling. Each sees only one half of it. The deferred action only works on the reader.

At the end of *Part Two*, Robbie and his remaining companion, Nettle, are sleeping in a cellar waiting for morning and for the promised evacuation boats. Robbie has been talking in his sleep, crying out "No, you are not guilty. No," perhaps in denial of his responsibility for the horrors he has witnessed, perhaps in denial of the rape of which he has been falsely accused. His final words in this part are addressed to Nettle: "Wake me before seven. I promise, you won't hear another word from me" (250). This could go either way, either as a prelude to his rescue, or, the reader realises much later, as a foreshadowing of his death.

TRAUMATIC DOUBLINGS

Part Three switches suddenly from Robbie's point of view to Briony's. The narration is once more spoken or written by a telepathic narrator in free indirect discourse that turns present experience into past tense narrative. This third section tells the story of Briony's training as a nurse and of her first attempts at professional writing. It is in this section that "CC," whom we surmise to be Cyril Connolly at *Horizon*, returns Briony's novella, *Two Figures by a Fountain*, with a long letter (294–97). This is Briony's first step toward a successful career as a published writer and her first draft of part of her "crime."

Part Three gives at length the truly gruesome details of Briony's treatment of the horribly wounded soldiers who have made it back from the retreat to Dunkirk: a young Frenchman with half his head blown away, who dies before her eyes, or a man with a gangrened leg, and so on. I find reading these descriptions traumatic in the everyday sense of being almost unbearable. Repetition is not necessary to cause trauma in this case, thank you very much, though I am haunted by my memories of McEwan's vivid descriptions. That is a form of duplication leading to a response not unlike Dominick LaCapra's "empathic unsettlement," a state in which

> [b]eing responsive to the traumatic experience of others, notably of victims, implies not the appropriation of their experience [...]. At the very least, empathic unsettlement poses a barrier to closure in discourse and places in jeopardy harmonizing or spiritually uplifting accounts of extreme events from which we attempt to derive reassurance. (41)

Throughout this part, the reader may be said to experience something very much like vicarious trauma, perhaps without possessively identifying with the character. This effect is enhanced by the realist idiom employed in the war part, in sharp contrast with the romance and Gothic elements identified in the first section. This combination of realist and anti-realist elements is characteristic of traumatic realism, as defined by Michael Rothberg (3–5).

Toward the end of *Part Three* Briony takes time off to attend surreptitiously the marriage of Paul Marshall and Lola in a suburban church outside London, in Clapham. She then goes to visit Cecilia and finds her living in a boarding house room with Robbie Turner. Robbie has survived Dunkirk. He has a brief leave from his continuing army service. Briony promises them both to make the legal deposition that will, they all hope, get Robbie declared innocent. She promises to write to her parents and to Robbie giving details of her crime of bearing false witness. *Part Three* ends with Briony returning to her nurse's duties and planning three actions:

> She was calm as she considered what she had to do. Together, the note to her parents [telling them she was recanting her testimony] and the formal statement [for the legal authorities] would take no time at all. Then she would be free for the rest of the day. She knew what was required of her. Not simply a letter, but a new draft, an atonement, and she was ready to begin. (330)

New draft of what? I asked myself. And why would that be an atonement? Then I noticed the letters and words below the end of *Part Three* and to the right: "BT / London, 1999." When I saw the initials and date suddenly I realised that the author of what I had been reading is not Ian McEwan or his invented telepathic reliable narrator. It is an invented narrative by a fictive character, Briony Tallis herself. She turns out to be a thoroughly unreliable narrator. To be more precise: all the text we have been reading so far has been written by Ian McEwan imagining himself writing as an invented character in a fiction. That character is also a fiction writer, the putative writer of what we have been reading. I had, I suddenly learned, been hoaxed, bamboozled, cheated into believing I was on firm ground and could trust the narration and the narrator. This was another kind of traumatic experience since it transformed suddenly the whole narration, doubled it.

That doubling required a new reading in the light of a dismaying revelation. I needed to superimpose a disillusioned reading on the first innocent one, just as Freud's Katharina sees in a new light her father's[6] molestation of her when she, now informed about sex, sees through a small window a repetition of that first act performed by her father with another girl, Franziska, the cook in the inn the uncle and aunt (actually her parents) run. The superimposition during a second reading of my two readings of *Atonement*, separated by a temporal gap, readings so similar (same words) and yet so different (altered meaning), fits the Freudian paradigm of trauma. It seems odd to claim, as I already have in my initial listing of possible traumas in realistic fiction, that disappointed presumptions about a narrative can be traumatic. Nevertheless, this has certainly been the case for me with *Atonement*. My trauma has turned me into that much-maligned thing, a suspicious reader. I won't take anything for granted anymore in novels I read, especially in recent fiction, fiction after Borges, Nabokov, and the rest of the "postmodern" novelists, though Cervantes, that forefather of all novels, does the same kind of thing in *Don Quixote*.

LE TEMPS RETROUVÉ

The final section of *Atonement*, titled *London, 1999*, is only eighteen pages long. It gives further shocking revelations. It is written in the first person by Briony at age seventy-seven on the day after she has been diagnosed with progressive "vascular dementia," said not to be as bad as Alzheimer's, but with many of the same symptoms, gradual memory loss and so on. Briony writes in the first-person present tense on the day she has gone back to her childhood home, now turned into a luxury hotel. She is a guest there at a big family birthday party in her honour. All the cast of characters from her early life who are still alive come to the party with all their children, grandchildren, and great grandchildren, mostly descendants of the twins, Lola's brothers. Paul Marshall and Lola, though still alive, are absent, as are Cecilia and Robbie, for reasons we are about to discover. The birthday party guests reappear in a resurrection that recalls the reception at the end of Marcel Proust's *À la recherche du temps perdu* (1913–27), though that parallel is not mentioned. Nor does McEwan mention the way the end of Briony's novel, when she resolves to write a text that will be the one we have been reading, echoes Marcel's resolve, at the end of the *Recherche,* to write what turns out to be the *Recherche,* all those thousands of pages we have just been reading. Inside and outside reverse bewilderingly, as when you reverse the finger of a glove, putting it inside itself, in the gesture that Jacques Derrida calls, using a medical term, "invagination."[7]

As in Proust's climactic gathering, so in Briony's birthday party all those of Briony's generation have immensely aged. Her brother Leon is in a wheelchair, with half his face paralysed, and so on. Various children in this extended family perform for Briony and for the other guests *The Trials of Arabella,* to general applause. Briony's adolescent play actually gets performed, at last. Briony writes the final two-page section of the text seated early the next morning at her desk in her hotel room. This was originally "Auntie Venus's room" when the family lived there. Briony remarks in her diary entry on the similarity between *The Trials of Arabella* and her long novel that, the reader now knows, makes up most of the text:

> It occurs to me that I have not traveled so very far after all, since I wrote my little play. Or rather, I've made a huge digression and doubled back to my starting place. It is only in this last version that my lovers end well, standing side by side on a London pavement as I walk away. All the preceding drafts were pitiless. (350)

Drafts? Pitiless? What is she talking about? The surrounding sentences explain. What the reader has been reading up until the last section is, Briony now tells us, the final draft, dated 1999, of a novel based on her life that has gone through numerous drafts: "The earliest version, January 1940, the latest March 1999, and in between, half a dozen different drafts" (349). Briony's motive, at least apparently, was to atone for her crime and for Lola's and Paul Marshall's complicity in it, by confessing to the crime in exact detail, as in the letters she had promised to write to her parents and to Robbie (349). That seems clear enough. It justifies the final draft as an extreme example of mimetic realism. Briony's novel is validated by its one-to-one correspondence to historical events that really happened, even though it all happens in a fiction. Briony goes on to assert that this means her novel cannot be published until both the Marshalls are dead, since they are notoriously litigious and "would not tolerate an accusation of criminal conspiracy" (349). Telling the truth, so she apparently thinks, would be an atonement, just as would be her letter to her parents telling them she had lied about Robbie, the legal deposition recanting her false testimony that she promises Cecilia and Robbie in their last meeting to write, and the "letter" to him with full details of her crime Robbie demands. Robbie in the last scene of the 1999 draft peremptorily insists that she write these three documents. In place of the requested letter, Briony will write a new draft of her novel, as she asserts in words already cited: "She knew what was required of her. Not simply a letter, but a new draft, an atonement, and she was ready to begin" (330). She is ready to begin, that is, the novel the reader has at that moment finished reading. That novel is the response to a demand from Robbie for a full and truthful accounting for what she has done.

Atonement is a tricky concept. If a truth-telling novel can work as atonement, then atonement in that case would be a special kind of performative speech act. It would be a particular way of doing things with words. I expiate my crime by circumstantially confessing to it in a novel. "Atonement" comes from a Middle English adverbial phrase, "at oon," meaning to reconcile or make "at one." Atonement is "at-one-ment." According to the long entry in the *Catholic Encyclopedia*, "[i]n Catholic theology, the Atonement is the Satisfaction of Christ, whereby God and the world are reconciled or made to be at one." In Judaic thought and practice, the Day of Atonement is Yom Kippur. This is a Jewish holiday observed with fasting and prayer as a way of expiating bad deeds committed during the previous year. The theological meanings hover, however faintly, behind any secular or vernacular use of the word "atonement," as in McEwan's title. Nevertheless, according to the *Merriam-Webster Dictionary*, the everyday use just means "reparation for an offense or injury." That is certainly what Briony is attempting to accomplish with her novel and with her legal recantation. This is in spite of the fact that at one point she thinks to herself that what she has done cannot be forgiven. Her perjury is by no means to be expiated by giving up her chance at Cambridge and becoming a war nurse: "she would never undo the damage. She was unforgivable" (269). Perhaps writing the confessional novel might do it. It might work as atonement and earn her forgiveness after all.

That hope is thoroughly dashed by things Briony says in the final section. Somewhat ominously, apropos of her having amalgamated into one hospital the three different hospitals where she has worked as a nurse during the war, Briony says: "A convenient distortion, and the least of my offenses against veracity" (236). What those greater offenses were, the reader discovers a few pages later. It turns out, apparently, though the phrasing is a little odd, that Robbie did not survive the evacuation of Dunkirk and that a German bomb in London killed Cecilia a few months later. The entire happy ending in the last episode of Briony's novel is a lie added in the final draft to change the "pitiless" but more veracious earlier drafts. This confession is phrased as the impropriety, in this case, of trying to persuade the reader of what was apparently, but not certainly, given the phrasing, the true outcome. What purpose would be served by that? (350).[8]

The purpose that would be served would be a fulfilment of a writer's obligation, in a story based on real historical events, to tell the truth. Can fictions give sense, hope, and satisfaction only by lying? Are all happy endings false testimony to life as it truly is? This passage is another trigger of trauma's deferred action. The reader may now remember those final words of Robbie's section: "Wake me before seven. I promise, you won't hear another word from me" (250). When we first read them they were a promise that he would no longer talk in his sleep. Now, in retrospect, they seem to foreshadow his death from septicemia during the night. No more words from him, then. Another such hint comes near the end of Briony's invented happy ending: "They stood outside the Balham tube station, which in three month's time would achieve its terrible form of fame in the Blitz" (329). Now, at the very end, in the last section, the reader learns that Cecilia (apparently) died in that bombing. I say "apparently" because Briony does not straightforwardly say Robbie and Cecilia died in 1940. She asks what purpose would be served by trying to persuade her readers of that grim end. She is, apparently, free to end her novel in any way she likes.

At this point, a page before the end, an exceedingly uncomfortable oscillation is set up inside the mind of the somewhat bewildered and traumatised victim of the text, me at least. This oscillation is something like our bewilderment before a famous Piranesi etching that does not make spatial sense, or before certain Escher etchings that are equally irrational, or before that celebrated Gestalt duck-rabbit, mentioned earlier. Or the oscillation is generated by a weird simultaneity of inside and outside like that in invagination, the finger turned inside the glove, already mentioned. The reader may suddenly remember, in another turn of the screw, that McEwan has made the whole text up more or less out of thin air. He can tell whatever story he likes. He can make it end happily or unhappily at will. *Atonement* is a fiction not obligated to truthful storytelling, though it borrows for fictive purposes all sorts of historical truths, especially the parts about the retreat to Dunkirk, about the flood of wounded from the evacuation, and details about the Blitz. I suspected that the bombing of the Balham tube station is a historical fact. Sure enough, the station, which had been turned into an air-raid shelter, received a direct hit from a German bomb on October 14, 1940, killing 64 people, as quoted on the memorial plaque in the station itself. There is "traumatic realism" for you! In *Atonement*, historical fact is absorbed into what is, as a story, so far as I know, a complete fiction.

On the other hand, within the confines of the fiction, on the other side of the mirror, so to speak, in fictive Wonderland, the events that Briony tells do have a historical basis. Cecilia and Robbie did make love in the library. Paul Marshall did rape Lola by the garden temple. Robbie was falsely convicted of the crime. Robbie did die at Bray Dunes on 1 June 1940. Cecilia did die in the Balham bombing the following October. That is why neither shows up at Briony's seventy-seventh birthday party. Briony has lied in her teeth again and again in her novel, however well-meaning her romance ending might be, however much motivated by an inability to wound the reader with the "pitiless" truth. Novelists are notorious liars, but they can lie only in relation to some historical truth outside the fiction. If they make the whole thing up, it cannot be a lie except insofar as it claims historical veracity, as indicated by Michael Rothberg who, when analysing the characteristics of traumatic realism, which uses anti-realist techniques (that may be borrowed from romance) so as to evoke the extreme character of a historical situation, insists on the contradictory nature of this idiom, demanding both documentation and self reflexivity, without ever being able to "free itself from the claims of mimesis" (Rothberg 137).

The final oscillation, however, returns the duck to a rabbit and claims that, like McEwan's text itself, Briony's mendacious fiction in all of its drafts is only a fiction. It has only such power as fictions do have. Within her fiction, as long as a copy remains, the lovers eternally survive, to live happily ever after, in fulfilment of the romance paradigm (350). Briony transfers to Cecilia and Robbie the epithets used in *The Trials of Arabella* to characterise the heroine and hero of that childish romance: "my spontaneous, fortuitous sister and her medical prince" (350). This echo signals once more the congruence of the two stories.

The problem with this final turn of the screw in Briony's claim that "the lovers survive and flourish," is that it puts the novelist in the position of God. That means, as Briony recognises, that his or her works cannot function as atonements in some "real world" outside the fictive one:

> There is no one, no entity or higher form that she can appeal to, or be reconciled with, or that can forgive her. There is nothing outside her. In her imagination she has set the limits and the terms. No atonement for God, or novelists, even if they are atheists. It was always an impossible task, and that was precisely the point. The attempt was all. (350–51)

Really? I don't see that attempting and failing to atone through a work of fiction is much consolation. McEwan, in remarks made on camera, in the added material in the DVD of the film, a segment called "Bringing the Past to Life: The Making of *Atonement*," fudges this in an interesting way. Briony's falsification of historical truth by having Robbie and Cecilia survive and live happily together ever after, he says, was done "almost in a cowardly way." I assume he means the aging Briony was too cowardly to confess to the truth. She says as much in the text (350). Nevertheless, says McEwan, by writing the lying ending she could "maybe get forgiveness that way." The novel's final sentences, quoted above, put that "maybe" in question. This is the ultimate trauma, the final turn of the screw: that the novel's speech act efficacy as atonement is suspended, nullified, made impotent. The novel says you cannot atone in a work of fiction. A novel is only made of fictive words. Fictive words, it appears, do not make anything happen, as J. L. Austin said. For a performative to be felicitous, Austin insisted, "I must not be joking, for example, nor writing a poem."[9]

The reverse of the title page has the following conventional (and conventionally untruthful) disclaimer: "This book is a work of fiction. Names, characters, businesses, organizations, places, events, and incidents either are the product of the author's imagination or are used fictitiously. Any resemblance to actual persons, living or dead, events, or locales is entirely coincidental." I call this disclaimer a lie because of course McEwan's carefully researched description of the retreat to Dunkirk does make a non-coincidental resemblance in words of real locales, as in many other cases in the novel: the Tube Station at Balham, the Imperial War Museum, Clapham Common, and so on. The disclaimer is intended to avoid successful lawsuits for libel, such as Briony knows she will risk if she publishes her novel before the Marshalls are dead. In spite of *Atonement*'s infelicity as atonement, however, it *has* worked as a felicitous speech act to generate in my imagination an alternative fictive world or several wavering confusingly interchangeable ones. It has brought about in me all sorts of emotions, including the traumatic ones I have stressed in my reading and the dizziness brought about by that oscillation between inside and outside that I have described as like an invaginated glove finger. We read a novel that seems objective, but turns out to be a fiction inside another encompassing truthful narrative that is apparently outside, but nevertheless is also inside a fictive text in its a shimmering totality. That text has only coincidental similarity to real places, people, and events.

This disquieting oscillation is by no means exclusively "postmodern." The same thing happens, as I have said, in *Don Quixote*, at the beginning of the Western print novel, or in a different way in *Tristram Shandy*. I shall go on being haunted by *Atonement*, re-enacting it in my mind, whenever I encounter something that recalls it, as traumatised soldiers remember obsessively their war experiences. One sees from this that the effects of reading should not be taken too lightly, and that reader's trauma may very well be triggered and amplified by the collaboration between the excruciatingly pointillist technique of realism and the beguiling extremities of romance.

NOTES

1. For an elegant brief analysis along these lines, this time based on Freud's case of Emma and on the *Project* of 1895, see Chase. "The first scene," says Chase, "is completely forgotten, and the second, in its insignificant detail, takes on all the affective significance of the first alien sexual gesture" (179).
2. As Anne Whitehead points out in *Trauma Fiction* (133), Freud studied shell shock in "Thoughts for the Times on War and Death" (1915) and "On Transcience" (1916), "Mourning and Melancholia" (1917), "The Uncanny" and "Beyond the Pleasure Principle" (1920). See also Luckhurst, on the birth and uses of the term.
3. On erring as a fundamental component of romance, see Patricia Parker's *Inescapable Romance*.

4. In an article devoted to the ethics of trauma in *Atonement*, and more concretely to the ethical implications of fictional testimony, Georges Letissier alludes to the family romance at the heart of the novel (221).

5. Catherine has been especially influenced by Ann Radcliffe's *The Mysteries of Udolpho* (1798), that archetype of Gothic romances. McEwan's epigraph for *Atonement* cites Henry Tilney's stern rebuke of Catherine: "Dear Miss Morland, consider the dreadful nature of the suspicions you have entertained. What have you been judging from?" and so on. After this revelation, the now more adult Catherine soon marries Henry Tilney, as the reader anticipates, in a romance ending after all. The opening of the next chapter (Ch. 25) specifies her moment of disillusionment: "The visions of romance were over. Catherine was completely awakened. Henry's address, short as it had been, had more thoroughly opened her eyes to the extravagances of her late fancies than all their several disappointments had done" (Austen 123).

6. I say "father" because though the case history says she was molested by her uncle, a remarkable footnote added for the edition of 1924 says it was actually her father. Freud sternly prohibits reliable scientific psychoanalysts from telling such lies: "Distortions like the one which I introduced in the present instance should be altogether avoided in reporting a case history" (Freud 2001a, 134).

7. Among other examples, see as especially relevant to my discussion of *Atonement*'s bewildering reversals of inside and outside, Derrida's "The Law of Genre" (234–46), and "Living On: *Border Lines*," (97–103). The pages about invagination in "Living On" are also available in revised form in *Parages* (123–27). In all these cases, Derrida is analysing the double invaginated structure of Maurice Blanchot's *récit*, *La folie du jour*. Blanchot's story has a narrative structure quite like that of McEwan's *Atonement*. "By definition," writes Derrida, "there is no end to a discourse that would seek to describe the invaginated structure of *La folie du jour*. *Invagination* is the inward refolding of *la gaine* [sheath, girdle], the inverted reapplication of the outer edge to the inside of a form where the outside then opens a pocket. Such an invagination is possible from the first trace on. This is why there is no 'first' trace. We have just seen, on the basis of this example refined to the point of madness, how 'the whole story [to which] they listened' is the one (the same but another at the same time) that, like *La folie du jour*, begins 'I am not learned; I am not ignorant [. . .].' But this 'whole story,' which corresponds to the totality of the 'book,' is also only a part of the book, the *récit* that is demanded, attempted, impossible, and so forth" (Derrida 2011, 124–25).

8. On *Atonement* rejecting the comfort of reassuring ideologies and neat narrative closure, hence privileging a vision of history as impossible to consign to the past, see Letissier 226.

9. Austin 9. As I have shown at length, however, in the first chapter of my *Speech Acts in Literature* (Miller 6–62), matters are not quite so simple for Austin's speech act theory, not to speak of those derived from Austin by Paul de Man, Jacques Derrida, myself, and others. The fictive is always a component of even the most conventional and lawful speech acts, as even Austin to some degree recognised.

WORKS CITED

Austen, Jane, *Northanger Abbey*. 1817–18. Chenango Folks, N.Y.: Wild Jot Press, 2009. Print.

Austin, J. L. *How to Do Things with Words*. 2nd ed. Eds. J. O. Urmson and Marina Sbisà. Oxford: Oxford UP, 1980. Print.

Blanchot, Maurice. *L'Entretien infini*. Paris: Gallimard, 1969. Print.

———. *The Infinite Conversation*. Trans. Susan Hanson. Minneapolis: U of Minnesota P, 1993. Print.

Chase, Cynthia. *Decomposing Figures: Rhetorical Readings in the Romantic Tradition*. Baltimore: The Johns Hopkins UP, 1986. 179–80. Print.

Derrida, Jacques. "Living On: *Border Lines*." Trans. James Hulbert. *Deconstruction and Criticism*. Eds. Harold Bloom, et al. New York: The Seabury P, 1979. 97–103. Print.

———. "The Law of Genre." Trans. Avital Ronell. *Parages*. Ed. John P. Leavey. Stanford: Stanford UP, 2011. 216–49. Print.

Freud, Sigmund. *Studies on Hysteria*. 1895. *The Standard Edition of the Complete Psychological Works of Sigmund Freud* Vol II. Trans. James Strachey et al. London: Vintage, Hogarth P and Institute of Psycho-Analysis, 2001a. Print.

———. "Family Romances." 1909. *Jensen's 'Gradiva' and Other Works. The Standard Edition of the Complete Psychological Works of Sigmund Freud* Vol IX. Trans. James Strachey et al. London: Vintage, Hogarth P and Institute of Psycho-Analysis, 2001b. 235–41. Print.

Lacan, Jacques. *Le Séminaire. Livre I. Les écrits techniques de Freud, 1953–1954*. Paris: Seuil, 1975. Print.

LaCapra, Dominick. *Writing History, Writing Trauma*. Baltimore and London: The Johns Hopkins UP, 2001. Print.

Letissier, Georges. "'The Eternal Loop of Self Torture': Ethics and Trauma in Ian McEwan's *Atonement*." *Ethics and Trauma in Contemporary British Fiction*. Eds. Susana Onega and Jean-Michel Ganteau. Amsterdam and New York: Rodopi, 2011. 209–26. Print.

Luckhurst, Roger. *The Trauma Question*. London and New York: Routledge 2008. Print.

Miller, J. Hillis. *Speech Acts in Literature*. Stanford, CA: Stanford UP, 2001. Print.

McEwan, Ian. *Atonement*. 2001. New York: Anchor Books, 2003. Print.

Parker, Patricia. *Inescapable Romance: Studies in the Poetics of a Mode*. Princeton: Princeton UP, 1979. Print.

Rothberg, Michael. *Traumatic Realism: The Demands of Holocaust Representation*. Minneapolis: U of Minnesota P, 2000. Print.

Whitehead, Anne. *Trauma Fiction*. Edinburgh: Edinburgh UP, 2004. Print.

Wright, Joe. *Atonement*. Working Title Films, 2007. Film

6 Purloining the Image of Trauma
Photography, Testimony and Self Articulation in Peter Roche's *Unloved*

Frédéric Regard

Unloved: The True Story of a Stolen Childhood is an autobiographical memoir. As its subtitle indicates, it defines itself as a "true story" and, as such, refers its readers to individuals whose verifiable existences are attested in the "Acknowledgements" (ix–x). *Unloved* conceives of itself as a testimony, an account made by a direct witness of true events, lived and felt directly, at a personal level. The events described are of a systematic use of cruelty to the helpless children of the Roche family, a cruelty assumed to be at the origin of Peter's—the I-narrator's—trauma, the symptoms of which are bouts of irrepressible anxiety plaguing his adult life. The trauma is not ascribed to the sudden irruption of a wound, physical or psychological, inflicted on Peter as a child; it is not limited in its duration, but characterised rather by its ongoingness: not just a sudden injury, but one which, as is always the case with child maltreatment, has a longer duration and is connected to growing up, in such a way that "the boundaries of violence, or the location and limit of trauma are overwhelmingly difficult to chart" (Gilmore 92).[1] The violence is endless—with flashbacks functioning as memory, but also as repetition, or anticipation of what is still to come—shattering time, preventing it from telling a different story, forbidding its restoration to narrative coherence, precipitating it into a crisis of "permanent simultaneity" (Gilmore 92). Under such circumstances, "trauma cleaves time into past and future in such a way that both coexist in the present" (Gilmore 93). Trauma means, thus, the impossibility of "romance," a term I will be using in Northrop Frye's sense: "a sequential and processional form," and "the nearest of all literary forms to the wish-fulfilment dream" (Frye 186–87). Anxiety signifies the impossibility of reshaping one's life on the model of the successful quest narrative, the impossibility of temporal differentiation, of a linear, progressive re-emplotting of one's life, leading through the overcoming of obstacles to the ultimate triumph of the human hero over his monstrous enemy.

According to Barbara Korte, one of the specific tasks for literary studies within Poverty Studies consists in analysing the "articulation" of misery memoirs by focusing in particular on "the issue of agency, one of the fundamental rights and capabilities that the poor are often denied."[2] Meditating on the example provided by *Unloved*, Korte argues that the turning point in the book is when Peter Roche, now a young man prone to ever-more severe bouts of anxiety, is officially diagnosed as suffering from Post-traumatic Stress Disorder, a verdict which triggers his determination to investigate the causes of his trauma and use the narration of his investigation as therapy. Crucial to this process of self-articulation is his rediscovery of a famous photograph of himself, aged two, taken in 1965 by Lord Snowdon for a fund-raising campaign of the National Society for the Prevention of Cruelty to Children (NSPCC). "Narration ultimately becomes [...] a way of achieving agency and authority over his life," Korte concludes, adding that, in a way that is typical of "articulation" in misery memoirs, Roche is not content with articulating his own emotions; he also intends to involve his readers emotionally and engage their sympathy. Korte's reading of *Unloved* seems to contradict Gilmore's emphasis on the ongoingness of certain forms of trauma: Roche's narrative seems to be evidence that there is no fundamental difference between various forms of temporality depending on the nature of trauma, that all traumas have a specific origin which, once traced, lends itself to narrativisation and, therefore, therapy. Korte is quite right to isolate the rediscovery of Lord Snowdon's photograph as a key moment in Roche's "articulation" of himself: it is indeed the representation of one particular event that is used by the narrator to re-establish a difference between past and future and, as it were, to fix the ghost of endless violence in the past. That is the paradox Roche's gripping narrative of self-exploration and recovery confronts us with: the photograph is evidence of the reality of endless, durational violence and, at the same time, of its potential relegation to a precisely datable chronological past.

My reading focuses on the central enigma of Roche's narrative of self-production: the disappearance and reappearance of this photographic image of himself, which does not only inexplicably disappear from Roche's parents' home, but also from the narrative itself. Even the account of the rediscovery of the lost photograph is tantalisingly introduced to be only deferred, as if the reluctance to confront the past were still at work in the very process of retrospective narration. As a matter of fact, this crucial visual object surfaces on only two occasions—three if one counts the cover of the 2007 Penguin edition, on which Lord Snowdon's picture was reproduced, henceforth permanently conditioning the reading of the text with its spectral paratextual presence. What complicates the matter further is that the photograph does not simply disappear; it is, as the subtitle suggests, "stolen" from the boy, a metonymic image of the normal childhood he has been bereaved of. My title for this article indicates however that I prefer to say "purloined," which I borrow not so much from Lacan's famous 1955 Seminar, as from its object of study, Edgar Allan Poe's tale, "The Purloined Letter." My hope in so doing is to retrieve the verb's full etymological meaning—which Lacan tends to overlook by assuming that the letter's arrival at its "proper" or true destination is only delayed (59)—and to recapture by the same token some of the tale's narrative force. "To pur-loin" is to remove from public view; to put out of the way, to conceal; to make away with, to misappropriate, under circumstances which involve a breach of trust. The OED traces the origins of the term to the Anglo-Nor-man *porloigner*, meaning to delay, to postpone, to prolong, to extend, and also to set aside, to reject far off. What this etymology suggests is precisely what led Jacques Derrida to offer a thorough critique of Lacan's Seminar, namely, the possibility for any letter *not* to reach its "proper" destina-tion and fail, therefore, to pass the test of truth and untruth. My notion of a purloined image is predicated on the signifier's constitutive force to allow itself to be caught in its own "drifting-off course," which Derrida construes as being replete with "effects of indirection" (1999, 186, 193). What I want to investigate, in short, is how a photograph that has been "put aside" returns into the narrative as the central but belated revelation of a secret that is not quite a secret, as a signifier that can only make sense through a dual operation of removal and prolongation.

By seeking to retrieve the traumatic source of his fits of anxiety through a recovery of himself as a photographed leftover of permanent abuse, the narrator of *Unloved* ascribes himself an impossible task. Indeed if, as Samuel Weber explains, "the trauma is always in excess of its recogni-tion or representation," exposing the psyche's inability to bind an excess of energy, then anxiety emerges as the conflict of contradictory processes by which the ego, in order to organise itself—to "articulate" itself—seeks "to represent the unrepresentable" (91). If, therefore, the photograph pro-duced by journalistic documentation is presented as the trace of something which necessarily falls out of conscious memory, both unrecognisable and immemorial, yet is still present in the mind, like a ghost whose prolonged force lies paradoxically in its deferral, the work of personal testimony implies the risk, and in fact the necessity, of narrative, which is also to say: literature. This is what Weber's reading of Freud's complementary notions of *Vorstellung* and *Entstellung* suggests (92): to confront the trauma is to make it into a *Vor-Stellung*, a re-presentation, something that is placed-in-front, both spatially and temporally, which the visual object indeed per-mits; but it is also to present a dis-figurement of the self, to present oneself as *Ent-Stellung*, an endless displacement of the self, which Roche's narra-tive strategy also precipitates.

TRAUMA, TESTIMONY AND LITERATURE

Unloved lends itself to being read as an almost unbearable succession of monstrous acts of cruelty to the helpless Roche children. The tortures and humiliations they are made to undergo include physical violence, lack of care—deprivation of food, clothes, heating, or hygiene—and linguistic abuse. The text describes how under such circumstances the children lose

their humanity, are turned by fear into "wild animals" (72), or reduced by
verbal violence to nothing but "little shits" (6, 94). Injurious speech coincides,
then, with the material effects of neglect: the Roche children—whose father,
working as public toilet cleaner, is called "bogbrush" by the other pupils at
school (36)—are literally transformed into shit, forced to wear unwashed
underwear, grubby shirts, and other "stinking rags" (53–54). What grips the
reader with real horror, however, is the terror the children are incessantly
subjected to. Peter himself is presented as the scapegoat of a nightmarish
nursery (29). Caught by his father in the act of storing bread in the basement,
the boy is smashed on his head with a metal bar and sent to hospital (41).
When Peter truants, his mother boils water and scalds his feet (59). A friend
of his brothers' head-butts him over and over again, until it is agreed that his
is a hard head indeed (84). As in all memoirs of trauma, this avalanche of
extreme cruelty forces the reader to assume a position of either masochism or
voyeurism (Gilmore 22). But such descriptions also aim to raise the reader's
sympathy, perhaps even turn him or her into a potential legal witness. In
Roche's case, the long litany of violence is meant first and foremost to explain
the various psychic disorders affecting the children of the family.

Peter, however, seems to be the only one to be officially diagnosed as suffering from "post-traumatic stress disorder" (319), which happens after his
wife Sally has left him for his brother Terry. From then on, he can no longer cope with his terrible anxiety attacks (196–97, 215, 242, 301). Peter's
trauma seems to have been occulted by himself, so that *Unloved* should be
construed not simply as the book of a man describing his miserable childhood, but more importantly as the story of a man writing in order to make
sense out of the "mess" that is inside his head (70), and simultaneously
to reestablish contact with other people, something he has always cringed
from (116–17). In other words, the narrator can portray himself as having
had a "psychotic behaviour" (208), or having been unable to concentrate on
work (239–40), retrospectively, only once he has been diagnosed with Post-
traumatic Stress Disorder. Writing is wondering about this black hole of
memory, trying to explain the present by an exploration of the past, retriev-
ing lost feelings, recapturing dim realisations (298). The problem arising
here is the credibility of a testimony which seeks to recreate a past the historicity of which is not attested, at least not until documentary evidence in
the form of the NSPCC photograph resurfaces in the final "Answers" chapter. It seems that even the third chapter, "The Photographers," describing
the irruption into the Roche home of Miss Zils, the NSPCC social worker,
and of "a man who kept hiding his face behind a strange black box" (28),
contains scenes which can only be the result of an ulterior reconstruction
of the past, insofar as the portrait that Roche draws of himself facing the
black box seems to be nothing less in fact than a description of the photograph placed on the cover of the book (28).

Despite the rhetorical strategy the narrator adopts—relying notably
on the present continuous and on internal focalisation—to convince his

reader that he is actually reliving the scene as if it were the resurgence of a personal memory, one may rightly suspect that the "desperately unhappy" child Roche is describing is the boy of the photograph he has seen, and that the details about his mother's attempts at clothing him properly (29) result more from deductive guessing by an adult commentator than from actual memories by a traumatised two-year old. This tension between first-hand experience and second-hand fabrication, between personal memory and *ekphrasis*, raises the suspicion that Roche's past may have been reconstructed, a suspicion somewhat encouraged by jarring frictions between the child's and the mature narrator's perspectives. *Unloved* readily accommodates childish, fantasised transfigurations of facts, without making sure that the sources of enunciation can be distinguished between the traumatised child persona and the more mature narrator persona. For instance, the narrator refers to Miss Zils as "Batman" (31). The unsettling effect of that particular style is further enhanced by Roche's intertextual references.

Korte convincingly argues that first-hand testimony in misery memoirs is very often filtered through a cultural history of poverty affecting our imaginary, such as Mayhew's journalism, Thomson's photographs, or Dickens's *Oliver Twist*. Awkwardly enough, Roche makes no secret of this: "If it sounds like the plot of *Oliver Twist*, that's because it was" (176). Elsewhere, he describes himself and a friend walking through the streets "like two Victorian kids on their way to sweep chimneys" (112). Many other references to the Victorian era and to Dickens in particular may be found throughout the memoir (262, 321, 323), and it is even permitted to suspect that when Roche mentions "another twist to the tale" (323)—the discovery that Lord Snowdon had sold the photograph to the *Sunday Times Magazine* (330)—he still unconsciously uses the reference to *Oliver Twist* to make it signify a classic form of innocence-stealing, deftly recontextualised in the London of the Swinging Sixties. Intertextuality is sometimes introduced by the children themselves, who refer to their predicament by implicitly quoting from poems by Robert Service and George Sims who seem to have joined their forces to design a gruesome tale of modern-day suburban Little Tom Thumbs (94). The world of fairy tales is never too far in any case. For instance, Peter's father is particularly fond of nicknames: Paul is "Dunce," Terry "Deafty," Francis "Spindle Legs," Laurence "Cabbage," Peter "Dwarf" (20). There is something cruel about such nicknames—"another form of bullying" (20)—but the bullying is to some measure attenuated by the suspicion that the names might have been invented as the parody of a Walt Disney production (*Snow White and the Seven Dwarfs*, released in 1937, had indeed given names to the dwarves of the Brothers Grimm tale). Some situations do give the impression that their nightmarish description is explicable in terms of some indigestion of animated cartoons (60). Roche's intertextual references thus serve to anchor his narrative in a given culture, a shared cultural past—marvellous plot devices, folk traditions, Gothic tales and various other "romantic" features—while also weighting his descriptions with an implied criticism of society, a typical characteristic of romance, the past being made thus both knowable and unfamiliar.[3] The "fictional" strategies adopted by Roche constitute in fact the interesting symptom of the popular culture through which he—and to a lesser extent his relatives—perceived his plight. Furthermore, what one expects of normal family life is made to clash so violently with the abnormality of Roche's parents—"my parents were not normal" (15)—that a certain degree of fantasy is to be expected: the situations are so monstrously impossible to believe that romance—particularly its archetypal codes of good and evil—is indeed what sometimes best translates this reality as lived and felt by the child. The quasi-hallucinatory quality of some of the scenes would, then, be an index of the hell into which Peter was thrown from the date of his birth, and a degree of "fictionalisation" would be an indication of the subject's profound disarticulation. In other words, fiction here would not be a sign of the traumatised child's recovered agency and "authority," but the very signature of indelible trauma.

It is precisely because trauma defies the law of realist representation that it demands our faith in the reliability of the facts reported. It is because trauma overwhelms the limits of acceptability that we are faced with the ethical responsibility of trusting the tale. The force of the testimonial relies in part on the suspicion that it might not be true, that the trauma memoir might after all be only literature. The unsettling, disconcerting, *unheimlich* quality of the account affects the reader too, demanding that she suspend her disbelief, or rather that she disbelieve *and* believe the tale. The paradox is in fact a dilemma: we cannot morally question the truth of Roche's narrative, and yet we must refuse to accept the unacceptable. This oscillation, between a moral and legal duty to believe testimony unconditionally, and a humanist refusal to accept the unacceptable, is an ethical moment. Derrida explains this in terms of the necessary haunting persistence of the possibility of literature within testimony: "if the testimonial is by law irreducible to the fictional, there exists no testimony that does not imply structurally in itself the possibility of fiction, simulacra, dissimulation, lie and perjury—that is to say the possibility of literature [. . .]" (2000, 29). If the possibility of fiction, or romance, were not contemplated, if the mature narrator's testimonial account of himself were not open to, at least, *the possibility* of a parasiting of its innermost convictions by simulacra, dissimulation, lie, or perjury, Roche's narrative of self-exploration would lose much of its gripping force. The dilemma must be allowed to persist in the form of this ethical hesitation between the necessity of proclaiming one's faith in the victim's words, and that of voicing one's disbelief in the face of the inhumanity of humanity.

DI(VISIBILITY)

Part of the narrator's skill in *Unloved* consists precisely in overtly contemplating the possibility that his rendering of facts might not be fully reliable, due notably to the recurrence of puzzling contradictions. For example, when Peter's brother Paul is savagely beaten by their father, Roche explains that he saw his brother's hands tied up in front of him, whereas Paul insists they were tied behind his back (50). When Roche evokes his father's death (161), he mentions "a brain haemorrhage brought on by years of smoking, heavy drinking and fighting." But immediately after, the selfsame narrator recalls his mother claiming that her husband had been hit over the head with a brick (163), a story the narrator dismisses but not entirely (163). Among the stories told by the mother there is one that is particularly "mad," about a dog eating rat poison, being then treated by forcing down its throat "the sticky, tarry stuff from the bottom of [her father's] pipe," then being thrown in a ditch, and coming back to their door on the following morning wagging its tail (245). The narrator just takes up his mother's story of this ghost-dog returning to life, without commenting on the plausibility of the tale. What is even more puzzling is that Roche himself will not hesitate to take full responsibility for other such stories. For instance, when the family move from Lambeth to Wandsworth, and Peter and his mother are the last ones to leave the house, they both distinctly hear the dead father shouting the mother's name (198).

The reality of the father's ghost—his voice being heard in the present of the enunciation, with the full responsibility of the utterance being inexplicably delegated to the dead person—is, of course, a blatant breach of contract in a narrative that purports to be a testimony, a speech act that any tribunal might use for indicting the Roche parents. Derrida insists that the testimonial mode requires an "I" that is assumed to be present to itself, and that the speech of neither a dead nor a mad person could be accepted as a viable testimony in any court of law. All temporal disjunctures must be mended: the past and the present must be clearly distinguished by a direct witness fully present to itself, capable of reconstituting the chronology of verifiable events without any gap, uncertainty, shift of perspective. Such is the condition for truth: there must be no "divisibility" (Derrida 2000, 32). Here, however, ghost stories divide time against itself, preventing the present from cutting itself off from the past. They divide the self, too, allowed to exist as speaking from one place and simultaneously answering calls from another, alive and dead, moving down the road to a new life and yet "stopping *dead*" (198). This divisibility of self is everywhere at work. Roche describes himself turning away from his dying father, pretending to the boys assembled in the street that he does not even know the man the ambulance is taking away (2), but he also describes himself saying the Lord's Prayer in front of his mother's coffin (313). Throughout his memoir Roche keeps calling his parents "Mum" and "Dad," which in a context of appalling child maltreatment is quite unsettling for the reader.

What makes the book so unwieldy in many respects is precisely this odd mixture of repulsion and attraction, as if the horror experienced by the child still exerted a fascination on the mature narrator, incapable of fully dissociating himself from the family in which he grew up, and from the abused, but still innocent, child he once was. This is a peculiar feature of *Unloved*, one that has induced me to shift constantly from the Christian name to the surname, from Peter to Roche, from the character in the story to the narrator of the text, from the objectified victim of traumatic violence to the agency invested with authority over the articulation of his life. For instance, Roche often describes Peter being anxious to meet "Dad" at the door when his father came back from work, only to "lash out at [him] for being too near the door" (61). Roche's comments are extremely perplexing, as the adult he has now become seems unable to suggest any rational explanation for his repeated, masochistic error. The autobiographical memoir maintains a permanent hesitation between a variety of contradictory postures, which often grammaticalises itself in the use of tenses. When Peter, now aged sixteen, meets Clara, he perceives that he has "turned a corner," and the dominant mode in which Roche describes this time of his life becomes the future, in stark contrast both to what precedes and to what follows (238). Sometimes, more disturbingly, temporal planes are collapsed, and the safe distance assumed to differentiate the mature narrator from the young character seems suddenly to break down, as when Roche describes Peter making the decision to burglarise the shop in which he is employed (241).

Towards the end of the book, Terry's betrayal of Peter with his wife Sally is met with sheer abuse from the narrator, in free direct speech again, as if Roche were still somewhat his younger self, unable to come to terms with his past and, worse still, unable to refrain from replacing his father by taking up his very words of abuse (317). When his new partner Lisa suggests that he find out why, if the NSPCC knew about his family, nothing was ever done to protect the children, the narrative resorts once again to free direct speech, conflating three different utterances, Lisa's, the protagonist's, and the narrator's (321). The use of free direct speech collapses the normally distinct sources of enunciation, so that it becomes an arduous task indeed to enter into a reassuring compact of truth and verifiability with a narrator whose reliability is constantly undermined by such divisibility. As a point of fact, the major reason why the ultimate goal of Roche's quest for the origin of his trauma is so long deferred, is that the focaliser is very often Peter, with Roche withdrawing into the background and even delegating the responsibility for the utterances to his younger self. The moment of truth is thus endlessly delayed, and much of the reader's curiosity—and frustration—is to be attributed to this uncertainty as to whose perspective is adopted as the inquest progresses towards its solution.

That is why the function of the photograph is of such importance to the structure of *Unloved*, as well as to the author's self-articulation: visibility keeps the process of divisibility under control. Once the photograph has been revealed and described in such a way that it is unmistakably the one the reader can see on the cover of the book, the suspicion of *Unloved* being a modern-day version of a horror tale can no longer be entertained. The photograph's documentary status validates the testimonial quality of the narrative, forbids hesitation to veer into disbelief. By suddenly making visible what has hitherto remained invisible, it gives the impression that it is simply recording a raw fact without making any statement about it: "photographed images do not seem to be statements about the world so much as pieces of it" (Sontag 1989, 4). The photograph in Roche's rearticulation of his past is the missing clue in a self-narrative that gradually reshapes itself into detective story: the protagonist of the tale is intent on solving the enigma of his life, on assessing the reality of a crime perpetrated against himself, while the narrator keeps playing a game of duplicity, guiding the reader but confusing him or her too, until the photograph is discovered, the crime proven, the culprits identified. Susan Sontag is well aware that any picture remains an artefact, but she argues that what ultimately lends photographs their evidential status is that they always seem to be "found objects," "unpremeditated slices of the world," trading therefore on the "magic of the real" (1989, 79). And indeed, Lord Snowdon's photograph has the status of a found object, forcing truth to be disclosed in an unpremeditated manner (337).

There are things that must be shown in order to be believed. Photography, Barthes remarks, just "does not know how to *say* what it gives to see."[4] Lord Snowdon's picture in *Unloved* is the irrefutable proof of the child's nightmare. What is written is always a betrayal of facts, but what is *shown* is the real itself, the sheer impossibility of romance. The child's sufferings are thus made almost palpable: we are indeed facing a case of child maltreatment. Roche explains that Peter's "survival strategy" (67) consisted mainly in making himself invisible (112); the NSPCC's strategy to ensure the survival of the little victims consisted, on the contrary, in making Peter's misery visible, exposing the scandal in a way that suffered no contestation, raised no suspicion, dispelled the possibility of any misunderstanding or misinterpretation. "In contrast to a written account, [. . .] a photograph has only one language" (Sontag 2003, 20). What this particular photograph univocally establishes is the incontrovertible reality of that particular child's sufferings. The blow is almost lethal, "like being hit over the head with a brick" (322), a comparison which, while curiously recalling Mrs. Roche's story about her husband's death, conveys the idea of a brutal explosion of the mother's "romantic" fantasy—a fantasy shared by Peter, from the age of six "well into his teenage years" (246)—of a privileged relationship of Peter's father with a Royal. Lord Snowdon had been documenting neglected children, certainly not visiting friends in Lambeth. Peter's pain is suddenly exposed as "something-that-has-been," to take up Barthes's phrase. The photograph does not direct the observer's eye to the signifier—to its potential unreliability—but to the thing signified itself: the "ça-a-été" of Peter's plight. Photography can never deny that the thing has been there: "every photograph is a certificate of presence" (Barthes 1981, 76, 87).

TRAUMA, IMAGE AND TEXT

Peter's image as an abused and neglected child is, therefore, the moment of indisputable truth, the final confrontation of the detective with the enigma of his life, when the character's life's black hole is, after so many narrative detours or ruses of the psyche, eventually freeze-framed by the I-narrator. Roche portrays himself as someone who can suddenly see, whose eyes are no longer blind, whose image as Peter, the invisible child, has returned into the world of visible things. No wonder, therefore, if Roche describes himself suddenly overwhelmed with the grief of sudden recognition. The mute, beaten, ill-fed, half-naked child and the mature married man, father of five, turned I-narrator, are eventually reunited, in a face-to-face that obliterates difference and abolishes distance, spatial as well as temporal. This is an experience of death, of the return of the dead, of one's own dead self: what Roche sees in the image is another self, the self that was once himself and that might still be him, but is nevertheless another—the image of both another *and* of oneself. In Barthesian parlance, Peter's image is Roche's "Spectrum": the Spectator's dead double, his revenant, returning to visibility to hold the viewer's gaze and remind him of his mortality: the traumatic image as a highly personal *memento mori* (Barthes 1981, 10 f.). This spectral experience is physical, in fact deeply corporeal. The reality of suffering, physical or psychological, is communicable through the image; the visual involves a cognitional process; the image is, literally, re-cognised.

The maudlin aspect of the misery memoir, intensified by tear-rending photojournalism, cannot be denied here. But the shock-photo also provokes on the part of the reader a response to injustice, empathy giving way to moral outrage, as this other is also recognised as potential self. LaCapra's admonition to distinguish between "ethical empathic unsettlement" and outright identification could prove extremely useful here (102). Indeed, if Peter's image precipitates in the reader what one would be tempted to describe as identification with the other, based on a sharing of his suffering, what takes place in reality is what I would call a form of *quasi* identification, as the suffering cannot possibly be shared, experienced on the same temporal plane, and is in fact immediately superseded by the demand that justice be done. It is not to be denied that a dialogical relationship is established whereby the self cannot exist without the other, and vice versa. Raw facts penetrate the onlooker's eye, prevent the gaze from being that of a distant observer, inducing the subject of the gaze to reincarnate him or herself in the suffering body of the other. But this can only take place transitorily: the viewer is not ultimately transformed into a truly fleshed-out other self, but does indeed recognise the other as a potential *alter ego*, not only as a suffering victim therefore, but also as an agency whose fundamental rights as a human being, and a British citizen, should be protected by law.[5] The purloined photograph of the "little shit" had been a call for help, a demand addressed to the unknown future viewer, and it is at long last answered by the reader-viewer's emotional but also ethical response.

Barthes remarks that there is always a certain degree of latency in any photograph's arresting force—what he calls its "punctum"—as the oddity which eventually "pierces the viewer" is something dependent on each individual. The punctum's existential mode is thus aleatoric (1981, 53–54). For today's reader-viewer, such an odd, disturbing supplement might be the nappy pin holding Peter's vest, a curious detail, normally connoting maternal care and yet here evidence of neglect, as it appears that the vest is not Peter's, but an oversized threadbare, buttonless garment, most probably wrapped hastily round the child to hide his filthy underwear, perhaps even his nudity, from the camera eye. For the narrator of *Unloved*, it is the *whole* photograph that seems to inflate into an enormous punctum; it is the complete image of himself as a victim of parental neglect that pierces him, like a wound inflicted on his whole self. What matters ultimately is not to decide whether or not Roche's tale of his first and final confrontation with this image should be trusted; *Unloved* is the story of an image that may always already have been there, but which is suddenly granted its full, piercing, wounding presence the moment Roche recognises Peter as himself and the reader-viewer shares the pain of recognition. This is the moment of the silent recognition of the trauma, the confrontation with a shock-image that, according to Barthes, is "pure denotation," a sheer absence of connotation, a blocking of meaning, a suspension of language: "The traumatic photograph [. . .] is the photography about which there is nothing to say" (1978, 30–31).

But the traumatic effect and its corollary of the demise of connotation are only provisional in *Unloved*. There is something more to say. This is one of the many consequences of the durational violence inherent in such traumas; it is also characteristic of the use of photography to document and investigate the past: the sheer force of the raw image seems to be insufficient in itself to establish the reality of the crime, the purely denotational image being thus implicitly denounced as suffering from an essential lack of connotation. The photo must be parasited by the text, analysed, interpreted, in direct contradiction, it seems, to photography's decoded, analogical ambition—a "structural paradox" which Barthes perceives to be also an "ethical paradox": the photograph must be both decoded and coded, objective and subjective, neutral and committed, natural and cultural (1978, 19–20). Roche's narrative of self-exploration and self-articulation is, therefore, resumed once the photograph has been rediscovered, as if the force of trauma also resided in its endless proclivity to suscitate commentaries on and textual supplements to its ever-elusive source. *Unloved* thus unfolds its investigation into the sources of the self on the assumption that photographs are signifiers like others, subjected to the same indeterminacy, and that, as a consequence, the meaning of photography is crucially dependent on words.

There were in fact two photographic versions of little Peter, drawn from two different archives, and telling two antagonistic stories about the same child. What the narrator gradually discovers is that Lord Snowdon's shock-image was contradicted by another picture, showing Peter in a brand-new duffle coat, enjoying himself on a swing (247, 328–29). Lord Snowdon's picture—no fewer than 16 pictures of Peter had in fact appeared in the *Sunday Times* (325–26)—is given the lie by this second photo, part of a collection of snapshots taken by Miss Zils for a 1966 issue of the *Child's Guardian*, the NSPCC magazine, which alongside Lord Snowdon's photo did indeed show Peter as a happy, well-dressed child. The implicit narrative linking the two archival documents is made explicit by the narrator: "The story the two photographs told was: 'This is that boy then and this is him now. Look how we have transformed his life'" (239). It is precisely this second picture of Peter which is mentioned the moment Miss Zils is introduced again into the narrative, when Peter and Clara visit the NSPCC office to enquire why social workers would have taken such "a liking" to the boy (249). Miss Zils reappears years later, at her home in south London (321), where the shock-picture is at last confronted, and Roche almost breaks down (322, 327). But the reader's frustration is kept high the first time Peter is reunited with his benefactor, not only because the significance of the NSPCC representative's involvement with his family is "lost on [him]" (248), but also because the conversation held under the reassuring auspices of the nice picture is inexplicably interrupted (249–50). No mention is made of any parental abuse or neglect, and Roche resumes the story of his adolescence as a delinquent, so that the readers are left uncertain as to which of the two versions of his childhood they should trust—two antagonistic images of the same individual which the technique of photography imposes as two equally valid pieces of documentary evidence.

The second picture certainly does not lie about the child; it is a true picture of him—not fabricated, not retouched—and yet it is a soothing one, invalidating the almost unbelievable cruelty scenario, while validating the more likely hypothesis of a fantasy of castigation. This would explain why Peter's parents were never brought to justice, or at least why Peter was never taken away from his family despite the NSPCC visits. A soothing image is one which, the OED suggests, blandishes, cajoles, pleases, humours, insofar as it also declares a statement to be true, verifies it, proves it. Miss Zils's photograph is soothing because it carries with it the force of a verified, "soothfast" statement. If the second picture says something, relieves the first photo of its purely denotational dimension, it is as a "soothsayer," which once again raises the suspicion that the first picture might have been a fabrication, a false sayer, or even an ill sayer. The reader turned inspector does indeed suspect a certain degree of manipulation, for the famous photograph, the one reproduced on the cover of *Unloved*, is quite obviously retouched, showing a filthy, unhappy toddler, whose environment has nevertheless been carefully obliterated, at best blurred, so that the child seems to be stepping forward from a misty, unrecognisable background, surrounded by a halo, presumably that of timeless martyrdom. But this is where, precisely, Roche's memoir reaches another, even more interesting, turning point.

Lord Snowdon's photograph seeks to disentangle itself from contingency, to reach an abstract, a-historical level, where poverty and neglect can be signified in general. The boy's face is transformed into what Barthes would have called "a mask," thus running the risk of being transfigured into a mere image, consumed poetically and no longer politically (1981, 34). The very extent to which a photograph can become unforgettable "indicates its potential for being depoliticized, for becoming a timeless image" (Sontag 107). If Peter's image became such an unforgettable icon of poverty in Britain, it was because its original use could from the very start be supplanted by subsequent uses. Still, this aestheticisation of personal suffering into abstract, decontextualised poverty is not what eventually causes Roche's anger and disgust. The real scandal, the real monstrous enemy that the investigator uncovers, the "twist to the tale" he resents most of all, that which makes him "crack up" (326), is the sudden realisation that "it had been a publicity stunt" (327).

PUBLICITY, IDEOLOGY, THERAPY

What Roche discovers as he visits various archives—Lord Snowdon's (325), the NSPCC's (328), the Newspaper Library at Colingdale (330)—is that the documenting of social abjection that was to make him into a star to all but himself, had been commissioned to Lord Snowdon because the Queen was the patron of the NSPCC and her brother-in-law had been looking for an opportunity to make a name for himself by publishing photos in "the first colour magazine ever to be published with a British newspaper" (323). Peter's image had become iconic, not because it had been published in a little charity magazine, but because royal patronage had made sure Lord Snowdon's documentary work appeared in the August 1965 issue of the glossy magazine, before it was eventually reproduced in the NSPCC journal, with no other caption but: "Courtesy of Lord Snowdon and the *Sunday Times*" (329). Peter's image was used to bring in donations to the NSPCC, and it worked quite well; but what gradually dawns on Roche as he investigates the story of his own image, is that his fate as a singular individual, as an abused and neglected child named Peter Roche, had been of little, if any, importance to "the fleet of shiny black cars" (325) that had parked one day of May 1965 outside his Lambeth home. To take up Sontag's words, "photography is essentially an act of non-intervention": it shoots an image but it does not interfere with what constitutes the interest of that particular image; it does not seek to change things, and, in that respect, it is complicit with what it shows (11–12).

The best proof of Lord Snowdon's and the NSPCC's indifference to the child's helplessness is the sudden revelation by Miss Zils that "a retired British army colonel" had contacted their central office to offer help to the boy whose pictures he had seen in the *Times Magazine*, but had been denied access to the child, so that when the colonel had died, his entire estate had gone not to Peter but to the Society (326). *Unloved* is also the narrative of a young boy's impossibility to experience his life through the grid of the "family romance," i.e., the fantasy of being freed from one's family and joining one of higher social standing (Freud 74–78). If we accept the theory that the novel as a genre always evinces the desire to change the real, on the model of family romances (Robert 35), then *Unloved* lends itself to being read as a *mise en abyme* of its novelistic potential, and simultaneously as the affirmation of its tragic obligation to cope with the inescapable reality of Peter's life. By supplementing the photograph with a belated commentary on its history as purloined image, Roche's text provides the reader-viewer with the original picture's missing caption—the long, complex caption of the moralist whom neither Lord Snowdon nor the NSPCC had had any desire to be when the lenses of their cameras had transformed Peter's image into a series of "fund-raising pictures" (330). The written statement seeks to neutralise the aestheticising tendency of the photograph; it forbids that this image of a poor boy's helplessness should once more be consumed by protected, affluent viewers: to take up categories formulated by Sontag, the text's *raison d'être* is to prevent "history" from being transformed into "spectacle" (110).

The real origin of the retrospective narrative is not, therefore, located where the reader thought it would be; the treasure of the quest is not buried where it should have been, guarded by the expected dragon of the archetypal romance (Frye 189, 193, 196). What causes Roche's tears to be shed at long last is less the recognition of the historical shock-photo than the sudden awareness of its subsequent iconisation, of its transformation into a *cliché* of child poverty for a consumer society. This is the second trauma of *Unloved*, the socio-cultural wound the book eventually manages to superimpose on the first, individual wound. What devastates Roche is a deprivation of uniqueness: less the recognition of himself as a maltreated child than the sudden realisation that neither the NSPCC nor Lord Snowdon, even less the media, had shown any real interest in *him*. *Unloved* claims that their interest had been of the predatory kind: "Limited-edition prints of it sell for £2,000, ironically in a West End gallery in one of the streets where I used to walk as a penniless, hungry child in rags" (338). The second trauma the text introduces to supersede the first can be easily located, therefore, as it leaves the medical field of unspeakable suffering to alight on the field of social, political injustice: even the plight of a poor neglected child could be "fetishised" into a commodifiable image, an object of speculation and exchange, the surplus value yielded by the circulation of the prints functioning as a negation—what Karl Marx would have called a "mystification"—of the intrinsic value of the unique individual.[6] Lord Snowdon's indifference to the child's fate only confirmed that his work had not been sincere, but voyeuristic, self-centred and above all capitalistically interested. This deprivation of uniqueness, made even more manifest by the documentary image's endless reproducibility, is felt to be more wounding than the maltreatment of which Peter was the victim at home, as if having one's image commercially used in a late-capitalist exploitation of feelings and emotions[7] were worse eventually than being physically or psychologically abused.

The adjective "disgusting" (330) should here be given its sense of moral disapproval, but its repetition emphatically signals the narrator's emotional involvement too, as if Roche and Peter were once again collapsed into one speaking entity, voicing a shared feeling of victimisation. Roche's rhetoric now projects the image of an adult victim who feels betrayed by the commodification of his image as an abused child, at best a simple illustration of poverty in the Britain of the mid-1960s, at worst a sentimental fundraising gimmick. So, the photograph, instead of unveiling Peter's secret in order to rescue him, "masks" him again, producing him twice as refuse: first, as it furnishes evidence of parental neglect; second, as it alters the significance of the image in a post-capitalist economy of semiotic exploitation. The child, from literal shit—absence of value—is metaphorised into sign of exchange—commercial value. The text leaves no doubt as to this second, cultural trauma, as the utterance shifts from the impersonal to the personal, from the objective to the subjective, in order to emphasise the displacement of cruelty, from abuse and neglect, to iconicity: "It had been a publicity stunt—I had been a publicity stunt—and it had worked well" (327). It is this semiotic betrayal of personal trauma that *Unloved* denounces in its closing lines (338).

Roche's articulation of his traumatising childhood may be perceived as a form of therapy, but if that is indeed the case, I suggest that the therapy consists less in confronting Peter's trauma than in shifting the terms of the confrontation, from a psychoanalytical to a political scene. What gradually emerges as one reads *Unloved* is a deep class antagonism, centring on the issue of a semiotic exploitation of the poor and helpless. Roche's exploration of his own transfigurations is also a way of unmasking the confusion about truth and beauty by exposing the elegant, well-meaning humanism of the few people who had shown any interest in his plight—what Sontag gently mocks as being the humanism of professional, fashionable photographers (112). Lord Snowdon's humanism and, to a certain extent, Miss Zils's, are exposed as the perpetuation of a social and political *status quo*, whereby the distress of the poor and miserable, thrown into unforgettable visibility also functions as asymmetrical relation, implicit differentiation and, ultimately, self-protection. What *Unloved* articulates, therefore, by contesting the ideological *status quo* implicit in the pictorial representation of the poor, is that testimony is also, and above all, an exercise in democracy. Roche's autobiographical memoir subtracts traumatic experience from humanist, condescending visual observation, and by adding subjective text to objective image, translates speechless trauma into social commentary.

In terms of media history and publishing policies, the class struggle that subtends *Unloved* takes therefore the form of a semiological war waged between two "prints": an iconic photograph of the sixties, taken by a celebrity for a trendy magazine, and an early twenty-first-century low culture best-seller, written by the man in the street. The photograph does not speak for itself; it has to be spoken by those whom it purports to represent. Roche's narrative of self-recognition and self-articulation thus redefines the function and status of the traumatic photograph by making it shift planes, from speechless denotation to social connotation. *Unloved* uses a shock-photo to bypass the issue of traumatic re-cognition of oneself as a child whose childhood was "stolen"; it exposes rather the stolen dimension of the image itself. Therapy in Roche's memoir does not take the form of a quest for the source of trauma: *Unloved* designs a therapy which consists for its author in purloining the image of trauma, the better to unmask the social and political context within which rigid class differentiation could historically persist between the silent suffering poor and those who professed to speak or act in their names, the charities and the Royals who sponsored or supported them.

NOTES

1. Gilmore is here taking issue with Cathy Caruth's definition of trauma in *Unclaimed Experience* (Caruth 11).
2. I wish to thank Professor Korte for generously sending me a copy of her talk. The definitive text should appear in the form of a revised article at a later date, under the following title: "Dealing with Deprivation: A Figuration Approach to Poverty Narratives on the Contemporary British Book Market."
3. On such issues, see Duncan 2.
4. "Telle est la Photo: elle ne sait pas *dire* ce qu'elle donne à voir" (Barthes 1980, 156, original emphasis; my translation). The 1981 translation is less explicit than the French original: "Such is the Photograph: it cannot say what it lets us see" (1981, 100).
5. On such a definition of the *alter ego*, see Ricœur 331f.
6. Marx's theory of commodity fetishism—instead of seeing a set of relationships between people, we see a set of relationships between things—may be found in vol. I of *Capital* (187).
7. According to Fredric Jameson, there emerged in the 1960s a form of aesthetic production which was "integrated into commodity production" (4–5).

WORKS CITED

Barthes, Roland. "The Photographic Message." *Image-Music-Text*. Trans. S. Heath. New York: Hill and Wang, 1978. 15–31. Print.

————. "Le Message photographique." 1961. *L'Obvie et l'obtus*. Paris: Éditions du Seuil, 1982. 9–24. Print.

————. *La Chambre claire. Note sur la photographie*. Paris: Gallimard/Le Seuil, 1980. Print.

————. *Camera Lucida—Reflections on Photography*. Trans. R. Howard. New York: Hill and Wang, 1981. Print.

Caruth, Cathy. *Unclaimed Experience: Trauma, Narrative, and History*. Baltimore: The Johns Hopkins UP, 1996. Print.

Derrida, Jacques. "Le Facteur de vérité." 1975. *La Carte postale. De Socrate à Freud et au-delà*. Paris: Flammarion, 1980. 439–524; "The Purveyor of Truth." Trans. Willis Domingo, James Hulbert and M.-R. L. *Yale French Studies 96* (1999): 124–97. Print.

————. "Demeure: Fiction et témoignage." *Passions de la littérature*. Paris: Galilée, 1996. 13–73. Print.

————. *Demeure: Fiction and Testimony*. Trans. E. Rottenberg. Stanford: Stanford UP, 2000. 13–103. Print.

Duncan, Ian. *Modern Romance and Transformations of the Novel: The Gothic, Scott, Dickens*. Cambridge and New York: Cambridge UP, 1992. Print.

Freud, Sigmund. "Family Romances." 1909. *Collected Papers* Vol. 5. Ed. James Strachey. New York: Basic Books, 1959. 74–78. Print.

Frye, Norhtrop. "The Mythos of Summer: Romance." *Anatomy of Criticism: Four Essays*. 1957. Princeton: Princeton UP, 1971. 186–93. Print.

Gilmore, Leigh. *The Limits of Autobiography: Trauma and Testimony*. Ithaca and London: Cornell University P, 2001. Print.

Jameson, Fredric. *Postmodernism, or, The Cultural Logic of Late Capitalism*. Durham: Duke UP, 1991. Print.

Korte, Barbara. "Poverty in Contemporary British Literature." Unpublished lecture. 25 August 2010, University of Turin. Print.

Lacan, Jacques. "Le Séminaire sur 'La Lettre volée'." *Écrits 1*. Paris: Éditions du Seuil, 1966. 19–78; "Seminar on 'The Purloined Letter.'" Trans. Jeffrey Mehlman. *Yale French Studies* 48 (1972): 38–72. Print.

LaCapra, Dominick. *Writing History, Writing Trauma*. Baltimore: The Johns Hopkins UP, 2001. Print.

Marx, Karl. *Capital: A Critique of Political Economy* Vol. 1. Trans. Ben Fowkes. 1867. Harmondworth: Penguin Classics, 1990. Print.

Ricœur, Paul. *Soi-même comme un autre*. Paris: Éditions du Seuil, 1990. *Oneself as Another*. Trans. Kathleen Blamey. Chicago: The U of Chicago P, 1992. Print.

Robert, Marthe. *Roman des origines et origine du roman*. 1972. Paris: Gallimard, 1981. Print.

Roche, Peter. *Unloved: The True Story of a Stolen Childhood*. London: Penguin, 2007. Print.

Sontag, Susan. *On Photography*. 1973. New York: The Noonday Press, 1989. Print.

————. *Regarding the Pain of Others*. New York: Farrar, Straus and Giroux, 2003. Print.

Weber, Samuel. *The Legend of Freud*. Expanded edition. 1982. Stanford: Stanford UP, 2000. Print.

Part III

Collective Trauma, History and Ethics

7 "Strangers to ourselves"
Story-telling and the Quest for the Self in Martin Amis's Trauma Fictions

Ángeles de la Concha

Readers familiar with Martin Amis's literary and critical work are ready—perhaps eager—for surprise and excess and indeed they are rarely disappointed. His novels hardly ever fit a clear-cut genre. Having declared war against cliché, he moves comfortably across conventions, literary and other, mixing and/or subverting them at leisure. Boldly independent and uncompromising, he has had no qualms in presenting himself through the mouthpiece of the narrator-character of *House of Meetings* as "a 'shock' writer who is telling the truth" (2007, 2). The incongruous combination of violence and excessiveness, characteristic of romance as a mode, conveyed by the word "shock," with the realistic aim of "telling the truth" situates Amis's work within the trend of traumatic realism, as defined by Michael Rothberg (140). It is from this incongruous standpoint, well beyond the scope of traditional realist fiction, that Amis has dealt openly with the physical and psychic traumas inflicted by dictatorships upheld by ideologies at opposite extremes of the political spectrum: from the Holocaust in *Time's Arrow* (1991) to the Siberian Soviet slave camps in *House of Meetings* (2006), with a brief stop at "In the Palace of the End" (2008), the sinister mansion of the body doubles of an Islamic dictator, inspired in Uday Hussein.

Amis has also dwelt on a more covert and historically silenced kind of trauma. In his detective novel *Night Train* (1997), he explores incest, called "the secret trauma" because it happens in the privacy of the home, unknown to all but the victim and the perpetrator. As Laura S. Brown has noted, only recently has this kind of sexual abuse received the consideration of trauma. As a result of the agreement of psychiatric clinicians that the first and foremost cause of the syndrome of Post-traumatic Stress Disorder was "*an event outside the range of human experience*," incest was left out of the category, on the grounds that it "wasn't unusual" for women (1995, 100, original emphasis). In fact, until very recently, sexual molestation has received little recognition, if not being used as butt of joke. In the realm of romance, for example, Northrop Frye tellingly suggests that "as a counterpart to greatness," when the central figure in romance is female, the mood is comic rather than tragic. "One might call it the quest of the perilous cunts," he comments glibly pointing at the Mrs. Heartfree episode in *Jonathan Wild* as an example of the romance heroine that "instead of killing dragons fends off fucks" (249).

In *Night Train*, Amis deals with that secret trauma metonymically, in an oblique way. The trauma of childhood sexual abuse only gradually comes to light as side effect of a suicide case investigation that grows to intertwine in strange ways the lives of the coarse mannish police woman in charge of it with that of the beautiful and professionally successful young woman who, against all reasonable evidence, has taken her life. As feminist research has unveiled, "for girls and women, most traumas *do* occur in secret" (Brown 101, original emphasis) and, in keeping with that secrecy, the protagonist sets off on a quest through the underworld of family terrors. Amis makes the tortuous workings of that secret trauma the catalyst that in the end resolves the case. In doing so he blurs the limits between genres, blending the detective novel with the *Bildungsroman*, with trauma fiction and with dark romance. Amis plays with the readers' expectations by subverting key genre conventions, thereby increasing the tension indispensable to the detective novel. This is particularly noticeable as regards the *Bildungsroman*, since the closure gives the lie both to the story of arduous growth into maturity of one of the two protagonists and to the tale of blooming "into a kind of embarrassment of perfection" (Amis 8) of the other. But it is even more so as regards romance, since self-inflicted death is the outcome of the reverse of "the archetypal quest form, according to which the hero moves from conflict and death struggle to self-realization" (Saunders 3). Significantly, it is precisely self-realisation that triggers the narrator-protagonist's decision to commit suicide.

As I shall argue, for Amis, sexual violence and abuse are located at the core of social violence. Moreover, in fictions where political trauma and romance intertwine, the male protagonists are, or have been, sex offenders. The perversion of love and its lack or loss, are clearly seen at the heart of unhealthy societies in which individual and collective traumas are sure to fly high. Amis exposes the connection between personal and social disease with power, usually in male hands, as prerequisite. This fact makes women and children the most vulnerable groups. In *Time's Arrow*, it is their nightmarish plight, disturbing presence and inarticulate sounds that resonate more audibly, in a sense—borrowing T. S. Eliot's coinage—working as objective correlative of the unspeakable collective horror of the Holocaust. Males find the resolve for the exertion of force and power they yearn for, and individually lack, in mass action. What they would dare not do alone becomes acceptable in the encouraging anonymity of the mass. Therein, they may not only give free rein to their worst instincts but are induced to do so, the resulting fantasy of limitless freedom, lawful transgression and exhilarating power becoming a potent addiction. As the young and still disassociated protagonist of *Time's Arrow*, Odilo Unverdorben, reflects on starting going out at night with his "herds of friends" "helping Jews":

"individually we have no power or courage, but together we form a glowing mass" (Amis 2003, 160). Likewise, the old narrator-character of *House of Meetings* retrospectively admits having sought safety in numbers, raping under the cover of his peer group, because "the peer group can make people do *anything*" (2007, 27, original emphasis).

In keeping with his self description as a "shock writer," Amis has often chosen to explore trauma not so much from the victims' side as from that of the perpetrators. This is an issue that has brought him a good deal of hostile criticism on the grounds that his work displays a concealed ideological connivance with what he, allegedly, sets out to expose, or that he has been carried over by a morbid fascination with excess. In the two novels and the short story that may be more clearly categorised as trauma fiction, he has made the offenders the narrators of their life stories, providing them with the opportunity to explain, and the reader with the possibility to understand, if that were possible. *Time's Arrow*, as is well known, is narrated by the ghost conscience, released at the moment of death, of a Nazi medical practitioner who had assisted the like of infamous Dr Mengele in his sinister experiments in Auschwitz. The narrator of the short story "In the Palace of the End" is one of the dictator's body doubles whose duty is not only to impersonate him in parades and other public events but to contribute to interrogation torture procedures and to sophisticated love making, the latter to make up for the dictator's sexual impotence. As for the narrator of *House of Meetings*, though imprisoned for seven long years in a Russian gulag, the victim of political arbitrariness and injustice, he acknowledges his willing participation in war rape.

A motif of romance common to all Amis's trauma fictions is love. Trauma and romance usually make a poignant coupling suggesting the intimacy of love and pain, the density of a liminal space harbouring life and bereavement, presence and absence, the real and the spectral. Yet, as in the case of trauma, we should not expect romance—or their blending—to run along familiar tracks. In *Time's Arrow* romance enhances trauma through a perversion of love that in the end takes its toll on the perpetrator himself. In *House of Meetings*, the narrator starts by announcing that what he is going to tell "is a love story." He quickly qualifies it as "Russian love. But still love" (2007, 7). Yet, the story of the love triangle that the narrator—now old and on the threshold of death—unfolds in the confession he writes for his stepdaughter is the glossing cover for his life, which, in retrospect, appears to him "a little heap of degradation and horror" (1). Close to the end, both of his life and his narrative, when he is on the point of clicking *SEND*, the story connects the personal to the political, pointing straight at its source: Russia, *"the nightmare country,"* the dream that, echoing Stephen Dedalus, he is *"about to escape"* (196, original emphasis). In the short story "In the Palace of the End," the building "in the shape of a titanic eagle" (2008, 31) flanked by the Interrogation Wing and the Recreation Wing—with the former devised for torture and the latter refurbished for romance—the narrator, who is alternatively on duty in both, becomes aware of the supreme perversion making love is put to and cannot help but wonder "why the body's genius for pain so easily outsoars its fitful talent for pleasure" (45).

Trauma and romance, as Lynne Pearce has persuasively argued (Pearce and Stacey 1995; Pearce 2007), show intriguing connections not only as regards the nature and some characteristic *topoi* of their respective genres but also and very specifically as regards their formal features and/or modal strategies, according to Fuchs's denomination (5). Among them, story-telling is one of the more obvious, since in both genres, narrative is the only means, first, to reach and put together the facts at the source of the flux of inchoate feelings that in inexplicable ways afflicts the individual; then, to find a pattern that may impose an order on the knot of symptoms and fragmented experiences through which that flow struggles to come into light. Sequence is of crucial importance as well, since it confers causality while uncovering through its breaks, gaps and slippages the hidden wounds and the damage made, allowing for the healing process, if at all possible, by giving shape and coherence to those symptoms and experiences. Accordingly, the narrative backward time sequence that is so striking a feature in *Time's Arrow*, while conferring hallucinatory contours to the protagonist's amatory life, as it interweaves with nightmarish half-grasped deeds and ghostly figures, is in the end truth revealing. From the critical stance of a disassociated self, the ghost narrator sees his other half, a stranger he hardly recognises and whose behaviour he misconstrues. He puzzles over his physical looks and ailments, over his deeds and nightmares. He watches love irreversibly fading into nothingness; sees a succession of women stepping out one after—or is it before?—the other; a housecleaner; a chain of undifferentiated nurses in the charged atmosphere of hospitals where "blood and bodies and death and power" erotically coalesce (2003, 87); of bodies "searched for undivulged openings, new incisions" (94); weird bald whores in the camp; an unfeeling wife who disowns him; sexual failure, impotence, a sweetheart vanishing into nothingness. Following the backward time sequence, the narrator makes his way to the place of origin, there teasing out the initially confusing pattern of thwarted romance.

First-person narratives, particularly those in the memoir form, partake of the confessional and, in the case of trauma, are also a form of bearing witness. Odilo's now estranged self allows the reader into scenes—before the split self—of wife battering and sexual abuse, of rough courtship and, yet before that, of ordinary childhood in a family where a powerless mother tried ineffectually to placate a crippled father's bitterness. Gender and domestic violence, with their inherent perversion of love and feeling, are thus signposted as the diseases at the heart of an unhealthy society that may make an "absolutely unexceptional moral being a criminal" (164).

A similar thesis, though running in a formal and ideological opposite direction, underlies *House of Meetings*, a work that is in a way a novelisation of Amis's earlier historical essay, *Koba the Dread: Laughter and the Twenty Million* (2002). Sexual and other atrocious forms of violence are there shown not as source but as outcome of Stalinist state terror, just as crippled interpersonal relations are presented as the result of the logic of the "slum family" to which contemporary Russia is likened. The narrative is also a memoir, a confession written from the standpoint of old age, and though the time sequence is nothing like the startling experiment in *Time's Arrow*, it yet shows the reluctance of traumatic memories to unfold smoothly. The narrator turns back obsessively to his crime. As Roger Luckhurst argues, taking his cue from Freud's efforts to understand the compulsion that forced the subject's psyche to return to the traumatic scene in waking hallucinations and nightmares, in returning to the "scenes of unpleasure" the psyche "hope[s] belatedly to process the unassimilable material, to find ways of mastering the trauma retroactively" (Luckhurst 9). Self-justification seeps through the narrator's frequent appeals to the sympathy of the addressee, his young step-daughter, who, of course, stands for the reader. He does so in many ways. Either straightforwardly, or under the guise of paternal advice or bitter comments on Russia's recent history of cruelty and spiritual barrenness, interspersed with disparaging remarks on the postmodern ills of her affluent contemporary culture's ideology—"Westernism" (Amis 2003, 50)—, or of broad generalisations meant to respectively sharpen and take the edge off collective and personal responsibility. As suits him; or so the reader cannot help surmise. The many gaps, the flashbacks and roundabouts, the seesaw association of his crime with historical political ill deeds and the flood of reflections and self and collective blaming they trigger make a meandering prose of blurring contours until the secret truth, the real trauma at the heart of impossible romantic love, finally spills over.

Trauma and romance show interesting connection points in the two novels. Firstly, their narrator-protagonists are in both cases perpetrators and also victims of the crimes that have been the cause of deadly trauma. Secondly, their narratives painfully make their way back to its origin, scrutinising its nature through a profusion of events in violently repetitive worlds. Thirdly, thwarted love is in both novels linked up to the nature of the offence. In *Time's Arrow*, the violence in the romantic world of courtship seeps into the world of domesticity and from there onwards to the street and later on to the camps. As Amis comments in the afterword to *Time's Arrow*, the alternative title he had thought of for the novel was *The Nature of the Offence*, a phrase of Primo Levi's (2003, 176) that was in fact left as subtitle. In explaining the sense in which that offence was unique, Amis describes its style as "reptilian," significantly the same word his narrator uses to describe the "erotic rapture" presiding over the perpetrator's affective and sexual relationship with his newly-wed wife, thus suggesting the regression from the human to the animal realm. Their romance is thus depicted in the visually powerful archetypal "coiling images of snake" (Frye 91). At their happiest, when bodies and their pleasures are enough, they make a couple of glistening lizards in a secluded "world of succulent lime" (Amis 2003, 159). Gradually, however, love and pleasure need a plus of sophistication and excess. "When human and reptile brains get together" logistics enters the scene and makes a change. The unreeling narrative shows their domesticity permeated by violence and the inverse chronological time sequence takes us back through the different stages of their courtship. The healthy natural Herta—no make-up and hairy legs—is Odilo's chimpanzee, with which he can engage in perverse games forcing it "to do housework naked, and on all fours" (159). She can be punched in the breasts if she sulks; made to lie "splayed and buckled, with her ankles on either side of the headboard" when attempting to conceive a child, with Odilo looking "as if he's trying to kill something rather than create" (158). The reptilian style and logistics of their sexual life and the killing-to-create mood that have become basic ingredients of Odilo's love life flow past the domestic world into the public sphere, there coalescing with those of his thousand equals, engaged in the ambitious enterprise of dreaming a race into being, of making a new people "from thunder and from lighting. With gas, with electricity, with shit, with fire" (128). Odilo's practices are common in both the romance and the social realms since, as the narrator points out, "as a moral being [Odilo] is absolutely unexceptional"; he is "innocent, emotional, popular, and stupid" (157); "liable to do what everybody else does, good or bad, with no limit, under the cover of numbers" (164). His youthful romantic feats, about which he boasts to his friends, prefigure—or explain—the violence pervading his sinister professional medical practices. The personal and the collective are inextricably woven. Odilo's interest in his wife's bowel movements, the games he forces her to play making her lie down as still as if dead, resonate through the fiercely "coprocentric" universe (132) and the day's deadly work in the camp; he believes that his dealings with the bald girls in the officers' bordello must have something to do with his wife; the death of his baby daughter blends confusingly with the *lots* of little babies in the extermination camp and with the baby he and Herta want to beget and cannot because of his impotence and her horror. In the metaphysical realm of the new race, creation is all. "Love and life must go on," muses Odilo. "Life and love must emphatically and resonantly go on: here, that's what we're all about. Yet there is a patina of cruelty, intense cruelty, as if creation corrupts" (130). In the novel's reverse universe, "you have to be cruel to be kind" (16). Life implies death. Death and life play confusing games. Dead bodies get back to life and the wounded walk back to their healthy selves.

In parallel, love grows backwards declining into extinction commensurate with the increase of logistical sophistication that makes the counter-creation prospect real. Thereof, amid the glimpsed chaos, the recurring nightmares, the fragmented narratives and selves, all metonymic of the ungraspable nature of the enterprise, we watch Odilo's growing sexual impotence, the break of his marriage and the extinguishing of all possible trace of love, romantic, filial, parental. The perversion of love and the frenzy of counter-creation go hand in hand, resulting in a particularly devious kind of trauma. In an interview with Cathy Caruth on the subject of trauma and survival, Robert Jay Lifton comments on Freud's view of the fear of death, of disintegration, as a displacement of castration anxiety, central to the Oedipus complex (Caruth 1995, 131). Though Lifton expresses some reservations as regards Freud's reintegrating the death experience into his instinctual theory, he acknowledges the relation between the knowledge of death, which extreme trauma procures, and the mythology of the hero, which in traditional psychology takes place in the confrontation with the father in the Oedipus complex. "The ordeal of the hero is a powerful confrontation with threat and death, and, really, the threat of annihilation," he says (135). Lifton's reservations are based on the possible detour of the real experience in the causation of trauma if too much pressure is put on childhood sexuality and/or repression, as traditional psychoanalytical therapy does. Therefore, he cautions against underestimating or misconstruing dream images. With respect to *Time's Arrow*, it is apposite to see Odilo's confrontation of Oedipal annihilation in the mythical enterprise he embarks on, that of creating a new perfectly pure race. Whereas as a child he had experienced castration fear under the form of "rhythmical upward sweep of his [father's] rattling hand" in front of an "intercessionary" but powerless mother (Amis 2003, 171), in his adult Nazi fantasy he becomes the god-father freely dealing with children against whose pain and suffering one has got to harden one's heart (91) because their threat is all too real. They are "bomb babies" wielding effective power, and they are numberless. Babies people his nightmares in an incessant warfare of cries, tears, threat. They follow him through his successive identities along his long life as survivor until, in keeping with the logics of reverse time narrative—and of the poetic justice available to the novelist—he will be defeated, sharing their final destiny, annihilated by his father in the second before being engendered.

In *House of Meetings* the perversion of love is also directly linked to State brutality and corruption as well as to culturally deep-rooted sexual violence. On the first page of his narrative, the narrator-character of *House of Meetings*, who is an aged and ailing Soviet defector to the United States, describes the love story he is about to tell his American step-daughter, Venus, as "triangular in shape": two half-brothers fall in love with the same Jewish girl in the emotionally and morally impoverished Russia of the 1940s, under Stalinist rule. The young woman, called Zoya, chooses the younger man, Lev, a physically insignificant youth and an ineffectual poet with his head in the sky, over the handsome, strong and able elder brother. The latter, who is the unnamed narrator, unfolds the story of love and rivalry that climaxes around a tryst that takes place in the coveted House of Meetings of Norlag, a slave-labor camp above the Arctic Circle where the three characters have been sent. The troubled love story thus threads its way across a tapestry of Russian history, portraying one of its darkest periods, with the interweaving of the individual and the collective endowing the novel with an epic ring. However, the moral of the story runs opposite to that of *Time's Arrow*. If in the latter the emphasis is drawn on the individual, in the former it is the state that firmly carries the brunt of the responsibility for the crimes of the individual, or so the narrator takes pains to make his step-daughter—and the reader behind her—believe. As mentioned above, the narrator is a rapist who marched along an army of rapists during the war. His first rape is described, in Amis's inimitable verbal panache, as a loss of virginity "to a Silesian housewife, in a roadside ditch, after a ten-minute chase" (2007, 27), the glib undertone doubtlessly a tribute to the girl's good humour and understanding. Furthermore, "in a pedagogic spirit," the addressee is offered yet another justification for both the individual and collective responsibility of the rape going well beyond the corrupt totalitarian Stalinist Russia to include a long-standing historical tradition endorsed by a whole continent: "the weaponisation of the phallus, in victory, is an ancient fact, and one we saw remanifested on a vast scale, in Europe, in 1999," he argues (27). To crown it all, in the midst of the vast landscape of human dilapidation and waste he draws, we, together with tender Venus, his nominal addressee, are requested to redress the balance in the matter of rape on the grounds that the raped have been given attention enough, and it is high time to pay a little attention to the consequences on the rapist. In the chain of self-justification, the first consequence is "post-coital tristesse," doubtless a sign of the rapist's deep-down decency and delicacy. The incapacity to see a woman whole is another sad consequence, a deformity embedded in a culture in which women are first and foremost bodies. Bodies to seduce and enjoy. Does culture not constantly impress upon us the beauty, inspiration and inexhaustible source of sexual pleasure inherent in the female body? Do not poets as refined and delicate as Andrew Marvell "atomise" women as "he did to the coy mistress"? (30). Amis has often declared his intention to explore men's narcissism, and *House of Meetings* is a good example of this. His protagonist is a huge, powerfully built, energetic and resourceful self-made man, blindly self-absorbed to the point of utter misunderstanding because of his inability to see beyond himself. Interestingly, one of the narrative threads is his obsession with the reason why his younger brother's wife—with whom he continues to be passionately in love—had chosen the ugliest and weakest of the two, something he cannot understand, given his obvious superiority in all manly attributes. The climax of the novel lies precisely in the insight which flares up at the point when the protagonist sees into the nature of his own crime even though he still keeps looking for self-justification, this time laying the blame on culturally ingrained female wiles. "Why women say no when they mean yes" is common saying, and to the narrator his beloved Zoya apparently showed that she was no cultural exception to this manoeuvring. Confessing the awful deed of her rape, he once again sues his readers for understanding, artfully laying the blame on Zoya under the appearance of exonerating her.

Until this moment, blame for individual barbarity—rape and murder— had been laid on the brutal policies of a corrupted criminal state and of huge impersonal forces unleashed by Russian history of dictatorships. "Mitigating" circumstances for his dealings with women were the army, the war and the particular Russian-German front: "four years on the dirtiest front of the dirtiest fight in history" (27). Late in life, though, he would have to accept the illusory fantasy of believing that with the end of war he could possibly go back to his earlier self, to the kind of man he was before the war and the slave camps had made him "a for-the-duration rapist" and "a coldblooded but also tumescent executioner" (91). Even then, justification crops up and in his confession it is still the raped woman herself, his life-long loved ex-sister-in-law, who is blameworthy. The "post-coital tristesse" he had glibly counted among the traumatic effects on the rapist reaches true tragic depth when he sees the horror in Zoya's face, worse yet because he realises that, in her half-conscious state, he had been taken for another, for his weakling brother Lev, the tender husband she had loved. After a while, he learns of her suicide following their ill-starred encounter. Though a survivor, the narrator—now old and terminally ill—has borne the trauma effects throughout his life. Its symptoms show in nightmares, total loss of sexual desire, guilt, conflicting self-deception and self-blame and, in the end, tormented wait for a death already closing in under the form of the lethal injection he has asked for and which, though freely chosen, has the ring of capital punishment. Thus, as in the case of *Time's Arrow*, for the perpetrator trauma and thwarted love become inextricably woven. Poetic justice ensures that its outcome is also sexual impotence and death in keeping with the sense of failure and loss that Corinne Saunders sees as characteristic of romances of the darker type (3).

In the two novels the protagonists make interestingly unusual trauma cases. Besides being perpetrators and victims of their own crimes, they are also survivors, which makes of them witnesses as well. Each narrative is, in its own way, a painful reordering of reality from various ethical stances, thus complicating an already conflictive, unacceptable experience. Each narrator is trapped in a self-created, self-deceptive, dissociated reality meant to help him tolerate aspects of that reality that he could otherwise simply not bear. Each protagonist-narrator—as Sandra L. Bloom argues that happens to traumatised individuals—eventually feels haunted by that incongruity, driven by "'the cognitive imperative', the need to bring order to disrupted and incomplete cognitive-emotional schemas" (Bloom 206) that until there and then had powerfully resisted the normal cognitive and verbal processes, by finding outlet in all kinds of secondary behaviours aimed at coping with the conflict. In the end, in both cases, their search for knowledge and truth revolves on a quest for their lost innocent selves from whom they have become utterly estranged. Only by telling their life stories, by the confession of their crimes, will they be able to integrate their splintered emotional experiences and awful deeds in a meaningful whole. In both cases it is death—coming close in *House of Meetings*, fully fledged in *Time's Arrow*—that triggers the narrative, in the form of an autobiographical account riddled with the struggle between knowing and not knowing. Although the urge to tell their stories may rise out of the need to know and to reintegrate the traumatic experiences into their conflicting dissociated selves, deep down, the telling partakes of an ethical thrust. As Michele L. Crossley argues, following Kierkegaard and Ricœur, "it is only through the process of telling our life stories, selecting and editing the past in order to direct our future, that we become ethical beings responsible for our own lives" (168). It is significant that the time chosen to start the narrative in both novels does not allow for a future, only for an opportunity for the offender to see. That may only happen when he can step out of his narcissistic self and see himself in the light of another's, or of his dissociated other's, gaze which gives him back his image as in a mirror.

Although both narrators are perpetrators, their stance is very different, commensurate with the nature of their respective crime. Odilo's is unfathomable in nature and scope. As María Jesús Martínez-Alfaro points out, following Emmanuel Levinas, "the Nazi subject tragically sought to define its humanity by depriving the other of it, and in the attempt, it became inhuman itself" (2011, 149). Hence there is no scope either for seeing another or for seeing himself, since there is no human self anymore. In the interview with Cathy Caruth mentioned above, Robert Jay Lifton notes the doubling that takes place in the traumatised person, suggesting that there are elements at odds in the two selves, including ethical contradictions: "This is of course especially true in the Nazi doctors, or people who doubled in order to adapt to evil," he says. But the victims also underwent a change of self, as Lifton remarks, quoting a sentence often uttered by Auschwitz survivors: "I was a different person in Auschwitz" (Caruth 1995, 137). As regards Odilo, the case is more extreme. As seen above, he is quite the same insensitive, rapacious and brutal person in and out of the camp so that when the dissociation takes place it is radical, with no possibility of reintegrating his better self, which is only released at the moment of death when his life unreels back so that he can see and bear witness. Through Odilo's recovered ontological status, Amis offers a disturbing recreation of one of the most characteristic features of trauma: the direct seeing of a violent event and the absolute inability to know it, the traumatic effect metonymically heightened by the expressionist subversive causality resulting from the reverse time sequence. In this way, the narrative incorporates in dramatic fashion the struggle between knowing and not knowing (Caruth 1996, 3–4) and, as befits an offender, not wanting to know. Thus, the narrator, who is the dissociated other self, has to extricate meaning from fragments, glimpses, images in dreams and recurring night-mares, against the backdrop of a frenzy of refusal:

> 'You don't want to know,' Tod whispers. She doesn't want to know. *I* don't want to know. No one wants to know. (Amis 2003, 66, original emphasis)

In *House of Meetings* the dissociation is mitigated from the ethical view-point. In the manner of old King Lear, the narrator's self-justifying dispar-agement depicts the offender as a man more sinned against than sinner. Also, as Oscar Wilde's poetic persona in *The Ballad of Reading Gaol*, he self-deprecatingly mourns for the woman he loved and murdered in her bed. In the end, notwithstanding the resistance strategies shared by the trauma and romance genres—the wandering; the dilation; "the haunting excessive return of past events" which, though typical of trauma (Caruth 1995; 1996), is also ascribed to postmodern romance (Elam 23); the half-knowing that Parker identifies in early romance (3) and Caruth explores in trauma stories focusing on the struggle between knowing and not knowing (1995, viii)—the story-telling succeeds in helping the nameless narrator see himself. Coming close to the end, both of the narrative and of his life, he finally drops his glib mask and is able to acknowledge the full import of his deed: "Of course, it would be nice to be able to blame it, the rape, on the war or on the camp or on the estate [. . .]. Now when I close my eyes I can only see a moribund murderer" (196).

"In the Palace of the End" offers yet another different exploration of the quest for the self. All the more so since the short story has to rely on the intensity of evocative images and metaphors to make up for its brevity. The dictator's doubles are bodily reconstructed in his image in order to become his perfect replicas, any insignificant failure being cause for "decommis-sion," a useful euphemism for execution. The narrator, who is one of them, shares with the two narrator-characters in the novels examined above the double nature of crime perpetrator and, simultaneously, trauma victim. In his case, though, doubling is not the result of psychic distortion as an unconscious strategy to survive but has been impressed on him by force. His narrative, as theirs, is both confessional and autobiographical: a release of feelings; a record of the loss of self; a witness testimony. The experi-ence is maddeningly "depersonalising," since he must absolutely give up his identity and take up that of a strange and feared other of whom there are so many replicas that entering a room "is to enter a hall of mirrors," as the offender-victim narrator puts it (Amis 2008, 34). Instead of an ethical endeavour, becoming one with that "other" is a terrifying physical and psy-chical ordeal inasmuch as, besides entailing the graphic replicating on his own body of the tyrant's ailments, wounds and mutilated limbs as results of his many enemies' murdering attempts, his duty as double includes the torturing of others in turn.

The narrator's story bears witness in a twofold way. On the one hand, the fact that it is grounded on real fact allows us a glimpse into the sophisticated horror of the underworld of torture, an obscure realm whose existence, though silenced, is all too well-known. On the other, it attests to the tragic nature of depersonalisation. Once accomplished, the recovery of the self proves an impossible task. Wherever the double looks for his old self, the image he gets back is that of the man whose replica he has become. The mirrors he smashes in despair for their mocking reflection of the hated self he has become, as well as the blank response he gets from the terrorised women with whom it is his duty to engage in vibrant romance, make of his story a traumatic black humoured version of Dorian Gray's. The portrait the narrator gives us of his obese, gruesomely mutilated self, painstakingly wooing his terrified partner in a vain attempt to rouse her sexually, makes of him a poignant tragi-comic specimen of Amis's inimitably grotesque, antihero cartoon figures. His narrative bears witness to absolute loss: of courage, of dignity, of beauty, of self. Irretrievable loss of self is the fate of the accomplice double. After strenuous effort to keep his head above the water, what the narrator faces, in Amis's idiosyncratic farcical black-humour terms, is "the dreaded 'toilet bomb'" up his ass (46).

Once more in his customary fashion against convention and cliché, Amis explores a very different kind of trauma in *Night Train*. This time he chooses a detective narrative, soon to subvert the genre,[1] since the supposed crime is promptly revealed as inexistent when the autopsy confirms the initial police report that the death under investigation was by suicide. Further, the search for the reasons underlying the incomprehensible suicide of Jennifer Rockwell, a young and beautiful astrophysicist with a seemingly perfect life, turns into a quest for identity when her mother asks Detective Mike Hoolihan, the police woman in charge of the case: "See, Mike, we were looking for a why. And I guess we found one. But suddenly we don't have a who. Who was she, Mike?" [. . .] "Who the hell was she, Mike?" (Amis 1997, 64). Furthermore, the moment the police woman accepts the task, she has the feeling that the search will have unforeseen consequences, not just for the dead woman's relatives but first and foremost for herself. In this way, the story widens to include yet another search: the quest for the self of the mannish Detective Mike Hoolihan, an expert in "suspicious deaths" (4), with a tough past.

In his autobiographic *Experience: A Memoir* (2000), Amis admits to his profound concern with suicide. Twice he describes it as "the most sombre of all subjects—the saddest story" (2001, 225, 280). Although he exonerates it from all moral blame on the grounds of the unendurable suffering that has led the suicide to that saddest of deaths, he is deeply sensitive to its effects on those around. Taking his cue from Chesterton's statement that "suicide was a heavier undertaking than murder," he states that "the murderer just kills one person. The suicide kills everybody" (281). Suicides are "worldkillers" (281). In *Night Train* Amis daringly explores the way in which the woman suicide "kills" the police woman investigating her. Both women stand in stark opposition yet in close relationship to each other. Jennifer Rockwell is the daughter of a retired police officer who had been Mike Hoolihan's Squad Supervisor and surrogate father figure since she was separated from her biological father as a child on account of sexual abuse. Jennifer has everything Mike lacks: a beautiful body, parental affection, an ideally happy love relationship, a prestigious job in astrophysics research. She is well off and unreservedly liked all around for her kindness and nicety. No less liked by the narrator, the police woman, who tells us from the start that she is part of the story and confesses her gratefulness for the young girl's caring presence and refusal to judge her during an alcohol addiction treatment she had undergone years before at her parents' place.

The narrator is her opposite. "A forty-four-year-old police with coarse blonde hair, bruiser's tits and broad shoulders, and pale blue eyes in her head that have seen everything" (Amis 1997, 43) is the first description she gives of herself, gradually followed by others, all of them the negatives of Jennifer's many accomplishments. The differences between them crop up throughout the narrative. Jennifer's beautiful, shapely five ten body (7, 24, 109) against her own coarse, asymmetrical five ten (3, 25, 43); Jennifer's ideal "dream couple" (38) against her string of woman-hater, woman-beater partners and her present "dickless sack of shit" (149). Jennifer's well-groomed, well-ordered rooms against her own cluttered, "slob cubed" place (77). Yet, ominously, both images start getting closer until they coincide in the end. At a point in her investigation, fed up with being taken by a man on the phone, Mike feels like changing her name "[t]o something feminine. Like Detective *Jennifer* Hoolihan" (105, emphasis added). Significantly, the sudden impulse is connected with her father's sexual abuse and with the image and harsh sound of the coming night train. Later on, as the investigation proceeds and she tries to enter into Jennifer's mind in an attempt to understand her inner self, she starts feeling that Jennifer herself is inside of her playing her flashlight, trying to reveal to her what she doesn't want to see (67). At this point, the reader may recall the words she had used to describe the young woman while reflecting on the case: "Brilliant, beautiful. Yeah, I'm thinking: *To-die-for* brilliant. *Drop-dead* beautiful" (7, emphasis added). Shortly after, when she has crossed out the more plausible motives she had compiled for the suicide and she is again idly engaged in writing down a list of their respective assets and liabilities, a lightening association strikes her: "On the evening Jennifer Rockwell died, the sky was clear and the visibility was excellent. But the seeing—the seeing, the seeing—was no good at all" (132). It is there and then that, by having unconsciously but so perceptively, connected their lives, Mike starts seeing the pattern of the clues Jennifer had left. It is not so much through reasoning as through physical sensation that she processes the facts she has been gathering. The revelation comes in the language of the non-verbal, of the body and the symbolic. Jennifer Rockwell's *fall* "burning out of a clear blue sky" (133) flares up Mike's body, making her understand what the suicide's ghostly figure, who had been a frequent presence in her dreams, wanted to tell her when that very morning she appeared at the foot of her bed "bent, lurching," "trying to throw up" (133).

Julia Kristeva opens *Powers of Horror: An Essay on Abjection* with the observation that: "There looms, within abjection, one of those violent, dark revolts of being, directed against a threat that seems to emanate from an exorbitant outside or inside, ejected beyond the scope of the possible, the tolerable, the thinkable" (1). She elaborates on the subject of self and desire and passionately claims for the need to establish the genuine self, to become an other, different from the self shaped in the image of the father's and the mother's desires, even if at the expense of death. Food becomes the sign of that desire that has to be expelled in order to allow for the true self to be born. So she cries out:

> "I" want none of that element sign of their desire; "I" do not want to listen, "I" do not assimilate it, "I" expel it. But since the food is not an "other" for me, who am only in their desire, I expel *myself*, I spit *myself* out, I abject *myself* within the same motion through which "I" claim to establish *myself* [. . .]. It s thus that *they* see that "I" am in the process of becoming an other at the expense of my own death. (3, original emphasis)

Watching Jenifer's ghost lurching to throw up, the detective understands her message and is then able to see the pattern of the clues carefully displayed, including the manner of her death: "The more violent the means, the louder the snarl at the living. The louder they said, *Look what you made me do* [. . .] three bullets, like the opposite of three cheers" (145, original emphasis).

What is fascinating in *Night Train* is that, through the complex web of connections between the two main characters, the narrator ends up seeing the nature and working of that violent revolt of being of Jennifer's other, narcissistic self. Moreover, that very sight triggers her own equally suppressed self's violent revolt, though for opposite reasons, in keeping with their radically opposed stances and selves. In reconsidering Jennifer's dreamland life, the tough police woman, whose eyes had seen so much, reflects on the relative nature of perfection: Jennifer's partner, Trader, "was 'the kindest lover on the planet'—but how kind is that? Miriam was the sweetest mother—but how sweet is that? And Colonel Tom was the fondest father. And how fond is that? Jennifer was beautiful. But how beautiful?" (144).

In her insightful essay "Bridging the Black Hole of Trauma," Sandra L. Bloom notes that "there is a great deal about reality that we simply cannot bear. There is a high price to pay for self-awareness" (201), and she then reflects on the issue of emotional contagion, arguing that managing our emotions is dependent on the interaction we have with others. Such interaction may be positive in a cathartic way, helping the healing of trauma; but it can also make the individual extremely vulnerable. In the narrator's case, it is her interaction with Jennifer, her opposite other, and the vision she gets of herself through the suicide's blind clues left for her to decode that trigger her own suicide. The pathetic woman "gored by her dad," "hanging on the arms of woman-haters and woman-hitters" (146), which she can see was Jennifer's image of her, fuels her intelligent other self to rebel and to establish her "I" at the expense of her own death. Thus, she grieves:

> Did she not see intelligence in me? Did she actually not? Did nobody see? Because if you take intelligence from me, if you take it from my face, then you really don't leave me with much at all. (146)

In addition to the unbearable image of herself that Jennifer presents Mike with, she makes her see at its crudest the scene of childhood sexual trauma and its successive reenactments throughout her life in a string of rough love-affairs which she fantasised she had overcome when in fact she had only managed to barely cure its symptom, her booze addiction.

As in the other fictions under analysis, trauma and romance are deeply connected in *Night Train*. In the introduction to her book *Romance Writing*, Lynne Pearce draws attention to the psychoanalytical interpretation of desire as "one of the most perverse and contradictory conditions known to human kind." As she further explains,

> For Freud its perversity lay primarily in the discovery that all individuals are destined to re-enact the needs and frustrations of their early childhood relationships (the Oedipus and Electra complexes) and only with considerable effort (and the successful operation of the superego) move on to successful 'mature' relationships with members of the opposite sex [. . .]. Freud was also the first theorist to realize the crucial importance of idealization and, indeed, narcissism in the creation of the love-object and thus begin to explain both the compulsive nature and ultimate 'impossibility' of romantic love [. . .]. This idealization, moreover requires the imposition of obstacles to enhance its desirability [. . .]. (Pearce 2007, 20)

The two instances neatly fit the two women's predicament. It is not just "needs and frustration" but also the sexual abuse and domestic violence of her early childhood relations that the police woman narrator reenacts once and again, repeatedly failing to establish mature relations. Her love relations invariably follow the pattern of the trauma scene with her father: he abusing her sexually, she viciously hitting back. At the opposite end of the spectrum is Jennifer's seemingly perfect love object, Trader. They are the dream couple. Not one obstacle in their way. And yet, the suicide staging she prepares—seated full naked on a chair, after the act of love, with three bullets in the head—and the related clue she leaves behind, show her awful mockery of it all.

As in the previous trauma fictions examined, traumatic realism and romance are intertwined by the formal features and modal strategies they share. The core of all the novels explored is the quest for the self. Fragmented story-telling, troubled by hunting past events and struggling between knowing and unknowing, is the means through which the wandering quest is conducted and, after much dilation, achieved. All narrators bear witness to crime; some, to the possibility of transforming guilt into self-responsibility; others, to the exorbitant outside and/or inside threat that drives them fatally to board the night train. To conclude, if all the narratives show compelling formal connections between traumatic realism and romance, given the nature and/or predicament of their narrators, they also bear witness to the impossibility of reconciling trauma and love.

NOTES

1. For a useful account of the critical reception met by *Night Train* as regards an alleged failure as a detective novel, as well as for an insightful analysis, see Martínez-Alfaro 2007.

WORKS CITED

Amis, Martin. *Time's Arrow, or, The Nature of the Offence*. 1991. London: Vintage, 2003. Print.
———. *Night Train*. London: Vintage, 1997. Print.
———. *Experience. A Memoir*. 2000. London: Vintage, 2001. Print.
———. *Koba the Dread: Laughter and the Twenty Million*. London: Jonathan Cape, 2002. Print.
———. *House of Meetings*. 2006. London: Vintage, 2007. Print.
———. "In the Palace of the End." *The Second Plane*. London: Jonathan Cape, 2008. 31–46. Print.
Bloom, Sandra L. "Bridging the Black Hole of Trauma: The Evolutionary Significance of the Arts." *Psychother. Politics. Int.* 8.3 (2010): 198–212. Wiley Online Library. Published online on 9 May 2010 at wileynlinelibrary.com DOI: 10.1002/ppi.223. http://www.sanctuaryweb.com/PDFs_new/Bloom%20Bridging%20the%20Blac20Hole%20Publihed%20Part%20I.pdf. Retrieved on 18 March 2012. Web.
Brown, Laura S. "Not Outside the Range: One Feminist Perspective on Psychic Trauma." *Trauma: Explorations in Memory*. Baltimore and London: The Johns Hopkins UP, 1995. 100–12. Print.
Caruth, Cathy. *Unclaimed Experience: Trauma, Narrative, and History*. Baltimore and London: The Johns Hopkins UP, 1996. Print.
Caruth, Cathy, ed. *Trauma: Explorations in Memory*. Baltimore and London: The Johns Hopkins UP, 1995. Print.
Crossley, Michele L. *Introducing Narrative Psychology: Self, Trauma and the Construction of Meaning*. Buckingham, Philadelphia: Open UP, 2000. Print.

Elam, Diane. *Romancing the Postmodern.* London and New York: Routledge, 1992. Print.

Frye, Northrop. *Northrop Frye's Notebooks for Anatomy of Criticism.* Ed. Michael Dolzani. Toronto: U of Toronto P, 2004. Print.

Fuchs, Barbara. *Romance.* London: Routledge, 2004. Print.

Kristeva, Julia, *Powers of Horror: An Essay on Abjection.* Trans. Leon S. Roudiez. New York: Columbia UP, 1982. Print.

Luckhurst, Roger. *The Trauma Question.* Abingdon, UK: Routledge, 2008. Print.

Martínez-Alfaro, María Jesús. "Experimental Fiction and the Ethics of *A Vérité*: The Encounter with the Other in Martin Amis' *Night Train*." Eds. Susana Onega and Jean-Michel Ganteau. *The Ethical Component in Experimental British Fiction since the 1960s.* Newcastle: Cambridge Scholars Publishing, 2007. 131–48. Print.

———. "Where Madness Lies: Holocaust Representations and Ethics in *Time's Arrow*." Eds Susana Onega and Jean-Michel Ganteau. *Ethics and Trauma in Contemporary British Fiction.* Amsterdam and New York: Rodopi, 2011. 127–54. Print.

Parker, Patricia. *Inescapable Romance: Studies in the Poetics of a Mode.* Princeton, NJ: Princeton UP, 1979. Print.

Pearce, Lynne. *Romance Writing.* Cambridge: Polity, 2007. Print.

Pearce, Lynne and Jackie Stacey, eds. *Romance Revisited.* London: Lawrence and Wishart, 1995.

Rothberg, Michael. *Traumatic Realism: The Demands of Holocaust Representation.* Minneapolis: U of Minnesota P, 2000. Print.

Saunders, Corinne. *A Companion to Romance, from Classical to Contemporary.* Oxford: Blackwell, 2004. Print.

8 Individual Choice and Responsibility for the Other

Two Ethical Paths in the Representation of Trauma in Jeanette Winterson's and Graham Swift's Postmodernist Romances

Christian Gutleben

When Hal Foster first theorised the notion of traumatic realism in 1996, it was to try and make sense of the contradictions of Andy Warhol's serial images, which Foster deemed "referential *and* simulacral, connected *and* disconnected, affective *and* affectless, critical *and* complacent" (130, original emphasis). As a concept intended to embrace these contradictions, traumatic realism is, then, paradoxical, defining as it does a system of repetitions that "not only *re*produce traumatic effects [but] also *produce* them" and that generate "a warding away of traumatic significance *and* an opening to it, a defending against traumatic effect *and* a producing of it" (132, original emphasis). The crucial point for Foster, then, is that traumatic realism simultaneously screens and produces the traumatic real. In a ground-breaking study written in 2000, Michael Rothberg takes up this notion of traumatic realism in an attempt to combine what he calls the realist and antirealist approaches of Holocaust representation. As he explains,

> By focusing attention on the intersection of the everyday and the extreme in the experience and writing of Holocaust survivors, traumatic realism provides an aesthetic and cognitive solution to the conflicting demands inherent in representing and understanding genocide. Traumatic realism mediates between realist and antirealist positions in Holocaust studies and marks the necessity of considering how the ordinary and extraordinary aspects of genocide intersect and coexist. (Rothberg 2000, 9)

In a passage which he stresses in a later study, Rothberg specifies that, in the "mode of representation and historical cognition" he calls traumatic realism, the extreme and the everyday "are neither opposed, collapsed, nor transcended through a dialectical synthesis—instead, they are at once represented together and kept forever apart in a mode of representation and historical cognition" (2002, 55).

ROMANCE, TRAUMA AND ETHICS

Applied to the issues of neo-avant-garde visual art and to "the dilemmas of Holocaust representation [. . .] in testimonial writing" (Rothberg 2002, 56), the concept of traumatic realism does not, at first sight, seem relevant in or even compatible with the field of romance, which "is generally associated with escapism, congruence and magic" (Ganteau 2003, 227). The emphatic referentiality of testimonial writing in particular seems incompatible with the flaunted fictionality of romance. However, romance's, and even more so postmodernist romance's relation to referential reality is far from unambiguous. Insisting on the stretchability of the genre, Diane Elam argues for a conception of postmodern romance which would

> open a sense of alternative spaces that are not simply utopian negations of the real, or the discovery of the hidden truth of the real. Romance and postmodernism evoke a difference that cannot be pinned down into simple opposition (realist/fantastic, historical/ ahistorical). (24)

By thus enlarging the scope of romance, Elam already suggests the possibility of including the referential real—and even the traumatically referential real. Lynne Pearce goes much further and suggests a kinship between romance and trauma because, for her, romance includes in "its deep structures the reiteration of events that—notwithstanding their subsequent resolution—are in themselves deeply traumatic" (2004, 527). Pearce thus speaks of "romantic trauma," which shares with traumatic realism the experience of "extreme temporal-spatial dislocation" and the necessity and difficulty of "narrativization" (2004, 529, 528). She later clarifies her argument when she explains that romantic love is "experienced by its subjects as a traumatic 'impossibility' that is worse than irrational" (2007, 2). Her hypothesis is a simple one, she asserts, "namely that, in the manner of trauma therapy, we turn to narrative to make first *visible* (indeed spectacular) and *causal* all that is essentially irrational, contradictory and *cause-less* about romantic love" (Pearce 2007, 17, original emphasis). It is, then, the suffering inherent in passion-love and the irrationality of love (or of the failure of love) that allow a possible correlation between romance and traumatic realism.

If trauma and passion-love are placed together in the realm of the irrational it is also because they are both non-events. The timeless and spaceless quality of love places it outside the boundaries of factuality (and even historicity) and is essentially characterised, as Paul Crosthwaite, paraphrasing Lacan, puts it, as "a *missed* encounter with the Real" (Crosthwaite 2009, 39, original emphasis): "The traumatic event, although real, took place outside the parameters of 'normal reality', such as causality, sequence, place and time. The trauma is thus an event that has no beginning, no ending, no before, no after" (Felman and Laub 69). From a phenomenological point of view trauma and passion-love are intangible and ungraspable and this elusiveness can be traced to the notion of excess. In its sheer extremity, trauma is said to exceed any understanding and any rationalisation just as romance "is federated by the notion of excess" (Ganteau 2004, 166). This notion of excess immediately posits both romance and traumatic realism as modes that seek to extend or reform the traditional laws of mimesis. Being ruled by excess, romance and traumatic realism necessarily stretch the limits of realism. As Rothberg points out, in traumatic realism the concept of realism is inevitably ambiguous because it is "a realism in which the claims of reference live on, but so does the traumatic extremity that disables realist representation as usual" (2000, 106).

The excessive nature of trauma and passion-love generates a fundamental paradox: because they defy understanding and narrativisation these excessive phenomena spur a quest for understanding and narrativising. In other words, "the *necessity of testimony* derives [. . .] from the *impossibility of testimony*" (Felman and Laub 224, original emphasis). Now, in order to represent the unrepresentable or to narrate the unnarratable, romance and traumatic realism constantly have to look for alternative and innovative forms of fiction. Just as trauma, including love trauma, obfuscates narrative knowledge, so the representation of that trauma must confound the conventions of fictional narrative. Anne Whitehead confirms the innovative necessity of trauma narratives when she asserts: "If trauma is at all susceptible to narrative formulation, then it requires a literary form which departs from conventional linear sequence" (6). The first device used by trauma narratives to test the limits of representation is generic hybridity. Generic impurity, which has already been mentioned in the case of romance, seems consubstantial with the narrativisation of trauma: "No genre or discipline 'owns' trauma as a problem or can provide definitive boundaries for it" (LaCapra 96). One of the main zones of convergence between romance and traumatic realism can, then, be found in the use of a multifarious, or rather "a genreless genre" (Elam 163), or even in the widely accommodating nature of a mode (see the Introduction to this volume). In their attempts to "testify to the impossible possibility of an aesthetics of trauma" (Luckhurst 81), romance and traumatic realism also try to renew the very language of representation, as we shall see in the cases of Winterson and Swift.

Before illustrating postmodernist romance's exploration of the limits of representation, it remains to be seen how the link between romance, the representation of trauma and ethics can be established. Let us start by specifying that, in the field of trauma, we are here dealing with the fictional—as opposed to the (allegedly) testimonial—representation of trauma: the emphasis of such fictional emplotment is, therefore, not (primarily) therapeutic; rather, it is placed on the determination to imagine and to narrativise the suffering of a being who represents in her/his inventedness an embodiment of the other. At the same time, the (re)creation of suffering in trauma fictions constitutes a reflexive attempt at understanding that suffering and a transitive invitation to tolerance and compassion. The fictional recreation of trauma is, then, almost by nature ethical, driven as it is by "the need to share and to 'translate'" (Kaplan 1). And since postmodern civilisation has been said to correspond to "the age of trauma" (Miller and Tougaw 1), "the true age of anxiety" (Bracken 181), "a post-traumatic imaginary" (Elias xi), it is the ethical duty of postmodernist fiction to reflect our traumatic *Zeitgeist*, to "recast the Other as the crucial character" and to "accord the Other that priority which was once unquestionably assigned to the self" (Bauman 84, 85). As to romance, Jean-Michel Ganteau has shown that it "is compatible with the ethical imperative. It is flourishing because it is the locus of alternative wisdom, despite—or precisely thanks to—its excesses" (2003, 238). The ethical dimension of romance consists of "rejecting the entrapment of 'the same' the better to vindicate an encounter with the other" (227). Insofar as it can be failed, short-lived or impossible, the romantic encounter with the other can be of a traumatic nature. Therefore, its narrativisation shares the ethical imperatives of trauma narratives. Clearly, then, the ethical concerns of both trauma narratives and romance are centred on the other and it is the forms of such a responsibility for the other that we shall now examine.

AN ETHICS OF ALTERITY

In postmodernist romance, love and romance itself are not only themes but also objects of a metadiscourse. In Winterson's *The Passion* love is compared to "another place whose geography is uncertain and whose customs are strange" (Winterson 1996, 68), while passion is said to consist in "set[ting] sail on an unknown sea with no certainty of land again (145). The semantic field of alterity and the topographic metaphor linking love to *terra incognita* clearly announce the concept of foreignness which is the object of an echoing repetition defining love and/or passion as "a foreign language" (68, 122). These metadiscursive considerations are not restricted to the thematic field, they extend to the generic field and can be considered as metafictional self-definitions of the genre they illustrate, since romance is notoriously "a world which is never [. . .] equivalent to our own" (Beer 3).[1] To force the reader to abandon the safety of her/his familiar knowledge and to discover various forms of otherness, such is the main ethical principle of romance. Incidentally, juxtaposing what is alien and what is familiar, what lies beyond the boundaries of the customary and what remains inside the realm of the familiar, is also the *modus operandi* of traumatic realism, as defined by Rothberg.

Romance stages the experience of otherness first and foremost within its diegetic world. The situations that are fictionalised, for example, the impossible love between the adoptive son of a monstrous Dog-woman and a fairy-tale-like dancing princess in seventeenth-century London, in Winterson's *Sexing the Cherry*; the shattering encounter of a Napoleonic foot-soldier and a web-footed bi-sexual cross-dresser in early nineteenth-century Russia and Venice, in *The Passion*; or the sacrifice of his undy-ing love offered by an apostate surveyor in Victorian England, in Graham Swift's *Ever After*, all forsake our contemporary society's received notions about the evocation of bygone amorous narratives. As Lynne Pearce has demonstrated, "extreme temporal-spatial dislocation" is part of the deep structure of romance (2004, 528), and this remote chronotope seems cru-cial, if only because it is metaphorical of the extreme possibilities to which it gives birth. Similarly, the fact that these instances of romance take place in the past, a typical narrative choice of romance, can be analysed as a temporal hypostatisation of foreignness, the past being the temporality of the present's otherness, of the unverifiable, of the potentially unknown and unknowable. If the encounter with otherness is enabled by the diegetic situ-ations, it is also the object of the heroine/hero's quest. The experience of love is in many respects the experience of the discovery of the other and this discovery, like most postmodernist romance's major issues, is metatextually verbalised. Thus, when one of *The Passion*'s homodiegetic narrators states that "our desire for another will lift us out of ourselves more cleanly than anything divine" (154), this desire to break free from oneself through the other *might* recall Emmanuel Levinas's need to escape the limits of the self, which he calls the ethical need for excendance (1982, 73–74), just as the "divine" nature of this liberation *might* recall Levinas's "excursion from the self (*la sortie de soi*)" (1995, 12). To depart from the self, to achieve "pneumatism," i.e., the ability to breathe through the other, is Levinas's recommendation to reach transcendence as "unclosure (*dé-claustration*)" (Levinas 1974, 278), and this transcendence through alterity *might* seem to apply to the lovers' desire to breathe in and through the other. But it must not be forgotten that for Levinas the other is not an incarnate, gen-dered being, it is a faceless face, "a non-phenomenon" (Levinas 1974, 141), the relation to which is necessarily one of fundamental "gratuitousness" (Levinas 1995, 111), that is, a relation manifestly incompatible with the romantic desire for concrete union with the other. Levinas's responsibility for the other comes before any cognition, while the romantic desire for the other comes after the shock of the epiphanic meeting. Levinas's caring for the other is distinguished by a disinterestedness which represents its own fulfilment and seems quite opposed to the lovers' sense of expectation and/ or frustration. The teleological longing for the other expressed by the pro-tagonists of romance may be mythical, but it cannot be ethical in the sense of Levinas's ethics of alterity. Rather, postmodernist romance's ethics of alterity is accomplished through a poetics of imagination, and this implies that the very language of romance is instrumental in the ethical quest. Tak-ing Winterson's *The Passion* and *Sexing the Cherry* as examples, one is struck by the daringness of the narrative choices. Choosing a seventeenth-century Dog-woman, her foundling son Jordan, a Napoleonic foot-soldier (Henri) and a Venetian bi-sexual croupier-cum-prostitute (Villanelle) as the main narrative instances means imagining first-person narrative voices the nature of which has not been taken sufficient heed of. What are Henri's diary, Villanelle's confessions, Jordan's journal and the Dog-Woman's account from a literary point of view? As recreations of languages of the past, they seem to belong to the category of pastiche. But pastiche is the imitation of a model and one of the main interests of these specific voices is precisely that they have no model. By lending a voice to characters whose voice has never been heard and by setting their speech in a specific historical and linguistic context, Winterson undertakes a paradoxical project: to imitate a language of which there are no (or very few) traces, to reproduce styles which have no prototype and to copy a model which has never existed. The resurrection of these voices from the past thus challenges the existing literary categories and constitutes in itself an attempt at probing the limits of representation. In her reconstitution of the past, Winterson does not repeat, recycle or recuperate existing versions of history: because she privileges unheard voices of marginal or eccentric actors, these voices cannot create an effect of repetition; on the contrary, they are opposed to the canonical discourses of the past and beget novelty also in the stylistic and poetic fields. Her texts, which have no hypotexts,[2] do not, therefore, partake of representation but of presentation, not of reproduction but of production, not of recreation but of creation. They owe less to *mimesis* (imitation) than to *poiesis* (creation) and appear, then, as worthy instances of a poetics of imagination.

What Winterson especially illustrates in order to both enact an ethics of alterity and to play with the limits of representation is the infinite otherness of the other. In *The Passion* this limitlessness is highlighted by the dual narrative organisation, each narrator commenting on the other's unaccountable inexplicability. Thus, when Villanelle reveals Henri's lunacy—"he was hearing voices [. . .] he woke up screaming night after night, his hands round his throat" (147)—, it is the male protagonist's alienation which is stressed and this alienation signifies the ultimate stage of becoming other. Just as the Henri of the final stages cannot be saved by Villanelle, he cannot be understood by her and her failure of reason to comprehend him stands for the rational failure to explain and, of course, to represent his radical otherness. How could Villanelle represent what she cannot understand, and how could Henri represent himself when his self has eluded him, and he has become alien to himself? Villanelle, the female protagonist, is presented as "deliberately mysterious" and, like the city she inhabits, "fantastic" and full of "mysteries that only the dead know" (113, 116, 118). The comparison between the heroine and her city, Villanelle and Venice, is pursued throughout the double narrative in order to show that to the amphibian "city of uncertainty" (58) there corresponds an ambiguous being now homoerotic

lover, now heterosexual prostitute. By thus emphasising the shifting identity of its heroine, the text circles around the idea of ungraspable otherness,
the various facets of Villanelle remaining not only unexplained but also (at
least superficially) unconnected.

Venice is also the city where the frontiers between the real and the fantastic are blurred,[3] and this deliberate confusion is brought to affect not
only the setting or the events but also the text's modalities. In her resolution
to give alterity a fictional existence Winterson does not hesitate to other
the very modes of her narration by resorting to magic realism. When Villanelle is reported to have walked on the water, or when she literally loses
her heart, which is then found by Henri in a "throbbing" blue jar (120), the
fictional reality, although consistent with the diegetic logic, clashes with
phenomenal reality and suggests alternative possibilities of representing the
other. These instances of magic realism, like traumatic realism, test the
limits of mimesis and seek "to disable established modes of representation
and understanding" and to "produce a rejuvenation of realism" (Rothberg
2000, 5, 99); they also point to the magic of Winterson's novels as a staple
of romance and its "world of mystery" (Frye 196). Testing the validity of
realism also amounts to questioning our understanding of reality and its
various forms of representation. Winterson's radical forms of representing the other evoke Michel Foucault's teratological representations of the
human, the purpose of which is "a critical ontology of ourselves" and a
challenge to "the limits that are imposed on us and an experiment with the
possibility of going beyond them" (50). Foucault "makes the monstrous
indistinguishable from the human" (Gibson 239), and the human acquires,
therefore, a shifting, fragile and plural ontology. It is the privilege of art
in general and of Winterson in particular to give an idea of this striking
ontological indeterminacy.

In the field of ethics, Graham Swift, in *Ever After*, displays a different but equally efficient strategy dedicated to demonstrating the infinite
otherness of the other. In order to show the sheer unknowability of the
Victorian other, Swift introduces a doubting, suffering land surveyor, Matthew Pearce, and a contemporary counterpoint, a double of the figure of
the reader, who constantly pinpoints the limits of our understanding of
the other, and particularly of the other in the past. The traces left by the
Victorian surveyor (a few notebooks and a letter) prove inevitably fragmentary and the reconstitution of the whole picture on the basis of these traces
is shown as an intellectual and hermeneutic impossibility. The innumerable questions raised by the contemporary interpreter about this figure and
his various imaginative versions of it stand for the limitless possibilities of
the otherness of the other. The challenge of reconstituting the other is the
central issue of *Ever After*, as is highlighted in an outstanding metacom-
ment: "It is a prodigious, a presumptuous task: to take the skeletal remains
of a single life and attempt to breathe into them their former actuality"
(1992, 90). This "attempt" is manifestly what the contemporary narrator

undertakes in his hermeneutic conjectures but it is also what Swift does when he creates his pastiche of a Victorian apostate's diary. The metaphor of resurrection contained in the quotation aptly applies to Swift's, and to Winterson's, restoration of bygone embodiments of alterity. By reviving neglected, forgotten or ill-treated forms of otherness and by putting them in the novelistic limelight, Swift and Winterson can be said to use a sort of *parousia*. The glorious return of the suppressed others certainly corresponds to the concept of *parousia*, and its enactment seems fundamental within the frame of an ethics of alterity since it effectuates an act of retributional justice. Besides, the time of the return—or of the returned—which derives from the concept of *parousia*, appears as a time that is neither completely past nor fully to come, and this temporal disjointedness might evoke the *Nachträglichkeit* of trauma.

The ethical mission is, then, carried out by the author—and not by the diegetic narrators or protagonists. It is the creation of voices excluded from the received system of representation which accomplishes the ethical opening to the other. To strive to imagine the feeling and the suffering of a Victorian husband torn between the truth of his apostasy and the truth of his love for his wife represents for Swift a true experience of *excendance*, an evasion from the ipseity of the self, "the ethical impulse towards or openness to the other that effects a release from the confines of the self (Gibson 37). In *Ever After* Swift not only imagines the putative life of a distant other, he also breathes life into a contemporary character that stands for the representative of our postmodern and post-traumatic condition.[4] By thus relating the known to the unknown, the familiar to the unfamiliar, the contemporary to the Victorian, Swift meets the "ethical demand" that, in traumatic realism, "ought to link the present to the past, the self to the other, and different histories of oppression to each other in such a way that coming to terms with the past necessitates coming to terms with the present in a public setting" (Rothberg 2000, 269).

In Winterson's and Swift's works, the ethics of alterity is, then, made manifest in the attempt to represent the other and particularly the other's trauma(s). As seems fitting in the context of romance, what is given pride of place is the suffering of love itself "the impossibility of fulfilment being the condition that sustains romance" (Boccardi 8). In *Sexing the Cherry*, love is associated to a "plague" that destroys an entire city (78) and, in *The Passion*, to a "beast" that devours the lover's heart (145). These predatory metaphors express the narrators' traumatic conception of love, as is suggested by the association of *The Passion* with Jesus Christ's passion. In these postmodernist romances love becomes a passion, a way of the cross, leading the characters on endless and fruitless peregrinations, imprisoning them in a monomaniac obsession or driving them literally crazy. And above all the trauma of unfulfilled or unrequited love, like any trauma, causes its victims to try and make sense of their senseless experience by repeating it in narrative. "This jotting urge, this need to set it down" (Swift 1992, 207) is shared by all the victims of the shock of passion-love. The explicit transition from victimhood to the status of narrator is not just a postmodernist ploy to endow the text with a metafictional dimension; it is the novelistic manifestation of the kinship between romance narrative and trauma discourse, for telling, since "turning [love] into a story is the oldest of the deep structures" of romance (Pearce 2007, 2).[5] As Luckhurst pithily puts it: "where trauma was, there narrative shall be" (82).

The narrators of *The Passion, Sexing the Cherry* and *Ever After* dwell on their need to "go on writing" (Winterson 1996, 159) and "to keep company with this notebook" (Swift 1992, 183), thus evidencing the therapeutic quality of their writing activity. But the act of narrating trauma proves fundamentally ambiguous: giving a voice to a trauma through a narrative may be a way of working it through but it is also—and perhaps primarily—a way of acting out this trauma. In this sense, narrativisation may be seen as an attempt to obliterate the trauma by remembering it; to cancel out the trauma by re-presenting it; to evacuate the trauma and yet recreate it. This paradox is central to the concept of traumatic realism such as it was originally conceived by Hal Foster as a logic of repetition which at the same time "dissolves" and "produces" the traumatic real (136).[6] When the diegetic narrators recount their traumatic experiences and thus reproduce them for their narratees, their undertaking in fact repeats the undertaking of the authors who, by creating their characters' traumas, at the same time force them upon and share them with their readers. The ethics of alterity, such as it is implemented in postmodernist traumatic romance, is then also always an ethics of sharing—for the writers and the readers alike.

Yet another characteristic feature of the postmodernist trauma romance is "the ordinary and the extraordinary," a mixture which Rothberg deems central to his conception of traumatic realism (2000, 149). Details of daily life thus tend to supersede the memory or the narrative of the unbearable. These objects or activities of the ordinary world Rothberg calls instances of "the traumatic index [which] points to a necessary absence" (2000, 104). The grafted cherry for Jordan, gardening for Henri, the butterflies for Matthew are all instances of such traumatic indexes and of their highly ambiguous relation to the real. The idea of breeding and cultivating (implicit in the activities of grafting and gardening) and the idea of natural beauty (contained in the contemplation of butterflies) represent life rather than death, fertility rather than sterility (particularly the sterility resulting from failed love), comforting reality rather than the enigma of passion. But the indexical fruit, flowers and insects are also attached to the lost object of love and point, therefore, to the traumatic blank which they were meant to replace. The narrative insistence on the everyday superficially effectuates a return to the real, perhaps counting on the solace of the real, but in fact inevitably reverts to the absent omnipresence of the trauma which evades or defies the real. The real and its representation cannot but be contaminated by the dominant traumatic modality.[7] The indexes of the narrators' everyday life are, of course, also marks of characterisation, tools used to particularise and humanise the other's specificity and, therefore, tools used to encourage the reader's ethics of alterity. Since, as Jean-François Lyotard has forcefully argued, the concept of the other is potentially problematic, the practitioners of romance sometimes prefer to turn to the self and the question of individual responsibility.

AN ETHICS OF INDIVIDUAL RESPONSIBILITY

That Winterson and Swift sometimes move away from an ethics of alterity can be illustrated in their more recent romances, *The.PowerBook* (2000) and *Tomorrow* (2007). Admittedly, the discourse about the other, the concern for the other, and even the unconditional love for the other are still major diegetic issues, but the point is precisely that they remain preoccupations of the first-person narrators and are not integrated into the novelists' art of composition. In these novels, the other remains at the (superficial) thematic level and does not affect the (deep) structure of writing. The other is talked about but not written. Ali/x,[8] *The.PowerBook*'s main narrative voice, and hence the instance responsible for the enactment of the bulk of the text, is deliberately presented as a mouthpiece, if not a double, of Winterson herself.[9] She cannot, therefore, represent a form of radical otherness for the extradiegetic novelist. Compared to Winterson, Ali/x appears to be a fictional version of the same and not of the other— even if, ontologically and ethically, the author and narrator remain clearly distinct, particularly because the narrative instance opens up her account to temporal and phenomenological diversity, whereas the authorial figure seems concentrated on questions and representations of her present civilisation. When Winterson imagines and writes Ali/x's thoughts, she does not seek to escape from the self and explore the other, she does not primarily strive for Levinasian *excendance*. Rather, she concentrates on the ethical problems of the self.[10] The change of ethical perspective seems quite manifest in the change of chronotopes. Whereas in *The Passion* and *Sexing the Cherry* the fictional misfits are staged in the remote past and in unfamiliar settings, in *The.PowerBook* the protagonist and framing narrator lives and writes in contemporary London (and in the same part of London as Winterson) and when she moves geographically it is to Paris or Capri, the typical romantic locations that are presented for their "cultural commodity appeal" (Pearce 2004, 524), in other terms, in the form of familiar or even hackneyed *topoi*. In this shift from the past to the present and from the unknown to the well-known the shift from an ethics of the other to an ethics of the self can be perceived.

Similarly, in *Tomorrow*, Swift gives up the defamiliarising exploration of a Victorian nonconformist psyche and fictionalises instead the moral qualms of a middle-aged and middle-class mother in contemporary

London. The whole narrative unfolds in the mind of Paula, the protagonist-cum-narrator, who lies awake in her bedroom. In spite of the inevitable analepses relating episodes taking place in an English sea-side resort, the whole narrative appears enclosed in the here and now, in the present and in the protagonist's mind. It is clearly the consciousness of a contemporary average person which constitutes the focus of the narrative, and it is the responsibility of the self which constitutes the ethical priority of the novel—even if the self, an unusual narrative perspective for Swift, is female. Like *The.PowerBook*, *Tomorrow* does not privilege an exodus from the self in its narrative composition. Paula's thoughts are the thoughts of any parent facing a dilemma with their children; they certainly do not provide an insight into Levinas's otherwise than being.[11]

Before examining this ethical mutation, let us consider the generic frame which is common to these two postmodernist romances. *Tomorrow*'s allegiance to the romance is signposted by two self-reflexive comments: "here's a bedtime story" and "it's a bedtime story: exactly" (9, 165). By combining two meanings of "bedtime story," one referring to the traditional narrative pact between parent and child(ren) and one literalising the phrase and taking bed as a metonymy for the amorous activities that take place in it, Swift highlights the two main generic features of romance, namely its narrative priority and its thematisation of love. A similar metageneric consciousness is at play in *The.PowerBook*, where the narrative conductor formulates these two equations: "I am the story" and "We were love" (5, 69). Again, the importance of narrative and the theme of love are advertised and combined, but here we have an increased degree of metatextuality because the equivalence that is established between the agent of the story and the story itself at once raises ontological questions about the concepts of subjectivity and identity. Winterson's outstanding self-reflexivity becomes blatant when she includes in the list of canonical romances her own *The Passion* just after *Wuthering Heights* and *Heat and Dust* (25–26), thus inscribing her novel in a generic lineage and at the same time displaying a radical metafictionality which sets it apart as a postmodernist, self-questioning and self-deconstructing version of the genre.[12]

What *The.PowerBook* also has in common with Winterson's previous romances is the traumatic undertones. Several versions of the narrator's origins are given but all of them insist on her unwanted birth, on her parents' lovelessness (187), and on the fact that she was given or taken away in infancy. This initial wound can be felt throughout the narrative in the fact that her love for her partner is not just a part of, or a supplement to, her family life but becomes a totalising obsessive purpose, a matter of life and death. As in *The Passion*, love is indistinguishable from suffering, always already potentially traumatic: "There is no love that does not pierce the hands and feet" (Winterson 2000, 79 and *passim*). If love is a metaphorical crucifixion, it can lead to actual death, as in the case of Francesca da Rimini and her lover Paolo, whose story Ali/x retells in the first person and in her own language. By telling this story in her own words, Ali/x seems to be talking about herself and she makes it clear that the legendary lovers' conception of love as a deathly risk is also hers.

What might be missing in Winterson's handling of traumatic romance compared to her previous novels is the historical dimension. Although there are various narrative excursions into the remote past, none of the embedded stories include a historical background. The trauma of passion-love is, then, never contextualised, never compared or extended to other forms of collective trauma—unless one considers cyberspace an alternative version of our contemporary consciousness. This absence of historical broadening is even more conspicuous in *Tomorrow*, which restricts itself to the domestic trauma of a family in danger of disintegration. Because of its restricted temporality and diegetic concerns (the novel never expands beyond the limits of the narrator's experiences and reminiscences), *Tomorrow* does not associate the particular to the general, the present to the past, as is customary in traumatic realism. This does not mean that trauma is absent from Swift's romance but simply that it is confined to the private sphere. In fact, what the narrator calls "the traumatic point" (180) concerns the coming day when she will have to disclose to her children that she has been lying to them about their true father. The narrator talks of "the eve of [. . .] execution," "the day that will change all our lives," "the most awful thing," "our last day," "the early hours of Doomsday" (1, 2, 36, 227), thus suggesting that the traumatic dimension stems less from the referential situation than from the narrator's rhetorics. Possibly, the novel's greatest weakness is that it uses the hyperbolic metaphors of shock and catastrophe to describe an experience which is neither unspeakable nor unheard-of[13]—and certainly not unheard-of in Swift's own œuvre. It is in the quest for the representation of this traumatic perspective that Swift proves resourceful, so consistently does he combine the story of an ordinary life with the rhetorics of romance. Swift's narrative takes the form of an "unexpurgated fairy tale" (87), where none of the facts of the protagonist's life are omitted and where all these facts become items or stages of the romantic teleology. Thus, for example, the narrator specifies: "Once upon a time your dad and I used to share a basement in Earl's Court" (17), thus integrating the description of a shabby flat into the discourse of the fairy tale for adults and illustrating Swift's idiosyncratic use of romantic realism or realistic romance. In Swift's novel the prosaic nature of daily experience becomes the stuff of romance and is, in the process, narrativised, aestheticised, questioned and viewed anew in the mirror of meta-romantic mimesis.

If the generic frame combining postmodernist versions of romance, realism and trauma remains constant in Winterson's and Swift's novels, the ethical priority, as already mentioned, varies considerably. Because the narrative and moral consciousness of both *The.PowerBook* and *Tomorrow* is unique and autodiegetic, the ethical concerns of these works are centred on the individual—and not on the other. In Swift's novel, the ethical problem revolves around "that whole issue of pretence" (223). Paula, the thinking and telling subject, ponders on the costs of a life of lies and on the risks of telling the truth as well. The paradox is that Paula and her husband created a united family by means of deception, and they might shatter this harmony by revealing the truth. Paula's choice to assume the responsibility to tell the truth is what the whole narrative justifies and explains in detail. Paula's narrative, which takes the form of a confession made by a mother to her children, is, then, alethic by nature, and the whole text is a performative demonstration of the ethics of truth(s). If the responsibility to tell is presented as an ethical duty, does this not mean that narrative itself, the narrative of traumatic realism, is an ethical priority? Could we not consider, then, that *Tomorrow*'s disclosure of an ordinary life is Swift's way of asserting the ethical necessity to favour micronarratives over metanarratives?

In *The.PowerBook* the ethical focus is on individual choice. The narrator has an existentialist conception of life according to which everyone is free to choose the course of his or her life: "We were universes dripping with worlds. All we had to do was choose" (230). In this fragment, the hyperbolic equivalence between microcosm and macrocosm and the provocative suggestion of a plural cosmos suggest the infinite possibilities of the self. "There are so many lives packed into one. [. . .] These lives of ours that press in on us must be heard [. . .], we are multiple and infinite" (103), insists the narrator, who stresses the plural potential of everyone's life only to make clear the individual responsibility to use and actualise this potential. In what Susana Onega calls the "vital choice between destiny and freedom" (232), Ali/x unambiguously advocates freedom, the freedom to decide which life one wants to select—and, of course, which life one wants to discard. The freedom to make radical choices is presented as all the more precious since it is strenuous and risky,[14] leaving Ali/x "scared to death" (205)—an idea reminiscent of what John Fowles, in his "existentialist terminology," called "the anxiety of freedom—that is [. . .] the realisation that being free is a situation of terror" (296).

The ethics of liberty, i.e., the possibility (which is also a responsibility) to make vital choices, is not only a heuristic concern of the narrative discourse, it is again performed in the course of the novel's diegetic unfolding. The framing plot bears upon the amorous meeting between the narrator and a glamorous married woman, and the diegetic crux resides in their life-changing decision to start a new life together or not. The narrator's progressive conviction of the necessity to make that decision and her efforts to convince her partner to make the same choice constitute, then, the main fictional stakes of this insubordinate romance. Using her diegetic material to illustrate and even to carry out an ethics of choice, Winterson demonstrates the intrinsic performativity of ethics. Winterson's ethical imperative is implemented not only in the embedding narrative but also in the embedded narratives. If the story of Francesca and Paolo, for example, is told in the first-person and in the present tense from the point of view of Francesca, it is to highlight the heroine's awareness of the risks she runs as she accepts her illicit lover. When she chooses "those few wide-open days" over "the grave of [her] married life" (127), she knows that the price to pay can be fatal, and when she and her lover are actually killed, she describes the death scene and the ensuing love in death as the logical consequence and even reward of her ethical choice. This description from beyond the grave, transgressing as it does the limits of realistic verisimilitude, represents one of Winterson's purple patches in her dealing with the sublime unrepresentable. Francesca's act of narration after her death in fact celebrates the (romantic) transcendental superiority of love over death— "We are light now as our happiness was, lighter than birds. [. . .] No one can separate us now. Not even God" (129)—and when one establishes the link between the act of narration and love, it becomes manifest that what is celebrated here is also the transcendental power of narration. Clearly, love and narrative remain the central ethical imperatives of Winterson's postmodernist romance.

Implemented and dramatised in the various stories told in *The.Power-Book*, Winterson's ethics of liberty also finds an illustration in her stylistic adventurousness. Beside the sublime attempt at speaking the unspeakable love beyond the grave, Winterson inserts a prosaic, literal, paratactic recipe for "salsa di pomodori" (182). And beside the repetitive speculations about love as "the mortal enemy of death" (70), she inserts a factual account of the minutiae of sex as "[j]ust fuck" (57). These juxtapositions of the sublime and the ordinary, the extreme and the everyday, can be seen as examples of Winterson's own version of the unlikely combinations of traumatic realism. Narrative contents and stylistic form are, then, associated in *The.PowerBook*'s demonstration of an ethics of liberty. A demonstration must be intended for an addressee, and indeed *The.PowerBook* has a strong addressive quality, particularly in the emphatic ethical message insisting on everyone's, that is, any reader's, freedom to choose his or her life. That the novel makes room for a hermeneutic ethics is manifest in the way it privileges chat-rooms and email sessions in its narrative forms. These conversations, argues Ginette Carpenter, "allow a degree of intimacy and feedback previously denied the writer. [. . .] Thus the fictional reader becomes a complicit companion in the unfolding of the narrative/s and the material reader is constantly aware of the activity of reading" (76). Because *The.PowerBook* "operates as both a representation *of* and metaphor *for* reading" (77, original emphasis), the reader is at the centre of the novelistic apparatus and s/he can never forget her/his ethical responsibility. Besides, the deliberate narrative indeterminacy with which the novel concludes forces the reader to make her/his own choices. It could, then, be argued that a hermeneutic ethics, again stressing individual responsibility, is part and parcel of Winterson's narrative programme.

CONCLUSION

As the comparative analysis of the works has shown, the ethical and aesthetic choices made in Winterson's and Swift's postmodernist romances are not really opposite but rather complementary. All the examples that have been examined here reveal a strong ethical component, and this ethical emphasis in turn signals romance's alertness to, and integration of the contemporary *Zeitgeist*. As Andrew Hadfield, Dominic Rainsford and Tim Woods argue, "the word 'ethics' seems to have replaced 'textuality' as the most charged term in the vocabulary of contemporary literary and cultural theory" (1). As already suggested, the ethics of alterity and the ethics of individual choice constitute complementary, rather than mutually exclusive, ethical priorities. Indeed, when Villanelle explains her decision not "to refuse passion as one might sensibly refuse a leopard in the house" (Winterson 1996, 145), she clearly inscribes her narrative discourse within the logic of an ethics of choice; and when Ali/x resurrects the voice of a seventeenth-century transvestite in order to give her a new dignity, she may be said to invoke an ethics of alterity. Finally, the ethics of alterity and the ethics of individual freedom intersect in the concept of responsibility: whether it be responsibility for the other or responsibility for the self, what is at stake is an ethical awakening enacted by the novelist and intended to contaminate the reader. An ethics of responsibility, both self-reflexive and transitive, is, then, what Winterson and Swift systematically implement in their postmodernist romances.

What the combination of these romances shows from an aesthetic point of view is the extreme malleability of the genre—or mode, which is an even more labile category. Adopting and adapting the form of the seventeenth-century tall tale, Victorian pastiche, historiography, fairy tale for adults, cyber-narrative, magic realism and, of course, traumatic realism, romance proves that it is open to the infinite variety of otherness in the field of generic poetics. These multiple generic borrowings also allow postmodernist romance to test the limits of novelistic representation. Above all, these architextual modulations testify to the chameleonic capacity of romance to adapt to the aesthetic and ethical imperatives of its time. This protean disposition is that of the novel itself, capable of integrating any form of representation in its all-encompassing rhetoric. It follows, then, that romance is not only at the origins of the novel but that it still constitutes its very essence.

NOTES

1. This is also what Ganteau explains: "as opposed to the novel, romance would tend to be concerned with things foreign in more than just one acceptation of the term, the foreign (from the Latin *fors, foris*) being associated with what is outside the walls of the city, what escapes common experience, what is more interested in the other than the same" (2004, 167).

2. I am of course, not asserting that there are no intertextual relations between Winterson's novels and other literary works. There are many, and they have been well documented (see Onega). The idea here is that, from a linguistic point of view, Winterson cannot be said to imitate a specific code.
3. For a detailed development of this idea, see Reynier.
4. For a more detailed analysis of the relations between the Victorian and the postmodern traumas in *Ever After*, see Gutleben 2009–10.
5. On the similarities between the narrative rhetorics of trauma and romance, see Pearce 2007, 17–19.
6. Foster's logic of repetition echoes Freud's concepts of repetition-compulsion and *Nachträglichkeit* (Freud 352–56) since these processes of acting out already represent, according to Freud, an attempt to overcome the trauma through reinterpretation and reenactment.
7. In *Sexing the Cherry* this traumatic modality is restricted to the sections about Jordan's unfulfilled love and cannot be said to affect the Rabelaisian Dog-Woman and her utter contempt for the futilities of love or the pangs of conscience.
8. "Ali/x" is a designation borrowed from Susana Onega.
9. For the similarities between *The.PowerBook*'s narrative voice and Winterson, see Onega 184.
10. This does not mean that there is not also an ethics of alterity at play in the novel. The point I am trying to make here is that the dominant in terms of ethics is shifting away from the other and concentrating on problems of the self. The persistence of an ethics of alterity can mainly be found in the embedded narratives, while the embedding narrative, that is, the frame and main substance of the novel, focuses on an ethics of individual responsibility.
11. Of course, like any work of fiction written in the first-person, *Tomorrow* represents a transfer from the writer's self to a new written other and an invitation for a transfer from the reader's self to a fictional other, but this form of otherness does not possess the radical degree indispensable for a true ethics of alterity. As I am attempting to show, the process of defamiliarisation—and of ethical questioning linked to defamiliarisation—remains minor and attenuated because the fictional other is closer to the known than to the unknown, to the familiar than to the foreign.
12. On the postmodernist nature of Winterson's romance see Keulks 146–62.
13. To give just two recent examples, Susan Barrett's *Fixing Shadows* (2005) and A. S. Byatt's *The Children's Book* (2010) both play on the *topos* of mistaken paternity without (over)using the rhetorics of trauma.
14. The congruence between an ethics of choice and an ethics of risk is repeatedly signalled in the novel (107, 177, 228).

WORKS CITED

Bauman, Zygmunt. *Postmodern Ethics*. Oxford: Blackwell, 1993. Print.
Beer, Gillian. *The Romance*. Critical Idiom. London: Methuen, 1970. Print.
Boccardi, Mariadele. "A Romance of the Past: Postmodernism, Representation, and Historical Fiction." *Études britanniques contemporaines* 26 (2004): 1–14. Print.
Bracken, Patrick. *Trauma: Culture, Meaning and Philosophy*. London and Philadelphia: Whurr, 2002. Print.
Carpenter, Ginette. "Reading and the Reader." *Jeanette Winterson: A Contemporary Critical Guide*. Ed. Sonya Andermahr. London: Continuum, 2007. 69–81. Print.

Crosthwaite, Paul. *Trauma, Postmodernism, and the Aftermath of World War II*. Basingstoke: Palgrave Macmillan, 2009. Print.

Elam, Diane. *Romancing the Postmodern*. London and New York: Routledge, 1992. Print.

Elias, Amy J. *Sublime Desire: History and Post-1960s Fiction*. Baltimore, MD: Johns Hopkins UP, 2001. Print.

Felman, Shoshana and Dori Laub, eds. *Testimony: Crises of Witnessing in Literature, Psychoanalysis, and History*. London and New York: Routledge, 1992. Print.

Foster, Hal. *The Return of the Real. The Avant-Garde at the End of the Century*. Cambridge, MA.: MIT Press, 1996. Print.

Foucault, Michel. *The Archaeology of Knowledge*. Trans. Alan Sheridan. London and New York: Routledge, 1991. Print.

Fowles, John. *The French Lieutenant's Woman*. 1969. London: Pan Books, 1987. Print.

Freud, Sigmund. *Project for a Scientific Psychology. The Standard Edition of the Complete Psychological Works of Sigmund Freud*. 1895. Vol. I. Trans. and ed. James Strachey in collaboration with Anna Freud, assisted by Alix Strachey and Alan Tyson. London: Hogarth Press, 1966. Print.

Frye, Northrop. *Anatomy of Criticism: Four Essays*. 1957. Harmondsworth: Penguin, 1990. Print.

Ganteau, Jean-Michel. "Fantastic but Truthful: The Ethics of Romance." *Cambridge Quarterly* 32.3 (2003): 225–38. Print.

———. "Hearts Object: Jeanette Winterson and the Ethics of Absolutist Romance." *Refracting the Canon in Contemporary British Literature and Film*. Eds. Susana Onega and Christian Gutleben. Amsterdam and New York: Rodopi, 2004. Print.

Gibson, Andrew. *Postmodernity, Ethics and the Novel: From Leavis to Levinas*. London and New York: Routledge, 1999. Print.

Gutleben, Christian. "Shock Tactics: The Art of Linking and Transcending Victorian and Postmodern Traumas in Graham Swift's *Ever After*." *Neo-Victorian Studies* 2.2 (Winter 2009–10): 137–56. Print.

Hadfield, Andrew, Dominic Rainsford and Tim Woods. "Introduction: Literature and the Return to Ethics." *The Ethics in Literature*. Eds. Andrew Hadfield, Dominic Rainsford and Tim Woods. London and New York: St Martin's P, 1999. 1–14. Print.

Kaplan, Ann E. *Trauma Culture: The Politics of Terror and Loss in Media and Literature*. New Brunswick, New Jersey and London: Rutgers UP, 2005. Print.

Keulks, Gavin. "Winterson's Recent Work: Navigating Realism and Postmodernism." *Jeanette Winterson: A Contemporary Critical Guide*. Ed. Sonya Andermahr. London: Continuum, 2007. 147–62. Print.

LaCapra, Dominick. *Writing History, Writing Trauma*. Baltimore, MD: Johns Hopkins UP, 2001. Print.

Levinas, Emmanuel. *Humanisme de l'autre homme*. Montpellier: Fata Morgana, 1972. Print.

———. *Autrement qu'être ou au-delà de l'essence*. Paris: Martinus Nishoff, 1974. Print.

———. *De l'évasion*. Montpellier: Fata Morgana, 1982. Print.

———. *Altérité et transcendance*. Montpellier: Fata Morgana, 1995. Print.

Luckhurst, Roger. *The Trauma Question*. London and New York: Routledge, 2008. Print.

Lyotard, Jean-François. *Moralités postmodernes*. Paris: Galilée, 1993. Print.

Miller, Nancy K., and Jason Tougaw, eds. *Extremities: Trauma, Testimony, and Community*. Urbana and Chicago: U of Illinois P, 2002. Print.

Onega, Susana. *Jeanette Winterson*. Manchester: Manchester UP, 2006. Print.

Pearce, Lynne. "Popular Romance and its Readers." *A Companion to Romance. From Classical to Contemporary*. Ed. Corinne Saunders. Oxford: Blackwell, 2004. 521–38. Print.

———. *Romance Writing*. Cambridge: Polity, 2007. Print.

Reynier, Christine. "Venise dans *The Passion* de Jeanette Winterson." *Études britanniques contemporaines* 4 (1994): 25–38. Print.

Rothberg, Michael. *Traumatic Realism: The Demands of Holocaust Representation*. Minneapolis: U of Minnesota P, 2000. Print.

———. "Between the Extreme and the Everyday: Ruth Klüger's Traumatic Realism." *Extremities. Trauma, Testimony, and* Community. Eds. Nancy K. Miller and Jason Tougaw. Urbana and Chicago: U of Illinois P, 2002. 52–70. Print.

Swift, Graham. *Ever After*. London: Picador, 1992. Print.

———. *Tomorrow*. London: Picador, 2007. Print.

Whitehead, Anne. *Trauma Fiction*. Edinburgh: Edinburgh UP, 2004. Print.

Winterson, Jeanette. *Sexing the Cherry*. 1989. London: Vintage, 1990. Print.

———. *The Passion*. 1987. London: Vintage, 1996. Print.

———. *The.PowerBook*. London: Jonathan Cape, 2000. Print.

9 "And to defeat that shadow ... he had to take it in *homeopathically*, in minute quantities of conscious reparation"

Adam Thorpe's Unsentimental Historical Romances

Maria Grazia Nicolosi

TWENTIETH-CENTURY TRAUMATIC HISTORY AND LITERARY CREATION

A noticeable phenomenon of the last two decades has been the growing public interest in the unprecedented events of twentieth-century traumatic history. The sheer amount of recent historical fiction revolving around the two world wars (Fussell; Tate; Torgovnick; Watson), no less than the founding of memorial museums and "oral history" archives all over the world (Winter), bear witness to the vast currency of this discourse. The impact of traumatic history on modernity and postmodernity has been acknowledged as a crucial problem for historical representation and understanding (LaCapra ix–x), just as it has dislocated "the imagination, stifling writers' creativity and destroying their confidence in the form" (Gasiorek 1).

The recent disclosure of Holocaust-related testimonies, in particular, has urged upon fictional narrative and historiography a new ethical agenda attentive to the perils and obligations of representation as well as to the danger of abusing memorialisation as "symbolic capital" (LaCapra 86–113).[1] A traumatised failure of a proper imaginative engagement with this historical heritage by survivors and later generations has resulted in the unthinkability of traumatic history within its own specific "condition of possibility." Pointing to the fact that ordinary discursive and affective responses fall short when tackling the question of how to render the un(re) presentable excess of limit events, theorists such as Jean-François Lyotard and Paul Ricœur have invoked some kind of "homeopathic" practice, to borrow Dominick LaCapra's clever metaphor (154). For Lyotard, it is the postmodern sublime which comes closest to "put[ting] forward the unpresentable in presentation itself" (Lyotard 81); for Ricœur, writing cannot but edge towards self-obliteration insofar as twentieth-century traumatic history is inherently in excess of language and representation (Ricœur 2004, 254–61). LaCapra underlines that the account of traumatic events in different genres/disciplines stirs paradoxes, for "no one genre or discipline 'owns' trauma as a specific problem or can provide [. . .] boundaries for it" (96). As he acutely argues, with limit events there exists a strong temptation to conflate historical trauma with structural trauma. Defined as a non-event, and as "an anxiety-producing condition of possibility related to the potential for historical traumatization" (82), structural trauma is a problematic precondition of historical trauma. However, insofar as it establishes the very "possibility of historicity, without being identical with history" (84), it ends up transvaluing traumatic events as being "epiphanous" (in modernist discourse), "sublime" (in postmodernist discourse), or even sacralised (80). According to James Berger, postmodern culture as a whole has been dominated by such an apocalyptic disposition (3–58); in fact, it has only made explicit the connection between trauma and catastrophe first articulated within Modernism. As Hannah Arendt observed about the predicament of Walter Benjamin, with Modernism the "citability" of the past had replaced its "transmissibility" (43). Having superseded the nineteenth-century notion of tradition, the discourse connecting trauma and historical catastrophe emerged as the new founding trope within the nihilistic rhetorics of Modernism. Yet, precisely the rupture of traditional forms of representation brought about by the historical deflagration of WWI turned the realist literary heritage into the displaced ground of cultural crisis, so that its aptly battered remains were symptomatically invested with a new symbolic value. In this sense, Modernism is rightly understood by Fredric Jameson as "cancelled realism" (266), as it attempted to "manage" the spectre of the realist tradition it had awakened first. By the same token, the artistic forms typically associated with Modernism have come to allegorise the un-representability of the last century's most unbearable legacy. Sensed to be the absolute zero point of Western civilisation, such a paradoxically originary traumatic rupture dissolved all former ties with the referential Real of history (Jameson 68).[2]

It is therefore against the backdrop of Modernism's referential crisis that many post-war historical novelists have sought narrative modes better suited to the times "after the end." While enlisting the formal innovations of the modernist novel among the literary resources of a "usable" past, they have often burst open the representational paradigms of postmodern "traumatic realism" (LaCapra 106, 185–86) through a sustained rewriting of narrative forms once peculiar to the repressed others of nineteenth-century realism. It has been the constantly mutating mode of romance (Bakhtin 84–258; Frye 186–206; Elam 4–8), as embodied by such heterogeneous genres as epic quests, ghost stories, thrillers, or even Harlequin romances, that has allowed for the articulation of a more intricate relation to reality, whereby the status of the referent has been problematised and the aporias of (fictional) temporality exposed. For Elam the peculiar strength of postmodern romance is precisely its radical undecidability and the disrupting hybridisation of time-honoured genres (22–24, 51–54); likewise, within the historical field, "trauma invites distortion, disrupts clear-cut definitions of genres" and "threatens to collapse distinctions" (LaCapra 96–97). The stylistic enactment of excess in romance is thus paralleled by the discursive inscription of traumatic symptoms through hyperbole in historiography (LaCapra 35). Indeed, this notion of excess has been capitalised upon in recent historical fiction in order to negotiate the multiple disjunctions between mimesis and the Real torn open by the horrors of twentieth-century traumatic history. Such a revised use of romance conventions by post-war historical novelists has obviously altered the rationale behind their construction of seemingly straightforward realistic plots. The possibility of their citation (in the "catastrophic" sense spelt out by Hannah Arendt) thus partakes of the discursive excess of romance (Jameson 104; Elam 51–73).

Alongside the representational problem of how to articulate a content at the furthest limit of any signifying system, contemporary historical fiction is also faced with the onto-epistemological problem of the present's troubling relation to its absent traumatic past, and the ethical one of "doing justice to the past" (Ricœur 1988, 152). It is this nearly unbearable burden, when suffered in terms of perverse fixation, that causes the phenomenological perception and the narrative representation of historical time to turn "monumental" (Nietzsche 1980, 16), i.e., petrified. In the case of the brand of postmodernist fiction christened "historiographic metafiction" by Linda Hutcheon (60–73), romance has seemed to provide a more resourceful narrative and rhetorical apparatus than either pure revivalist or pure modernist narratives to engage a conversation between history as non-representable "absent cause" (Jameson 146) and narrativity. Recently published British fiction where the phenomenon I have indicated undoubtedly holds true could make up an endless list. Just a few examples will suffice: Graham Swift's *Waterland* (1983), Pat Barker's *Regeneration Trilogy* (1991; 1993; 1995), Ian McEwan's *Black Dogs* (1992) and *Atonement* (2001), Sarah Waters's *The Night Watch* (2006) and *The Little Stranger* (2009). In these works, all variously engaged with the most unspeakable traumas of twentieth-century history, a proliferation of romance genres—self-consciously employed as questioning devices—has taken over narrative zones previously left unexplored in historical fiction.

ADAM THORPE'S UNSENTIMENTAL "HISTORICAL ROMANCES"

By his own admission, the poet and novelist Adam Thorpe is extremely sensitive to the epistemological and ethical problems underlying the representation of traumatic history; he is also acutely aware of the methodological complications encroaching on our aesthetic practices when dealing with the imaginative re-creation of the painfully troubled otherness of a still unsettled past (Hagenauer 221–30). The "burden" of history, conceived of as "eternal return" (Nietzsche 1969, 24), conspires to *ghost* historical representation (Derrida 123) in the "historical romances"[3] I intend to survey. On the one hand, Thorpe's narrative modality combines implausible postures of intradiegetic narration with multiply refracted focalisation: as a consequence, his fragmentary and dispersed narrating voices urge the reader to re-enact the characters' traumas by mimetically positioning him/her in complicitous proximity with the representational (and phenomenological) aporias brought to them by their symptomatic allegiance to "monumental history." On the other hand, the *un*realistic expectations activated by a large array of romance conventions—deployed under the versatile guises of crime-, ghost-, love story, Gothic tale of doubling, murder mystery, folk legend, classical myth, or family romance—are calculated to undo the most unquestionably *fated* heritage of the past, wherein history literally keeps repeating itself within an over-arching evil scheme.

By redeploying fated history as the virtually endless generativity of arbitrary plot constraints, romance as a mode offers the readers of Thorpe's novels rich alternative options to the "hauntingly possessive ghosts" (LaCapra xi) of the traumatic past. As long as they are willing to embark on the hermeneutic and affective work demanded, they can bring to fruition—in the space of their own lived experience[4]—history's unintended outcomes. As we shall see, Thorpe's fiction utilises as its own material the narrative performance conventionally ascribed to its referential other(s). Whether it reads like surreal war memoirs, implausible ghost stories, clichéd love triangles, hackneyed social comedies of village life, unexplained murder mysteries, "posthumous" films, anachronistic pageants, or blunt satires of pastoral mysticism, each of these genres dictates by turns a specific mimetic test of the respective risks of monumental history and of the inherently anachronistic historical impulse of romance (Elam 75).

A failure to appreciate Thorpe's tropological approach to historical discourse has vexed the reception of his fictional work since the publication of his first novel, *Ulverton* (1992). Although ostensibly chronicling the hypothetical history of an invented English village from 1650 to 1988, the transition from one chapter to the next across the twelve episodes of which it consists is advertised as a doubly traumatic affair. Discursively, it is characterised by conspicuous self-reflexive formal ruptures; in terms of plot, each episode dwells on a reiterated history of violence whose unaccountability is troped as some unresolved mystery which has affected the lives of successive generations of locals and outsiders. Inbuilt in the final revelation through which the readers learn that all the "stories" have in fact been concocted by "[t]his bloke Thorpe. Alan Thorpe" (1993, 379) is a surfeit of romance *topoi* which offers an ironically qualified key to the disclosure of a half-forgotten, half-remembered, mostly.fabricated history.

Rejecting any sensational coverage of the large-scale horrors of the two world wars and focusing instead on single episodes which take on their paradigmatic significance in the metonymic register of fittingly partial supplement to the unrepresentable Real, Thorpe's later fiction has continued exploring the legacy of traumatic history, much in the terms established by his debut novel. Throughout, the transformative potential borne by romance's flexible handling of genre conventions has allowed the novelist to devise an *excessive* representational space (Elam 76–79) wherein ample narrative room has been made for the implausible occurrence, so germane to the endemic "anachronism" of romance, to materialise in the least predictable historical forms (Elam 69–75), i.e., away from a metaphysical understanding of traumatic history as the "experience of necessity" (Jameson 101).

The bold experimentalism of *Still* (1995) borrows its structure from a layering of the codes and tropes of film scripting onto those of extreme stream-of-consciousness techniques. At the turn of the new millennium, the protagonist is engaged in filming a lengthy docudrama about Edwardian England until the climactic outbreak of WWI. The collective catastrophe interlocks in crucial ways with the character's obsessive search for his origins, and the equally obsessive diagnosis of the reasons why both his romantic and professional pursuits have failed him. The disturbance that trans-generational trauma brings to the ordinary experience of (historical) time is such that the singularity of the event comes apart. WWI always happens again, re-enacted in the eternal present*s* of WWII, Vietnam and any other major historical disasters: "We'll come back to the end that we already know, at the end. [. . .] But it'll all be the same, exactly the same" (Thorpe 1995, 152–53). The film's failure to perform its intended "homeopathic" cure ends up freezing the protagonist-narrator's ritual of reparation into the phantasmatic hallucinatory presence of melancholia. The trace of those who are no longer (the WWI dead) is thus imparted a paradoxically absent persistence, haunting even the time to come in the way of an unsolved enigma: "I'm making a film that doesn't exist. [. . .] Maybe this film that doesn't exist will play to an empty room. Empty except for myself, which is really empty. What a great metaphor for the brain." (Thorpe 1995, 232).

Although Thorpe's later novels have adopted less complex narrative strategies, they are concerned with similar representational, onto-epistemic and ethical problems. Consistently with the "uncertain generic construction of romance" (Elam 82), the five sections making up *Pieces of Light* (1998) cast the historical and private events in Hugh Arkwright's life—straddling two continents and two world wars—within incompatible and yet equally compelling narratives. Each retelling—be it as mystery, ghost story, folk legend, or unfulfilled family romance—yields a contradictory version of the "facts." The protagonist is haunted, in a kind of two-timed narrative loop suggestive of a doubly displaced, unspeakable traumatic wound, by the "ghost" of his stepmother and by the phantasmatic smell of wild garlic, alternatively mistaken for WWI mustard gas (Thorpe 1999, 326) and

WWII nerve gas (305–07). The protagonist's search for origins reveals, on a seemingly lesser scale, that personal trauma is historically motivated and always branching out towards the collective trauma of colonialism and war. His imagination of the future as an exact repetition of the past thus illustrates the lures and dangers of "antiquarian history" (Nietzsche 1980, 19) for those living through trauma, perversely enacting a mockery of Nietzsche's "eternal return."

Because *Nineteen Twenty-One* (2001) is circumscribed to the historical moment conveyed by the title, at first sight, it would seem less caught in the deadlock of traumatic repetition. This impression would appear to be reinforced by the fact that its protagonist, the aspiring novelist Joseph Monrow, is engaged in the writing of the "great War book" (Thorpe 2005a, 304) and that his effort towards making sense of that single unprecedented shock is meant to accomplish the ultimate "homeopathic" reparatory act. Nevertheless, from his phantasmally vacant writing position—for Joseph did miss the trenches by chance (44)—his struggle to bestow a publicly resonant significance on his creative act cannot but be in vain. Indeed, the aspiring novelist fails to historicise his own traumatic experience in the first place. During his "trench tour" across the surreally spectral landscape of post-war ruins at Ypres and the Somme area, he rather becomes aware of his stereotypically romantic worldview and the profound gulf between the mass-scale destruction and death and his desultory reaction to it. Projected on this least propitious of settings, the disjunction between the protagonist's unsentimental romance and the ethical imperative of mourning publicly the WWI dead (166, 168) reveals how haunted by a dead past his literary ritual of reparation is doomed to be. The conflation of historical and structural trauma causes the singular contingency to collapse into a pathological literalisation of the timeless mythical encounter between life and death. This conflation is what elevates to the rank of atemporal universality an ironically scaled-down version of epiphanic revelation borrowed from the apocalyptic modernist discourse of history as catastrophe (153).

Through a triangular orchestration of "posthumous" inner voices, *The Rules of Perspective* (2005) splices up backwards the sundry fragments of the last day of three groups of people that WWII and chance brought together in the German town of Lohenfelde. The narrative shifts back and forth from a group of civilians to members of the occupying Anglo-American army, to an anonymous hidden Jewish girl. In parallel fashion with the former novels, here again, grand rituals of reparation are endlessly repeated, only to be miserably brought to an end with the characters' last breath under collapsed heaps of unromantic rubble (Thorpe 2005b, 337). The discordant temporalities separately inhabited by each of the three groups converge in one uncanny fold of suspended time, wherein none of the characters is yet dead but stands still on the threshold, as it were. The narrative is lent a disquieting sort of ghostly closure when the readers shudder into a belated recognition that this flickering encounter between life and death has failed to relieve the characters from their unaccountably meaningless deaths (118). Consistently with the traumatic ghosting of historical representation borne out by "the event at the limits" (Friedlander 3), the narrative focus increasingly turns on the least embodied presence of all, that of the Jewish girl. Her textual body—hardly her own, for she borrows incongruous verbal scraps from the other characters and from a number of crowning giants of the German-Jewish literary tradition—is only posthumously restored to an ambiguous memorial place in the reader's present.[5]

Set in contemporary rural France, *The Standing Pool* (2008) weaves together several narrative threads in a sinister chronicle of mysterious incidents occurring in a country-house possessed with a disturbing life of its own. Violence seethes just beneath the surface, for the looming shadow of WWII is construed as *the* primal crime: "a hangover from the war. All those German atrocities. Sins of the fathers" (Thorpe 2009, 121). The burden of past evils thus lingers on, marking the collectivisation and transgenerational legacy of traumatic history, darkening the present with the delayed consequences of a compulsion to repeat that reaches out to the horrors of the Iraqi War and those attending the ruthless oil exploitation of postcolonial Africa. The traumatic impact of un(re)presentable, belated suffering triggers trans-generational identification with the experience/ voice of the victim, which has taken roots so deeply as to become properly the unwitting mourner's own: "You remind me of the Germans when they shot *me* in the back of the neck" (395, emphasis added). The pattern of repetition without variation, which sets apart the traumatic "event at the limits" (Friedlander 3) as being stalled within a temporal vacuum which annuls all distance across different generations, obliterates the distinction between self and other; as a consequence, the mourner's melancholy narrative is both dispossessed of and possessed by the past that he is bound to re-enact "from another part of his head" (399). Once again, the burden of monumental history turns what existed in the unmediated Real as a living memorial into the Imaginary's inadequate symbolic substitute endowed with the enigmatic traits of a failed private mourning rite. Even though the final realisation that the novel's chillingly climactic massacre (406) has in fact merely occurred within the pages of a "Comic Book" works to readjust the status of the referent, the mediation by the discourse of romance only serves to intensify the reader's unease. This arises not solely from the multiple rehearsals of excruciatingly traumatising events, but especially from an inability to decide what generic conventions could best manage such narrative excesses. Despite the fact that the quite unexpected bathetic ending forces the reader to revise any former tragic configuration, the discourse of fate—translated in terms of narrative necessity—disables the discursive/ ideological conditions upon which the reader might be willing to buy the novel's putative closure. As a consequence, its rather hesitant and belated turn to "comedy" only sporadically dispels the feeling of very real tragedy and impending doom under whose spell the characters are left.

TRAUMATIC ABSENCE OF THE HAUNTING PAST

As Freud famously conjectured in such early essays as "Remembering, Repeating and Working Through," "Mourning and Melancholia," "Fixation to Traumas—The Unconscious," "The Uncanny," and expanded on in "Beyond the Pleasure Principle," compulsive repetition signals a defensive mechanism the psyche puts up as a response to trauma. Leaving aside Freud's ground-breaking contribution to the diagnosis of shock-induced memory pathologies, I will pause on the paradoxical configuration this mechanism assumes in his theory, as it comes remarkably close to the description of the temporal and discursive disruptions proper of romance. To the traumatised self a void manifests the unbearable displaced content that is no longer or not yet there: "New, more deep-seated drive-impulses—still nascent rather than fully established—can emerge as repetition" (Freud 1955, 39). Likewise, romance depends on delayed repetition for the logical/discursive breakdown wrought by traumatic events to show in its remotest effects; and it gestures to absence, too, in its narrative withdrawal from any direct textualisation of those disarranging effects. A mimetic as well as a figural failure is, therefore, shared by the symptomatic discourse of trauma and by the stylistic peculiarities of romance, both crucially revealing of a traumatic intermission. LaCapra concurs with this interpretation when he specifies that writing trauma eventuates a chronotopic dispossession, "if only because trauma cannot be localised in terms of discrete, dated experience," but it depends on a "shattering break or caesura in experience which has belated effects" (186). Like the plight of those living through trauma who, haunted by the ghosts of the past, dwell in a strangely evacuated, anachronic present, romance's estranged disposition towards the past is unfailingly marked out by "anachronism" (Elam 31–45). Contrary to the common-sense belief that, by receding into the past, the reality/vividness of events fades, with trauma and historical romance quite the opposite occurs in complex ways (Caruth 1996, 153–54). As one of Thorpe's characters perceptively realises, "It remained a kind of abstraction. [. . .] But as time went on, and it dwindled into the past, she believed in it more and more. It became this concentrated point of intensity in her life" (Thorpe 2009, 47).

Benveniste's well-known linguistic distinction between *histoire* and *discours* (Benveniste 206–07) would seem to suggest that, if pure historical narration were ever possible, it would emanate from a paradoxically self-effacing, irretrievable narrating origin (208). In this sense, it would reduplicate the mimetically and figurally blank locus of trauma, on the one hand, and that of historical romance, on the other. From this double fading, there descends a certain ghostly nature of *histoire*, as though the uncanny structure of trauma inhered in history *per se*, if only on the plane discursively articulated within the elusive configurations of romance. Even LaCapra, who protests—for quite commendable socio-political and ethical reasons—against any blurring of distinctions between specific "historical losses" and existentially constitutive "trans-historical absence" (xiii–xiv), admits that the confusion, when it occurs, is witness to the overwhelming impact of traumatic events (46, 49–52). In his turn, although regarding it as a purely "internal limit," Ricœur similarly underlines how "narration exceeds itself to the point of exhaustion, in attempting to draw near the inscrutable" (1988, 271). As Elam argued, confusion and excess are to be regarded as hallmarks of romance, particularly in its postmodern varieties (1–15). Far from being regretted, these properties make for a very suitable envoy to deliver on the scene of history the hopeful promise of change. Thanks to the tropes of romance, contingency—no longer understood within the limits of linear causality, where it truly reflects the time of catastrophe—can do its work outside the stalled pattern of traumatic repetition.

Indeed, anyone in the grip of traumatic history can hardly aspire to be the narrative's originating locus, let alone a vehicle of its transmission to posterity, unless s/he embraces the tentative opportunities offered by the tropological resources of romance. As Ricœur emphasises, it is "[f]iction [that] gives eyes to the horrified narrator" (1988, 188), who would otherwise find it impossibly hard to choose the appropriate representational stance between bare historical description—"counting the cadavers" (188)—and narrative vindication—"telling the story of the victims" (188).[6] As a narrative mode "standing for" a past that is absent, the ethical strength of romance—being more than blunt mimetic representation but less than direct metonymy—lies in its "capacity for provoking an illusion of presence, but one controlled by critical distance" (188). Much like Marc Bloch's characterisation of vestigial historical documents (oral testimony, personal memories) and residual monuments (debris and ruins) as "witnesses in spite of themselves" (2004, 178), in Thorpe's historical romances the least plausible voices are placed into the moral witness's position. Precisely because they are *not* up to the ethical demands implicit in that role, the romance mode they variously dramatise comes to manifest what is *not there*, namely, history as "absent cause."

On this larger scale, the exile from one's own being, enacted through the interruptive temporality of romance, shows where the risk of its latent melancholia might lie. Insofar as "[r]omance can never do justice to the past because the dead can never speak on their own behalf" (Elam 75), the "work of mourning for the past" (Elam 68) that romance performs may propel some unconscious desire to "invest trauma with value and make its reliving a painful but necessary commemoration or memorial" (LaCapra 22). In this case, the discourse of romance would reinstate the traumatic past to ghostly presence as the nearly inconceivable, literally unre-presentable, frozen moment wherein time would finally come to stand "still." As the narrator of *Pieces of Light* uncannily discerns, "When time stops, spirits can be summoned. They slip in and out between one moment and the next" (Thorpe 1999, 267). The obsessive reiteration of the lexemes "spirits," "phantoms" and "ghosts" in Thorpe's historical romances, travelling from the stylistic function of metaphysically dense echoing refrain to the thematic and structural significance of a veritable symbolic leitmotif, and beyond to full-blown narrative subgenre, abundantly bears out the melancholic slant attached to romance when articulating "the absent of history." As Michel de Certeau convincingly argues,

> Through these combinations with an absent term, history [. . .] manifests the very condition of discourse: *a death*. [. . .] Its work consists in creating the absent, in making signs scattered over the surface of current times become the traces of "historical" realities, missing indeed because they are other. (46, original emphasis)

From this literally phantasmatic (narrative) configuration there arises the unsolved tension—textualised as contradictory demands elicited by different generic conventions—between the depiction of "ghosts" as matter-of-course romance paraphernalia and a sceptical construal that lends the uncertain experience of sighting/being a ghost (Thorpe 2005a, 148–49) an unstable figural status. Such radical undecidability is troped as both the absolute metaphysical absence of the expired past[7] and the uncanny posthumous trace of its haunting presence:

> *I am not at all certain I am alive. What is being alive?* [. . .] *The birds are alive, but that is no proof of my own existence: just as words in a book can bring pictures, but the words are not alive, they are an illusion of life* [. . .]. *What proof is there that, anyway, everything we experience is not invented by us?* (Thorpe 2005b, 50, 60, original italics)

If this is the case, if "writing plays the role of a burial rite [. . .]; it exorcises death by inserting it into discourse" (de Certeau 100), no narrative could be expected to "redeem" us from the burden of the haunting past, except as a Derridian supplement, which, by paradoxical counter-evidence, proves past existence to have already been a simulacrum (Derrida 48). However, the bracketing of a too distressing historical reality is never comfortably displaced onto *absent* textual simulacra in Thorpe's diegetic world. In most cases the ethical implications are so outrageous that no metafictional sleight of hand can lay them to rest, as with the Jewish girl in *The Rules of Perspective*: indeed, her diary entries—not incidentally appearing in a different typeface, as if to mark out the aporetic liminality she inhabits—repeatedly doubt even the negative ontology shared by the other characters: "*I am not even a ghost*" (2005b, 12, *passim*, original italics).

LEARNING THE LESSON OF HISTORY
AS HOMEOPATHIC REMEDY

Compulsive repetition, eternised instant, iterative past—the ghostly temporality of trauma—disable the possibility to live fully in the present. Nietzsche's "eternal return" could well be the time of traumatic history, as Thorpe's novels seem to indicate: "Oncle Fernand is used to this, he was in the war. He has been in every war since then [. . .]. They're all the same" (Thorpe 2009, 409). Leafing through history's frustratingly identical re-enactments of its least uplifting pages, Thorpe's historical romances insinuate that, as the historian Nick Mallinson puts it in *The Standing Pool*, "'[t]he first lesson of history is the good of evil.' [. . .] Actually, history is tragic. No one ever learns from it" (2009, 187). Thus, the hopelessly short-sighted wish of the idealistic WWI writer Joseph Monrow in *Nineteen Twenty-One*[8] and the outrageously twisted historical interpretation of a current crisis, to opposite effects, of the sleazy antique art dealer Alan Sandler in *The Standing Pool*[9] prove both horribly wrong. Their antithetical views are ultimately predicated upon the *same* misconception about the historical imagination, that is to say, about the cultural and ideological conditions needed for a personally and collectively lived past to be recognised as being of our own making. Thus, the contemporary narrator of *Still* reiterates his great-uncle's censure of the college educators for their failure to take their share of historical responsibility at the outbreak of WWI. In the narrator's own words:

> [T]his is the mythology of the faces burdened with their own futures, the bastards and the brilliants [. . .]. Yet the fact remains that my great-uncle condemns them all from the grave. For they [college educators] did nothing. They are about to do nothing. Big deal. Isn't that the lesson of history? (Thorpe 1995, 105)

Thorpe's question harks back to Nietzsche's warning about the "abuses of history"—what instigated the peculiar "historical malady" of modern man, living "in a never to be completed imperfect tense" (Nietzsche 1980, 9)—and the philosopher's urge to forgetfulness, i.e., to live "unhistorically":

> Cheerfulness, a good conscience, belief in the future, the joyful deed— all depend, in the individual as well as the nation, on there being a line that divides the visible and clear from the vague and shadowy: we must know the right time to forget, as well as the right time to remember, and instinctively see when it is necessary to feel historically and when unhistorically. (Nietzsche 1980, 7)[10]

Nietzsche seems to have embraced the peculiar notion—enacted in Thorpe's fiction—that the "diseased" modern historical imagination entertains a paradoxically *willed* relation to history and memory. His urge to "forget-fulness" could thus indicate a way of getting over, against all odds, the rep-etition-compulsion ingrained in traumatic history. Thus, the most severely traumatised character of *The Standing Pool*, Jean-Luc Maille, believes that what he calls "[t]he foreign riff-raff," that is, the occupying Nazis in the past, just like the English tenants in the present, "are still in occupation if a single person is left [alive]," so that "Oncle Fernand will be forced back up the track and shot through the nape once more" (2009, 410–11).

In order to avoid mimetically re-enacting the past, as is wont to be, it should be "forgotten": "It requires great strength to be able to live and for-get how far life and injustice are one" (Nietzsche 1980, 21). Not absolutely, however: Ricœur ascribes to Nietzsche's view of history the nature of Pla-to's *pharmakon*, "oscillating between poison and remedy" (Ricœur 2004, 287). As Thorpe's historical romances would appear to suggest, learning the lesson of history may entail that the repetition-compulsion be played off against singularity "homeopathically," as both symptom and antidote:

I've played this scene a thousand time [. . .] I know it by heart, I know every word before it comes [. . .] But you're gonna see it once, once only. Unique printing. Nothing happens in this world MORE THAN ONCE. It's called entropy [. . .]. (1995, 306–07)

"You can't kill a man twice [. . .]. Only once." (2009, 415)

In this connection, Ricœur considers diverse approaches to such a dilemma by taking Plato's discussion of "the Same, the Other, the Analo-gous" in *Sophist* as an explanatory model of different historical concep-tions (1988, 143). Within the logic of the Same, "[t]he past is intelligible only as persisting in the present" (144); by means of "a de-distanciation, an identification with what once was," it stages a "re-enactment of the past" (144). At the opposite end, when the emphasis is laid on the otherness of the past, its temporal distance is restored through the affirmation of its irreduc-ible difference (147). Conversely, the metaphorical logic of the Analogous conceives of history as "'being-affected' by the past" (207), so that "[t]he complex interplay of the Same and the Other" allows for the past "to be re-enacted in the mode of identity," even as it remains "absent from all our constructions" (155).

As we have seen, neither the figment of the past as irretrievably lost, nor that of its persistence in the present due to the arrested temporal sameness of Nietzsche's eternal return describes Thorpe's "historicizing method" (Jameson 115), which is rather epitomised by the paradox of the trace: "visible here and now as a vestige" of something passed/past which it does not cause to appear (Ricœur 1988, 119). As we have seen, Thorpe's histori-cal romances narrativise a complexly ubiquitous and erratic "sense of the past," which Benjamin defined vividly: "History is the subject of a structure whose site is not homogeneous, empty time, but time filled with the presence of the now" (252–53). Such an aesthetic and ethical agenda underlying Thorpe's re-writing of the past is what justifies the writer's otherwise distressing return to the same traumatic chronotopes troped in excess of the "event at the limits" (Friedlander 3). If one intends to chart what narrative strategies Thorpe has devised to counter a representation of history as endlessly repeated horror and tries to assess what narrative configurations emerge from his rejection of the limitations entailed by the referential impasse of traumatic realism, one may usefully attend to the complex narrative function the novelist has conferred on the interplay between repetition and the unintended results of chance triggered off by the hermeneutic dispositif of emplotment (Ricœur 1984, 31–51).

The tradition of genre criticism and rhetorical tropology, started by Aristotle and revived by such critics as Northrop Frye, Frank Kermode, Mikhail Bakhtin, and Fredric Jameson, has handed down to the school of historiography, of which Hayden White is a prominent member, the conceptual model that identifies the structuration of sets of historical events on the grounds of the distinctive encoding of certain plot types, namely, Romance, Tragedy, Comedy, or Satire (White 5–11). Accordingly, the historical imagination is understood as being shaped by certain tropological categories, inasmuch as the meaning of events is figured out in terms of Metaphor, Metonymy, Synecdoche, and Irony (31–38). Having emphasised how close to each other Marx's and Nietzsche's philosophies of history are in many respects (276–79), White points out one crucial distinction: whereas Marx's historiographical model privileged "the *mode of explanation* to be used in characterizing its structures and processes" (279, original emphasis), Nietzsche's interest centred on "the *mode of emplotment* to be chosen for the creative explication of a phenomenal field that appeared not to be governed by any law whatsoever" (279, original emphasis). While in Marx an implicitly deterministic idea of causation confines historical agency and ethical responsibility to the repetition of the same script either as tragedy or as farce,[11] in other words, in terms of mutually exclusive generic histories, Nietzsche is willing to take heed of the otherness of history as the field of chance irreducible to rational laws.

Depending as it does on a fundamentally *anachronistic* structure (in Elam's sense), romance allows for the simultaneous inscription of historical narration into multiple generic histories. Instead of complying with the logical and representational demands of a Marxian scheme of historical determinism, the discontinuities tolerated by romance construct faulty Nietzschean laws of causation within the irreversible arrow of chronological time. The co-emergence of diverse temporal ontologies is what suddenly jolts off track the representation of history as ineluctable catastrophe in Thorpe's historical romances, no longer compelled to rehearse the unspeakability of trauma by compulsively repeating it *in the same order*: "Towards the end of his life [. . .], Jean-Luc's father would talk about nothing else

but the war: always the same stories, in the same order, as if he were bur-
rowing back, finding the reason why it all happened" (2009, 163).[12]

Romance as a mode of emplotment is associated with metaphor by
White.[13] By slightly extending White's metahistorical model, Ricœur further connects romance with the temporalising function of the trace, which
"stands for" the past while taking its place (1988, 151). According to this
reading, the metaphorical structuration of romance depends on deferred
repetition in order to bring to light what was blocked out from the ordinary temporal horizon, eminently on account of traumatic experiences.
Romance thus serves the unsentimental function of unlocking a narrative
gateway out of the deadly repetition entailed by the petrified memorialisation of the past. The interesting implication, one particularly fruitful
when applied to Thorpe's historical romances, is that repetition, by pointing to its own mechanisms of displacement, that is, to the figural borders
where the excessive discourse of romance resides, causes loss and absence
to operate as the trace for the otherness of the traumatic past to be able to
register in narrative discourse. In this acceptation, romance is the mode of
emplotment best suited "to keep otherness from slipping into the unsayable" (Ricœur 1988, 184).

The role of romance as "the imaginary aspect of standing-for" the absent
"other" (Ricœur 1988, 185) could be figured out—borrowing from one
of Thorpe's characters a telling oxymoronic phrase—as "the uncontrolled
and deliberate accident of it" (2005b, 89–90), in other words, as some sort
of contingency control device prompted by the peculiarly undecidable liminality of romance as a mode of emplotment. Of course, this dream of control cannot but be formulated as an ineradicable paradox, for contingency
is emphatically placed on the side of historical necessity by Thorpe.[14] In
Ricœur's words,

> [W]e are affected by history and [. . .] we affect ourselves by the his-
> tory we make. It is precisely this tie between historical action and a
> received past, which we did not make, that preserves the dialectical
> relation between our horizon of expectation and our space of experi-
> ence. (1988, 213)

Similarly, Thorpe makes of loss and finitude, through the mediating role
of historical time, the necessary price to be paid in order to live historically. Frye reminds us that conventional narrative structures, teleologically
transcending past trials towards self-realisation and final revelation, carry
a redemptive meaning (158–206). However, with their resistance to har-
monising endings, where comedy does not unambiguously win over tragedy, Thorpe's historical romances reject any facile redemptive closure. This
resistance, on the writer's part, could well account for his mildly enigmatic,
unfinal and anti-climactic denouements, often narrativised as happy endings of sorts, without actually being felt to be so by the characters, not even

ironically. For example, in *Nineteen Twenty-One*, the incongruous rekindling of Joseph Monrow's unsentimental romance with a German woman he had experienced his sexual initiation with in post-war Ypres inverts all expected inversions:

> A shape in front of the window. [. . .] He went rigid with terror [. . .]. The sheer surprise. It was her. [. . .] Then the laughter took hold of him [. . .]. He could not stop laughing while she looked on in astonishment. (2005a, 370, 371)

Regretting his own guilt-ridden marriage proposal earlier on—"It was as if her sense of destiny was gigantic, much too big for him" (359)—Joseph is now taken aback, no less than the readers themselves, because totally unprepared for the "happy ending" the German woman unexpectedly announces.

Likewise, Nick Mallinson's urge "to burst into laughter, a fit of hilarity swelling in his belly" (Thorpe 2009, 325) hardly tolerates a realistic reading in terms of a mere hysterical reaction to his daughters having gone missing: in fact, comedy and tragedy—"ominousness," "entertaining evilly nasty thoughts" (325)—inconclusively fight out for control of the narrative outcome: "two sides of the same coin: one awful, one fine. It was a question of how life flicked it, how it fell" (326).[15]

CONCLUSION

As has been claimed, the "reversal of the movement of history would require an apocalyptic erasure of modernity. Crossing the threshold of catastrophe is part of the teleology of fascist discourse" (Mengham 182). Thorpe has gone a long way to demystify this apocalyptic erasure of modernity as a falsely consoling lie functioning tropologically in the service of melancholia. In his diegetic universe, the debt to the past and to the dead is precisely what allows the lived experience of loss to offer the only authentic measure of reparation human beings may hope for: "That was how it had to be: a memory. A regret, even. Your life shapes itself around the empty spaces of regret" (Thorpe 2005a, 192).

This space is that of mourning, what LaCapra would call "a homeopathic socialization or ritualization of the repetition compulsion [. . .] that allow[s] for a measure of critical distance" (66). In this manner do Thorpe's historical romances manage to endow his unsentimental representations of traumatic vicissitudes in time, edged with the posthumous traces of vanished people and vanished acts, or even with absence, with a certain miraculous persistence, in other words, with some sort of paradoxical embodiment. Benveniste perceptively noticed how the logical-grammatical infractions of narrative, typified by the counterintuitive use of tenses and deixis, establish an anomalous connection between narrativity and the moment of writing as an absent present in the past simple (219). This paradox exceeds the mere linguistic plane and extends into the metaphysical hermeneutic of history; in this sense, it turns out to be the enabling condition for the transformation of all-encompassing trans-historical absence, which haunts the contagiously annihilating act of narrating trauma with the ghostly shadows of death, placelessness and silence, into a constitutive moment of return, through what Franz K. Stanzel would call the narrators' "corporeality" (qt. in Chatman 82–87) back to "'real' objects, to 'historical' times and places" (Benveniste 219).

NOTES

1. While endorsing the widely accepted notion of "unique event" with respect to the Holocaust (Friedlander 1–21), LaCapra shifts the sense from unrepeatable to outrageous limit experience. This shift has the merit of emphasising the paradoxically disarranging/deranged temporality of traumatic history as something unique that nevertheless is repeated (160).
2. For a view of the Real, or the literal, in Lacanian terms as inherently traumatic and therefore unknowable and unrepresentable, except figuratively or allegorically, see Caruth 1995, 3–12, 128–57, and Felman and Laub.
3. The label is here employed in the sense specified by Elam with reference to Walter Scott's romances, where traditional romance features are juxtaposed, combined and even commingled with plot requirements spuriously engendered by the contradictory demands placed upon them by the realistic conventions of the historical novel (Elam 51–79).
4. This is the hermeneutic moment called "mimesis$_3$" by Ricœur, when the fictional world connects in existentially significant ways with the real one of the readers through the act of "refiguration" (1984, 76–82).
5. "Exhibited alongside the painting [at the "Peace exhibition" held in Lohenfelde in 1964] is a notebook [. . .] containing the diary of an unknown Jewish girl in hiding [. . .]. [T]his anonymous diary is a moving testament to courage in the face of the Fascist horror" (Thorpe 2005b, 341).
6. LaCapra comes close to Ricœur when he regards the ethical task of historiography to be that of restoring to victims the dignity they were deprived of, or also when he acknowledges the ultimate inadequacy of its symbolical compensation for events that can never be fully compensated (178).
7. "As if Raoul Lagrange is everywhere. But he is nowhere, really" (Thorpe 2009, 252).
8. "At least Germany, he thought, would never make the same mistake again" (2005a, 307).
9. "The invasion [of Iraq] would be regarded as a fine, honourable decision in a hundred years' time, and [. . .] any other view was a failure of historical imagination" (2009, 364).
10. Ricœur pauses on the Nietzschean bid to forget arguing that, by forcing the "burden" of the past on individual consciousness, the "ability to remember" of the "modern historical culture" has in fact rendered individual and collective memory, no less than their respective pathologies, structurally interchangeable (1988, 236). The ascendancy, at the turn of the nineteenth century, of this psychopathological aspect of historical culture is what incensed Nietzsche for the reasons outlined above; on the other hand, this

same notion has authorised LaCapra to extend the scope of his unorthodox psychoanalytic approach to the discussion of historical trauma (141–45).

11. "Hegel remarks somewhere that all facts and personages of great importance in world history occur, as it were, twice. He forgot to add: the first time as tragedy, the second as farce" (Marx and Engels qt. in White 320).

12. Interestingly, Freud employs the very phrases here illustrating how traumatic experiences repeat themselves *exactly* and unwittingly to describe the antithetical case of a child's pleasurable experience of controlled repetition: "If he has been told a pretty story, he wants always to hear the same story instead of a new one, insists inexorably on exact repetition and corrects each deviation which the narrator lets slip by mistake" (Freud 1955, 62).

13. See "Michelet: Historiography Explained as Metaphor and Emplotted as Romance" (in White 149–62).

14. "The black loop's [symbolising the ominous fate of WWI casualties] settled like a halo [. . .], no one can erase it, [. . .] and say, start again, don't die, just hide your head on that last day" (Thorpe 1995, 147).

15. Thorpe's distrust of teleologically oriented narrative is fully allegorised by the unresolved discrepancy between the carefully timed, pre-planned suicide of the protagonist of *Still* and his film's aborted end: "In the closing minutes of the film as shown and apparently 'interrupted' there were several mentions of Hoovers in connection with death and certainly with the end of the film. [. . .] this calls into question the idea that he [. . .] had no notion that his film overran by ten hours or that it would be forcibly halted in mid-showing" (1995, 454, 455).

WORKS CITED

Arendt, Hannah. "Introduction." In Walter Benjamin, *Illuminations*, 7–58. Print.
Bakhtin, Mikhail. *The Dialogic Imagination*. Ed. Michael Holquist. Trans. Caryl Emerson and Michael Holquist. Austin: U of Texas P, 1981. 84–258. Print.
Barker, Pat. *Regeneration*. London: Viking, 1991. Print.
———. *The Eye in the Door*. London: Viking, 1993. Print.
———. *The Ghost Road*. London: Viking, 1995. Print.
Benjamin, Walter. *Illuminations*. Ed. and intro. Hannah Arendt. Trans. Harry Zohn. 1968. London: Pimlico, 1999. Print.
Benveniste, Émile. *Problems in General Linguistics*. 1966. Trans. Mary Elizabeth Meek. Coral Gables, Fla.: U of Miami P, 1971. Print.
Berger, James. *After the End: Representations of Post-Apocalypse*. Minneapolis: U of Minnesota P, 1999. Print.
Caruth, Cathy, ed. *Trauma: Explorations in Memory*. Baltimore, MD: The Johns Hopkins UP, 1995. Print.
———. *Unclaimed Experience: Trauma, Narrative, and History*. Baltimore, MD: The Johns Hopkins UP, 1996. Print.
Chatman, Seymour. *Story and Discourse: Narrative Structure in Fiction and Film*. Ithaca, NY: Cornell UP, 1978. Print.
de Certeau, Michel. *The Writing of History*. 1975. Trans. Tom Conley. New York: Columbia UP, 1988. Print.
Derrida, Jacques. *Specters of Marx*. 1993. Intro. Bernd Magnus and Stephen Cullenberg. Trans. Peggy Kamuf. London and New York: Routledge, 1994. Print.
Elam, Diane. *Romancing the Postmodern*. London: Routledge, 1992. Print.

Felman, Shoshana and Dori Laub. *Testimony: Crises of Witnessing in Literature, Psychoanalysis and History.* New York and London: Routledge, 1992. Print.

Freud, Sigmund. "Beyond the Pleasure Principle." 1920. *The Standard Edition of the Complete Psychological Works* Vol. XVIII. Ed. James Strachey. London: Hogarth P, 1955. 7–64. Print.

———. "Remembering, Repeating and Working Through." 1914. *The Standard Edition of the Complete Psychological Works* Vol. XII. Ed. James Strachey. London: Hogarth P, 1958. 145–56. Print.

———. "Mourning and Melancholia." 1915/1917. *The Standard Edition of the Complete Psychological Works* Vol. XIV. Ed. James Strachey. London: Hogarth P, 1957. 243–58. Print.

———. "Fixation to Traumas—The Unconscious." 1917. *The Standard Edition of the Complete Psychological Works* Vol. XIV. Ed. James Strachey. London: Hogarth P, 1971. 273–85. Print.

———. "The Uncanny." 1919. *The Standard Edition of the Complete Psychological Works* Vol. XVII. Ed. James Strachey. London: Hogarth P, 1957. 217–56. Print.

Friedlander, Saul. "Introduction." *Probing the Limits of Representation: Nazism, and the "Final Solution."* Ed. Saul Friedlander. Cambridge, Mass.: Harvard UP, 1992. 1–21. Print.

Frye, Northrop. *Anatomy of Criticism: Four Essays.* 1957. Harmondsworth: Penguin Books, 1990. Print.

Fussell, Paul. *The Great War and Modern Memory.* 1975. New York: Oxford UP, 2000. Print.

Gasiorek, Andrzej. *Post-War British Fiction: Realism and After.* London and New York: Edward Arnold, 1995. Print.

Hagenauer, Sabine. "An Interview with Adam Thorpe." *"Do you consider yourself a postmodern author?": Interviews with Contemporary English Writers.* Ed. Rudolf Freiburg and Jan Schnitker. Münster, Hamburg, London: Lit Verlag, 1999. 219–35. Print.

Hutcheon, Linda. *A Poetics of Postmodernism: History, Theory, Fiction.* London and New York: Routledge, 1988. Print.

Jameson, Fredric. *The Political Unconscious: Narrative as a Socially Symbolic Act.* Ithaca, NY: Cornell UP, 1981. Print.

LaCapra, Dominick. *Writing History, Writing Trauma.* Baltimore, MD.: The Johns Hopkins UP, 2001. Print.

Lyotard, Jean-François. *The Postmodern Condition: A Report on Knowledge.* Trans. Geoff Bennington and Brian Massumi. Minneapolis: U of Minnesota P, 1984. Print.

Marx, Karl and Frederick Engels, *The Eighteenth Brumaire of Louis Napoleon Bonaparte. Selected Works in Two Volumes.* Moscow: Foreign Languages Publishing House, 1958. Print.

McEwan, Ian. *Black Dogs.* London: Jonathan Cape, 1992. Print.

———. *Atonement.* London: Jonathan Cape, 2001. Print.

Mengham, Rod. "Fiction's History: Adam Thorpe." *British Fiction Today.* Eds. Philip Tew and Rod Mengham. London: Continuum, 2006. 177–85. Print.

Nietzsche, Friedrich. *Thus Spoke Zarathustra: A Book for All and None.* 1883–1885. Trans. T. J. Hollingdale. Harmonsworth: Penguin, 1969. Print.

———. *On the Advantage and Disadvantage of History for Life.* 1874. Trans. Peter Preuss. Indianapolis: Hackett, 1980. Print.

Ricœur, Paul. *Time and Narrative* Vol. 1. 1983. Trans. Kathleen Blamey and David Pellauer. Chicago and London: The U of Chicago P, 1984. Print.

————. *Time and Narrative* Vol. 3. 1985. Trans. Kathleen Blamey and David Pellauer. Chicago and London: The U of Chicago P, 1988. Print.

————. *Memory, History, Forgetting.* Trans. Kathleen Blamey and David Pellauer. Chicago and London: Chicago UP, 2004. Print.

Swift, Graham. *Waterland.* London: Heinemann, 1983. Print.

Tate, Trudi. *Modernism, History and the First World War.* Manchester and New York: Manchester UP, 1998. Print.

Thorpe, Adam. *Ulverton.* 1992. London: Minerva, 1993. Print.

————. *Still.* London: Quality Paperbacks Direct, 1995. Print.

————. *Pieces of Light.* 1998. London: Vintage, 1999. Print.

————. *Nineteen Twenty-One.* 2001. London: Vintage, 2005a. Print.

————. *The Rules of Perspective.* London: Jonathan Cape, 2005b. Print.

————. *The Standing Pool.* 2008. London: Vintage, 2009. Print.

Torgovnick, Marianna. *The War Complex: World War II in our Time.* Chicago: Chicago UP, 2005. Print.

Waters, Sarah. *The Night Watch.* London: Virago, 2006. Print.

————. *The Little Stranger.* London: Virago, 2009. Print.

Watson, Janet S. K. *Fighting Different Wars: Experience, Memory, and the First World War in Britain.* Cambridge: Cambridge UP, 2007. Print.

White, Hayden. *Metahistory: The Historical Imagination in Nineteenth-Century Europe.* Baltimore, MD.: The Johns Hopkins UP, 1973. Print.

Winter, Jay. *Remembering War: The Great War and Historical Memory in the 20th Century.* New Haven, CT, and London: Yale UP, 2006. Print.

10 Greek Romance, Alternative History and Political Trauma in Alan Moore and Dave Gibbons's *Watchmen*

Andrés Romero-Jódar

The decade of the 1980s proved to be an unprecedented melting pot of ideas and experimentation on the technical and narrative possibilities of comic books and graphic novels.[1] Works like Art Spiegelman's *Maus* (1978–91), Bryan Talbot's *The Adventures of Luther Arkwright* (1979–89), Raymond Briggs's *When the Wind Blows* (1982), or Neil Gaiman's *The Sandman* (1988–96), revolutionised the medium of narrative iconical productions and, in the Anglo-American context, laid the foundations for the recently-born graphic novel. Alan Moore and Dave Gibbons's *Watchmen*, originally issued in instalments between 1986 and 1987, stands out as one of the most influential graphic novels. Drawing on and simultaneously subverting the chronotope of the Greek romance, commonly employed in superhero comic books, this trailblazing text brings to the fore key political issues of our contemporary world by making use of the ethos of romance as a mode, while, at the same time, relying on a parodic rewriting of history. Thus, *Watchmen* can be considered a postmodern romance combining features of British historiographic metafiction with others associated with speculative fiction and science fiction, common to narrative iconical texts.

This essay aims to analyse how *Watchmen* constructs an alternative history of our contemporary world in which a peevish capitalist society is haunted by traumatic memories of the horrors provoked by politicians and suffered by the common citizen. By employing narrative techniques proper to trauma narratives like fragmentation, repetition and indirection, *Watchmen* constitutes a telling example of what can be labelled as "political trauma" (in contradistinction to other forms of individual and collective traumas such as "structural trauma," "punctual trauma," "cultural trauma," and "collective trauma," as defined by Dominick LaCapra, Greg Forter, Jeffrey C. Alexander and Kai Erikson, respectively). The defining trait of political trauma is that it destroys the social structures which confer meaning on the existence of the individual subject within a certain community. Political traumas, as will be argued, involve the frustrating discovery of mischievous truths lying underneath significant decisions taken by the representatives of a society and the rulers of a community. A political trauma is triggered by the unveiling of conspiracies in the corridors of power and the discovery of mass-scale manipulations of public opinion. A key early example of political trauma fiction is George Orwell's *Nineteen Eighty-Four* (1949). Moore's graphic novel forms part of a large set of texts produced throughout the decade of the 1980s that belong in this tradition.[2]

My starting hypothesis is that, in *Watchmen*, the traumatic memories of such atrocious genocides as the Holocaust and the bombing of Hiroshima and Nagasaki, directly caused by the political decisions of greedy and immoral representatives of society, are rethought not only as atrocities that traumatised whole communities (becoming cultural traumas for the Jews and the Japanese). They are primarily represented as examples of immoral political behaviour of greedy individuals in positions of power. Both genocidal events are rendered feasible through the massive use of propaganda and thought control, hidden under a morally dubious political discourse. And they provide the background to the irrationality and the state of paranoia that characterised the last years of the Cold War. Against this political and cultural context, *Watchmen* sets to represent the situation of Alan Moore's England in the 1980s, reflecting those political traumas that stem from the reactionary politics of Margaret Thatcher and her Conservative Governments between 1979 and 1990.[3]

GREEK ROMANCE AND ALTERNATIVE HISTORY

The narrative of *Watchmen* transports the reader to a fictional 1985 United States where Richard Nixon has been re-elected for the third time in a row. A most conspicuous feature of that society is the existence of masked adventurers who, allegedly, watch over the welfare and rightful morality of the community. They take the role of the police in fighting crime and social unrest. In 1959, after Dr. Jonathan Osterman suffered a work accident in an atomic research centre, he became the almighty Dr. Manhattan, a real superhero. Through the intervention of this god-like figure, the United States managed to win the Vietnam War in just two months (Moore and Gibbons 4: 20: 1).[4] However, neither this superman nor his masked counterparts are capable of stopping the race towards nuclear destruction brought about by the Cold War between the United States and the Soviet Union. This graphic novel depicts a society that, despite the presence of caped crusaders in its streets, dwells on the verge of nuclear self-annihilation for political reasons.

This alternative version of 1980s U.S. history is narrated through continuous flashbacks that represent the memories of the many characters that contribute to the narration. The linearity of time is shattered by the constant intrusions of the past into a present time in which a government agent and former vigilante called Edward Blake, also known as the Comedian, has just been murdered. Blake becomes the first victim of a mass-scale conspiracy that will lead to the destruction of the centre of New York and the massive killing of innocent citizens. Trying to save humanity from world-wide devastation, Adrian Veidt, a business tycoon and former masked adventurer, contrives a plot to stop the Cold War. In a secret research centre, his company works on a new technology that will teleport an artificially-made creature to New York so as to make the confronting governments believe that extraterrestrial aliens are invading the world. Veidt successfully makes politicians stop threatening each other and join forces against the common external (but non-existent) enemy. However, the process of teleportation not only acts as a political deterrent, it also kills three million New Yorkers.

The mental sanity of Edward Blake collapses when he discovers Veidt's conspiracy. Blake, then, painfully realises that every single truth he believed in is a lie. Having been a puppet during all his life, he was actually preparing the ground for people like Veidt, the epitome of popular capitalism, to take control of society from an economical perspective. Politically traumatised Blake is incapable of coping with the truth of having discovered the plan to kill three million of his own people for, allegedly, a better cause and, in an irrational reaction, he looks for consolation in his former enemy, a decadent and terminally ill villain called Edgar William Jacobi (Moloch). Subsequently, Veidt will arrange the killing of them both, thus providing the starting point of the narrative of *Watchmen*.

The history of that alternative world is plagued with traumatic memories of real historical events. The Second World War and the Holocaust, in the form of the name of a music band called *Krystalnacht*, and the bombing of Hiroshima, fashioned in the sprayed black silhouettes of the Hiroshima couple, are recurrent motifs in the world of *Watchmen*. Similarly, the Cold War is represented at its most tense point, becoming the reason for Blake's initial murder and the central topic of the graphic novel. As Margaret Ann Gray points out, this graphic novel "interrogate[s] the psychological, moral and social impact that the existence of nuclear weapons has on a generation who cannot see beyond the final exclamation mark of a mushroom cloud" (253). The 1980s fear of absolute annihilation through nuclear power in the real context of Moore's Thatcherite England is present in the fiction of the graphic novel.

As a narrative iconical text making use of superheroes, the most noteworthy aspect of *Watchmen* is the subversion of the chronotope of the Greek romance on which superhero narratives in comic books usually rely. Mikhail Bakhtin defined the chronotope (literally, "time space") as "the intrinsic connectedness of temporal and spatial relationships that are artistically expressed in literature" (84). Applying this concept to the ancient novel, Bakhtin differentiated among three categories: the Greek romance, the adventure novel of everyday life, and the ancient biography or autobiography. Drawing on the ideas of the Russian formalist, I established somewhere else a generic distinction between comic books and graphic novels according to the first two types (Romero-Jódar 102–06). I contended that comic books, as a genre, rely on the chronotope of the Greek romance, in which the protagonist, after the closure of the narration, "*keeps on being the same person* and emerges from this game, from all these turns of fate and chance, with his *identity* absolutely unchanged" (Bakhtin 105, original emphasis). The static nature of their identity allows comic-book characters to participate in never-ending adventures that do not modify their essential characteristics and, consequently, fit the needs of a market that creates long-running series, such as *Superman, Batman, Asterix*, or *Flash Gordon*.[5]

By contrast, the graphic novel may be said to rely on the chronotope of the adventure novel of everyday life. According to Bakhtin, this type of narrative depicts those exceptional moments in the character's life that "shape the definitive image of the man, his essence, as well as the nature of his entire subsequent life" (116). Therefore, "the most conspicuous element in [the graphic novel] is the possibility of *change*" (Romero-Jódar 104, original emphasis). According to this definition, Moore and Gibbons's *Watchmen* can be considered a graphic novel: its characters change and die, evolve and transform their essential identity alongside the unfolding of the narrative.

To the 1980s readership of narrative iconical texts the finding of a group of superheroes in a graphic novel was rather surprising. Until the 1980s, superhero characters were usually engaged in comic-book narratives that relied on a static Greek romance chronotope, created to repeat adventures *ad infinitum*. Comic-book readers were acquainted with the adventures of DC-Comics and Marvel-Comics characters, whereas graphic novels usually depicted complex stories aimed at mature audiences—such as Will Eisner's *A Contract with God* (1978). *Watchmen* defied the expectations of the readership, as its superhero characters were forced to face the passing of time in a narrative that took them to impending destruction.

Nonetheless, Moore and Gibbons's graphic novel can be said to employ romance, if not as a genre, as a mode. Jean-Michel Ganteau points to the renaissance of the romance as a mode in contemporary literature and highlights its characteristics in the following terms:

> Formally, romance is associated with emphatic closure, loosely strung, episodic plots, shallow characterization and a general bias in favour of polarisation and simplification (use of archetypes, allegories, etc.), along with a preference for congruence (some detractors might call that cheapness) and expressionism. All this is held together by the notion of excess, which may be why romance has often been defined in contrast to the novel: because it eschews verisimilitude, prefers the exotic to the familiar and the far to the near. (226)

The excessiveness of *Watchmen* is perfectly in keeping with this categorisation. Despite the complexity of the story, the plot is separated in clear-cut episodes that usually centre on single characters. For instance, Chapter Four recalls Dr. Manhattan's story; Chapter Six centres on Kovaks's life and how he became the masked vigilante Rorschach; and Chapter Eight describes the awkward relationship of Dan and Laurie, other two former masked adventurers. Obviously, this defies Ganteau's contention in the above quotation that the romance offers a "shallow characterization." The characters of *Watchmen* are given a deep psychological and emotional background that escapes the requirements of the romance and are more in consonance with those of the adventure novel of everyday life.

Nathaniel Hawthorne, on considering representation in romances in the preface to *The House of the Seven Gables* (1851), established a distinction between the novel and the romance, and stated that:

> [the romance] has fairly a right to present [...] truth under circumstances, to a great extent, of the writer's own choosing or creation. If he think fit, also, he may so manage his atmospherical medium as to bring out or mellow the lights, and deepen and enrich the shadows of the picture. (v)

Thus, the romance allows for the manipulation of the environment so as to produce a certain expressionistic effect even if the setting becomes completely fantastic. In contrast to this, Alan Moore sets a high value on the truth-telling capacity of all artistic forms, including fantasy fiction: "With fiction, with art, with writing, it is important that even if you are dealing with areas of complete outrageous fantasy, that there is an emotional resonance. It is important that a story ring true upon a human level, even if it never happened" (Vylenz).

Needless to say, the story in *Watchmen* never happened, and the world portrayed in the graphic novel never existed. However, by creating an alternative world, Moore and Gibbons's text comments on social issues which belong in our world, such as Hiroshima, the Holocaust, the Cold War, and Thatcherism. Thus, *Watchmen* questions the notion of mimesis as representation of reality in the same fashion as the romance, as a mode, does, according to Ganteau: "Romance turns its back on the realistic tradition and the realist idiom to suggest an alternative field of investigation and an alternative way of *presenting* as opposed to representing, a way of creatively questioning mimesis" (237, original emphasis). The romance element in *Watchmen* may be said to become a vehicle for social comment in that it metafictionally ironises upon the realistic account of its own traumatic socio-political context.

The bond between this use of romance as a mode and the truthful representation of trauma in fiction strongly recalls Dominick LaCapra's concept of "plausible feel." According to this historian, narratives in fiction may also involve truth claims on traumatic historical events "by giving at least a plausible 'feel' for experience and emotion which may be difficult to arrive at through restricted documentary methods" (LaCapra 13). *Watchmen* offers a "truthful" emotional depiction of the contemporary context when the graphic novel was created, as it portrays the social anxiety and unrest provoked by the unstable political situation of the 1980s. This account of a world that is truthful "upon a human level" (Vylenz), aimed at representing the social conditions in England during the decade of the 1980s, is carried out by means of the conscious use of repetitions and flashbacks and through displacement and indirection. Hence, *Watchmen* may be said to echo Anne Whitehead's tenet that, in trauma narratives, "temporality and chronology collapse, and narratives are characterised by repetition and indirection" (3).[6] *Watchmen* presents a new-but-disturbingly-familiar world that is haunted by the memories of past wars, genocides and nuclear devastation, as the race towards nuclear annihilation seems to be reaching an end. Thus, Moore and Gibbons offer a fictional recreation of the political situation of the 1980s in the real world. The use of this alternative history that places the action in the United States, instead of England, and goes back one year from the authors' present time, implies a complete rewriting of history that may be said to have "a realism-undermining effect of *déjà vu* that enhances the fictionality of [the] created world" (Onega 102). The fact that *Watchmen* rewrites official history in order to reflect upon the nature of power and nuclear responsibility places Moore and Gibbons's work in the trend of historiographic metafiction. As Linda Hutcheon argues, historiographic metafictions are "self-reflexive and yet paradoxically also lay claim to historical events and personages" (5). They "suggest that truth and falsity may indeed not be the right terms in which to discuss fiction. [. . .] There are only *truths* in the plural, and never one Truth; and there is rarely falseness *per se*, just others' truths" (109, original emphasis). *Watchmen* consciously rewrites history, but the various events taking place (such as Dr. Manhattan's appearance in the world) do not prevent humanity from being on the verge of destroying itself. Further, *Watchmen*, as a historiographic metafiction, challenges institutions in the readers' ontology, and warns us readers about the dangers of taking a single perception of the world for the only possible reality. Thus, Adrian Veidt's imposition of his will leads to the final destruction of the community, the "death of neighbourhood culture" (Jameson 54), and the triumph of capitalism over individual freedom. In summary, *Watchmen* rewrites history so as to take a political stance on a social situation that is leading to a general traumatisation of society. Said differently, the trauma that affects the world of *Watchmen* must be seen in the context of Moore and Gibbons's conception of England and Thatcher's Conservative Governments throughout the 1980s.

WATCHMEN AND THATCHERISM

The decade of the 1980s in England was a stern reactionary period in which the New Right and a new conception of aggressive capitalism emerged out of the "rejection of socialism in its first stage and as the engine for free-market economics once the Socialist state had been rolled back by a Thatcher administration" (Holmes 9). Among the different aspects of Thatcher's governments that might be mentioned, I would like to draw attention to four concepts that will prove relevant for the reading of *Watchmen* as a representation of Thatcherite politics: privatisation, popular capitalism, social unrest, and nuclear fear. "Between 1979 and early 1989," Peter Ridell affirms, "about two-fifths of the previously state-owned industries were sold to the private sector" (87). This emphasis on privatisation and property owning was enhanced by a conservative political discourse promoting a popular capitalism:

> Popular capitalism has proved to be a powerful political slogan for the Conservatives. The reality of a property-owning democracy may have much more to do with the long-term post-war build-up of owner occupation, and inheritance, than the post-1979 initiatives of giving council tenants the right to buy their homes or attractively priced share offers. [...] The true significance may be to give greater control to individuals over their own lives. [...] Popular capitalism has become a central part of the individualist challenge to collective provision—while the extension of ownership has given people something to defend. (Ridell 126)

The changing conservative society of the 1980s, as promoted by Thatcherism, was leading to a political organisation where the central government stopped being involved in everyday life. State power was basically reduced to the provision of "defence and law and order" (Holmes 13), and there was no involvement in social issues related, for example, to government-owned companies or the national health services. The basic social unit was neither the community nor the collectivity, but rather, the individual and the illusion that he or she could take full control of his or her own life. As Margaret Thatcher famously claimed, "there is no such thing as society. There are only individual men and women, and there are families" (Ridell 171).

Obviously, as a left-positioned writer and self-confessed anarchist, Alan Moore's response to this type of politics was far from positive. His most straightforward response to Thatcher's government appeared in *V for Vendetta* (1982–88). Nevertheless, it is my contention that *Watchmen*, despite taking place in an alternative United States, represents Moore's reaction to Thatcher's economic politics of privatisation, popular capitalism, and extreme individualism. Adrian Veidt turns into the real monster in *Watchmen* when the readers discover his conspiracy to kill three million innocents for, allegedly, a better good (stopping the Cold War). As the narrative unfolds, Veidt progressively becomes an excellent representative of Thatcherite economics in terms of privatisation and popular capitalism. As an individual capitalist, he stopped being a caped crusader in the 1960s in order to found his own company and become a business tycoon. With this move, he opposed his fellow caped crusaders, particularly Rorschach, who saw Adrian's rejection of moral watching as an example of ideological prostitution (Moore and Gibbons 1: 17: 6–8).

Drawing on these ideas, and conceiving Adrian and his companies as the epitome of privatisation and popular capitalism, it is easy to see that in every single chapter of the book there is a massive presence of Veidt or his companies' logos in different forms and shapes. It would be excessive and pointless to enumerate all occurrences of Veidt's company logo in the graphic novel; nevertheless, Chapter One may be mentioned as a good example: from the very first page of the graphic novel, the attentive reader can see the symbol (a triangle inside a circle) of Pyramid Deliveries painted on the top of a purple truck (Moore and Gibbons 1: 1: 5). Pyramid Deliveries happens to be one of Veidt's companies and will play an essential role in the conspiracy that leads to the final destruction of New York. Afterwards, on page 10, panel 2, the reader catches the first glimpse of another ubiquitous image in the text: the advertising of *Nostalgia*, a perfume owned by Veidt. And finally, on page 15, panel 9, a terrified customer wearing a hooded top with the "V" symbol of Veidt's company on the chest, escapes from the menacing Rorschach, who has just arrived at the bar with the aim of gathering information about Blake's death. Significantly, Adrian Veidt's symbol appears in the story much before the character is introduced to the reader.[7]

Although the world of *Watchmen* seems to live in terror of nuclear powers and political decisions, the single entity that, in the end, manages to control every aspect of daily life is a private company. Adrian Veidt, thus, becomes the extreme representative of the Thatcherite aspirations towards privatisation and popular capitalism. Subsequently, the whole community and every aspect of the individual citizen's life are in the hands of one single person. And this person, Adrian Veidt, decides whether the working individual in the street (the newsvendor, the taxi driver, the psychologist) must live or die for a higher cause. Consequently, this graphic novel can be seen as a fictional experiment on Thatcherism as applied to a community. From this perspective, Moore and Gibbons's work reveals striking similarities with George Orwell's *Nineteen Eighty-Four* (1949): *Watchmen* may be said to stand in the same relation to Thatcherism that *Nineteen Eighty-Four* stood to Stalinism.

In the 1980s, the politics of privatisation and popular capitalism created an enormous amount of social unrest in England. As Peter Ridell points out, "the level of offences, particularly of violence, was substantially higher than a decade earlier and remained one of the public's main worries" (171). Further, the emphasis on individualism and the neglect of social responsibilities may be said to have increased criminality. The growing social unrest produced an encouragement of the figure of the "active citizen," who sought to protect him- or herself by creating Neighbourhood Watches.

The individual citizens would, thus, assume the role of the police in order to maintain the security of their own neighbourhood. As Ridell argues, there was a "spread of the Neighbourhood Watch scheme from two in 1982 to over 60,000 by the end of 1988, covering 750,000 people" (172).

In the unassuaged capitalist society of fictional New York of *Watchmen*, the group of masked vigilantes are strongly reminiscent of the Neighbourhood Watches in real England under Thatcherism. Like their English counterparts, the New York masked vigilantes are "active citizens" encouraged by the Conservative government, but unlike them, they fail to realise the larger issues behind their system and even behind the creation of the first group of caped adventurers, the Minutemen. The first superhero group of vigilantes in the world of *Watchmen* was created in 1939, as a marketing campaign to revamp Sally Jupiter's popularity and presence in the media. Sally's agent, an individual named Laurence Schexnayder,

> realized that without the occasional gimmick to revitalize flagging public interest, the fad for long underwear heroes would eventually fade, reducing his girl Sally's chances of media exposure as The Silk Spectre to zero. Thus it was Schexnayder, in mid-1939, who suggested placing a large ad in the Gazette asking other mystery men to come forward. (Moore and Gibbons 2: 31)

The Minutemen had no social aim. It was just another capitalist strategy to advertise a product (in this case, an actress hiding under the mask of a superheroine). Obvious as this may seem, this situation creates a constant state of paranoia in the citizens who, when confronted with the truth, start questioning every movement and motivation behind the government's interests. Orwell in *Nineteen Eighty-Four* relies on a similar state of paranoia to depict the situation of a dystopian society. When Winston Smith remembers the dropping of an atomic bomb on Colchester, the narrative agent gives voice to the feeling of manipulation and conspiracy lurking behind the official truth. As the narrator explains:

> In his childish way Winston grasped that some terrible thing, something that was beyond forgiveness and could never be remedied, had just happened. [. . .]. Someone whom the old man loved, a little granddaughter perhaps, had been killed. Every few minutes the old man kept repeating:
> "We didn't ought to 'ave trusted 'em. I said so, Ma, didn't I? That's what come of trusting 'em. I said so all along. We didn't ought to 'ave trusted the buggers.'
> But which buggers they didn't ought to have trusted Winston could not now remember. (Orwell 38)

Conspiracy theories were abundant in the 1980s, inheriting many of the ghosts created during the Cold War and the anti-Communist paranoia of the 1950s and 1960s in the United States. The assassination of John F. Kennedy in 1963, the assassination attempts of Ronald Reagan in 1981, or of Margaret Thatcher on 12th October, 1984[8] produced thousands of interpretations leading to different conspiracy theories when the official versions were not believed by the common citizen. Paralleling these conspiracy theories and their mechanisms to hide the truth from the public, Adrian Veidt in *Watchmen* not only carries out a plan to kill three million citizens, he even manages to hide his involvement by faking assassination attempts against himself (in Chapter Five). His purpose is to give the citizens the impression of being in control of their own life. Rorschach, Nite Owl, or even President Nixon should never find out the strategies informing Veidt's conspiracy to control the world. The discovery of the hidden truth leads to the traumatising belief that the structures on which their social order relies are dysfunctional and prove to be a blatant lie. When Edward Blake discovers Veidt's control of the world, his mind crumbles down and becomes dysfunctional, echoing the dysfunctionality of the social structures of the political order that he has unveiled. This type of shocked response to a suffocating and overwhelming social experience I shall label "political trauma."

POLITICAL TRAUMA

Drawing on Freudian psychoanalysis, Cathy Caruth defined trauma as an event that "is experienced too soon, too unexpectedly, to be fully known, and is therefore not available to consciousness until it imposes itself again, repeatedly, in the nightmares and repetitive actions of the survivor" (4). This traumatic event or experience is of such an unprecedented and shocking condition that it "overwhelms the individual and resists language and representation" (Whitehead 3). The representation of traumatic events and traumatic memories has been widely explored and different types of traumas have already been classified according to different criteria. Thus, Dominick LaCapra distinguishes two types of individual traumas: structural trauma and historical trauma (81). Structural traumas are anxiety-producing conditions that may lead the subject to a traumatising situation expressed in the form of obsessive melancholia. By contrast, historical traumas—or "punctual traumas," according to Greg Forter—are "historical events of such singularity, magnitude, and horror that they can be read as shocks that disable the psychic system" of the individual (259).

When analysed from the perspective of its effects on communities, traumas can be approached as "pathologies of culture" (Samuels 9). Kai Erikson offered the term "collective trauma" and defined it as "a blow to the basic tissues of social life that damages the bonds attaching people together and impairs the prevailing sense of community" (187). Additionally, Jeffrey C. Alexander explains that "cultural trauma occurs when members of a collectivity feel they have been subjected to a horrendous event that leaves indelible marks upon their group consciousness, marking their memories forever and changing their future identity in fundamental and irrevocable ways" (1). In other words, whereas collective traumas destroy the community, cultural traumas fashion its essential social structures.

To give some examples, an individual may be "structurally" traumatised when he or she becomes morbidly obsessed with his or her own mortality and falls prey to "an anxiety producing condition" (LaCapra 82). By contrast, the subject can be "historically" or "punctually" traumatised in response to an extreme event that disables his or her psychic system (Forter 260). This would be the case of accident and atrocity survivors, whose psychic system is unable to cope with the memories of the event. Additionally, a group of individuals may see their community destroyed by a collective trauma, as is the case of Palestinian refugees in the West Bank and the Gaza Strip (and effectively depicted in the graphic novel *Palestine* by Joe Sacco, in 2001). Or the group may shape their identity according to the traumatic events they had to go through as a community. Such would be the case of the Sephardic and Ashkenazi Jewish communities, who base their communal identities on similar traumatic myths of origin.

In *Watchmen*, the unveiling of the final truth, Adrian Veidt's conspiracy to kill three million innocent citizens to stop the Cold War, produces in Edward Blake's mind an effect comparable to traumatic dissociation regarding his socio-cultural context. He is unable to put into words the reality that he has just discovered: everything he believed in was a smoke screen to cover a mass-murder conspiracy. His work for the American Government, his involvement in Vietnam, his fights against strikes and riots, and even his cruelty as a masked crusader prove all lies to cover up the awful truth about capitalism: Veidt controls the world and he is more than willing to kill half of the population of New York for the greater good of stopping the Cold War. Blake is mentally shocked and psychically injured neither by an unexpected event of the type described in Caruth's definition of trauma, nor by a collective experience in line with Erikson's or Alexander's definition of collective and cultural traumas. He is shocked and traumatised to the point of losing his speech abilities due to his inability to cope with the terrible lies coming from the political system, government and people in power he has backed.

Upon making this discovery, Blake, the amoral and Nazi-like agent of the U.S. Government, suffers a nervous breakdown and bursts into tears while confessing his sins to his arch-enemy, the decadent evil and terminally ill Moloch (Moore and Gibbons 2: 23: 4–6). This type of overwhelming shock is what I call political trauma. Blake has violently realised that the social structures are a smoke screen covering up a greedy system controlled by capitalist interests. The unveiling of the conspiracy destroys Blake's beliefs in the system he has been forcefully backing so far.

The studies of trauma in literature have offered an enormous variety of terms to refer to different types of traumas, and many times the terminology employed by the critics tends to overlap and create ambiguities, making it difficult to establish clear-cut categories. The political trauma that affects Blake's mind can be easily considered cultural, if we understand "cultural" as related to the culture of a community. Nonetheless, the ambiguous meaning of Jeffrey C. Alexander's term, "cultural trauma," does not allow considering this type of overwhelming event in this category, since, according to Alexander, cultural trauma is the cohesive element that unites the members of a community around a "negative myth of origin" (LaCapra 162) or a "chosen trauma" (Volkan and Itzkowitz 232). In contrast to this, Blake's political trauma implies the destruction of such a myth, as the established social cohesion is proved to be based on a blatant lie. Consequently, although the trauma suffered by Blake is directly related to his own cultural context, this trauma does not become the source of his definition as part of a community.

In order to understand their narrow interconnection, Alexander's "cultural trauma," Erikson's "collective trauma," and political trauma should be considered within the broader spectrum of "pathologies of culture" (Samuels 9). The traumas that affect collectivities always have social, political, cultural, and individual components. It is pointless to establish boundaries between them, as they unavoidably overlap. Nonetheless, a fictional text can centre on one of those aspects and emphasise the cultural union of the group through a traumatic myth of origin (with a cultural trauma); or it can reflect the shattering of the community affected by a collective trauma. What *Watchmen* does instead, is to represent the destruction of the individual's beliefs in the political and social system when Blake unveils the conspiracy contrived by the single individual who controls the whole society. What is more, those clear-cut categories prove inefficient in *Watchmen*, since Edward Blake actively fulfils the role of perpetrator of certain traumas that affect groups and individuals alike, such as the assassination of Kennedy (Moore and Gibbons 9: 20: 5), the Vietnam War (4: 19: 5), or the violent repression against citizens on strike (2: 16: 4). He is also involved in another character's punctual trauma when he rapes Sally Jupiter (2: 6: 9), and he displays the inhuman cruelty proper of a serial killer when he shoots to death a Vietnamese pregnant woman in cold blood (2: 15: 2). However, his Nazi-like psyche shatters when he realises that every atrocity he committed in the name of his government was, in fact, part of a secret conspiracy to give more power to one single individual, and not to his country. Until then, Blake's crimes had been part of a system that, no matter how corrupt and immoral, he proudly boasted of knowing. The moment he discovers Veidt's plan, his mind fails to cope with the dysfunctional structures of his community, and he is plunged into a state of mental unbalance and apathetic inaction. His worldview and his cultural unconscious are shattered, as his belief in the political system—that is, in the distribution of power and the institutions ruling society—is utterly destroyed. As Robert K. Merton has pointed out, the after-effects of the destruction of social structures may lead the individual to a state of anomie, or lack of moral standards that can subsequently give way to extreme episodes of violence and/or suicide (248). In the case of political trauma, the violence exerted on the individual is exclusively psychological and directly aimed at the destruction of his or her assumptions about the system ruling social organisation.

Andrew Samuels, in his book *The Political Psyche*, offers a working definition of the concept of politics that is worth quoting in full:

> By 'politics' I mean the concerted arrangements and struggles within an institution, or in a single society, or between the countries of the world for the organization and distribution of resources and power, especially economic power. Politics concerns the way in which power is held or deployed by the state, by institutions, and by sectional interests to positively perhaps, enhance the quality of human life. Politics implies efforts to change or transform these arrangements and efforts to maintain them. Economic and political power includes control of processes of information and representation to serve the interests of the powerful as well as the use of physical force and possession of vital resources such as land, food, water or oil. (3)

Politics is, then, a communal agreement, a social contract aimed at ruling the life of a community according to the values and principles of the community's culture. The people's representatives, the politicians, are supposed to keep watch over these principles in order to guarantee the citizens' freedom according to the set of social rules. What Edward Blake discovers, along with the readers of *Watchmen*, is a diametrically opposed world: politicians greedily fight to control the world by threatening each other during the Cold War. However, along with Blake, Rorschach, Nite Owl, Dr. Manhattan and the rest of caped crusaders, these politicians fail to see that their world is, in fact, in the hands of Adrian Veidt, one single individual whose interests rely on money and power and, ultimately, on imposing his own world-view on the rest of humanity. When Veidt's conspiracy is unveiled, the characters that discover the truth may be said to be forced to face the principle of "doublethink" that governs their political life, just as it governed the dystopian life of Winston Smith in *Nineteen Eighty-Four*. As the protagonist explains, the term "doublethink" was coined and employed to refer to

> the power of holding two contradictory beliefs in one's mind simultaneously, and accepting both of them. [...] The process has to be conscious, or it would not be carried out with sufficient precision, but it also has to be unconscious, or it would bring with it a feeling of falsity and hence of guilt. (Orwell 244)

Winston Smith, a Party intellectual of the country of Oceania, who is in charge of manipulating memories as recalled in newspapers and other media, starts questioning the political system to the point of believing that his own government may have been secretly killing the working classes (the "proles") with the aim of making people believe in a false war. Thus, "the rocket bombs which fell daily on London were probably fired by the Government of Oceania itself, just to keep people frightened" (176).

The Government in Orwell's novel favours doublethink by means of the constant repetition in the media of contradictory slogans such as "War is Peace," "Freedom is Slavery," and "Ignorance is Strength" (31). *Watchmen* presents the same type of paradoxical and dissociative thinking related to political issues and the general socio-political context in which the text was created. As Alan Moore has explained, "*Watchmen* also grew out of the political shadowy landscape of the 1980s, when the Cold War was at probably its hottest in twenty or thirty years, and when nuclear destruction suddenly seemed a very real possibility" (Vylenz). And he situates the roots of the dissociative thinking characteristic of doublethink in the political context of Thatcherite government. Indeed, the Cold War politics of gathering massive killing nuclear weapons in order to keep peace was extremely difficult to explain in plain terms to the common citizen. Margaret Thatcher, in the above-mentioned Conservative Party Conference speech, delivered on 12th October 1984, explained the gathering of nuclear forces in the following terms:

> With the huge array of modern weapons held by the Soviet Union, including chemical weapons in large quantities, [a war in Europe] would be a cruel and terrible conflict. The truth is that possession of the nuclear deterrent has prevented not only nuclear war but also conventional war and to us, peace is precious beyond price. We are the true peace party. (Thatcher)

Peace and war, two contradicting concepts, are simultaneously held true in the mind of the common citizen, consciously knowing that, contradictory as they may be, they are necessarily complementing each other. As the old Latin saying goes, *si vis pacem, para bellum*. War and peace coexist in the same utterance, thus providing an excellent example of Orwellian doublethink. However, what leads to the political traumatisation of the citizens is the realisation that the acceptance of doublethink is only beneficial for those few in power. The discovery of the conspiracy to control the world according to the wishes and interests of a minority leaves the common citizen with a feeling of immorality, falsity and guilt when he or she feels that he or she is the first, and usually the only one, to suffer the consequences of political decisions.

As stated before, political trauma is the result of the collapse of social structures provoked by the destruction of deeply engraved political, social and cultural assumptions in the subject's mind when he or she is made to face the horror of not being in control of his or her own life. In *Watchmen*, it does not matter whether the text rewrites history by re-electing Richard Nixon, or making the United States triumph in the Vietnam War. Horrors like the bombing of Hiroshima and Nagasaki, the Holocaust and even the eventual destruction of New York are bound to occur when one single person conspires to impose his or her will over the rest of society. When the official discourse breaks up and doublethink stops being effective, the political self falls into a state of anomie and distrust. The common citizen understands that those who are bound to suffer the final destruction brought about by the Cold War are not the politicians, but the working classes and the neighbourhoods they belong in. In *Watchmen*, when the Comedian discovers Veidt's conspiracy, he is unable to understand the meaning of such behaviour. This strongly recalls the words of Winston Smith in *Nineteen Eighty-Four*: "I understand HOW: I do not understand WHY" (Orwell 91, capitals in the original). The failure to understand political decisions that involve and affect the lives of millions of citizens provides the basis for political trauma.

As can be gathered from Orwell's quotation, the individual is unable to grasp an essential part of meaning, to the extent of being incapable of fully understanding and, consequently, of representing the traumatic event. This undecidability of apprehension, evincing the struggle between the desire to know and not to know, which is characteristic of the acting out phase of trauma (Whitehead 121), is provided in *Watchmen* by means of a displacement of romance as the mode for depicting political trauma as part of the pathologies of culture. The displaced/ironic romance structure of adventures and superheroes works as a vehicle for creating the "plausible feel" of the 1980s dystopian society, employing LaCapra's terminology. *Watchmen*, thus, proves to be an example of what this historian has labelled "traumatic realism." According to LaCapra the emergence of traumatic realism in our post-WWII world "differs from stereotypical conceptions of mimesis and enables instead an often disconcerting exploration of disorientation, its symptomatic dimensions, and possible ways of responding to them" (186). Romance as a mode, with its excesses and tendencies for the supernatural, serves in this graphic novel as the medium to render the social depiction of a traumatised world.

CONCLUSION

Moore and Gibbons's *Watchmen* revolutionised the medium of comic books by subverting the Bakhtinian chronotope of the Greek romance employed in superhero narratives before and during the 1980s. This narrative iconical text introduced superhero characters into the chronotope of the adventure novel of everyday life, thus developing the graphic-novel subgenre. Nevertheless, *Watchmen* has recourse to romance elements, such as the use of episodic plots and excessive expressionism, in order to depict an alternative version of history that comments on the political situation of our capitalist world in general and, more concretely, of Thatcherite England. From this perspective, *Watchmen* reveals its condition as an allegory of the Thatcherite economic policy of privatisation and popular capitalism, comparable to Orwell's dystopian recreation of Stalinism in *Nineteen Eighty-Four*. The traumatic component in the iconical narrative enhances the consideration of *Watchmen* as representative of "political trauma," that is, a narrative dealing with the traumatic collapse of the socio-political structures in the psyche of the individual.

NOTES

1. The research carried out for the writing of this article is part of a research project financed by the Spanish Ministry of Science and Innovation (MICINN) and the European Regional Fund (ERFD) (code HUM 2007–61035). The author is also grateful for the support of the Government of Aragón and the European Social Fund (ESF) (code H05).
2. Among the many examples of British fictional works centring on political traumas in the 1980s, could be mentioned Bryan Talbot's *The Adventures of Luther Arkwright* (1978–89); Pat Mills and Joe Colquhoun's *Charley's War* (1979–85); Pat Mills and Kevin O'Neill's *A.B.C. Warriors* in *2000AD* (1979–2010); Gerry Finley-Day and Dave Gibbons's *Rogue Trooper* in *2000AD* (1981); Raymond Briggs's *When the Wind Blows* (1982); Alan Moore and David Lloyd's *V for Vendetta* (1982–88); Iain Banks's *The Wasp Factory* (1984); Alan Moore's *AARGH (Artists Against Rampant Government Homophobia)* (1988); and Alan Moore's *Brought to Light: Thirty Years of Drug Smuggling, Arms Deals, and Covert Action* (1988). The decade also witnessed the production of widely popular films dealing with political trauma, such as Ridley Scott's *Alien* (1979) and *Blade Runner* (1982); James Cameron's *The Terminator* (1984) and *Aliens* (1986); or Paul Verhoeven's *Robocop* (1987).
3. The political commitment of Alan Moore's writing was overtly expressed in Moore and Lloyd's *V for Vendetta* (1982–88). Nevertheless, the best examples of Moore's political denunciation can be found in two works released in 1988: *AARGH (Artists Against Rampant Government Homophobia)* and "Shadowplay: The Secret Team," a short iconical text included in the graphic docudrama *Brought to Light: Thirty Years of Drug Smuggling, Arms Deals, and Covert Action*. At the beginning of 2010, Alan Moore and other collaborators started publishing *Dodgem Logic*, a magazine centred on political and social issues related to Northampton.
4. Comic books and graphic novels are sometimes unnumbered. *Watchmen* was released in twelve instalments, each containing one chapter of the graphic novel, and each chapter has its own page numbers from one to twenty-eight. The 1987 collected edition of the twelve issues in book format keeps this numeration, so there is no continuity from one chapter to the next. This makes textual reference in an essay like this rather problematic. The system I am using here (4: 20: 1) refers to the story chapter, chapter page, and the panel the example is taken from.
5. Northrop Frye, in his essay "The Mythos of Summer: Romance," places comic strip characters in the mode of romance: "at its most naïve it [romance] is an endless form in which a central character who never develops or ages

goes through one adventure after another until the author himself collapses. We see this form in comic strips, where the central characters persist for years in a state of refrigerated deathlessness" (186).

6. Brandy Ball Blake analyses *Watchmen* from the perspective of trauma. Nevertheless, she centres on Dr. Manhattan and interprets the chapter devoted to this character as representative of the doctor's traumatised mind. Even though I believe that analysing this graphic novel from the perspective of Trauma Studies can yield insightful results, I do not consider Dr. Manhattan a traumatised character. When, in a fatal accident, John Osterman becomes Dr. Manhattan, he becomes capable of perceiving time and manipulating matter in the fourth dimension. All the broken and fragmented representations of time in his chapter may be said to point to his ability to apprehend time in the supra-human perception of the fourth dimension. That is, the narrative techniques employed do not depict traumatic memories but a perception of time that is beyond human comprehension.

7. The presence of Veidt's symbols in tiny details of the visual narrative is overwhelming. *Nostalgia*, Veidt's perfume, appears in many different contexts throughout the graphic novel: as an advertisement (1: 10: 2; 2: 1: 2; 3: 7: 2; 7: 14: 1), or being used by other main characters (2: 3: 4; 3: 24: 7; 8: 1: 2; 8: 22: 6). By means of the advertisement on the back cover of *Tales of the Black Freighter*, the comic book that the boy reads and becomes the *mise en abyme* of Adrian's conspiracy, Veidt is also teaching boys how to succeed in society by following "The Veidt Method" (3: 1: 4; 3: 25: 5; 10: 13: 1; 12: 6). Thus, Veidt's company seems to control every aspect of the world in *Watchmen*, from delivery companies (5: 8: 1; 10: 17: 1) to fashion and clothing (as can be seen in the hat of a passer-by, 4: 24: 4); from pills to mitigate migraine (6: 13: 2) to the TV set in Hollis Mason's apartment (8: 27: 2).

8. The narrative of *Watchmen* begins on 12th October 1985. The date may have many different meanings. On the one hand, 12th October is Columbus Day in the Americas, commemorating the arrival of the Spanish discoverers. Thus, *Watchmen* may be seen as representative of the new world that is being created in the United States. On the other hand, it is also one year after the terrorist attack against Margaret Thatcher and her Conservative Government in Brighton. *Watchmen* may thus be seen as Moore's speculations on how the world has changed following the premises established by Thatcher in her "Speech to Conservative Party Conference," delivered on that very same day, 12th October 1984, emphasising the importance of privatisation, denationalisation and the preventive use of nuclear weapons.

WORKS CITED

Alexander, Jeffrey C. "Toward a Theory of Cultural Trauma." *Cultural Trauma and Collective Identity*. Eds. Jeffrey C. Alexander, Roy Eyerman, Bernhard Giesen, Neil J. Smelser and Piotr Sztompka. Berkeley, Los Angeles and London: U of California P, 2004. 1–30. Print.

Bakhtin, Mikhail. *The Dialogic Imagination. Four Essays*. 1981. Texas: University of Texas Press, 1988. Print.

Banks, Ian. *The Wasp Factory*. London: Macmillan, 1984. Print.

Blake, Brandy Ball. "*Watchmen*: The Graphic Novel as Trauma Fiction." *ImageText: Interdisciplinary Comics Studies* 5.1 (2009). http://www.english.ufl.edu/imagetext/archives/v5_1/blake/. Retrieved on 26 March 2012. Web.

Briggs, Raymond. *When the Wind Blows*. Harmondsworth: Penguin Books, 1982. Print.

Cameron, James. *The Terminator*. Hemdale Film, 1984. Film.

———. *Aliens*. Twentieth-Century Fox, 1986. Film.

Caruth, Cathy. *Unclaimed Experience. Trauma, Narrative and History*. Baltimore and London: The Johns Hopkins UP, 1996. Print.

Eisner, Will. *A Contract with God, and Other Tenement Stories*. 1978. New York: DC Comics, 1996. Print.

Erikson, Kai. "Notes on Trauma and Community." *Trauma. Explorations in Memory*. Ed. Cathy Caruth. Baltimore and London: The Johns Hopkins UP, 1995. 183–99. Print.

Finley-Day, Gerry, and Dave Gibbons. *Rogue Trooper: Future War*. 1981. London: Titan Books, 2007. Print.

Forter, Greg. "Freud, Faulkner, Caruth. Trauma and the Politics of Literary Form." *Narrative* 15.3 (2007): 259–85. Print.

Frye, Northrop. *Anatomy of Criticism, Four Essays*. 1957. Harmondsworth: Penguin, 1990. Print.

———. "The Mythos of Summer: Romance." *Anatomy of Criticism, Four Essays*. 1957. Princeton: Princeton UP, 1990. 186–206 . Print.

Gaiman, Neil, *et al. The Sandman* (10 volumes). 1988–96. New York: DC Comics. Print.

Ganteau, Jean-Michel. "Fantastic but Truthful: the Ethics of Romance." *The Cambridge Quarterly* 32.3 (2003): 225–38. Print.

Gray, Margaret Ann. *"Love your Rage, not your Cage": Comics as Cultural Resistance: Alan Moore 1971–1989*. Unpublished PhD Thesis, History of Art. London: University College London, 2010. Print.

Hawthorne, Nathaniel. *The House of the Seven Gables: A Romance*. 1851. Cambridge: Cambridge UP, 1879. Print.

Holmes, Martin. *Thatcherism: Scope and Limits, 1983–87*. London: Macmillan, 1989. Print.

Hutcheon, Linda. *A Poetics of Postmodernism: History, Theory, Fiction*. New York and London: Routledge, 1988. Print.

Jameson, Fredric. "Postmodernism, or the Cultural Logic of Late Capitalism." *New Left Review* 146 (1984): 53–92. Print.

LaCapra, Dominick. *Writing History, Writing Trauma*. Baltimore and London: The Johns Hopkins UP, 2001. Print.

Merton, Robert K. *Social Theory and Social Structure*. 1949. London: Collier-Macmillan, 1968. Print.

Mills, Pat and Joe Colquhoun. *Charley's War* (9 volumes). 1979–85. London: Titan Books, 2004–12. Print.

Mills, Pat and Kevin O'Neill. *A. B. C. Warriors. Book One*. 1979. London: Titan Books, 1983. Print.

Moore, Alan and Bill Sienkiewicz. "Shadowplay: The Secret Team." *Brought to Light: Thirty Years of Drug Smuggling, Arms Deals, and Covert Action*. California: Eclipse Comics, 1988. Print.

Moore, Alan and Dave Gibbons. *Watchmen* (1986–87). New York: DC Comics, 1987. Print.

Moore, Alan and David Lloyd. *V for Vendetta* (1982–88). New York: DC Comics, 1990. Print.

Moore, Alan, *et al. AARGH (Artists Against Rampant Government Homophobia)*. Northampton: Mad Love, 1988. Print.

Onega, Susana. "Self, Text and World in British Historiographic Metafiction." *Anglistik* 6.2 (1995): 93–105. Print.

Orwell, George. *Nineteen Eighty-Four.* 1949. London and New York: Penguin, 2009. Print.

Ridell, Peter. *The Thatcher Era and Its Legacy.* 1989. Oxford and Cambridge: Blackwell, 1991. Print.

Romero-Jódar, Andrés. "The Quest for a Place in Culture: The Verbal-Iconical Production and the Evolution of Comic-Books towards Graphic Novels." *Estudios Ingleses de la Universidad Complutense* 14 (2006): 93–110. Print.

Sacco, Joe. *Palestine.* 2001. London: Jonathan Cape, 2003. Print.

Samuels, Andrew. *The Political Psyche.* London and New York: Routledge, 1993. Print.

Scott, Ridley. *Alien.* Twentieth-Century Fox, 1979. Film.

———. *Blade Runner.* Warner Bros. Pictures, 1982. Film.

Spiegelman, Art. *The Complete Maus.* 1978–91. London: Penguin Books, 2003. Print.

Talbot, Bryan. *The Adventures of Luther Arkwright.* 1979–89. Milwaukie: Dark Horse, 2007. Print.

Thatcher, Margaret. "Speech to Conservative Party Conference." 1984. *http://www.margaretthatcher.org/document/105763.* Retrieved on 14 April 2011. Web.

Verhoeven, Paul. *Robocop.* Orion Picture Corporation, 1987. Film.

Volkan, Vamik D. and Norman Itzkowitz. "Modern Greek and Turkish identities and the psychodynamics of Greek-Turkish relations." *Cultures under Siege: Collective Violence and Trauma.* Ed. Antonius C. G. M. Robben and Marcelo M. Suárez-Orozco. Cambridge: Cambridge UP, 2000. 227–247. Print.

Vylenz, Dez. *The Mindscape of Alan Moore.* 2003. Shadowsnake Films, 2008. Film.

Whitehead, Anne. *Trauma Fiction (A Selection).* Edinburgh: Edinburgh UP, 2004. Print.

Part IV
Therapeutic Romance

11 From Traumatic Iteration to Healing Narrativisation in *Shalimar the Clown* by Salman Rushdie
The Therapeutic Role of Romance

Anne-Laure Fortin-Tournès

Repetition is inherent in trauma, Cathy Caruth tells us. Trauma causes the mind to hold on to the moment of the traumatic event, so that it is lived over and over again compulsively, since trauma is "a response, sometimes delayed, to an overwhelming event or set of events, which takes the form of repeated, intrusive hallucinations, dreams, thoughts or behaviours stemming from the event" (Caruth 1995, 4–5). Caruth locates the pathology of trauma in the repetition of the event since, to her, trauma consists "solely in the structure of its experience or reception: the event is not assimilated or experienced fully at the time, but only belatedly in its repeated possession of the one who experiences it" (5). Thus, trauma consists in the revival of an event that has not been fully assimilated at the time it took place. The fact that trauma is to be "associated with the effects of associations triggered by an event, as much as by the event itself" (Kaplan 35), makes it impossible for the subject to find a coherent sequence that would ascribe meaning to the traumatic occurrence. In the absence of such coherent sequence, the subject lacks temporal and logical markers with which to channel reality into an acceptable and meaningful whole. My contention is that in the case of a number of British writers after the terrorist attacks on Washington and New York on 9/11 2001—and Salman Rushdie in *Shalimar the Clown* is a case in point—that coherent sequence is provided by the narrative of romance. I will base my understanding of the narrative of romance on Jean-Michel Ganteau's definition of romance as including the themes of love, fighting and the quest, as well as mystery and the manifestations of the past (16–17).[1]

The double bind of trauma resides in its articulation of temporality and repetition. Caruth, in her influential reading of Freud's *Moses and Monotheism*, argues that "events, insofar as they are traumatic, assume their force precisely in their temporal delay" (1996, 9), what Freud calls *Nachträglichkeit*, or "deferred action," a notion which designates trauma as manifesting itself belatedly, between two events, in a deferral of the act of understanding which introduces a period of latency (Freud 9). This concept of *Nachträglichkeit* implies that trauma takes place in its return, in its painful repetition. And yet, it is only through repetition that trauma can be overcome. Narrativising trauma is the key to working it through, because traumatic memory must be turned into narrative memory for trauma to become acceptable. Two types of memory are, therefore, involved in the experience of trauma: traumatic memory, which consists in bearing "true" witness to the event by reproducing its painful impact; and narrative memory[2] which is a displaced form of reproduction of the event that allows the subject to situate it in the proper place and time of its occurrence and to inscribe meaning in the traumatic event. Before narrativisation takes place, the traumatised subject lives in a sort of frozen present time, and is caught in a ceaseless imaginative reiteration of the traumatic experience, in the guise of fragmented and incomprehensible traumatic memories. Under these circumstances, narrativising the event amounts to an "uncoiling of trauma, an undoing of its never-ending circularity, and its integration into a completed story of the past" (Versluys 4). Repetition in trauma is, therefore, both a symptom and a cure; repetitive and painful post-traumatic disorders bear witness to the subject's suffering, whereas the narrativised repetition of the event works as a Freudian "talking cure." This dual mode of repetition—a senseless and painful form of acting out, on the one hand, and a narrativised, healing form of working through, on the other—sheds light on the processes whereby contemporary British fiction deals with the traumatic event by acting it out formally in its linguistic texture, while working it through narratively, by means of a coherent, even if meandering plot.

It might appear as something of a paradox to focus on the representation of 9/11 outside American fiction, given the flow of American "post 9/11" novels. Yet, what characterises the terrorist attacks of 2001 is precisely the fact that they can be considered as "the first worldwide historical event" to have taken place in a globalised world (Habermas 83). For 9/11 to qualify as a global event, the attacks must have been intended by the terrorists to have global impact, and the terror they waged on America indeed duly spread like waves to other continents, owing to the way the media reported on them. Therein lies the difference between 9/11 and previous acts of political terrorism, according to Jean Baudrillard: "Current terrorism is not the descendant of a traditional history of anarchy, nihilism and fanaticism. It is contemporaneous with globalization" (87). Globalisation is the new configuration of the world that transforms social interaction and prevents writers from remaining inured to world events, as Rushdie claims in *Shalimar the Clown*: "Everywhere was now a part of everywhere else [. . .] The world was no longer calm" (37).

Even as U.S. fiction vastly records and registers the attacks, British fiction, too, though in a less profuse way, does tackle the issue of terrorism after 9/11 and of novelists' traumatic reactions to it (Fortin-Tournès 62–76). Interestingly enough, the fact that most British writers felt the need to write about them even though they had experienced the 9/11 attacks only vicariously, demonstrates that vicarious trauma is real (Kaplan 39–40). As

Martin Amis argues in *The Second Plane*, the 9/11 attacks have put a tab on the freedom of the writer: "in the West, writers are acclimatised to freedom—to limitless and gluttonous freedom. And I discovered something. Writing is freedom; and as soon as that freedom is in shadow, the writer can no longer proceed" (51).

According to Amis, the trauma of 9/11 came to restrict the freedom of writing, because it rendered writers speechless when it came to broaching the issue of terrorism (51). British and American writers alike found it impossible to escape the "massive collective experience" of "an encounter that makes no sense, an event that fits in nowhere" and for which no "coherent narrative" could at first be found (Laub 204). In other words, both British and American novelists perceived 9/11 as traumatic, as a "blow against our commonly held beliefs about the value of life" (Amis 204), representing such a shock that it temporarily silenced them. The massive mediatisation of the event greatly contributed to their feeling of confusion and paralysis, which led to a traumatic loss of literary voice. In "The voice of the lonely crowd," one of the essays contained in *The Second Plane*, a collection of essays and short stories aimed at making sense of the terrorist attacks, Amis declared that: "an unusual number of novelists chose to write some journalism about September 11" because the "so-called work in progress had been reduced, overnight, to a blue streak of autistic babble" (12). In "Terror and Boredom: The Dependent Mind" (47–93) Amis acknowledged that the impossibility of writing any fictional work relating to 9/11 in a satisfying way led him to stop his production of a promising draft because of its narrator's "unreliability" (66). As a matter of fact, the rough summary of that draft, which appears at the beginning of the essay, strikes the reader as an outrageous caricature of Muslim fundamentalism, complete with polygamy, hatred against women and sexual repression. Even though readers conversant with Amis's fiction are now familiar with his subversive subjects and style, it clearly appears that Amis dropped this particular fictional project because it had failed in its attempt to think through and grasp 9/11 in relation to Muslim fundamentalism so soon after the events (Badiou 46). However, if we now turn our attention to the two pieces of fictional writing in the collection, which are respectively entitled "In the Palace of the End" (31–46) and "The Last Days of Muhammad Atta" (95–124) we realise that those stories fictionalise both the end of romantic love and its persistence in residual form, which means that they borrow from the well-established narrative tradition of the romance[3] to channel the violence of terrorism into a recognisable form. If, as Amis argues in "Terror and Boredom: The Dependent Mind" in *The Second Plane* (51) the 9/11 attacks have put a tab on the freedom of the writer, then borrowing from well-established and even hackneyed forms appears as a viable option to work through the trauma of 9/11.

In the pages that follow, I would like to consider "In the Palace of the End" and "The Last Days of Muhammad Atta" together with Rushdie's

Shalimar the Clown, as testimonies to the traumatic memory or legacy of 9/11, so as to investigate the solutions both writers come up with in order to process trauma through writing. My contention here is that beyond the mere linguistic acting out of 9/11 as trauma, these fictional works attempt to overcome trauma by making a number of conscious literary choices, among which the choice of establishing a dialogical relation with the literary tradition of romance writing, as a residue unassimilable to, and yet always present in realism, in other words, with romance understood in its "unstable relationship with the historical realism it displaces" (Elam 78). I will base my case on a reading of Freud's theory of trauma that pays particular attention to the dialectics between the meaningless and painful and compulsive repetition of a traumatic event during the phase of acting out, and its liberating channelling through the constraints of narrative during the phase of working through (LaCapra 21–22), and on a definition of romance narrative as revolving around the conjoined narrative streaks of the quest, love and adventure, and the complex relation to history which the romance establishes (Elam 35).

ACTING OUT TRAUMA

Trauma theory has provided the postmodernist literary critic with heuristic tools to understand the broken syntax and disrupted narratives that characterise the contemporary novel. In the wake of Cathy Caruth's, Dominick La Capra's, Marianne Hirsch's, Anne Whitehead's or Dori Laub's seminal analyses, we can now understand that the formal innovations of the postmodernist work of fiction literally make sense as repetitions and enactments of the symptoms of the trauma they seek to re-present. Viewed in this perspective, the postmodernist novel can be construed as a mirror held up for the reader to contemplate historical and subjective trauma; its disrupted chronologies, fragmented narratives and broken syntactic rules self-consciously designate themselves as an equivalent for the broken links in the traumatised subject's failed attempt to make sense of trauma.

Such mirror-like, mimetic repetition of the traumatic event through textual re-presentation undoubtedly applies to Amis's and Rushdie's attempts at fictionalising 9/11, its causes and its aftermath. In *Shalimar the Clown,* the most violent and traumatic passages in the novel take place when the narrator evokes the destruction and tearing apart of Kashmir by conflicting political and religious influences, which were contemporary to, if not responsible for, the development of jihadist groups in the region and across the border. Significantly enough, it is through a very self-conscious politics of style that Rushdie conjures up the reality of Kashmiri people's traumatic experience, the use of a broken syntax enabling him to convey the sense of pain, anger and anxiety that accompanies trauma. It is to be noted that the trauma was also Rushdie's own, since a large part of his family stems from

Kashmir. Thus, when asked about what triggered his desire to write *Shalimar the Clown* as a post-9/11 novel, in the sense that the novel registers the happening of the event and bears witness to the state of the world after 9/11, Rushdie declared:

> Another germ is that my family is from Kashmir originally [. . .] and I have felt very personally and emotionally what has happened in that beautiful place in this last half century and I wanted to find a way of exploring that. What I didn't want to do was to write a novel directly about 9/11 events or al-Qaeda, because my real motivation was to write a novel about Kashmir [. . .]. What happens in Kashmir is not only about Kashmir: in some ways you can read it like a microcosm of what is happening everywhere else in the world. (Johnson)

The trauma of strifes in Kashmir which lies at the roots of Rushdie's desire to undertake the writing of *Shalimar the Clown* takes on additional significance and import for being both personal, as it resonates with Rushdie's own individual history, and collective history, the trauma of Kashmiri people echoing other similar stories of insurgency and resistance in border countries throughout the world, such as Alsace during the Second World War, from which Max Ophuls, the slaughtered ambassador, originates. Such resonance between individual and collective trauma may explain why the passages dealing with Kashmir convey a particularly vivid sense of the reality of trauma in their visual evocations of the violence exerted both by the Indian army and by Pakistani terrorist groups. Their evocative power lies in the fact that they write violence in—linguistically, syntactically and rhythmically—by mimicking what trauma does to its victims. In the Kashmiri part, Rushdie tinkers with language so that it becomes mimetic of its object. He manipulates syntax itself and distorts the temporal frame of his narrative, piling up flashbacks upon flashforwards, so as to imitate the temporal distortions induced by trauma. Significantly, the trauma of Kashmiri people is conveyed not only through the text's repeated borrowing from the semantic field of violence and strife, but also through its writing into the very syntax. At those crucial moments when the novelist evokes the extremities of pain and suffering endured by Kashmiris, punctuation disappears and the linguistic tempo accelerates so that language stammers and verges on the inarticulate:

> There were six hundred thousand Indian troops in Kashmir but the pogrom of the pandits was not prevented, why was that. [. . .] There was one bathroom per three hundred persons in many camps why was that and the medical dispensaries lacked basic first-aid materials why was that and thousands of the displaced died because of inadequate food and shelter why was that maybe five thousand deaths because of intense heat and humidity because of snake bites and gastroenteritis and

dengue fever and stress diabetes and kidney ailments and tuberculosis and psychoneurosis and there was not a single health survey conducted by the government why was that and the pandits of Kashmir were left to rot in their slum camps, to rot while the army and the insurgency fought over the bloodied and broken valley, to dream of return, to die while dreaming of return, to die after the dream of return died so that they could not even die dreaming of it, why was that why was that why was that why was that why was that. (296)

The passage, which begins with the slow yet persistent repetition of the same question "why was that," quickly accelerates to adopt a staccato rhythm when gruesome details are accumulated to evoke the horrors of population displacement as a result of religious strife. Acceleration culminates in the climax of the question "why was that" repeating itself as if in a prolonged shout of pain which would be denied the alleviating possibility of an answer, a particularly successful stylistic feat that perfectly evokes the mechanisms of painful senseless repetition in trauma.

Similarly, Rushdie's handling of repetitive rhetorical questions proves very effective when evoking the absurdity and cruelty of the raiding and torture of Kashmiri villagers by the Indian army in the 1980s, because it reproduces the very mechanism of the apparent meaninglessness of traumatic repetition:

Who raped that lazy-eyed woman? Who raped that grey-haired lazy-eyed woman as she screamed about snake vengeance? Who raped that woman again? Who raped that dead woman? Who raped that dead woman again? (308)

It is quite clear that Rushdie's textual politics of relying on the repetition of recurring unanswered questions inscribes trauma in the very texture of the novel, as it mimics the process of traumatic neurosis, whereby the traumatising event returns in the form of flashbacks and dreams or hallucination, thus painfully repeating itself in the subject's psyche until the subject can organise those repetitions into a coherent whole which signals the beginning of recovery. Through repetition and rhetorical questioning, the trauma of Kashmiri people, and of the author himself, who witnessed the shocking destruction of everything they loved and believed in, becomes the reader's own empathic, secondary trauma. We are able to share in the novelist's sense of revolt because we are made to experience, albeit vicariously, some of the horrors inflicted on the Kashmiris, through the mimetic syntax that Rushdie creates.

Interestingly enough, Rushdie links strife and torture in Kashmir with the development of terrorism in the 1990s by establishing a clear link between the Kashmiri plot and the wider issue of terrorism which he addresses through the assassination of American former diplomat Max Ophuls. The novel can be read as an allegory of 9/11 understood not only as an attack against the US, but also, and more largely, on the Western world, since Max Ophuls's power of seduction over Shalimar's wife Boonyi lies in his capacity to embody the wealth and freedom of that world, given his American nationality, his French background and the important part he played in the Resistance during WWII. The fact that the American diplomat is brutally slaughtered in broad daylight by a Kashmiri turned terrorist therefore refers to 9/11, as has been underlined by a number of critics.[4] In the Kashmiri plot, warring Muslims and Hindus in Pachigam, the small village located at the centre of Kashmir, appear as the symbolic embodiments of the disappearance of tolerance which Rushdie places at the roots of terrorism. Ophuls's assassination, for its part, is attributed as much to personal motives (Shalimar's revenge) as to wider political reasons. However, the descriptions of Ophuls's assassination and of strife in Kashmir correspond to different stylistic choices. The discovery of Ophuls's death by his daughter and her ensuing state of shock are conveyed through negations that combine with simple and short, almost breathless sentences, monosyllabic words, and the use of free indirect speech to express India's state of shock:

> She didn't open the door. Her father wasn't there, just a mess that needed cleaning up. Where was Olga? Somebody needed to inform the janitor. There was work for a janitor to do. (40)

Rushdie's usually ornate style is deflated and neutralised in this passage to give the reader a sense of India's devastated self as a result of her traumatic loss, in the wake of her father's murder.

But beyond Rushdie's mimetic politics of writing oscillating between excess and restraint, to convey linguistically the acting out of trauma, I would like to investigate the ways in which his novel might be said to go into action itself by working trauma through. In order to do so, I will look at the narrative strategies elicited by Rushdie to overcome the repetitive senselessness of trauma and to shed some light on terrorism, and on 9/11 *qua* event. "Working through" in this context designates the liberating process whereby the scattered and fragmented experience of the traumatic event is channelled into a narrativised version of it, so that traumatic anxiety finds an outlet and recovery can be envisaged. If Rushdie's textual politics of acting out trauma results in a scattering of the fragments of the event along the numerous narrative, syntactic and temporal fractures of the text, the novel's narrative strategy reorganises those scattered fragments into some form of coherent sequence, which allows trauma to be worked through. The centrifugal structure of the novel, which mimics the scattered fragmentation of the traumatised self, is doubled up by a centripetal structure which works towards a healing of the scattered and ruptured self. The narrative of romance plays a constitutive role in this centripetal structure, as it provides the missing logical and chronological links through which senseless terror can be made sense of. Indeed, romance appears as the main motive for the terrorist's act: Shalimar commits murder out of betrayed love and revenge. The plot is built around Shalimar's quest, which begins after the American diplomat's seduction of his wife, Boonyii, when Shalimar sets out to slaughter them both and also India Ophuls, their illegitimate daughter. Although the idea that a revenge quest might be the only motivation behind terrorism does not stand up to rational analysis, it certainly invites fictional treatment and provides a circuitous structure in which the event can write itself. Although the centripetal narrative of romance, which unifies the scattered fragments of the destruction of Kashmir and of the rise of global terrorism in *Shalimar the Clown*, branches out into several episodes as befits the traditional structure of romance (Ganteau 17–18), those episodes actually come down to two main interconnected plots, revolving around the centrality of love and the love quest. Indeed, not only are love and its developments central to the plot around Max Ophuls, they are also crucial to the plot revolving around his daughter. It is because Max Ophuls falls in love with Boonyi Kaul, Shalimar's wife, and steals her away from her husband, that the clown decides to kill Max, thus in turn traumatising India. Symmetrically, India Ophuls's falling in love with Kashmir and a Kashmiri called Yuvraj helps her on her way to her recovery from the combined traumas of her mother's and of her father's deaths. Thus is the narrative of romance redoubled to work through the trauma of terrorism. Those two narratives of romance include traditional motifs of the mode such as larger-than-life heroes and heroines, drama, adventure, the marvellous verging on the fantastic, and the themes of honour and loyalty (Pearce 2). But it is not so much the motifs as the narrative of romance itself that enables the novel to process and overcome the trauma of 9/11. Indeed, narrative is essential to romance, as Lynne Pearce argues in *Romance Writing*: "Romance and narrative have always gone hand in hand, and what romantic love seeks to conceal, romance (the genre) reveals through its wonderful and spectacular stories" (2–3).[5] Moreover, the narrative of romance is essential to the processing of trauma because it provides the modal framework and narrative structure needed to reorganise the different scattered fragments of the plot into a significant whole.

WORKING THROUGH TRAUMA

In Rushdie's novel, the narrative of romance plays a neutralising and soothing role which makes it possible for the novelist to put into words the extreme terror and violence that threaten to destroy language. The narrative of romance enables Rushdie to rewrite trauma into a coherent and recognisable, albeit slightly displaced, whole, by providing a local cause for the despair and anger underlying terrorism. Fiction allows precisely for that freedom, which consists in pondering over a phenomenon in a non-conceptual way, by displacing it and recontextualising it in the fictional plot. This process of decontextualising and recontextualising a phenomenon or an event partakes of the fictional freedom that allows a novelist to create a convincing alternative to the real world, with a capacity to reflect on the violence of that world. Thus, Shalimar the terrorist's own personal frustration, pain and anger are shown as causes that might be extrapolated to the terrorists of 9/11, if repoliticised, in so far as Shalimar's victim, Max Ophuls, embodies hateful Western imperialism in Shalimar's eyes.

Furthermore, the narrative of romance enables Rushdie to intertwine love and violence in his novel: the tradition of romance is built precisely around the thematisation of the cliché of thwarted love.[6] The transformation of Shalimar the passionate lover into a ruthless terrorist and assassin becomes possible within the structure of the romance narrative. Boonyi Kaul had already thematised such possible association between romance and murder when she placed her story under the sign of romantic love, ironically connecting passionate love with death. On the occasion of Shalimar and Boonyi's first night together, Boonyi had gently mocked her lover when he declared he would kill her if she ever left him, saying: "What a romantic you are [. . .]. You say the sweetest things" (Rushdie 61). The ironic contrast between romance and killing underlying this seminal passage ominously articulates romance and violence, just as it is programmed in the epigraph borrowed from *Romeo and Juliet*, which invites the reader to draw an equation between Shalimar and Boonyi and the "star-crossed lovers" in Shakespeare's play. Romeo and Juliet appear as two archetypal romance lovers insofar as their destiny is dictated by their family names. This epigraph thematises the romance *topos* of impossible love and prepares the reader for the link between love and terrorism that will be made throughout the novel. Thus, borrowing from the tradition of romance allows Rushdie to channel darker and traumatic realities into a recognisable and meaningful narrative structure. By providing a narrative for those darker *unheimliche* forces, romance in *Shalimar the Clown* makes sense of, and provides an explanatory motif for Shalimar's change from a beautiful and gifted young man at the beginning of the novel, into a cold-hearted terrorist who, after having carried out a number of attacks in Northern Africa, sets out on his revenge quest and slaughters both Max Ophuls and Boonyi. Although the discrepancy and the displacement that the narrative of romance introduces in the terrorist's motives remain perceptible to the reader—who knows that there are many more complex political, social, and even psychological motivations behind terrorism—, this simplification does not prevent the novel from effectively taking up the issue of terrorism and inviting the reader to think about its possible motives, for it is by borrowing its narrative structure from that of romance that *Shalimar the Clown* can re-inscribe the original trauma of violence and murder into a temporal sequence.

Alain Badiou has shown quite forcefully that the event represents a rupture in time.[7] The reason why the traumatic event is traumatic is because it disturbs the flow of time as it comes to interrupt the sequence between a before and an after, thus making it difficult for the subject to reorganise facts into a logical and chronological sequence. The narrative of romance in its very sequential temporality reorganises and reorders the scattered fragments of experience. This centripetal effect brought about by the temporal sequencing of romance narrative is made visible in the novel, or rather born out of a failure of the discourse of the law to solve the problem of terrorism. When India brings Shalimar to trial, it is quite obvious that the narrative of the law helps her on her way to psychological recovery. Indeed, as the reader proceeds towards the end of the novel, India succeeds in bringing Shalimar to court, which enables her to reorder the sequence of her father's death according to the logic of facts. It is to be noted that the text underlines the therapeutic effect of that legal representation of reality according to the temporality of facts. Significantly enough, India's traumatic nightmares cease to bother her after the trial has started. She can at last face her tormentor and express her anger. However, the therapeutic effect is limited because the trial brings out the truth of facts but bypasses the reconciliation process that is needed for psychic wounds to be healed. Shalimar refuses to answer India's questions and to abandon his revenge plans, making it very unlikely for a fair trial to take place, where India might be able to confront him with his deeds and obtain repentance, a possible prelude to reconciliation. Thanks to the narrative of the law, India gets more direct conscious access to the traumatic event she experienced when witnessing her father's assassination. But it is only through the second narrative of romance, that of India's love for and in Kashmir,[8] that trauma will be fully worked through. On top of bearing witness to Rushdie's belief in the importance of the fair legal treatment of terrorists, the narrative of the law in its liberating function for India Ophuls is but a step towards her full recovery. She will need romance, and Rushdie himself will need to include a second narrative of romance in the last part of his novel, to complete the writing process of trauma. This second romantic plot appears as a further injunction for the reader to interpret romance narrative as a possible way of working through trauma in a post-9/11 world, where Western economic dominance is exerted through imperialistic forms of power.

CONCLUSION

The pervasive mode of romance in *Shalimar the Clown* may not have gone down so well with reviewers or critics of the book. For instance, in the chapter he dedicated to this novel in his essay about Rushdie's fictional work, D.C.R.A. Goonetilleke derisively stated that: "[t]he novel seems a vintage Hollywood romance" (175). In a similar vein, John Updike in his *New Yorker* review of the novel wrote that it resembled "a Bollywood movie with its emphasis on tacky tinsel visual effects to create a mythical reality" (Updike). In both cases, what seems to irritate the critics is the salience of the motifs of romance in Rushdie's novel. Yet, it is not so much the motifs as the very logical and chronological structure of the narrative of romance that enables Rushdie's *Shalimar the Clown* to process trauma to our literary satisfaction. Love as articulated by the narrative of romance is indeed a way for the novelist to write himself out of the speechlessness with which the trauma of 9/11 has threatened writing, because romance caters for the darker possibilities of love, in consistently thematising thwarted love. Moreover, the meaningful borrowing from a well-established, well-structured and recognisable tradition enables the writer to channel the traumatic reality of 9/11 into a coherent, understandable form. The novel clearly shows, albeit in a fictional way, that the post-9/11 state of shock described by Amis in his collection of essays *The Second Plane* is something which Rushdie himself experienced in the wake of the attacks as something of an even larger scope, a difficulty turned global, as a response to the arguably first global traumatic event. Romance, in the form of the love story between Shalimar and Boonyi on the one hand, and between India Ophuls and Yuvraj the Kashmiri on the other hand, makes it possible for Rushdie to explore the apparent senselessness of terrorism, because it reorders events and facts into a coherent and consecutive sequence. Contrary to the literary critics who riled Rushdie's novel on account of its sentimental plot, romance in *Shalimar the Clown* plays an essential role in Rushdie's capacity to narrate our traumatised world and to give an account of what seems to escape understanding and rationalisation, namely the ability of terrorism to devalue life to the point of worthlessness. Romance enables Rushdie to rely on a well-established narrative tradition to shape and mould the shapeless reality of terrorist attacks. This narrative makes it possible for him to place fictional words on the motivations of terrorist action which Amis deemed irrational: "Terrorism undermines morality. Then, too, it undermines reason" (22). For Rushdie, romance is, therefore, a way to capture the elusive dimension of an event the purpose of which resided in its capacity to defy reason so as to provoke terror. It is precisely because *Shalimar the Clown* can be read as a well-rehearsed saga repeating stories of love and revenge that Rushdie can confront the horrors of terrorism through writing, and the readers themselves begin to come to terms with the event.

NOTES

1. "Formally, the romance is rhizomatic in form; it is replete with episodes and parentheses, presents the reader with characters that tend to be types, and favours such binary formal structures as the allegory or the archetype. In aesthetic terms, the romance favours the exotic and the remote over the realistic and the mundane" (Ganteau 16–17, my translation). Barbara Fuchs gives a similar definition of the notion of the romance. Gillian Beer defines the Romance as a "cluster of properties: the themes of love and adventure, a certain withdrawal from their own societies on the part of both reader and romance hero, profuse sensuous detail, simplified characters (often with a suggestion of allegorical significance) a serene intermingling of the unexpected and the everyday, a complex and prolonged succession of incidents usually

without a single climax, a happy ending, amplitude of proportions, a strongly enforced code of conduct to which all the characters must comply" (8).

2. The distinction is borrowed from van der Kolk-and van der Hart (163).

3. In her thorough analysis of the genre and the mode of romance, Barbara Fuchs traces back our common understanding of romance to the narrative poems that emerged during the twelfth century, featuring the quest for love as a central motif: "In the narrow literary sense, romance is the name given to a particular genre: the narrative poems that emerge in 12th century France and quickly make their way around Europe. These popular poems were known as romances because they were written in the vernacular, or romance, languages derived from Latin, as opposed to Latin itself, which was the traditional language of learning; these poems are typically concerned with aristocratic characters such as kings and queens, knights and ladies, and their chivalric pursuits. They are often organized around a quest for love or adventure, and involve a variety of marvellous elements. This is the genre from which we derive our popular sense of romance" (4).

4. Natasha Walter has cogently argued that Rushdie's characters are often meant to embody the fate of nations: "Once we [. . .] return to the point of the murder we realise what was hidden from us the first time it was played out: the grand symbolism of the act. So the resentful Muslim, in revenge for what he sees as the corruption wreaked by the west, is being used by greater political forces to try to cut down the American Jew; leaving in his wake a confused individual, neither western nor eastern, who is nevertheless determined to understand and to survive" (2005).

5. Romance in *Shalimar the Clown* arguably provides a happy coda to the novel, in spite of the fact that the story of love around Boonyi and Shalimar turns sour because, towards the end of the novel, India Ophuls, the daughter of the slaughtered former ambassador to India, visits Kashmir and falls in love with a Kashmiri called Yuvraj.

6. "The traumatic, invisible moment of rejection experienced by most lovers at some point in their relationships is converted into a spectacular adventure with a happy ending. So intrinsic is this resolution to romance that romantic love has been defined as a quest for obstacles" (Pearce 4). In the case of *Shalimar the Clown*, the happy ending requires the building of a second plot, as will be shown.

7. "What happens—and inasmuch as it happens, goes beyond its multiple-being—is precisely this: a fragment of multiplicity wrested from all inclusion. In a flash, this fragment [. . .] affirms its un-foundedness, its pure advent, which is intransitive to the place in which 'it' comes. The fragment thereby also affirms its belonging to itself, since this coming can originate from nowhere else" (Badiou 2010, 103). In Badiou's classification of events, however, the traumatic event at stake in Rushdie's novel is more a disaster than an event in the positive sense of the term. Yet, its suddenness and unprepared character give this particular disaster the structure of an event.

8. The fact that she changes her name from "India" to "Kashmira" (324) shows that her destiny is allegorical, and her individual trauma endowed with collective resonances.

WORKS CITED

Amis, Martin. *The Second Plane: September 11: 2001–2007.* London: Vintage, 2008. Print.

Badiou, Alain, *Circonstances, 1: Kosovo, 11 septembre, Chirac/Le Pen*. 2003. Paris: L. Sheer, 2008. Print.

———.*Theoretical Writings*. Trans. Ray Brassier and Alberto Toscano, 2004. New York and London: Continuum, 2010. Print.

Baudrillard, Jean. *The Spirit of Terrorism*. London and New York: Verso, 2002. Print.

Beer, Gillian. *The Romance*. London: Methuen, 1970. Print.

Caruth, Cathy. *Unclaimed Experience, Trauma, Narrative and History*. Baltimore: The Johns Hopkins UP. 1996. Print.

Caruth, Cathy, ed. *Trauma, Explorations in Memory*. Baltimore: The Johns Hopkins UP, 1995. Print.

Derrida, Jacques and Jürgen Habermas. *Philosophy in a Time of Terror*. Chicago: The U of Chicago P, 2003. Print.

Elam, Diane. *Romancing the Postmodern*. New York and London: Routledge, 1992. Print.

Fortin-Tournès, Anne-Laure. "*Saturday* by Ian McEwan: The Resurgence of the Event in Allegorical Form." *L'Atelier* (January 2010): 62–76. http://latelier.u-paris10.fr. Retrieved on 7 March 2011. Web.

Freud, Sigmund. *Moses and Monotheism*. 1939. New York: Vintage Books, 1976. Print.

Fuchs, Barbara. *Romance*. New York and London: Routledge, 2004. Print.

Ganteau, Jean-Michel. *Peter Ackroyd et la musique du passé*. Paris: Michel Houdiard, 2008. Print.

Goonetilleke, D.C.R.A. *Salman Rushdie*. Basingstoke and New York: Palgrave Macmillan, 2010. Print.

Greenberg, Judith. *Trauma at Home. After 9/11*. Winnipeg: Bison Books, 2003.

Habermas, Jürgen. *Philosophy in a Time of Terror*. Chicago: U of Chicago P, 2003. Print.

Hirsch, Marianne. "I took pictures: September 2001 and Beyond." *Trauma at Home, After 9/11*. Ed. Judith Greenberg, 2003. 69–86. Print.

Johnson, Sarah. "Salman Rushdie and a Story of Paradise Lost." Radio Netherlands (Transmission Date: Sunday 30 July 2006). http://www.martinfrost.ws/html files/july2006/rushdie_lost. Retrieved on 8 March 2011. Web.

Kaplan, E. Ann. *Trauma Culture, the Politics of Terror and Loss in Media and Literature*. New Brunswick, NJ: Rutgers UP, 2005. Print.

LaCapra, Dominick. *Writing History, Writing Trauma*. Baltimore: The Johns Hopkins UP, 2001. Print.

Laub, Dori. "September 11, 2001–An Event without a Voice." *Trauma at Home, after 9/11*. Ed. Judith Greenberg, 2003. 204–15. Print.

Pearce, Lynne. *Romance Writing*. Cambridge: Polity. 2007. Print.

Rushdie, Salman. *Shalimar the Clown*. New York: Random House. 2005. Print.

Updike, John. "Paradises Lost, Rushdie's *Shalimar the Clown*." *The New Yorker* 5 September 2005. http://www.newyorker.com/archive/2005/09/05/050905crbo_books?printable=true#ixzz0vN9Ccz5n. Retrieved on 1 December 2010. Web.

van der Kolk, Bessel A. and Onno van der Hart. "The Intrusive Past: The Flexibility of Memory and the Engraving of Trauma." *Trauma: Explorations in Memory*. Ed. Cathy Caruth. 1995. 158–82. Print.

Versluys, Kristiaan, *Out of the Blue*, New York: Columbia UP, 2009. Print.

Walter, Natasha. "The Children of Paradise." Review of *Salimar the Clown* by Salman Rushdie. *The Guardian* 3 September 2005. http://www.guardian.co.uk/books/2005/sep/03/fiction.salmanrushdie. Retrieved on 11 July 2011. Web.

Whitehead, Anne. *Trauma Fiction*. Edinburgh: Edinburgh UP, 2004. Print.

12 Checking Out

Trauma and Genre in Ian McEwan's *The Child in Time*

Brian Diemert

Romance, Northrop Frye claimed, is the "structural core of all fiction" (15), but how can one represent the overwhelming experience of trauma in any narrative, let alone fiction? There are, as Hayden White observed, "fictions of factual representation" (121–34) that coordinate and arrange events within a structure of fulfilment: expectations are met and endings are securely placed, but trauma "issues a challenge to the capacities of narrative knowledge [. . .]. [T]rauma is anti-narrative" (Luckhurst 79). In history, trauma exists on a vast scale: racial, national, and individual horrors have been experienced in incomprehensible forms. But trauma itself has been a contested term (Luckhurst 1–15): is it physiological, psychological, or both? What constitutes trauma and is traumatic? Is the same thing equally traumatic for all who experience it? Can it be collectively experienced or only individually? (As a corollary, is guilt its complement?). Is it contagious? Can we speak of "trans-generational haunting"; that is, can trauma be passed on to later generations? (Luckhurst 69). Whether one is witness to genocidal atrocity or a car accident (even a railway accident[1]), trauma can be experienced, and it can obviously involve whole populations (as with the Shoah, Hiroshima, Cambodia, Armenia, Rwanda). Ultimately, however, such collective moments depend upon their being shared discursively (van Alphen 37), which may or may not bring its own problems. Ian McEwan has spent much of his career probing manifestations of trauma in his novels. The Nazi experience haunts *Black Dogs*; incestuous rape, murder, various cruelties inhabit other works; indeed, it is not for nothing that early reviewers labelled Ian McEwan "Ian Macabre" (Walsh): trauma may well be his subject. *The Child in Time* (1987), his break-through third novel,[2] explores the aftermath of a traumatic event (the abduction of a toddler in a supermarket) that remains an aporia, as the crime is never solved. In McEwan's world, there are no safe spaces: trauma can be initiated in the most mundane of settings. And, yet, *The Child in Time* uneasily places trauma within the structure of romance; its repetitions, correspondences, and coincidences are amply evident in a text offering the happy ending of romance.

An easy point of comparison with *The Child in Time* is Graham Swift's *Waterland*, in which narrator Tom Crick works tirelessly to account for his wife Mary's inexplicable action of abducting a baby from the now ironically named Safeway grocery store. Crick, a history teacher facing dismissal ostensibly because of budgetary constraints that mean the loss of history as a discrete and teachable subject, ceaselessly burrows into the past to recount stories that seem to have bearing on the present, but explaining is, as his student Price says, "a way of avoiding the facts while you pretend to get near them" (145). Crick's narration might best be characterised as an example of "dissociation," which narrative theorist Mieke Bal, in her discussion of traumatic narration, contrasts with Freud's concept of repression insofar as "dissociation doubles the strand of the narrative series of events by splitting off a sideline" while "repression interrupts the flow of narratives that shape memory," creating an ellipsis in the narrative which "stalls" the discursive process (van Alphen 27). In other words, "dissociation splits off material that cannot then be reincorporated into the main narrative" (Bal ix). Swift's book narrates trauma through dissociation, but the moment of occurrence, Mary's abduction of the baby, remains outside the narrative—a space she explains in logocentric terms: "God told me" (232). In both novels, events and time conspire to create an unredeemable moment that is suspended and apart from narrative while yet being integral to it. In this way, both novels obsess over time and its distortions (Introduction to this volume 8).

The unredeemable moment is, of course, the place of trauma, which "cannot be integrated into diachrony; it is a blockage, 'a bit monstrous, unformed, confusing, confounding'," Roger Luckhurst summarises Jean-François Lyotard's *Heidegger and 'the Jews'* (qt. in Luckhurst 81), and Lyotard's view is widely held. Bal speaks of the "blockage" as a "stutter" or, echoing Freud, an unresolved repetition (as in Freud, "Remembering" 150–51). Trauma is the gap within a narrative that resists narrative: "Traumatic memories remain present for the subject with particular vividness and/or totally resist integration. In both cases, they cannot become narrative" (Bal viii). The frequently cited Cathy Caruth argues further that "traumatic experience [. . .] suggests a certain paradox that the most direct seeing of a violent event may occur as an absolute inability to know it" (Caruth 91–92). The problem here is epistemological: how do we "know" an experience? And, van Alphen adds, the event "depends on discourse to come about: forms of experience do not just depend on the event or history that is being experienced, but also on the discourse in which the event is expressed/thought/conceptualized" (24). In this sense, the event is already a representation because, as Bal said, "to enter memory, the traumatic event of the past needs to be narratable" (x). But trauma is "anti-narrative" (Luckhurst 79): its very excess ruptures established forms of expression and eludes discursive formulas.[3] So, in this respect, trauma lies outside narrative while also being the spur to narrative: "all literature is probably a version of the apocalypse [. . .] literature [. . .] represents the ultimate coding of our crises, of our most intimate and most serious apocalypses" (Kristeva 207–08). While the application of this insight to a kind of macro-history is doubtful—Dominick LaCapra argues against a vision of history as trauma (xi)—, at the level of individual experience, disruption forces narration: the quiet community that encounters the unexpected stranger, the sudden death in a family, the collapse of a marriage, fortune, structure, a stolen child—in each case, stories proliferate.

Trauma's disruption in the ordinary course of life is felt in its aftermath: no one expects the next moments of one's life to be irrevocably altering, but that is the traumatic moment when all preconceived narratives of the future are broken. Trauma breeches the divide between the inner life's expectation and the outer life's reality (Luckhurst 3): what is expected and imagined, if only in the banal anticipation of a future that is much like the present, is no longer possible. In a sense, two narratives, of the expected and the unexpected, of romance and irony, conflict to produce a phased stasis that is the space of trauma.

Much of trauma literature and the commentary on it deal with the Holocaust as "the worst imaginable collective trauma" (Luckhurst 65)—sexual abuse being "the worst individual trauma" (Luckhurst 65)—, and these subjects dominate the discussion and theory of trauma in literature. McEwan's *The Child in Time* explicitly involves neither—though both shadow the narrative—but the book can be usefully considered in light of these discussions, for *The Child in Time* picks up from *Waterland* to place trauma in a life and a love story. Stephen Lewis, loading groceries on to a check-out belt, turns to discover that his daughter, Kate, has disappeared. Few things can be more distressing than a child's loss, as McEwan has acknowledged (Groes 124), and he probes the awful consequences. For all of his thematic highlighting—the recurrent referencing to time conceived in scientific, psychological, historical and textual terms—, the moment of Kate's loss shatters Stephen's and his wife Julie's lives together and apart[4]:

> Later, in the sorry months and years, Stephen was to make efforts to re-enter this moment, to burrow his way back through the folds between events, [. . .] and reverse his decision. But time—not necessarily as it is, for who knows that, but as thought has constituted it—monomaniacally forbids second chances. There is no absolute time, his friend Thelma had told him on occasions, no independent entity. Only our particular and weak understanding. [. . .] They [Kate and Stephen on the morning of her disappearance] stepped outdoors as though into a storm. (10)

The final simile refers to the bustling traffic and noise of London's urban space, but its meaning expands metaphorically.

Brief consideration of McEwan's book, of his fiction, and of Swift's *Waterland*, pushes us to recognise trauma as precisely that which cannot be assimilated to explanatory structures of any kind—whether historical, psychological, generic, legal, religious, scientific, or the rest—none is satisfactory, and it is here that trauma's problematic relationship to narrative and particularly romance is most clearly revealed. That is, while trauma and romance are characterised by excess (Introduction 7; Elam 12), trauma is trauma because, as Caruth influentially argues, it defies narrative and so cannot be assimilated within the psyche. Nonetheless, contemporary cliché retails this futility with variants of Freud's "working through" (1982), such as "closure" or "coming to terms"—all of which imply the secure placement of the traumatic event within a psychic narrative. From media's perspective, the notion of "closure," expressed in the arrest, incarceration and, in many jurisdictions, execution of a criminal perpetrator, conveniently recognises the formal requirement of a story to end, to be replaced by a new representation of trauma. In this sense, the concept of "closure," however artificial, narrativises trauma and locates it in a context that assimilates trauma to meaning: trauma is pared, and what is left is its representation. The gesture essentially sacrifices trauma to romance: the incomprehensible, the unnarratable, is given "the structural core of all fiction" (Frye 15). Romance, in its broadest forms, disrupts mimetic codes to present basic structures in which "the world we want and the world we don't want" are polarised (Frye 5). Good and evil, innocence and experience, fear and loneliness, among many, are clearly exposed and explained in romance: meaning is found to exist; trauma is horrible but treatable. Life goes on, resolving itself in comprehensible patterns—that is the romance narrative.

McEwan's *The Child in Time* sketches trauma's terrain uneasily with a narrative arc that emphasises the possibilities of repetition, recurrence, and return—all features of the traumatic experience as articulated by Freud but also the staples of romance (Whitehead 84–86; Introduction 8)—for ultimately, in the novel, Stephen and Julie are to have another child. After nine gestative chapters, the novel's end appears to offer comfort. Stephen, whom we have followed, has "come to terms" and, in a remarkably layered scene involving a truck accident, is figuratively reborn (105–15). Not only does he artfully drive his car through "a six foot gap formed between a road sign and the front bumper of the motionless lorry" (107),[5] but he rescues the somewhat comical truck driver by using a jack to help pry him from his crushed cab. All of this occurs on Stephen's way to visit Thelma and Charles Darke, who has regressed to boyhood. The obvious (re)birthing aspects of the accident, however, mask several important features of its place in McEwan's narrative. Here, again, the novel emphasises an aspect of time's relativity through a process of "dilation" that Patricia Parker sees as typical of romance (76) insofar as "the rapidity of events was accommodated by the slowing of time" (McEwan 2005, 106) throughout the brief duration of the accident—five seconds, it is assumed (108)—, and "in this slowing of time, there was a sense of a fresh beginning" (107). Tellingly, even the truck's driver exaggerates the amount of time he spent trapped in the wreckage (114). The accident epitomises a Freudian traumatic experience (similar to a railway accident) that offers Stephen a close encounter with death (a traumatic variant of the loss of his child).[6] For Stephen, the accident is a turning point, the moment the romance narrative offers to signal the rebirth of the hero: nearly dead, Stephen begins his recovery to become a force of new life. (A parallel moment of possible re-birth is found in Stephen's recovery from his uncanny vision of his parents' discussing Stephen's own gestation). Similarly, late in the novel and as a part of a nearly two-page long account, Julie rapidly re-presents a comparable narrative arc from her perspective in terms that echo the novel's telling of Stephen's life. Her consideration of abortion is particularly relevant given Stephen's experience of seeing, perhaps intervening, as Stephen's mother suggests (207), in his parents' discussion of his own birth (207). Julie's narrative is unnatural, a sort of "convenient conversation" (and so perhaps ironical), but is nonetheless important to our sense of narrative satisfaction.[7] In this moment the elasticity of romance, its contrariness and illogicality are revealed.

These events, of course, conform to the romance pattern—essentially comic in its orientation—but in McEwan's case, heavily marked by the unassimilated trauma that is Kate's loss—is she "the child in time"? And to unpack this concept reveals the many ways in which trauma has been theorised—does she continue to exist in time, in another dimension of time, or is she suspended in and out of time? Perhaps Stephen only dreams of her continued existence, or, perhaps, all possible moments continue to exist including one in which her existence is assured? (69). Of course, there may be a more general interpretation of the title—is the child any child, the child inside us all, the child in Darke who asserts himself, the child in Stephen who turns *Hashish*, his first novel as he originally conceived it, into *Lemonade*, the prefatory material Darke published that cemented Stephen's place as a writer for young readers? Stephen imagines Kate's continued growth as "the essence of time itself." And he thinks that: "Without the fantasy of her continued existence he was lost, time would stop" (2). Consequently, at one point, he poignantly believes he has found her: "The thick bangs bobbed against her white forehead, her chin was raised, she had a dreamy appearance. He was looking at his daughter" (165–66). While the adjective, "dreamy" (and a faint echoing of Yeats's "Among School Children"[8]) might alert us to Stephen's mistake, the fact that he even makes it reinforces our sense of Stephen's desperate desire to keep Kate within the most basic of narrative structures (chronological time) so as to mitigate the trauma of her loss. Again, McEwan exposes the essential contradiction here between trauma and narrative. Trauma is unassimilable. No narrative can contain it, much less erase it, as McEwan's later novel *Atonement* (2001) illustrates through Briony Tallis's surprising, though futile—and according to J. Hillis Miller's argument in this volume, traumatising for the reader—rewriting of the past.

Julie's account, filling out the final pages of *The Child in Time*, is motivated by the insistence of the romance mode on resolution, not realism (she is, after all in the final stages of labour, so one doubts her coherence), and it gives readers satisfaction, especially in the repetition of earlier motifs (such as her consideration of abortion), but it does raise several questions (beyond the obvious ones about the police investigation and Kate's fate). The book's ending is very moving, but Julie's incredible speech points, again, to the essential conflict between trauma and narrative, between trauma and "deeper patterns of time" (254). Julie has reconciled herself—"I had to stop running from her in my mind" (254)—and has accepted the past:

> 'She was a lovely daughter, a lovely girl.' [. . .] It was then, three years later, that they began to cry together at last, for the lost, irreplaceable child who would not grow older for them, whose characteristic look and movement could never be dispelled by time. They held on to each other [. . .] they started to talk through their crying as best they could [. . .]. In the wild expansiveness of their sorrow they undertook to heal everyone and everything [. . .]; and while they could never redeem the loss of their daughter, they would love her through their new child, and never close their minds to the possibility of her return. (256)

The moment of traumatic effraction is unredeemable by definition, but the new birthing is, in the narrative, implicitly the reward of acceptance and of working through: the result of ceasing to run. Not even McEwan's ironical reflection on Julie's and Stephen's commitment to universal healing dampens the moment's effect. That the abduction remains unresolved hardly raises doubts, as Dominic Head suggests (12), about McEwan's confidence in narrative resolution (at least at this point in his career), but the narrative's convenient ending may do so. In this case, the excessive qualities of romance—its presentation of a world in which things work out—points towards both resolution (the "happy" ending) and to the place of unnarratable trauma. *The Child in Time* is not, after all, a crime story (we read nothing of a police investigation), so Kate's unresolved disappearance stands as little more than the space of loss into which narrative moves. It is the spark, analogous to lost jewels, stolen papers, a body in the library, a missing child, that opens a story of consequences, but is fundamentally and coldly insignificant in itself.

McEwan's comforting if bittersweet conclusion is far from unique in fiction that deals with even the most extreme of traumas. Canadian novelist and poet Anne Michaels's *Fugitive Pieces* presents us with an analogous vision to McEwan's that anticipates the consequences of trauma. Interestingly, Michaels's book also adopts a romance paradigm and offers a reassuring and quite beautiful ending to a novel that deals with trauma on the largest canvas. Her conclusion hints at a reconciliation between Naomi and Ben, whose unfocused anger has abated. Of course, the traumatic moment—in Michaels's case the Shoah—remains paradigmatically unassimilable. It exists outside of the narrative, like the fading photograph

Ben finds (Michaels 251–52).[9] Stephen and Julie's more assured reunion (Naomi and Ben's reconciliation is anticipated but not narrated) still has, in narrative terms, the unassimilated loss of Kate behind it. Thematically, the traumatic moment of Kate's disappearance stands in time's stream as an obstacle to Stephen's and Julie's lives and to Thelma's theorising about time, which, the narrator explains, "monumentally forbids second chances" (McEwan 2005, 10). Stephen can never do over the moment of Kate's disappearance, but in a novel built on patterns of return—theorised by Thelma Darke, experienced by Stephen in the vision of his parents (64–66), neurotically enacted by Darke, and found in the book's recurring imagery and language (among other places)—Kate's abduction remains the narrative's aporia thematising the unutterability of trauma.

In *Waterland*, Mary Crick's theft of a baby in the supermarket is similarly treated. For all of Tom Crick's accounts, his explanation is recessive and elusive—perhaps it is, like any event, ultimately beyond rational power to articulate: "Events elude meaning, but we look for meaning" (Swift 122). Swift, of course, does not present the trauma of that event from an immediate perspective (neither the baby, nor his family, nor the criminal are central here). And to a great extent the abduction, though gravely consequential for Crick, is of a different order, certainly less traumatic, than the account in *The Child in Time*. For one thing, Crick's circular attempts to account for a horrifying action, however dissociative they may be, do offer readers some sense, albeit not definitive, of where Mary's moment can fit into a personal narrative. This situation is quite different from that of *The Child in Time*, where the extreme emphasis on time as a repeating and folded thing fails to account for the randomness of Kate's disappearance or to bring her back. The two books, then, paradoxically, can be read dialectically with McEwan's being an answer to Swift's. They formally represent trauma in two different modes—dissociation and stutter, a Freudian compulsion to repeat (Luckhurst 9), but both implicitly challenge a poststructuralist theory that suggests experience is only recognised discursively, and so is the "product" of language, through their adherence to the law of chronology.

Within McEwan's œuvre, the moment of chance, the moment that alters everything for his characters, is heavily probed: freakish events (a balloon accident, a car accident, a misunderstood letter, or a slippery rug) inevitably alter the course of characters' lives and disrupt their expected narrative lines while simultaneously spurring the narrative we read. Neither Swift nor McEwan find solace in metanarratives and both acknowledge the impossible task of explaining a traumatic event. In Swift's view, any explanation is another story requiring further explanation; for McEwan, any representation or explanation of trauma is pointless because it is without narrative (hence, his challenge). To speak the event is to reduce it, to formalise it (place it in form and narrative coding), and to locate it in history's pattern of cause-effect relations.

In this sense, those who fell to silence in the wake of the Shoah (Adorno's "no poetry after Auschwitz"[10] is often seen to typify this reaction, however misunderstood) recognise the experience as rupture, a chasm in the course of history: "By its uniqueness, [. . .] the Holocaust defies literature."[11] Yet individual history, we recall, is made up of chasms; as Crick observes: "History begins only at the point where things go wrong: history is born only with trouble, with perplexity, with regret" (Swift 92). From another point of view, a narrative line without deviation or disruption "is void of interest, energy, and the possibility of narration" (Brooks 139)—history, in this sense, is the break that becomes memorable because it is a break. This circumstance points precisely to the doubled difficulty of representing trauma which stands apart from the normal flow of disruption both in memory and in narrative (Luckhurst 3). In the recollection of history, silence too easily becomes forgetting, but in the face of the unsayable, narration fails.

It is to McEwan's credit that he presents these difficulties in *The Child in Time* on a manageable scale. The question of scale, however, may be undecided for there can be little doubt that McEwan sought to introduce Stephen Lewis's trauma by alluding to the twentieth-century's great trauma of the Holocaust through Stephen's early encounter with the "licensed" beggar. Not only is she presented with severely cropped hair and a badge, but McEwan also notes the crudity of bad government, which separates "public policy from intimate feeling," and Stephen's speculation that she has been "deloused" (3). Stephen and Julie suffer the event of Kate's loss, but the backdrop is a vague, dystopian world whose government is hostile to children (suggesting broader culpability in Kate's disappearance). Still, there can be little doubt that McEwan's description of the beggar is meant to alert us to a relationship between the personal and the political, the individual and the community. Michaels, on the other hand, chose to let the Holocaust stand behind her characters as the explanation for all they experience and do.

McEwan, too, often turns to history to offer a backdrop for his characters. The anti-war demonstration in *Saturday* (2005), or the Cold War in *The Innocent* (1990) offer two clear examples, while *Black Dogs* (1992), his book to follow *The Child in Time*, is cast against the fall of the Berlin Wall and, more significantly, the Holocaust. In *Black Dogs* moments in time stand apart (such as the fall of the Berlin wall), but the past resonates/echoes in the present (the apocryphal account of the dogs) while the conditions that created these circumstances remain (Bernard is violently assaulted at the wall). In *The Child in Time*, however, McEwan imagined a dystopian world of Thatcherite extremes that complicates his contextual space. His imagining of the prospect of nuclear conflict during the 1996 Olympic games (a decade in his future while writing the novel) is, perhaps, odd to us now because we live in a post-Cold War world, but there is still an uncanny reverberation here in so far as the Atlanta Olympics were marred by a bombing (albeit non-nuclear).

The Child in Time, then, not only anticipates McEwan's later work, but it gives us what may be his first mature probing of the traumatic in narrative. In Stephen and Julie's life "the lost child [is] between them" always (72), and no power of magical thinking, no amount of pretending, can bring her back. This point is most poignantly seen in Stephen's preparation for and re-enactment of Kate's birthday (146–50). Of course, he recognises the gesture as fiction, a sad game because no narrative can atone for the loss, yet he performs the preparatory ritual. Trauma is shown to disarm metanarrative and mock metafiction. Literary theory has occasionally offered a vision of the world as pure text,[12] but trauma upends such a suggestion. Tom Crick circles his subject, even reports his conversations with Mary about the baby, but the explanation eludes Crick. Mary's account is more direct— "God told me to" (Swift 232). McEwan's dealing with the aftermath of trauma repeatedly shows how such explanations bump against the fact of Kate's loss. Thelma Darke explains time (135–39) in some detail but none of it means that the moment of Kate's loss can be avoided, however "variable" time is.

For McEwan, Kate's disappearance is the canker in a narrative—its beginning—that develops and repeats images of return (it is the absent presence). Darke praises Stephen's book, *Lemonade*, about childhood experience, for its perception of childhood as timeless (32), Julie remarks during Stephen's first visit, "Here we are again" (70), and Stephen, after his narrow escape (107), rescues the truck driver in a scene calculated to suggest birth (112). While not exactly a stutter, for each incident of repetition is unique and moves the narrative forward, these patterns of recurrence stumble over the fact that nothing brings Kate back.

McEwan's narrative enacts the psychological process described by Freud in his discussion of trauma. Swift's representational strategy is somewhat different and is built on dissociation rather than the repressive stutter that echoes in McEwan's text. Within Swift's pattern there can be no end, no conclusion—its final question is, "someone best explain" (Swift 310). McEwan's book, though, is driven by the arc of the romance narrative and, consequently, compelled to resolve its tensions in Stephen and Julie's reunion and in the rebirth of family. As Frye notes, romance "brings us into a present where past and future are gathered" (179). Instead of "someone best explain," we get "boy or girl?" and the overwhelming feeling, whatever doubts we may have, because loss too can be repeated and the "sorry months and years" (10) remain, that trauma has been worked through.

NOTES

1. Freud exemplified the experience of delayed trauma by describing the phenomenon in terms of a railway accident in *Moses and Monotheism* (84). Luckhurst summarises the etiology of the railway accident in the nineteenth century (21–23).
2. The book is widely acknowledged as a shift in McEwan's œuvre. See Dominic Head's gathering of critical opinions in *Ian McEwan*. Malcolm Bradbury's

The Modern British Novel 1878–2001 is quoted in Head, 7. Similar opinions can be found in *The Fiction of Ian McEwan*, edited by Peter Childs. McEwan acknowledges the book as a shift in interview (Groes 115–16).

3. Extremely, then, no event can be contained in discourse. Geoffrey Hartman writes: "memories can only perpetuate themselves by entering a figurative space, an inverted present different from the 'anterior present' they evoke. [. . .] Writing, in seeking to recapture the unique or to image what is absent, hardens it, so that we are left with the consciousness of language as incorporating a void [. . .]. That void is at once very personal and quite impersonal: the loss of a sister, but also what language, as a condition of its possibility, passes over or sublimates [. . .]. Thus literary space is marked by ellipsis." (111–12).

4. As Susan J. Brison says, "trauma [. . .] unravels whatever meaning we've found and woven into ourselves" (49). Roger Luckhurst offers a similar description: "Trauma is a piercing or breach of the border that puts inside *and* outside into a strange communication. Trauma violently opens passageways between systems that were once discrete, making unforeseen connections that distress or confound" (3, original emphasis).

5. The fact that the space is described as six feet, too narrow by far for almost any car I know, but a rather traditionally measured space for a grave, indicates McEwan's clear archetypal thinking: the once dead Stephen is now to be reborn to become a source of life.

6. I have little doubt that McEwan was thinking about Freud's description of deferred action in relation to a railway accident as it is presented in *Moses and Monotheism*. Stephen's second journey to visit Julie, as she prepares to deliver a child, includes his presence in the engine of a train. Again, repetition occurs in the narrative (Stephen's second trip to Julie), but whereas the first involved the trauma resulting from his seeing his parents in a pub, The Bell, in which they determined that Stephen's own birth would be assured, the second puts Stephen in the position of a childhood fantasy, driving a train while moving towards his new child's birth.

7. The ending's satisfying nature may, in its very artificiality, be a self-conscious sop to the romance genre's requirements. Such endings, while not unique in McEwan's work, are precisely the kind of thing frustratingly denied to readers of *Atonement*.

8. In "Among School Children," Yeats's speaker 'dream[s] of a Ledaean body" (line 9), and is suddenly confronted with the vision of his beloved as a child: "And thereupon my heart is driven wild: / She stands before me as a living child" (lines 23–24).

9. Ben is the child of Holocaust survivors who, he discovers from an old photograph, had lost the children they had before Ben was born. In Robert Harris's *Fatherland* (1992) an old snapshot functions similarly as the emblem of a reality that stands apart from the lives of characters. Katharine Burdekin's *Swastika Night* (1937) anticipates the power of a photograph to unmask hidden elements in the Nazi regime. While not dealing with any of these texts, Marianne Hirsch's "Projected Memory: Holocaust Photographs in Personal and Public Fantasy" (in Bal 3–23), offers a stimulating gloss on a common feature in these and, no doubt, other narratives. Furthermore, as Frédéric Regard shows in this volume, photography plays a central testimonial role in Peter Roche's autobiographical memoir, *Unloved: The True Story of a Stolen Childhood*, a trauma narrative unrelated to the Shoah.

10. The actual remark, "Nach Auschwitz ein Gedicht zu schreiben, ist barbarisch"—"To write poetry after Auschwitz is barbaric" (1981, 34)—is found in Adorno's 1949 essay, "Kulturkritik und Gessellschaft." The essay

was published singly in 1951, and then collected in *Prismen* (1955). See also Steiner 53.

11. Luckhurst cites Elie Wiesel's widely quoted statement, in *The Trauma Question*, 69. See Wiesel 10. The question of the uniqueness of the Holocaust is heavily politicised and Wiesel's assertion is part of that argument.

12. The notion seems to derive from Derrida's discussion of Rousseau in *Of Grammatology*: "*There is nothing outside of the text* [there is no outside-text: *il n'y a pas de hors texte*]" (158). Several post-structuralist theorists have developed the idea. See, for example, van Alphen on the Holocaust. He argues "that experience of an event or history is dependent on the terms the symbolic order offers. It needs these terms to transform living through an event into an experience of the event. [. . .] experience is the transposition of the event to the realm of the subject. Hence, the experience *of* an event is already a representation of it and not the event itself. [. . .] it could not be experienced, because a distance from it in language or representation was not possible. In this view, experience is the result or product of a discursive process. Thus, the problem of Holocaust experiences can be formulated as the stalling of this discursive process. Because of this stalling the experience cannot come about" (27, original emphasis).

WORKS CITED

Adorno, Theodor. *Prisms*. Trans. Samuel and Shierry Weber. 1955. Cambridge, Mass.: MIT P, 1981. Print.

Bal, Mieke. Introduction to *Acts of Memory: Cultural Recall in the Present*. Eds. Mieke Bal, Jonathan Crewe and Leo Spitzer. Hanover and London: Dartmouth College UP of New England, 1999. vii-xvii. Print.

Bradbury, Malcolm. *The Modern British Novel 1878–2001*. London: Penguin, 2001. Print.

Brison, Susan J. "Traumatic Narratives and the Remaking of the Self." *Acts of Memory*. Eds. Mieke Bal, Jonathan Crewe and leo Spitzer, 1999. 39–54. Print.

Brooks, Peter. *Reading for the Plot: Design and Intention in Narrative*. New York: Vintage,1984. Print.

Childs, Peter, ed. *The Fiction of Ian McEwan*. Houndmills and New York: Palgrave Macmillan, 2006. Print.

Caruth, Cathy. *Unclaimed Experience: Trauma, Narrative, and History*. Baltimore: Johns Hopkins UP, 1996. Print.

Derrida, Jacques, *Of Grammatology*. Trans. Gayatri Chakravorty Spivak. 1967. Baltimore: Johns Hopkins University Press, 1976. Print.

Elam, Diane. *Romancing the Postmodern*. London and New York: Routledge, 1992. Print.

Freud, Sigmund. *Moses and Monotheism*. Trans. Katherine Jones. 1939. New York: Vintage, 1958. Print.

———. "Remembering, Repeating and Working-Through." 1914. *The Standard Edition of Complete Psychological Works of Sigmund Freud*. Trans. James Strachey Vol. XII. Cambridge, Mass.: Harvard UP, 1982. 147–56. Print.

Frye, Northrop. *The Secular Scripture: A Study of the Structure of Romance*. Cambridge, Mass. and London: Harvard UP, 1976.

Groes, Sebastian, ed. *Ian McEwan, Contemporary Critical Perspectives*. New York: Continuum, 2009. Print.

Hartman, Geoffrey. *The Fateful Question of Culture*. New York: Columbia UP, 1997. Print.

Head, Dominic. *Ian McEwan*. Contemporary British Novelists. Manchester and New York: Manchester UP, 2007. Print.

Kristeva, Julia. *The Powers of Horror: An Essay on Abjection*. Trans. Leon S. Roudiez. 1980. New York: Columbia UP, 1982. Print.

LaCapra, Dominick. *Writing History, Writing Trauma*. Baltimore and London: Johns Hopkins UP, 2001. Print.

Luckhurst, Roger. *The Trauma Question*. London: Routledge, 2008. Print.

Lyotard, Jean-François. *Heidegger and 'the Jews'*. Trans. A. Michel and M. Roberts. Minneapolis: U of Minnesota P, 1990. Print.

McEwan, Ian. *Black Dogs*. New York: Vintage, 1992. Print.

———. *Atonement*. London: Jonathan Cape, 2001. Print.

———. *The Child in Time*. 1987. Toronto: Lester and Orpen Dennys, 2005. Print.

Michaels, Anne. *Fugitive Pieces*. Toronto: McClelland and Stewart, 1996. Print.

Parker, Patricia. *Inescapable Romance*. Princeton: Princeton UP, 1979. Print.

Steiner, George, *Language and Silence: Essays on Language, Literature, and the Inhuman*. New York: Atheneum, 1967. Print.

Swift, Graham. *Waterland*. 1983. London: Picador, 1984. Print.

van Alphen, Ernst. "Symptoms of Discursivity: Experience, Memory, and Trauma." *Acts of Memory*. Eds. Mieke Bal, Jonathan Crewe and leo Spitzer, 1999. 24–38. Print.

Walsh, John. "Ian McEwan: Here's the twist." *The Independent* 20 January 2007: http://www.independent.co.uk/news/people/profiles/ian-mcewan-heres-the-twist-432 893.html. Retrieved on 24 May 2011. Web.

White, Hayden. "The Fictions of Factual Representation." *Tropics of Discourse: Essays in Cultural Criticism*. 1978. Baltimore: Johns Hopkins UP, 1985. 121–34. Print.

Whitehead, Anne. *Trauma Fiction*. Edinburgh: Edinburgh UP, 2004. Print.

Wiesel, Elie. *One Generation After*, New York: Random House, 1970.

Yeats, W. B. "Among School Children." *Collected Poems of W.B. Yeats*. 1950. London: Macmillan, 1978. 242–44. Print.

13 "Redeemed, Now and For Ever"

Traumatic and Therapeutic Realism in Peter Ackroyd's *The House of Doctor Dee*[1]

Jakob Winnberg

Reading the very first page of Peter Ackroyd's 1993 novel, *The House of Doctor Dee*, for the first time, the experienced and attentive reader is quite probably ready to hazard the guess that it houses a narrative about childhood, secrets and forgetfulness. Once the same reader has read the whole novel, s/he should also be able, upon going back to that same page, to discern the signs there of a romance quest that gradually reveals the intimate connections between those three themes, but also reveals that the connective node they share is that of trauma. For this is how the bulk of that first page reads—with a generous helping of ellipses added:

> I had heard nothing about [the house] until after [my father's] death [. . .]. The house was in [. . .] an area I scarcely knew [. . .]. I took the tube [. . .] [as] since childhood I have always enjoyed riding under the ground. [. . .] Each time the automatic doors close I experience a deeper sense of oblivion—or is it forgetfulness? (1)

The mystery house is, of course, a staple of the Gothic romance, as is its location in an unfamiliar area; meanwhile, the simultaneous reference to childhood joys and things kept secret by parents, as well as to oblivion and forgetfulness related to what is "under the ground," points in the direction of traumatic events that have been repressed; whereas the question posed by the narrator—is it oblivion or more correctly forgetfulness?—shows us, as it were, that what has been kept in the sewers is starting to spill up onto the streets; the narrator is starting to doubt whether he is in full control of the writing of his own life-script.

So far this is a fairly familiar, not to say unduly facile, psychoanalytic reading in the Freudian vein. Indeed, the central trauma of *Doctor Dee* is of the individual, childhood variety: the abuse of the twentieth-century narrator, Matthew Palmer, by his father. However, even here the novel stretches beyond the stuff of therapists' couches to engage with more collective cultural traumas. In fact, the root of Palmer's childhood traumas is the legacy of the sixteenth-century scientist and sorcerer, John Dee, whose incessant and ruthless quest for illumination and ultimate, divine knowledge, as well as the retrieval of a lost golden spiritual age of England (needless to say, a remnant of Atlantis), has been carried on by subsequent generations, including Palmer's father, with unsavoury consequences. More significantly, though, Dee himself, having one foot in esotericism and the other in empiricism, may be read as a metonym of the traumatic historical rift constituted by modernity, which among its consequences had the loss of mythic time and the so-called disenchantment of the world.[2] It is the retrieval of mythic time and the re-enchantment of the world that Palmer's father is concerned with—and Palmer is pivotal in this context, as his father believes him to be the *homunculus*, an artificially grown hominoid that Dee allegedly managed to create. It transpires towards the end of the novel that Palmer is indeed an orphan, found and raised by the "father" together with the "mother," both of whom Palmer has firmly believed are his biological parents. If Palmer's father is correct in his assumption, Palmer is not only the "child" of Dee's aspirations, but a *bona fide* piece of the past and thus the promise of its restoration—in effect, a means of healing the wound (*trauma*) in history.

Yet, lest we forget, modernity also brought with it new certainties: the cementation of the nation state, of national culture and identity—and probably nowhere more so than in the case of Britain, with England as its centre. However, such verities were relatively short-lived, in turn becoming subject to the trauma of what might be called post-modernity, involving postcolonial and postimperial processes in conjunction with globalisation. Thus, there was a doubling of trauma, and it is this that the novel ultimately struggles with, on the level of its master-narrator: Peter Ackroyd, who discloses himself at the end of the novel in the act of attempting a visionary merging of the historical past and his own present on the plane of fiction; nothing less than an attempt at healing the historical rift and redeeming the world by transcending time.

This is, indeed, the same task that Eliot and Joyce set themselves in *The Waste Land* and *Ulysses*, respectively, and one that called for new notions of lyrical and novelistic realism—and particularly in Eliot, these notions translated into the forms of what might arguably be labelled "traumatic realism" *avant le mot*: fragmentation, dissonance, melancholy repetition. However, these forms were also immediately in search of harmony, of healing, of a corresponding "therapeutic realism" tenable on the premises of a waste land of ruins, or, in the words of Joyce/Stephen Dedalus, the nightmare of history—and for both Eliot and Joyce, the means of healing was the superimposition of the mythic.

I would argue that we find the same movement (with particularly strong echoes of Eliot) in Ackroyd—and not just in *Doctor Dee*, but in most of his novels, if not all: a poetics of splitting, but also of merging, which operates on both the diegetic and the aesthetic levels of the narrative, and which simultaneously constitutes a poetics of trauma and of (an attempt at) its overcoming, traumatic realism begetting therapeutic realism.³ Rather than a clearly recognisable modernist aesthetic, however, Ackroyd employs the mutable form of the romance to realise this poetics. Importantly, it is the romance features of the text that allow it to ultimately present a scenario for the overcoming of Palmer's trauma, a scenario that promotes an alternative to Dee's ruthless quest. For, at the end of the novel, Dee is alternatively illuminated: first by a vision, presented by the ghost of his father, of the nightmare of "the world without love," and subsequently by an Arcadian vision, offered by the ghost of his wife, of "the world with love," a place for being-without-asking, care-for-the-other and feeling rather than knowing (205, 247). This vision would seem to hold the key as well to the contemporary narrator's overcoming of his traumas, as Dee's and Palmer's worlds merge at the end of the novel, and Dee's sixteenth-century vision of "the world with love" thus seems to be brought into Palmer's twentieth-century wasteland. Ultimately, their worlds merge with that of Ackroyd himself, as he violates the author/narrator distinction by speaking directly of his novelistic creation from within it, subsequently multiplying the merged worlds and voices, as seemingly all inhabitants of London and, by inference, possibly every reader (through the book as interface) are included in Ackroyd's own vision of London as "the mystical city universal" (277). Consequently, in this grand mystical vision, Ackroyd emerges as not just a writer in the mutable romance tradition but as a descendant of the romantic visionaries—in other words, romantic in a double sense.⁴

Yet, this vision seems to approach a monadic union in absolute immanence, and would thus seem to break with the anti-totalising provisionality and maintenance of the opening to alterity that has been taken as a defining mark of traumatic realism, in the sense of a mode of representation that is faithful to the particulars of trauma.⁵ Therapy, healing, seems to reside only in this perfect retrieval and conflation of everyone and everything on the same plane, in the same node—which hardly makes for therapeutic realism either, or for a realistic therapeutic goal, even when that goal is, as here, only claimed to be attainable through artistic (which is to say fictional) vision. Indeed, it is Ackroyd's self-consciousness as an artist, his understanding of his medium and of the ontological status of his vision, that saves the novel from sliding down a slippery slope into utter kitsch and divine madness: the metaleptic and metafictional move that precedes Ackroyd's concluding vision effects something more akin to a therapeutic realism to match the novel's traumatic realism, by making the readers question how true the vision of being "redeemed, now and for ever" actually rings (277).⁶ By questioning the historiographic status of his own fiction, Ackroyd implicitly questions the status of his final vision as well.⁷

However, the status of that vision may also be questioned in ways Ackroyd does not begin to acknowledge. As touched upon above, Ackroyd struggles with the loss of unified national identity, here as in his *œuvre* in general, which constitutes a sustained excavation of English cultural history, more often than not taking the even more myopic form of archae-ologies of London, and finding its apotheosis in his non-fictional work, *Albion* (2002). Lest we forget, it is *London* that will become "the mystical city universal" (Ackroyd 1994, 277). Like Dee, it seems, Ackroyd is strug-gling to retrieve a golden age of England; as Jean-Michel Ganteau puts it, "Ackroyd's artistic project is a quest for the English music that is the expression of English culture and of Englishness" (2005, 241). In this proj-ect, Ackroyd is, as Raphaël Ingelbien argues, affected by "[t]he quandary of a romantic-conservative imagination faced with the crisis of English cultural and political conservatism" (168). What is more, Ackroyd comes across as locked in a somewhat narcissistic melancholia, as his "English-ness is a silent, private communion with an imagined past," albeit one that "reconciles an outlandish mysticism with a Blakean sense of community" (Ingelbien 169, 170).

Now, from the perspective of trauma studies, the question is, thus, ultimately whether Ackroyd's struggle is a sign of health; whether it con-stitutes a melancholy attempt at restoring what has been irredeemably lost—if it was ever quite there to be found—or an act of mourning, of letting-go, entailing a positive reorientation. This question builds upon the post-Freudian distinction between melancholia and mourning as responses to both personal and cultural traumatic loss, with the universal birth trauma as paradigmatic foundation (Wheeler 19–24, *passim*; Lasch 163–64). Melancholic individuals seek to restore the original oceanic feeling of unity in the womb, a quest that is easily projected onto one's whole culture as the wish to restore some golden age.[8] Mourning, con-trastingly, is the path to a liberating emancipation from agonism, involv-ing a letting-go of the lost object. This point is seized upon by Wendy Wheeler in her discussion of the possibility of replacing a melancholic modernity with "a new modernity." As Wheeler explains, "[l]oss of any treasured thing—and particularly of 'big' things like certainty, tradition, and God—is profoundly traumatising. The melancholic's response is a refusal to let go" (165). The mourner, however, "is able to transform the shattered fragments of an earlier self and world, and to build something new from those fragments and ruins," something which requires "a radi-cal reformulation [. . .] so that old and familiar ways of understanding things are reconfigured, and old certainties and values understood in quite different ways" (165).

This question about the therapeutic value of Ackroyd's romance in rela-tion with trauma forms the coda of this chapter, which is reached by route of, first, an elaboration on how the elements of romance in the novel partake in its traumatic realism; second, a deeper analysis of the trau-matic core of the novel; third, an explanation of how the novel within its traumatic realism holds a vision of the overcoming of trauma; and finally, a fleshing out of the concept of therapeutic realism and its pertinence to the novel.[9]

POSTMODERNIST ROMANCE AND/
AS TRAUMATIC REALISM

The phrase "traumatic realism" was probably first used by Hal Foster in his 1996 study, *The Return of the Real*, in an attempt to come to terms with Andy Warhol's serial representations and their ostensibly blank conflation of celebrities, consumer goods and disaster scenarios, which, Foster argues, "may point less to a blank subject than to a shocked one, who takes on the nature of what shocks him as a mimetic defence against this shock" (130–31). Importantly, there is a critical element to Warhol's aesthetics of repetition-compulsion as well because "if you enter [the implicit logic of consumer culture] totally, you might expose it [. . .] through your own excessive example" (131). The term, "traumatic realism" has subsequently been used by Michael Rothberg in his study of Holocaust representation to denote "a form of documentation and historical cognition attuned to the demands of extremity" (14). Traumatic realism, then, would seem to be a hybrid mode of representation of the extraordinary and the excessive—a definition that it would interestingly share with the romance. As Diane Elam puts it, in her struggle to (not) define what she considers intrinsically indefinable, in romance "the division between high and low culture [. . .] becomes blurred," and there is a "persistence of excess," but above all, romance "exists as a contradictory term from the start" (1, 2, 5).

Keeping in mind Elam's caution against cementing any notion of romance, I nonetheless think it safe to state that *Doctor Dee* shares much with a more common notion of romance as dealing in tales of the fantastic and the extravagant, of adventures and quests, often involving mythic elements and harking back to medieval traditions. Following Suzanne Keen, one might call *Doctor Dee* "a double romance of the archive," meaning a romance centred on a scholarly quest and, in this case, one in which the quest is doubled on account of its having two narrators on investigatory missions—one might add to this the fact that Dee's and Palmer's worlds as well as their ultimate fates in significant respects double one another (128). It is also a romance of the more particular Gothic kind, as it runs the gamut of features typical of Gothic fiction: the motif of the double that Keen touches upon, the supernatural, haunted houses, secrets and hereditary curses. However, it blends these traditional Gothic romance traits with modernist anachrony and fragmentation, as well as, at the end, metafictional frame-breaking complete with an admission that the novel is, to a significant extent, a piecing together of previous texts:

> Is [the past] [. . .] created in [. . .] writing, or does it have some substantial reality? [. . .]. [N]o doubt you expected [this novel] to be written by the author whose name appears on the cover [. . .], but in fact many [. . .] words and phrases are taken from John Dee himself [. . .] [or] his contemporaries. [. . .] I have taken a number of obscure

texts and have fashioned a novel from their rearrangement. (Ackroyd 1994, 275)

It is thus unquestionably a postmodernist romance, fitting with both Linda Hutcheon's characterisation of postmodernist fiction as essentially historio-graphic metafiction and Brian McHale's definition of it as ontological play. Yet, Elam's notion of postmodernist romance as marked by "an *ironic* coexistence of temporalities" has relatively little purchase on Ackroyd's novel (3, emphasis added). Elam's grand example of the postmodern romance is, of course, Umberto Eco's *The Name of the Rose*, with its planting of the Holmesian William of Baskerville in medieval Europe.[10] There is, significantly, none of that overt winking knowingness in *The House of Doctor Dee*, which instead comes across as all but anachronistically earnest for all its ostensibly ludic elements. Amy J. Elias's term "metahistorical romance" is perhaps more fitting in the context of not just *Doctor Dee*, but similar novels of Ackroyd's such as *Chatterton* and *English Music*.

Notwithstanding the particulars of genre classification, all the elements of postmodern Gothic romance mentioned above partake in the novel's effectuation of a traumatic realism. To begin with anachrony and frag-mentation, it has become an *idée reçue* that, as Anne Whitehead puts it, "[i]f trauma is at all susceptible to narrative formulation, then it requires a literary form which departs from conventional linear sequence" (6). Indeed, *Doctor Dee* belongs with the recent spate of trauma narratives that, as Roger Luckhurst notes, have "played around with narrative time, disrupting linearity, suspending logical causation, running out of temporal sequence, working backwards towards the inaugurating traumatic event, or playing with belated revelations that retrospectively rewrite narrative sig-nificance" (80). These narrative moves constitute a poetics of trauma that evinces a fidelity to "the temporal paradoxes of trauma's belated effects" (Luckhurst 81). Related to this fidelity is, again, the figure of the double and of doubling, for, as Cathy Caruth argues, trauma is always "a double wound [. . .] experienced too soon, too unexpectedly, to be fully known and is therefore not available to consciousness until it imposes itself again, repeatedly, in the nightmares and repetitive actions of the survivor." (3–4). It is thus the doubling of trauma, the repetition-compulsion attendant with trauma, that makes possible the acknowledgement of it and of its signifi-cance—and this structure finds its metaphorical expression in haunting, ghostly echoes, *Doppelgängern*, and the like.

This brings us to the other more properly Gothic elements of the novel. The hereditary curse is, of course, another metaphorical representation of the way in which trauma can be doubled, repeated, passed on through generations if it remains unhealed, as is the motif of haunting. A prime example of the latter is Toni Morrison's *Beloved*, discussed by Luckhurst as a paradigmatic trauma fiction (90–97). Luckhurst's example of "trauma Gothic," however, is Stephen King. In his discussion of King's fiction,

Luckhurst observes that "trauma psychology frequently resorts to the Gothic or supernatural to articulate post-traumatic effects" (98). With reference to Lenore Terr, Luckhurst explains that the Gothic is an exemplary mode of trauma representation since:

> Post-traumatic experience is intrinsically uncanny, finding cultural expression in ghostly visitations, prophetic dread, spooky coincidence or telepathic transfer: 'Traumatic anxiety is a ghost! It moves through the generations with the stealth and cunning of a most skilled spectre.' (98)

As Robert Miles points out, there is also "broad agreement that the Gothic represents [. . .] the self finding itself dispossessed in its own house" (3)—a notion that sits easily with Ackroyd's novel, where the situation is further aggravated by the fact that it is not the self's house to begin with, as Palmer has inherited it from his father, and it is unclear what its exact origins are. Add to this Miles's observation that the Gothic has been read as dealing with "a rift in the psyche," which is "in some sense a collective psyche, one shaped by social and historical forces" (2), and we are closing in on my main argument: that *Doctor Dee* does not simply deal with individual trauma, but also with a more collective, shared trauma of modernity. Indeed, Wheeler makes explicit the connection between the Gothic and the trauma of modernity:

> [W]hat had once been socially and psychically contained within the realm of the sacred flies loose in frightening ways in secularising societies [. . .] [and] popular culture gives expression to these changes in the form of gothic fiction and art [. . .]. [T]he explosion of ghosts, vampires and undead [. . .] in the 1790s is 'something brought about by modernity itself.' (Wheeler 28)[11]

So, let us examine these horrors brought about by modernity itself, as they find expression in Ackroyd's novel.

TRAUMATIC REALISM—LOSS AND MELANCHOLIA

In order to begin to discuss trauma on the diegetic level of this novel at all, one has to posit a distinction between its sixteenth-century plot and its twentieth-century plot—even though these ultimately prove inseparable. As one reads the novel, it quickly becomes clear that the former haunts the latter: events and statements of the sixteenth-century plot are echoed in the twentieth-century plot, much in the way they are in an earlier Ackroyd novel like *Hawksmoor* (1985), and Palmer experiences flashes of ghostly apparitions. The echoes of the past are redolent of the repetition-compulsion concomitant with trauma, whereas the apparitions appear to be residual hauntings, or *restligeists*, which a popular assumption of paranormal folklore holds are "playbacks" of traumatic events. From this perspective, then, it would appear that not just a single instance, but substantial aspects, of Doctor Dee's life are tantamount to an unresolved trauma—which supports my contention that Dee himself represents a traumatic cultural rift: the loss of a divine order and the entry into a rational order, together with a melancholic relation to this loss that perpetuates rather than heals the trauma.

Still, the more readily detectable central trauma of the twentieth-century plot is of the common childhood variety, and resides in the—apparently sexual—abuse the twentieth-century narrator was subjected to by his father. The memory of this event has been repressed, and to such a point that Palmer confesses to "remember[ing] very little about my childhood" (Ackroyd 1994, 80). In fact, the truth of the abuse is revealed only towards the end of the novel (together with the revelation that he was adopted), and only because Palmer's mother misconstrues him as remembering it himself: "I only caught him with you once, but I threatened to take him to the police" (177). Yet, the root of this trauma turns out to reside in the sixteenth-century plot, for if Palmer's father did in fact sexually abuse his (adopted) son, he had a very particular, instrumental reason for the abuse that had little or nothing to do with the fulfilment of any carnal desires: as a devout follower of the esoteric teachings of Doctor Dee, Palmer Sr. believed that intercourse (in the carnal sense) with his son would yield intercourse (in the communicative sense) with the spiritual dimension. As the son himself ruminates upon his mother's revelation: "I knew now why I had forgotten my childhood, and so forgotten myself. I knew why there were no people in my memories. I had been lost from the beginning" (177). Significantly, the protagonist virtually does the job for the critic of reading the Gothic elements of the novel through the lens of this realisation:

> I had grown up in a world without love [. . .] and so I had none for myself or for others. That was why I had seen ghosts rather than real people. That was why I was haunted by voices from the past [. . .]. That was why I had dreamed of being imprisoned in glass, cold and apart. The myth of the homunculus was just another aspect of my father's loveless existence. (178)

That is, the Gothic elements are effects of Palmer's traumatic upbringing and, thus, partake in the novel's traumatic realism.

But again, to read Palmer's traumatic upbringing as simply the result of a perverse form of divine madness would be to miss a pivotal subtext of the novel. Reading Dee as not just occultist, but also scientist and child of a fledgling modernity, we may see that the novel exposes modernity itself as trauma. In effect, Dee is the rift in history, where the pre-modern mythos gives way to the modern ethos. Viewed from that perspective, the semi-incestuous rape of Palmer may be read as a metonymic figure for the melancholy desperation of modernity—the attempt to reinstate a mythical-spiritual order that modernity will not support, and the violence that results from that attempt.[12] Dee, whose fictionalisation in Ackroyd's novel matches the known facts concerning the historical John Dee, personifies both esotericism and empiricism: he is a master of mathematics *and* alchemy, astronomy *and* astrology, navigation *and* divination—all of which are at that historical point fully capable of adding up to provide theories and methods for attaining a transcendent understanding of ultimate truths, of the hidden divine dimension of the world.[13] Bent on salvaging what has been lost and restoring the validity of the past, Palmer's father suggests that they will add up again, as may be gleaned from the notebooks that Palmer eventually finds, which describe the life and destiny of Dee's *homunculus*:

> It knows that contemporary science [. . .] will return to its origins, purified, and then expound the mysteries of the past. The doctrines of the alchemists and the astrologers [. . .] will then be revived within the great vision of quantum theory. [. . .] [T]he theory of the four elements is also accurate in a spiritual sense and will one day be employed by theoretical physicists. (125)

As much as these statements thrill the imagination, they also represent a fundamentally melancholic perspective, a refusal to let go of what has been lost and enter into the mourning capable of clearing the path for a viable reconstruction of one's relation to the world.[14]

TOWARDS THERAPEUTIC REALISM

As my reading suggests, traumatic realism does not in and of itself constitute a therapeutic move; as Foster is quick to add in his discussion of Warhol's seminal work: "Warhol's repetitions are not restorative [. . .]. [T]hey are not about a mastery of trauma. More than a patient release from the object in mourning, they suggest an obsessive fixation on the object in melancholy" (131–32). However, *Doctor Dee* does move beyond mere traumatic mimeticism into a more properly therapeutic realm. Towards the end of the novel, Dee is faced with two visions that present him with a choice between aspirations to worldly and spiritual power, on the one hand, and *kenosis* and *caritas*, the humble work of communal care, on the other. In the vision of "The City," Dee is given a glimpse of the future of London, "which will grow larger and still larger upon fraud and usury and bribery and extortion and other such tricks" and which "is the true city universal" (208). Dee's crushing conclusion is that he has "tried to conquer time and nature only to be impaled upon them" (209). The vision ends with the image of an Eliotean waste land, "some trees leafless, and others torn up by the roots, in a confused landscape of broken stone," and Dee's father driving home the point that this "world without love [. . .] [is] one you yourself have fashioned" (218).

In the second vision, of "The Garden," a woman appears, "so clear and transparent that I could see a man child within her," and Dee understands this child to be himself (245). Indeed, Dee takes the woman to be his mother, but swiftly realises that it is his wife. Guiding Dee through the vision, his wife bids him to "make an end to this knowledge born out of fear and ambition" and instead "look inwardly" so as to see that the "star man" that he has "sought for [. . .] is within [him], where he has always been, but he cannot be found by experiment or speculation." (245, 248, 256). Accordingly, he must now place his faith "in love and not in wisdom, in surrendering and not in power" (256). In a Prospero-like gesture, Dee then resolves to "abjure the path of worldly knowledge and seek that original spirit which dwelt within me" (257).

Despite this final vision, it is with the legacy of "The City" that Palmer has grown up, as seen above. Yet, Palmer's response to his realisation of this fact is that "[n]ow everything had to be changed," and so he enters upon the quest of a "place where the elements might be reconciled—where ghosts and real people, lost cities and present ones, my past and present lives, my mother and myself, could be reunited in love" (178, 180). He subsequently finds this place, opening a door between past and present so that he and Dee may merge. Somewhat paradoxically, as it happens, the cause of the trauma (Dee, through the legacy of his transcendental quest) is also the key to its overcoming (Dee, through the legacy of his redeeming vision). What might appear to be a fractured narrative mirroring the fracturing effects of trauma is actually subsumed under a poetics of healing. The past is healed retrospectively and the present prospectively—only with the advent of Dee's doubling in Palmer can the wound become known and history fold back upon itself—or, equally true, "fold ahead"—to bring about a therapeutic merging. Out of the waste land of a burgeoning modernity, allegorised in Dee's vision of "The City," comes the promise of the "Shantih shantih shantih." (Eliot, "The Waste Land" line 434). In *Doctor Dee*, the "fragments" that Eliot had "shored against [his] ruins," (431) the "different voices" in which "he do the police,"[15] become merged in a vision approaching blissful unity. If Eliot, standing "on Margate Sands," could "connect nothing with nothing" (300–02), Ackroyd, sitting (one presumes) in the midst of busy London, seems able at least to "create [a] bridge across two shores" (277).

This is, of course, as far as we know, a vision that must remain poetic, a transcendence that can only take place in the sphere of imagination. All the same, one might wonder how this aspect of the novel tallies with the starting hypothesis for the project that led to the present book, which held that "by probing at the limits of representation both in word and image, and by favouring a failure of understanding, romance is especially well equipped to challenge totalising devices and provide an accommodated mimetic mode naturally akin to the evocation of traumatic realism" (Ganteau and Onega 12).[16] If, as Ganteau suggests, the ethics of romance resides in its rejection of "the entrapment of 'the same' the better to vindicate an encounter with the other" (2003, 227), that ethico-poetics is in Ackroyd's novel a route to an ultimate merging of others into sameness. There is a profound difference between the immanence of the individual open to alterity, the Many, and the transcendence of the individual into the immanence of the same, the One. In other words, one's own interiority, one's immanent perspective, is something one is stuck in and cannot quite transcend—yet, one can be more or less open to the other and let alterity impact on one, which is at least an intimation of a transcendence of one's singular interiority. Contrarily, transcendence of one's specific situatedness, were such transcendence possible, would mean that others would cease to be others and instead meld with one on a higher plane of immanence—a fitting metaphor here would be the hive-mind, with all its ethical implications.[17]

Yet, before we accuse Ackroyd not only of therapeutic sentimentalism but also of totalising violations of alterity, we need to nuance our reading of his ultimate vision by making that reading more honourably *close*.

THERAPEUTIC REALISM—MOURNING AND ACCEPTANCE

And so we come to my point about "therapeutic realism," a phrase which, at the same time as it plays on "traumatic realism" for semi-specular effect, is meant to imply a mode of narrative representation that is realistic as pertains to therapeutic vision. This realism is most directly evident in Ackroyd's doubting his control of the narrative and the veracity of his vision, much like Palmer at the very start of the novel, in a kind of doubling, circular move. We find here a discordance at the heart of the therapeutic, revealing the more profound sense of therapeutic realism: a realistic view of the therapeutic, which cannot heal all, at once and forever. Therapy, like trauma, may entail repetition, continual reopenings, and therapy's promise of closure may have to remain a promise. We are never "redeemed, now and forever" (Ackroyd 1994, 277).

I have chosen as part of my title for this chapter that phrase from the ending of the novel. There is a touch of irony in that move, for my quotation is markedly partial, out of context. The last two sentences of the novel, seemingly issuing from Ackroyd himself, read: "Come closer, [. . .] so that we may become one. Then will London be redeemed, now and forever, and all those with whom we dwell—living or dead—will become the mystical city universal" (1994, 277). Redemption may not be read as a *fait accompli* here, as it is deferred by a "Then will . . . " And, given Ackroyd's metafictional, metahistoriographic, indeed metavisionary doubts, his entreatment to Dee (and by extension Palmer and hosts of others) to lose himself in a monadic meld may lack both confidence and persuasive powers—not to mention an actual addressee, for, as Ackroyd himself acknowledges, his Dee is a fiction. We are indeed witnessing "a silent, private communion with an imagined past" (Ingelbien 168).

At any rate, Ackroyd's romantic vision comes across as spinning on a see-saw shared with a more properly postmodernist incertitude. In short-hand, one might say that the vision deconstructs itself. If Ackroyd is, some-what paradoxically, trying to transcend into perfect immanence, he ends up, then, in what Ihab Hassan has called "indetermanence"—a conjunction or continual play of indeterminacy and immanence, immanence lodged in indeterminacy. Thus, what Ingelbien refers to as Ackroyd's "outlandish mysticism" should not be taken literally; rather, Ackroyd espouses what Patricia Waugh refers to as "[t]he postmodern self-conscious awareness of the finitude of the material and the plasticity of the imagination (now pro-ducer of fictions by which to live rather than mediator of absolute vision)" (11). The Ackroyd who wrote disjointed language poetry in his youth and name-checked Derrida in *Notes for a New Culture* maintains his grip on the Ackroyd who writes mythopoeic fantasies of transcendence and unity. What Susana Onega observes of Ackroyd's first novel, *The Great Fire of London*, thus, *mutatis mutandis*, holds true for *Doctor Dee*: "the god-like Author himself" remains "imprisoned within the cardboard walls of the novel and incapable of conceiving his own transcendental escape," and his vision might be a "distorted and subjective 'misreading'" (30). Indeed, this predicament is itself intrinsically romantic—for, as John Williams points out, Ackroyd's suspended visions recall "Keats's attempt to commune with the song of the Nightingale, and his melancholy recognition that 'The fancy cannot cheat so well / As she is famed to do'"; or, in the more general terms of Waugh, that "to engage with the world through the non-instrumental form of the aesthetic, is to glimpse, painfully, a plenitude which may be lost forever, even if its existence was only ever imaginary in the first place." (Waugh 78; Williams 35).

In other words, we remain, after all the therapeutic moves of the novel, in the agonism of the melancholic. The novel does halt before the fulfilment of its basically infantile vision of plenitude, remaining in an "indeterma-nence" that leaves alterity intact and might open up a space for acceptance and mourning. However, the operative word here is "might," because halt-ing before the wish-fulfilment of the melancholic, the novel does not even begin to tread the path of the mourner, ready to accept loss and discard his cultural nostalgia, much like Dee discards his transcendental quest. As Ingelbien puts it, "[t]he persuasiveness of Ackroyd's ending depends on the relevance of Blakean poetics to present-day England" (170)—or to the present-day *world*, one hastens to add. To put it differently, what Jeffrey Roessner notes of *English Music* gels with *Doctor Dee*: its "most striking feature [. . .] is the incongruity between its postmodern narrative tactics and the conservative ideal of British identity it celebrates" (104).

Significantly, though, Ackroyd makes Dee the mouthpiece of his autocriticism in this regard, as he has the doctor query him in the final pages of the novel: "Why not write of your own time? Why do you fly from it? Is it because you fly from your own self?" (275). It need hardly be said that flying from one's own self is one possible consequence of trauma. Ultimately, then, perhaps the novel's therapeutic realism resides in its attunement to the fact that, as Waugh puts it, "[t]o live in a state of 'hesitation', irresolution or paradox, is, indeed, intensely difficult. It is, as Freud argued, indicative of a hard-won maturity" (32). Yet, it is the only possible route for successful mourning and to a new, less agonistic modernity. Indeed, as Wheeler argues, "[i]t is only out of what is true for modernity that a new truth language and a new modernity can arise" (133). In the final analysis, "with postmodernism, the critique of modernity recognises that gestures of 'radical surpassing—romantic utopianism' are no longer possible, and have even constituted the most totalitarian of modernity's teleological narratives" (Wheeler 59–60).

However, while the novel clearly wavers at the end, implicitly evidencing some amount of recognition of the insight that "the fantasy of a finally triumphant, romantic closure" must now be replaced by "the reality of the lesser, stoical or faithful, goal of an open-ended continuing" (Wheeler 88), it also steers well clear of tackling such a process of replacement. That, it seems, would be a different pilgrimage, for a different Palmer—or for a different Ackroyd.

NOTES

1. Initial research for this article was part of a project financed by the Swedish Research Council.
2. Wendy Wheeler brings out this traumatic dimension of modernity when she charts the long history of "[t]he sense that there is something injurious to the social whole in modernity" (11). The main problem with "Enlightenment modernity," as Wheeler puts it, is that it "could not offer a sufficiently wide and rich cosmology in place of what had been lost" (3).
3. This aspect of Ackroyd's œuvre—the interplay of splitting and doubling, self-conscious fragmentation and mythic unification—has, of course, been noted previously (Onega).
4. Before the advent of the Romantic movement, the term "romantic" was indeed used in the sense of "similar to what one might find in a romance," i.e., adventurous, extravagant, fantastic or improbable.
5. See, for instance, the Introduction to the present volume.
6. For an elaborate and appreciative discussion of the kitsch aspect of Ackroyd's work, see Ganteau 2005.
7. There is a similarity here to the Eliot who "shores his fragments against his ruin, hoping to make them cohere through the discovery of a deep aesthetic logic expressing universal mind in some version of a collective unconscious. The faith is not strong, but the desire is everywhere in evidence" (Waugh 78).

8. As Christopher Lasch explains, mental life begins "with the blissful feeling of 'oceanic' peace and union," swiftly substituted by an "experience of overwhelming loss [that] becomes the basis of all subsequent experiences of alienation, of historical myths of a lost golden age, and of the myth of the primary fall from grace" (163–64).
9. In the process, I will not be able to begin to do justice to the richness and power, indeed the poignancy, of this novel, which is considerable. As much as I do admire it, however, I think it also lends itself to a reasoned critique.
10. See Eco's own *Postscript* to *The Name of the Rose*, which understands postmodernism largely as Eco's own form of ironic appropriation.
11. Wheeler's quotation is from Dolar 7.
12. The novel, thus, warns readers that while the alleged disenchantment of the world by modernity may be lamentable, attempts at re-enchantment might not necessarily be laudable. As I argue in fuller detail below, Ackroyd himself steers close to such an attempt, with questionable consequences.
13. He is, of course, in no way a singular anomaly in this respect; even a hundred years later, in the Age of Reason proper, Isaac Newton shared such Rosicrucian leanings.
14. Given its *in vitro* conception, the promotion of the *homunculus* as saviour becomes even more damning when one considers Wheeler's argument that "a significant part of [modernity's] failure of symbolic power results from an evacuation of symbolic forms of maternity from our culture, and from the acting out of a masculine fantasy of replacing the mother, which is particularly associated with the subject of Enlightenment (Mary Shelley's *Frankenstein* is probably its first striking fictional representation)" (41).
15. I am referring here to the original title of "The Waste Land": "He Do the Police in Different Voices."
16. See the Introduction to this volume.
17. We thus have two significantly different modes of transcendence: one transient, akin to a flicker, constituting the ethical moment, and one decisive, final and totalising. Speaking of the former mode, Emmanuel Levinas stresses that "[t]ranscendence owes it to itself to interrupt its own demonstration. [. . .] It is necessary that its pretension be exposed to derision and refutation" (1998, 152). Thus, the former is a "transcendence-without-being," whereas the latter is a "transcendence-into-another-being"—as Levinas puts it, true ethical transcendence "is to be distinguished from the negativity by which discontent man refuses the condition in which he is established" (1969, 40). Indeed, there would seem to be a connection here to Ackroyd's cultural nostalgia in the novel, as Levinas points out that "[t]he alterity of a world refused is not the alterity of the Stranger but that of the fatherland which welcomes and protects" (41).

WORKS CITED

Ackroyd, Peter. *Hawksmoor*. 1985. Harmondsworth: Penguin, 1993. Print.
———. *Chatterton*. 1987. Harmondsworth: Penguin, 1998. Print.
———. *English Music*. 1992. Harmondsworth: Penguin, 1993. Print.
———. *The House of Doctor Dee*. Harmondsworth: Penguin, 1994. Print.
———. *Albion: The Origins of the English Imagination*. 2002. London: Vintage, 2004. Print.
Caruth, Cathy. *Unclaimed Experience: Trauma, Narrative, and History*. Baltimore, MD: John Hopkins UP, 1996. Print.

Eco, Umberto. *Postscript to The Name of the Rose.* Trans. William Weaver. London: Harcourt Brace Jovanovich, 1984. Print.

———. *The Name of the Rose.* Trans. William Weaver. 1980. London: Vintage Classics, 2004. Print.

Dolar, Mladen. "'I Shall Be with You on Your Wedding-Night': Lacan and the Uncanny." *October* 58 (Fall 1991): 5–23. Print.

Elam, Diane. *Romancing the Postmodern.* London: Routledge, 1992. Print.

Elias, Amy J. *Sublime Desire: History and Post-1960s Fiction.* Baltimore and London: The Johns Hopkins UP, 2001. Print.

Eliot, T. S. "The Waste Land." *The Complete Poems and Plays: 1909–1950.* New York: Harcourt Brace, 1952. 37–55. Print.

Foster, Hal. *The Return of the Real: The Avant-Garde at the End of the Century.* Cambridge: The MIT P, 1996. Print.

Ganteau, Jean-Michel. "Fantastic but Truthful: The Ethics of Romance." *Cambridge Quarterly* 32.3 (2003): 225–38. Print.

———. "Peter Ackroyd, Kitsch and the Logic of Impersonal Imitation." *Impersonality and Emotion in Twentieth-Century British Literature.* Eds. Christine Reynier and Jean-Michel Ganteau. Montpellier: Presses Universitaires de la Méditerranée, 2005. 239–49. Print.

Ganteau, Jean-Michel and Susana Onega, "S.21. Traumatic Realism and Romance in Contemporary British Fiction." ESSE/10 Conference (Torino 24–28 August 2010). PDF file, *European Society for the Study of English* web, http://www. essenglish.org/cfp/ESSE-10-Torino.pdf, 12. Retrieved on 15 May 2011. Web.

Hassan, Ihab. "Culture, Indeterminacy, and Immanence: Margins of the (Postmodern) Age." *The Postmodern Turn: Essays in Postmodern Theory and Culture.* Columbus: Ohio State UP, 1987. 46–83. Print.

Hutcheon, Linda. *A Poetics of Postmodernism: History, Theory, Fiction.* London: Routledge, 1988. Print.

Ingelbien, Raphaël. "Imagined Communities/Imagined Solitudes: Versions of Englishness in Postwar Literature." *European Journal of English Studies* 8.2 (2004): 159–71. Print.

Keen, Suzanne. *Romances of the Archive in Contemporary British Fiction.* Toronto: U of Toronto P, 2001. Print.

Lasch, Christopher. *The Minimal Self: Psychic Survival in Troubled Times.* London: Picador, 1985. Print.

Levinas, Emmanuel. *Totality and Infinity: An Essay on Exteriority.* Trans. Alphonso Lingis. Pittsburgh: Duquesne UP, 1969. Print.

———. *Otherwise Than Being, or, Beyond Essence.* Trans. Alphonso Lingis, Pittsburgh: Duquesne UP, 1998. Print.

Luckhurst, Roger. *The Trauma Question.* London and New York: Routledge, 2008. Print.

McHale, Brian. *Postmodernist Fiction.* London: Routledge, 1987. Print.

Miles, Robert. *Gothic Writing 1750–1820: A Genealogy.* 2nd ed. London and New York: Routledge, 2002. Print.

Morrison, Toni. *Beloved.* 1987. London: Picador, 1988. Print.

Onega, Susana. *Metafiction and Myth in the Novels of Peter Ackroyd.* Columbia: Camden House, 1999. Print.

Roessner, Jeffrey. "God Save the Canon: Tradition and the British Subject in Peter Ackroyd's *English Music.*" *Post-Identity* 1.2 (1998): 104–24. Print.

Rothberg, Michael. *Traumatic Realism: The Demands of Holocaust Representation.* Minneapolis: U of Minnesota P, 2000. Print.

Waugh, Patricia. *Practising Postmodernism/Reading Modernism.* London: Arnold, 1992. Print.

Williams, John. "Peter Ackroyd's *Chatterton*, Thomas Chatterton, and Postmodern Romantic Identities and Attitudes: 'This Is Essentially a Romantic Attitude'." *Romanticism: The Journal of Romantic Culture and Criticism* 15.1 (2009): 33–40. Print.

Wheeler, Wendy. *A New Modernity?: Change in Science, Literature and Politics.* London: Lawrence & Wishart, 1999. Print.

Whitehead, Anne. *Trauma Fiction.* Edinburgh: Edinburgh UP, 2004. Print.

Contributors

Rosario Arias is Senior Lecturer in English Literature at the University of Málaga (Spain). Her main areas of research are neo-Victorian fiction, haunting and spectrality, memory and revisions of the past. She has been a Visiting Researcher at Brunel University (London). She has published a number of articles and book chapters in, for example, *The Journal of Gender Studies, LIT: Literature, Interpretation, Theory* and *Variations: Literaturzeitschrift der Universität Zürich*, and *Stones of Law— Bricks of Shame* (U of Toronto P, 2009). She has recently co-edited (with Dr Patricia Pulham, University of Portsmouth) *Haunting and Spectrality in Neo-Victorian Fiction: Possessing the Past* (Palgrave, 2010).

Brian Diemert is Professor of English and American Literature, Brescia College, Canada. He received his BA in English and History from St. Jerome's College at the University of Waterloo, his MA in English from Queen's University, and his PhD, also in English, from the University of Western Ontario. A member of Brescia's English Department since 1988, his main areas of academic interest are British and American literature from the first half of the twentieth century. He is also interested in detective fiction and cultural studies. Diemert is the author of *Graham Greene's Thrillers and the 1930s* (McGill-Queen's 1996). He has published many essays on various authors, such as Graham Greene, F. Scott Fitzgerald, T. S. Eliot, and E. L. Doctorow, and topics such as rock music and Cold War discourse.

Ángeles de la Concha is Professor of English Studies at the Spanish National University of Distance Learning (UNED) in Madrid, where she teaches early modern drama and contemporary fiction. She he has co-authored *English Literature in the Second Half of the 20ᵗʰ Century* (2006) and *Ejes de la Literatura Inglesa Medieval y Renacentista* (2010); she has edited, introduced and contributed to *Shakespeare en la imaginación contemporánea. Revisiones y reescrituras de su obra* (2004) and *El sustrato cultural de la violencia de género. Literatura, cine, arte y video-juegos* (2004); and has co-edited as well as introduced and contributed to *Mujeres y niños primero. Discursos de la maternidad* (2004). She has published numerous articles and book chapters on gender issues and feminist theory, on contemporary women writers, and on postmodern fiction, particularly historical fiction and rewritings of the canon. Her current research focuses on the impact of cultural and literary representations of gender violence, a subject on which she has also taught several courses in the UNED MA in "Cultura y Violencia de Género," which she founded and directed until 2009; also on fiction about the impact of 11/9 and "glocal" terror.

Anne-Laure Fortin-Tournès is Professor of British literature at the University of Maine (Le Mans) in France. She wrote her PhD on the representation of violence in contemporary British fiction at La Sorbonne Nouvelle and published a series of articles on postmodernism and the notion of the event. In her post-doctorate thesis she broadened her approach to include the contemporary philosophies of the event and their relation to British literature. She published books on Martin Amis and postmodernism (Presses Universitaires de Rennes 2003), on the figures of violence (2005), and on text/image relations (Parcours/Détours 2008). Her research currently focuses on the representation of trauma through text/image relation.

Jean-Michel Ganteau is Professor of Contemporary British Literature at the University Paul Valéry Montpellier 3 (France), where he is in charge of the postgraduate and doctoral programmes. He is the editor of the journal *Études britanniques contemporaines*. He is the author of two monographs: *David Lodge: le choix de l'éloquence* (Presses Universitaires de Bordeaux, 2001) and *Peter Ackroyd et la musique du passé* (Michel Houdiard, 2008). He is also the editor, with Christine Reynier, of four volumes of essays *Impersonality and Emotion in Twentieth-Century British Literature* (Publications Montpellier 3, 2005), *Impersonality and Emotion in Twentieth-Century British Arts* (Presses Universitaires de la Méditerrannée, 2007), *Autonomy and Commitment in Twentieth-Century British Literature* (PULM, 2010), and *Autonomy and Commitment in Twentieth-Century British Arts* (PULM, 2012). He has also co-edited two volumes of essays with Susana Onega, *The Ethical Component in Experimental British Fiction since the 1960s* (Cambridge Scholars Publishing, 2007) and *Trauma and Ethics in Contemporary British Literature* (Rodopi, 2011). He has edited special issues of various journals (*Études anglaises, Cahiers victoriens et édouardiens*). He has published many articles on contemporary British fiction, with a special interest in the ethics of affects (as manifest in such aesthetic resurgences and concretions as the baroque, kitsch, camp, melodrama, romance), in France and abroad (other European countries, the USA) as chapters in edited volumes or in such journals as *Miscelánea, Anglia, Symbolism, The Cambridge Quarterly*, etc.

Christian Gutleben holds a chair of British literature at the University of Nice-Sophia Antipolis. His research focuses on the theory and practice of postmodernism with a special concern for the relations between postmodernism and Victorianism. He is the author of several monographs (on the British campus novel, on neo-Victorianism, on Graham Greene) and the co-editor, along with Marie-Luise Kohlke, of the Neo-Victorian Series at Rodopi. He is also the Director of the academic journal CYCNOS.

Georges Letissier is Professor of British literature at the University of Nantes (France). His research focuses on both Victorian literature and culture and contemporary fiction. Chief among his areas of concern are the links between fiction writing and historiography and between science and literature. He has recently published an article on Dickens: "'The wiles of insolvency': Gain and Loss in *Little Dorrit*," *Dickens Quarterly* 27.4 (December 2010) and another one on Darwinism in the neo-Victorian novel: "Trauma by Proxy in the 'Age of Testimony': Paradoxes of Darwinism in the Neo-Victorian Novel" (*Neo-Victorian Tropes of Trauma*, Marie-Luise Kolkhe and Christian Gutleben, Rodopi, 2010). He has edited a study on rewriting for Cambridge Scholars Publishing (*Rewriting/Reprising, Plural Intertextualities*, 2009) and co-edited with Michel Prum: *L'héritage de Darwin dans les cultures européennes* (L'Harmattan, coll. Racisme et Eugénisme, 2011). He was involved in several projects related to the celebration of Dickens's bicentenary in 2012.

J. Hillis Miller is UCI Distinguished Research Professor of English and Comparative Literature at the University of California at Irvine. He taught for 19 years at Johns Hopkins, then 14 years at Yale, and has been at Irvine since 1986. He is the author of books and articles on nineteenth- and twentieth-century literature and on literary theory. His most recent books are *Others* (Princeton, 2001), *Speech Acts in Literature* (Stanford, 2001), and *On Literature* (Routledge, 2002), *Literature as Conduct: Speech Acts in Henry James* (Fordham, 2005), *For Derrida* (Fordham, 2009) and *The Conflagration of Community: Fiction before and after Auschwitz* (Chicago, 2011).

Maria Grazia Nicolosi is Senior Lecturer at the University of Catania, Italy, where she teaches English language and literature to undergraduate and postgraduate students. She holds a Doctorate from the University of Pavia and is a graduate from the Universities of Catania and Bayreuth. Her PhD thesis was devoted to the novels of Adam Thorpe, and she has published several articles on German and English philosophers, novelists and poets such as Michele Bachmann, Hermann Brochs, Jenny Diski, Günter Grass, and Adam Thorpe.

Susana Onega is Professor of English Literature at the University of Zaragoza (Spain) and the Head of a research team currently working on ethics and trauma in contemporary fiction (http://cne.literatureresearch. net). She has written numerous articles and book chapters on contemporary British literature and narrative theory, and several monographic sections, including "Structuralism and Narrative Poetics" (*Literary Theory and Criticism: An Oxford Guide*, 2006, 259–79). She is the author of *Análisis estructural, método narrativo y "sentido" de The Sound and the Fury de William Faulkner* (Pórtico, 1980), *Form and Meaning in the Novels of John Fowles* (UMI Research Press, 1989), *Peter Ackroyd: The Writer and his Work* (Northcote House, 1998), *Metafiction and Myth in the Novels of Peter Ackroyd* (Candem House, 1999), and *Jeanette Winterson* (Manchester UP, 2006). She is the editor of *Estudios literarios ingleses II: Renacimiento y barroco* (Cátedra, 1986) and of *"Telling Histories": Narrativizing History / Historicizing Literature* (Rodopi, 1995). She has introduced, edited and translated into Spanish John Fowles' *The Collector* (Cátedra, 1999) and has co-edited with José Angel García Landa *Narratology: An Introduction* (Longman, 1996), with John A Stotesbury *London in Literature: Visionary Mappings of the Metropolis* (Carl Winter, 2001), with Christian Gutleben *Refracting the Canon in Contemporary Literature and Film* (Rodopi, 2004), with Annette Gomis *George Orwell: A Centenary Celebration* (Carl Winter, 2005), and with Jean-Michel Ganteau, *The Ethical Component in Experimental British Fiction since the 1960s* (Cambridge Scholars Publishing, 2007), and *Ethics and Trauma in Contemporary Narrative in English* (Rodopi, 2011).

Lynne Pearce is Professor of Literary Theory and Women's Writing at Lancaster University and has recently come to the end of her term as Principal Investigator for the AHRC-funded research project, "Moving Manchester: How the experience of migration has informed writing in Greater Manchester from 1960 to the present" (2006–10) (see www.lancaster.ac.uk/fass/projects/movingmanchester). Her principal publications include: *Woman/Image/Text: Readings in Pre-Raphaelite Art & Literature* (1991); *Reading Dialogics* (1994); *Feminism and the Politics of Reading* (1997); *Devolving Identities: Feminist Readings in Home & Belonging* (ed.) (2000); *The Rhetorics of Feminism* (2004); *Romance Writing* (2007). In the field of romance studies, she is also joint editor of *Romance Revisited* (1995) (with Jackie Stacey) and *Fatal Attractions: Rescripting Romance in Literature and Film* (1998) (with Gina Wisker).

Frédéric Regard is Professor of English Literature at the University of Paris 4-Sorbonne (France), where he holds the Chair of Modern English literature and is the head of the Lire-SEMA research laboratory. He has widely published in the field of modern and contemporary British literature, with a special focus on feminine writing. His main publications are *La Naissance de l'oeuvre romanesque de William Golding* (CIEREC, 1990), *1984 de George Orwell* (Gallimard, 1994), *L'Ecriture féminine en Angleterre* (Presses Universitaires de France, 2002), *La Force du féminin. Sur trois essais de Virginia Woolf* (La Fabrique, 2002), *La Littérature anglaise* (PUF, 2007), *Histoire de la littérature anglaise* (PUF, 2009). At present he is working on a full-scale project on Josephine Butler entitled *Josephine Butler et la grande croisade contre les lois sur les maladies contagieuses* (ENS Éditions) to be published in 2012.

Andrés Romero-Jódar holds a BA and an MA in English Philology, and a BA in Spanish Philology from the University of Zaragoza (Spain). He is a Research Fellow at the Department of English and German Philology of the University of Zaragoza, and is a member of the excellence research group entitled "Contemporary Narrative in English" headed by Professor Susana Onega. With the support of a scholarship granted by the Spanish Ministry of Science and Innovation, he is currently working on his Doctoral Thesis on sequential art, iconical genres and representation of trauma in graphic novels in English. He has published on these and related subjects in national and international academic journals such as *Atlantis, Estudios Ingleses de la Universidad Complutense, Revista Canaria de Estudios Ingleses, Revista Alicantina de Estudios Ingleses, Revista de Literatura* (CSIC), *Tropelías, Journal of Popular Culture* (Wiley) and *Studies in Comics* (Intellect).

Jakob Winnberg is presently Lecturer and Head of English at Katedralskolan upper secondary school in Växjö, Sweden, and an independent scholar. He holds a PhD in English from Gothenburg University, where he has also been a Research Fellow. He has lectured in numerous Swedish universities and colleges, and has been a visiting Research Fellow at the Université Paul-Valéry, Montpellier III, France. His research focuses on the theories and practices of modernism and postmodernism, with special attention to the aesthetics, ethics and politics of affect. He has published articles and presented papers on works by Peter Ackroyd, Martin Amis, J.G. Ballard, A.S. Byatt, Angela Carter, Bret Easton Ellis, Thomas Pynchon, Graham Swift, Alice Walker and Jeanette Winterson. He is the author of one monograph, *An Aesthetics of Vulnerability: The Sentimentum and the Novels of Graham Swift* (2003), and is completing another, tentatively titled *The Waxing and Waning of Affect in Postmodernist Fiction*.

Index

Forster, Margaret, 54, 63
fragmentation, 181, 229, 232–33;
  acting out and, 1; hyperbolical,
  9; of the traumatised self, 209;
  self-conscious, 240n3 (*see also*
  dissociation, doubling, split self,
  splitting)
Freud, Sigmund, 4–6, 8, 11n3, 23,
  49n6, 52, 56, 62, 72–74, 81, 83,
  85–86, 90–92, 96, 99, 104n1,
  105n6, 109, 120, 131, 133,
  141, 169, 178n12, 206, 217–19,
  222–24, 231, 240; "Beyond the
  Pleasure Principle," 104n2, 169;
  "Family Romances," 62; "Fixation to Traumas—the Unconscious," 169; (Freudian) slip,
  93, 178n12; *Moses and Monotheism*, 203, 224n1, 225n6;
  "Mourning and Melancholia,"
  49n6, 169; *objet ideal*, 85;
  Oedipus and Electra complexes,
  141; "On Transience," 104n2;
  "Remembering, Repeat-
  ing and Working Through,"
  169; *Studies on Hysteria*, 90;
  "The Uncanny," 73, 104n2,
  169; "The Wolf Man," 52;
  "Thoughts for the Time of War
  and Death," 204n2. *See also*
  Breuer, Josef; compulsion; cure;
  family romance; *Nachträglichkeit*; psychoanalysis; repetition;
  repression
Friedlander, Saul, 168, 174, 177n1
Frye, Northrop, 2–3, 18, 23, 60,
  107, 120, 127, 132, 150, 163,
  174–75, 196–97n5, 216, 219,
  224; *Anatomy of Criticism*,
  60; "The Mythos of Summer:
  Romance," 196–97n5; *The
  Secular Scripture*, 18, 23
Fuchs, Barbara, 2–4, 9–10, 17, 32n8,
  213n1, 214n3, 130
Fukuyama, Francis, 36

G

Gaiman, Neil, 181; *The Sandman*, 181
Gamble, Sarah, 19, 21, 29; *See also*
  Armit, Lucie
Ganteau, Jean-Michel, 5, 7, 11n1,
  32n1, 34, 145–47, 158n1,
  184–85, 203, 210, 213n1, 231,
  240n6; and Susana Onega,

1, 3–4, 238. *See also* Onega,
  Susana
genre(s), 2, 4, 34, 56, 120, 127–28,
  130, 138, 145–47, 154, 158,
  163–65, 184, 214n2, 216;
  airport bookstore, 5; classification, 233; comic books as a,
  184; conventions, 128, 165;
  criticism, 174; genreless, 146;
  Gothic, 8, 21, 53, 57, 71–72, 91;
  graphic-novel sub-, 195; hybrid,
  51; non-fictional, 6; of biofiction, 54; of generic uncertainty,
  8; of romance, 4, 8; of the fairy
  tale, 5; popular, 34; romance,
  56, 71, 164, 210; sub-, 4, 171;
  trauma and romance, 137. *See
  also* mode
ghost(s), 21–22, 30, 36–38, 40, 44,
  46, 53, 55–56, 58, 62, 108–09,
  113, 140, 165, 169, 171, 189,
  230, 234–35, 237 (*see also*
  apparition(s); phantom; spectre;
  spirit(s); undead; vampires);
  conscience, 129; -dog, 109;
  fiction, 48n1; image, 22; motif,
  21, 28; narrator, 113; romance
  trope, 42; stor(ies), 1, 5, 15,
  19, 21, 30, 35, 40, 48, 113,
  163, 165–66; tale(s), 39, 42,
  44, 48. *See also* cryptophoria;
  Doppelgänger(n)
Gibbons, Dave, 6. *See* Moore, Alan
  Moore, and Dave Gibbons
Giddens, Anthony, 72, 86
globalisation, 1, 204, 209
Golding, William, 26; *Lord of the
  Flies*, 26
Gothic, (the), 3, 19–21, 34, 47, 51, 56,
  61–64, 234; atmosphere, 56;
  elements, 98, 233, 235; fiction,
  232, 234; genre, 21, 53; mansion, 19; novel(s), 49n6, 91, 93;
  romance(s), 22, 51–52, 56, 93,
  105n5, 228, 232–33; tale(s),
  111, 165; *topos*, 45; trauma,
  233
graphic novel(s), 1, 181, 183–84, 186,
  188, 191, 195, 196n4, 197n6,
  197n7. *See also* comic book(s)
Gray, Margaret Ann, 183
Greene, Graham, 245
guilt, 40–41, 56, 59, 62, 97, 135, 142,
  193–94, 216; survivor's, 41–42

H

hallucination(s), 18, 21, 26, 41, 131, 203, 208. *See also* delusion(s); nightmare(s)

Harris, Robert, 225n9; *Fatherland*, 225n9

Hassan, Ihab, 239

haunting, 3, 5, 8–9, 17, 233; excessive return, 137; ghost, 40; motif of, 233; past, 169, 171; power, 20–22, 26; presence, 4, 28, 52–53, 64, 171; reader- haunting places, 47; residual, 235; trans-generational, 5, 22, 216. *See also* spectrality

hauntology, 34

Hawthorne, Nathaniel, 8, 185; *The House of the Seven Gables*, 8, 185

healing, 31, 52, 79, 141, 145, 152, 203, 206, 209–12, 221, 224, 229–31, 235–36; form, 204; (phase) of trauma, 9, 52, 141; poetics of, 237; process, 79, 130. *See also* working through

Heat and Dust (Ruth Prawer Jhabvala), 154

Henke, Suzette, 63

Hirsch, Marianne, 30, 206, 225n9; "Projected Memory: Holocaust Photographs in Personal and Public Fantasy," 225n9

historiography, 8, 11, 34, 158, 162, 164, 174, 177n6–78, 247

history, 3–4, 6, 8, 11, 22, 25–27, 34–35, 37–38, 41, 47, 59, 82, 105n8, 120, 135, 149, 162–65, 169–77, 183, 186, 206, 216–18, 222–23, 226n12, 229, 235, 237, 240n2; alternative (version of), 181–82, 186, 195–96; and literature, 59; and memory, 173; and romance, 82; antiquarian, 167; as catastrophe, 167 (*see also* catastrophe); as eternal return, 165; as trauma, 218; (Freudian) case, 105n6; collective, 25, 207; contemporary, 47; cultural, 111, 230–31; English, 48; hermeneutic of, 177; in the making, 26; individual, 25, 207, 223; interpretation of, 6; literary, 7; macro-, 218; media, 122; Modernist, 22: monumental, 165,

168; narrative of, 9; nightmare of, 229; of anarchy, 204; of cruelty, 131; of romantic love, 74; of trauma, 27; of violence, 165; of Western literature, 75; oral, 162; positivist, 48; representation of, 174; repressed voices of, 17; rewrit(ing of), 181, 186, 195; Russian, 134–35; spectre of, 38; teacher, 48, 217; traumatic, 162, 164, 166, 168, 170, 172–73, 171n1, 172, 178n10, 185, 190, 206, 218, 221, 229; U.S., 182; world history, 4, 6–7, 178n11

Hoffmann, E. T. A. , 83; *The Sandman*, 83

Holocaust, 1, 4, 87, 90, 128, 177n1, 182–83, 185, 195, 218, 223, 226n11-n12 (*see* Shoah); fiction, 6; narratives, 4, 162 ; -related testimonies, representation, 144–45, 232; studies, 144; survivors, 144; trauma of, 223

horror(s), 1, 84, 96–97, 110, 113, 129, 132, 135, 138, 164–65, 168, 174, 181, 190, 194–95, 208, 324; collective, 128; Fascist, 177n5; individual, 216; of terrorism, 213; tale, 114

Høystad, Ole M., 46–47; *A History of the Heart*, 47

Hughes, Hellen, 34

Hunt, Nigel, C., 42; 49n7

Hutcheon, Linda, 164, 186, 233. *See also* metafiction, historiographic

hybridity, 7; generic, 52, 146. *See also* genre(s)

hysteria, 90. *See also* Freud, Sigmund

I

identity, 20, 25, 29, 60, 63–64, 137, 154, 184, 191, 229; British, 240; gender, 72; lesbian, 35, 56; loss of, 32n2; mode of, 173; national, 230; obscured, 2; quest for, 138; search for, 54; sexual: 54, 63; shifting, 150; surrender of, 20

ideology, 75, 119, 131; of progress, 6; patriarchal, 1

illogicality, 9, 220

image(s), 20, 24, 31, 52, 116–22, 136–41, 184, 188, 237–38; after-, 42, 48; coiling, 131;

N
Te'

30